Cisco Networking Academy Program

# Fundamentals of Network Security Lab Companion and Workbook

Cisco Systems, Inc.
Cisco Networking Academy Program

**Cisco Press**
800 East 96th Street
Indianapolis, IN 46240 USA

# Cisco Networking Academy Program
# Fundamentals of Network Security Lab Companion and Workbook

Cisco Systems, Inc.
Cisco Networking Academy Program



Published by:
Cisco Press
800 East 96th Street
Indianapolis, IN 46240 USA



ISBN: 1-58713-123-4
Printed in the United States of America 1 2 3 4 5 6 7 8 9 0
First Printing March 2004

## Warning and Disclaimer

This book is designed to provide information based on content from the Cisco Networking Academy Program *Fundamentals of Network Security* course. Every effort has been made to make this book as complete and as accurate as possible, but no warranty or fitness is implied.

The information is provided on an "as is" basis. The author, Cisco Press, and Cisco Systems, Inc. shall have neither liability nor responsibility to any person or entity with respect to any loss or damages arising from the information contained in this book or from the use of the programs that may accompany it.

The opinions expressed in this book belong to the author and are not necessarily those of Cisco Systems, Inc.

**This book is part of the Cisco Networking Academy® Program series from Cisco Press. The products in this series support and complement the Cisco Networking Academy Program curriculum. If you are using this book outside the Networking Academy program, then you are not preparing with a Cisco trained and authorized Networking Academy provider.**

**For information on the Cisco Networking Academy Program or to locate a Networking Academy, please visit www.cisco.com/edu.**

## Trademark Acknowledgments

All terms mentioned in this book that are known to be trademarks or service marks have been appropriately capitalized. Cisco Press or Cisco Systems, Inc. cannot attest to the accuracy of this information. Use of a term in this book should not be regarded as affecting the validity of any trademark or service mark.

## Corporate and Government Sales

Cisco Press offers excellent discounts on this book when ordered in quantity for bulk purchases or special sales.
For more information please contact: U.S. Corporate and Government Sales 1-800-382-3419
**corpsales@pearsontechgroup.com**
For sales outside the U.S. please contact: International Sales **international@pearsoned.com**

## Feedback Information

At Cisco Press, our goal is to create in-depth technical books of the highest quality and value. Each book is crafted with care and precision, undergoing rigorous development that involves the unique expertise of members of the professional technical community.

Readers' feedback is a natural continuation of this process. If you have any comments regarding how we could improve the quality of this book, or otherwise alter it to better suit your needs, you can contact us at networkingacademy@ciscopress.com. Please be sure to include the book title and ISBN in your message.

We greatly appreciate your assistance.


| | |
|---|---|
| **Publisher** | John Wait |
| **Editor-in-Chief** | John Kane |
| **Executive Editor** | Mary Beth Ray |
| **Cisco Systems Representative** | Anthony Wolfenden |
| **Cisco Press Program Manager** | Nannette M. Noble |
| **Production Manager** | Patrick Kanouse |
| **Senior Development Editor** | Chris Cleveland |
| **Technical Editor** | Henry Benjamin |
| **Senior Project Editor** | Sheri Cain |
| **Copy Editor** | Jill Batistick |

Corporate Headquarters
Cisco Systems, Inc.
170 West Tasman Drive
San Jose, CA 95134-1706
USA
http://www.cisco.com
Tel: 408 526-4000
800 553-NETS (6387)
Fax: 408 526-4100

European Headquarters
Cisco Systems Europe
11 Rue Camille Desmoulins
92782 Issy-les-Moulineaux
Cedex 9
France
http://www-europe.cisco.com
Tel: 33 1 58 04 60 00
Fax: 33 1 58 04 61 00

Americas Headquarters
Cisco Systems, Inc.
170 West Tasman Drive
San Jose, CA 95134-1706
USA
http://www.cisco.com
Tel: 408 526-7660
Fax: 408 527-0883

Asia Pacific Headquarters
Cisco Systems Australia, Pty., Ltd
Level 17, 99 Walker Street
North Sydney
NSW 2059 Australia
http://www.cisco.com
Tel: +61 2 8448 7100
Fax: +61 2 9957 4350

**Cisco Systems has more than 200 offices in the following countries. Addresses, phone numbers, and fax numbers are listed on the Cisco Web site at www.cisco.com/go/offices**

Argentina • Australia • Austria • Belgium • Brazil • Bulgaria • Canada • Chile • China • Colombia • Costa Rica • Croatia • Czech Republic • Denmark • Dubai, UAE • Finland • France • Germany • Greece • Hong Kong • Hungary • India • Indonesia • Ireland Israel • Italy • Japan • Korea • Luxembourg • Malaysia • Mexico • The Netherlands • New Zealand • Norway • Peru • Philippines Poland • Portugal • Puerto Rico • Romania • Russia • Saudi Arabia • Scotland • Singapore • Slovakia • Slovenia • South Africa • Spain Sweden • Switzerland • Taiwan • Thailand • Turkey • Ukraine • United Kingdom • United States • Venezuela • Vietnam • Zimbabwe

## Table of Contents

## Foreword

Throughout the world, the Internet has brought tremendous new opportunities for individuals and their employers. Companies and other organizations are seeing dramatic increases in productivity by investing in robust networking capabilities. Some studies have shown measurable productivity improvements in entire economies. The promise of enhanced efficiency, profitability, and standard of living is real and growing.

Such productivity gains aren't achieved by simply purchasing networking equipment. Skilled professionals are needed to plan, design, install, deploy, configure, operate, maintain, and troubleshoot today's networks. Network managers must assure that they have planned for network security and for continued operation. They need to design for the required performance level in their organization. They must implement new capabilities as the demands of their organization, and its reliance on the network, expands.

To meet the many educational needs of the internetworking community, Cisco Systems established the Cisco Networking Academy Program. The Networking Academy is a comprehensive learning program that provides students with the Internet technology skills essential in a global economy. The Networking Academy integrates face-to-face teaching, web-based content, online assessment, student performance tracking, hands-on labs, instructor training and support, and preparation for industry-standard certifications.

The Networking Academy continually raises the bar on blended learning and educational processes. All instructors are Cisco Certified Academy Instructors (CCAIs). The Internet-based assessment and instructor support systems are some of the most extensive and validated ever developed, including a 24/7 customer service system for Networking Academy instructors and students. Through community feedback and electronic assessment, the Networking Academy adapts the curriculum to improve outcomes and student achievement. The Cisco Global Learning Network infrastructure designed for the Networking Academy delivers a rich, interactive, and personalized curriculum to students worldwide. The Internet has the power to change the way people work, live, play, and learn, and the Cisco Networking Academy Program is in the forefront of this transformation.

This Cisco Press title is one of a series of best-selling companion titles for the Cisco Networking Academy Program. Designed by Cisco Worldwide Education and Cisco Press, these books provide integrated support for the online learning content that is made available to Academies all over the world. These Cisco Press books are the only authorized books for the Networking Academy by Cisco Systems, and they provide print and CD-ROM materials that ensure the greatest possible learning experience for Networking Academy students.

I hope you are successful as you embark on your learning path with Cisco Systems and the Internet. I also hope that you will choose to continue your learning after you complete the Networking Academy curriculum. In addition to its Cisco Networking Academy Program titles, Cisco Press also publishes an extensive list of networking technology and certification publications that provide a wide range of resources. Cisco Systems has also established a network of professional training companies—the Cisco Learning Partners—who provide a full range of Cisco training courses. They offer training in many formats, including e-learning, self-paced, and instructor-led classes. Their instructors are Cisco certified, and Cisco creates their materials. When you are ready, please visit the Learning & Events area on Cisco.com to learn about all the educational support that Cisco and its partners have to offer.

Thank you for choosing this book and the Cisco Networking Academy Program.

Kevin Warner
Senior Director, Marketing
Worldwide Education
Cisco Systems, Inc.

# Introduction

*Fundamentals of Network Security Lab Companion and Workbook* acts as a supplement to your classroom and laboratory experience with the Cisco Networking Academy Program, whose curriculum empowers you to enter employment or further education and training in the computer-networking field.

This book is designed to further train you beyond the online training materials that you have already used in this program, along with the topics pertaining to the Securing Cisco IOS Networks (SECUR) and Cisco Secure PIX Firewall Advanced (CSFPA) exams. These exams also count towards the Cisco Certified Security Professional (CCSP) certification. This book closely follows the style and format that Cisco has incorporated into the curriculum.

This book consists of labs that are based on those in the current Cisco Networking Academy Program, with some additional information. Most of the labs are hands-on and require access to a Cisco router lab or a simulator. Additional paper-based labs, which are practice exercises for complex topics, are included to supplement the online curriculum.

## The Audience of This Book

This book is written for anyone who wants to learn about network security and the overall security processes. The main target audience for this book is students in high schools, community colleges, and four-year institutions. Specifically, in an educational environment, this book could be used both in the classroom as a textbook companion and in computer labs as a lab manual.

## How This Book Is Organized

Table I-1 outlines all the labs in this book, the Target Indicator (TI) in the online curriculum, the difficulty rating (1 to 3, with 3 being the most difficult), and the time it should take to do the lab.

**Table I-1 Master Lab Overview**

| Lab Number (TI) | Title | Difficulty (1-3, with 3 Being the Most Difficult) | Estimated Time (Minutes) |
|---|---|---|---|
| 1.1.5 | Student Lab Orientation | 1 | 15 |
| 1.2.8 | Vulnerabilities and Exploits | 1 | 20 |
| 1.3.3 | Designing a Security Plan | 2 | 30 |
| 2.1.6 | Configure General Router Security | 1 | 15 |
| 2.2.1 | Controlling TCP/IP Services | 1 | 15 |

| Lab Number (TI) | Title | Difficulty (1-3, with 3 Being the Most Difficult) | Estimated Time (Minutes) |
|---|---|---|---|
| 2.3.2 | Configuring NAT/PAT | 2 | 15 |
| 2.4.2 | Configure Logging | 1 | 15 |
| 2.4.3 | Setting Time and NTP | 2 | 15 |
| 2.4.5 | Configure SSH | 2 | 20 |
| 3.2.4 | Standard, Extended, Named, and Context ACLs | 3 | 30 |
| 3.2.5 | Lock-and-Key ACLs | 3 | 30 |
| 3.2.7 | Time-Based ACLs | 2 | 20 |
| 3.8.3 | Configure Cisco IOS Firewall CBAC on a Cisco Router | 3 | 35 |
| 4.2.3 | Configure AAA on a Cisco Router | 2 | 20 |
| 4.3.1 | Install and Configure CSACS 3.0 for Windows | 2 | 30 |
| 4.5.2 | Configuring Authentication Proxy | 2 | 30 |
| 5.2.5 | Configure IOS Firewall IDS | 2 | 15 |
| 5.3.8 | Configuring Syslog | 3 | 30 |
| 5.4.5 | Configure SNMP | 2 | 15 |
| 6.4.5 | Configuring Cisco IOS IPSec Using Preshared Keys | 2 | 30 |
| 6.6.6 | Configure IPSec Using Digital Certificates | 2 | 30 |
| 7.3.6 | Configure Remote Access Using Cisco Easy VPN | 2 | 20 |

| Lab Number (TI) | Title | Difficulty (1-3, with 3 Being the Most Difficult) | Estimated Time (Minutes) |
|---|---|---|---|
| 8.3.3 | Configure the PIX Firewall | 2 | 25 |
| 8.5.3 | Configure the PIX Firewall as a DHCP Server | 1 | 15 |
| 9.6.3.1 | Configure Access Through the PIX Security Appliance | 2 | 25 |
| 9.6.3.2 | Configure Multiple Interfaces | 3 | 25 |
| 10.1.2 | Configure ACLs in the PIX Security Appliance | 3 | 40 |
| 10.4.4 | Configure Object Groups | 2 | 35 |
| 11.3.5 | Configure AAA on the PIX Security Appliance Using Cisco Secure ACS for Windows 2000 | 3 | 40 |
| 12.1.7 | Configure and Test Advanced Protocol Handling on the Cisco PIX Security Appliance | 2 | 20 |
| 12.4.3 | Configure Intrusion Detection | 2 | 30 |
| 13.3.3 | Configure LAN-Based Failover (Optional) | 2 | 30 |
| 13.5.3 | Configure SSH, Command Authorization, and Local User Authentication | 2 | 25 |
| 13.6.2 | Perform Password Recovery | 2 | 20 |
| 14.6.6 | Configure a Secure VPN Gateway Using IPSec Between Two Cisco Secure PIX Security Appliances | 3 | 45 |
| 14.7.5 | Configure a Secure VPN Using IPSec Between a PIX and a VPN Client | 2 | 30 |

| Lab Number (TI) | Title | Difficulty (1-3, with 3 Being the Most Difficult) | Estimated Time (Minutes) |
|---|---|---|---|
| 14.8.2 | Configure IPSec Between Two PIX Security Appliances with CA support | 2 | 30 |
| 15.6.3 | Configuring the PIX Security Appliance with PDM | 3 | 45 |

**This Book's Features**

Many of this book's features help facilitate a full understanding of the networking and routing covered in this book:

- **Vocabulary Exercise**—Each chapter in this book begins with a section in which the student should review and provide definitions for some of the key terms affiliated with the technology within the chapter.

- **Labs**—Each lab in this manual provides an objective, or a goal of the lab. The lab lists the equipment required and provides a scenario that allows you to relate the exercise to real-world environments. Each lab also provides a list of supplementary resources (web-based and print) that the student can refer to enhance their understanding of the concepts of the lab. In addition, each lab provides a table listing the key commands used within the lab.

- **Review Questions and Quiz Questions**—To demonstrate an understanding of the concepts covered, chapters conclude with short-answer review questions and a multiple-choice quiz that elicit particular points of understanding. These questions help verify your comprehension of the technology being implemented.

The conventions used to present command syntax in this book are the same conventions used in the *Cisco IOS Command Reference*:

- **Bold** indicates commands and keywords that are entered literally as shown. In examples (not syntax), bold indicates user input (for example, a **show** command).

- *Italic* indicates arguments for which you supply values.

- Braces ({ }) indicate a required element.

- Square brackets ([ ]) indicate an optional element.

- Vertical bars ( | ) separate alternative, mutually exclusive elements.
- Braces and vertical bars within square brackets (such as [x {y | z}]) indicate a required choice within an optional element. You do not need to enter what is in the brackets, but if you do, you have some required choices in the braces.

Do theses

# Chapter 1

## Overview of Network Security

With the growing number of vulnerabilities being found and exploited in different operating systems, it is imperative that administrators secure the network. By keeping up to date with the vulnerabilities and knowing the network's weak points, an administrator is in a better position to protect the network and the company's assets. A few good online resources for administrators are the Security at the Cisco Systems website (http://www.cisco.com/security/) and the CERT Coordination Center website (http://www.cert.org).

Because network security is new to most readers, this chapter introduces you to some new concepts and terms. The need for network security is discussed, along with the goals and key elements of securing the network.

You learn about the different vulnerabilities and threats that exist and what can be done to protect the network. Using some of the same tools that attackers use, you can determine what weaknesses exist and then correct the weaknesses. By knowing what to look for, you can determine what needs to be fixed and how to fix it.

By designing a security framework that fits the company's needs and applying that policy to the network, you can deflect most attacks to the network.

### Vocabulary Exercise

confidentiality

_______________________________________________

_______________________________________________

integrity

_______________________________________________

_______________________________________________

authentication

_______________________________________________

_______________________________________________

availability

_______________________________________________

_______________________________________________

reconnaissance

_______________________________________________

_______________________________________________

packet sniffer

_______________________________________________

_______________________________________________

DoS

DDoS

Ping of death

smurf attack

security policy

firewall

intrusion detection

IDS

# Lab 1.1.5: Student Lab Orientation

Estimated Time: 15 Minutes

Number of Team Members: Two teams with four students per team

## Objective

In this lab, the student covers the following objectives:

- Review the lab bundle equipment.
- Understand the security Pod topology.
- Understand the Pod naming and addressing scheme.
- Load the IOS Firewall image.
- Load the default lab configurations.
- Cable the standard lab topology.
- Test connectivity.

## Overview

This chapter describes the basics of cabling and configuring the standard lab topology for this course. Students become familiar with the physical and logical topology that is used throughout the course. To avoid problems with the lab exercises, proper lab setup and connectivity is required before configuring security. In real-world scenarios, it is important to check the network for proper operation before proceeding with more advanced configurations.

There are four basic lab topologies used in this course.

Figure 1-1 illustrates the lab network environment using IOS Firewall routers for Chapters 1–6.

**Figure 1-1 IOS Firewall Lab Visual Objective: Chapters 1–6**

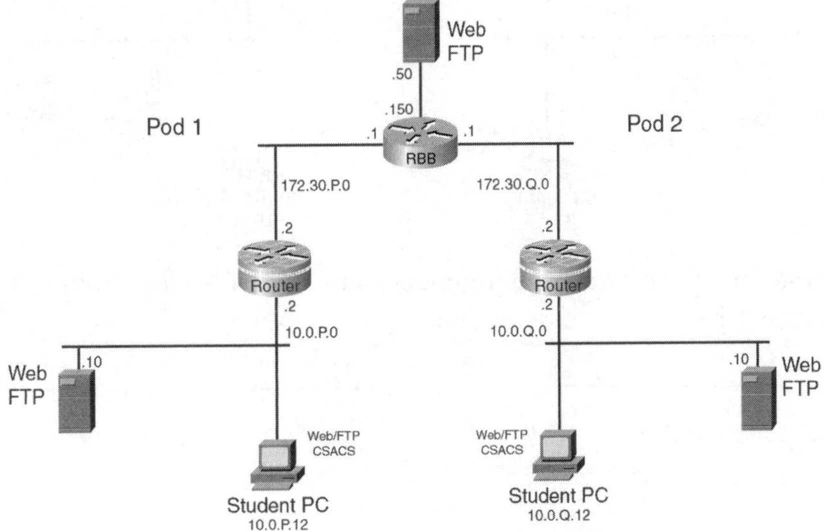

Figure 1-2 illustrates the lab network environment using the VPN Client and IOS Firewall for Chapter 7.

**Figure 1-2 VPN Client-to-IOS Firewall Lab Visual Objective: Chapter 7**

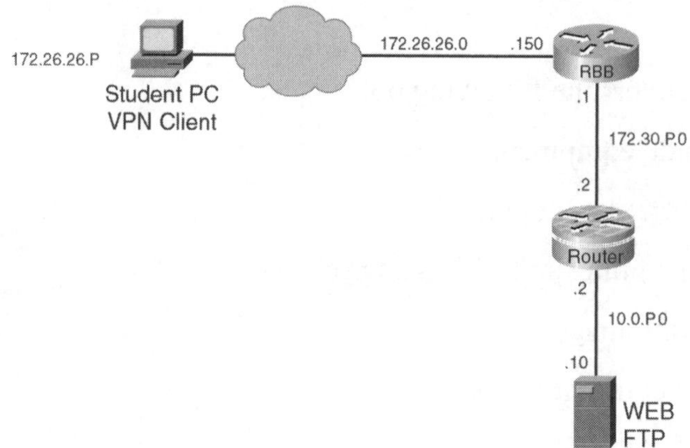


Figure 1-3 illustrates the lab network environment using PIX Security Appliances for Chapters 8–13.

**Figure 1-3 PIX Security Appliance Lab Visual Objective: Chapters 8–13**

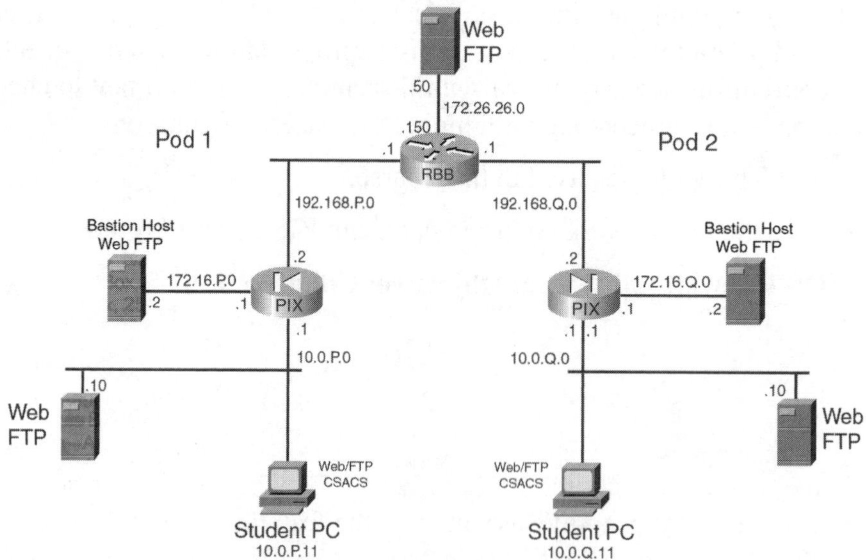


Figure 1-4 illustrates the lab network environment using the VPN Client and PIX Security Appliance for Chapter 14.

**Figure 1-4 VPN Client-to-PIX Security Appliance Lab Visual Objective: Chapter 14**

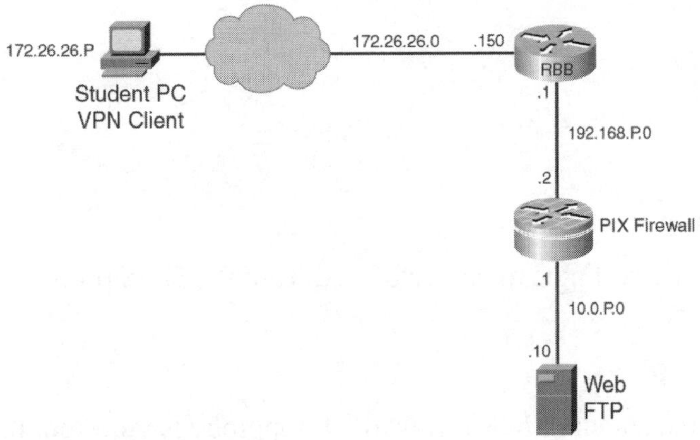

As documented in Table 1-1, three basic setups exist for each topology.

**Table 1-1 Lab Topology Setup**

| Name | Trust Level | Common | Network | Physical Port |
|---|---|---|---|---|
| Inside | Trusted | Private | LAN | Ethernet/FE/GE |
| Outside | Untrusted | Public | WAN (Internet) | Ethernet/Serial |
| DMZ | Protected | Partnernet | LAN | Ethernet/FE/GE |

In most labs, the physical interface is not specifically stated as Ethernet0, Fa0/0, E0/0, and so on. Instead, a lab instructs students to configure the outside interface, the inside interface, or the DMZ interface. Students have to configure the interfaces based on the router model and interface characteristics.

Note that both topology figures indicate a specific numbering, naming, and addressing scheme. The basic lab topology includes two Pods. Each Pod consists of a router, a firewall, a student PC, and an inside server. The **P** value in the addressing and naming scheme refers to the Pod router that will be assigned to a team consisting of one to four students.

The **Q** value in the naming and addressing scheme is used when testing the security or connectivity with the peer team. For example, assume that the team on the Pod 1 router is asked to ping the neighbor router at 172.30.**Q**.2. In this case, the **Q** is substituted with a 2.

The basic tasks in most labs are as follows:

- Configure security on the Pod device, such as a router or firewall.
- Test the security on the Pod device.
- Test the security of the peer team's device.
- Test LAN and WAN services through the Pod device and through the peer device.

When testing connectivity and security configurations, be careful to observe the prompt. Some possible prompts are as follows:

- C:\
- Router>
- http://10.0.P.12
- ftp://172.26.26.50

This is important because testing can be performed from the DOS prompt, the router prompt, the web browser, and so on.

## Tools and Resources

To complete this lab, the standard IOS Firewall lab topology is required. It is comprised of the following:

- Two Pod routers
- Two Pod firewalls
- Two student PCs
- One server with Intel Pro Server and a NIC with VLAN support
- Backbone switch and router
- Two console cables and HyperTerminal
- Assorted Cat5 patch cables
- (Optional) Label machine

## Command List

This lab uses the commands listed in Table 1-2:

**Table 1-2 Commands for Lab 1-1**

| Command | Description |
|---|---|
| **copy run start** | Stores the current configuration in RAM into NVRAM |
| **copy tftp flash** | Downloads a new image from the TFTP server to Flash memory |
| **copy tftp start** | Downloads a configuration from the TFTP server into the NVRAM |
| **enable** | Turns on privileged commands |
| **show interface** | Displays statistics for all interfaces configured on the router |

| Command | Description |
|---|---|
| **show ip interface** | Displays the status and global parameters associated with an interface |
| **show ip route** | Displays the contents of the IP routing table |
| **show running-config** | Displays the current configuration in RAM |
| **show startup-config** | Displays the saved configuration, which is the contents of NVRAM |
| **show version** | Displays the configuration of the system hardware, the software version, the names and sources of configuration files, and the boot images |

### Task 1: Examining the Devices

**Step 1.** Physically examine each device. Notice the available interfaces available on the IOS router and PIX Firewall.

**Step 2.** Notice that the devices are labeled with an adhesive label. Table 1-3 provides a list of devices that should be labeled.

**Table 1-3 Devices to Label**

| Routers | PIX Security Appliances | Student PCs | Backbone Devices |
|---|---|---|---|
| Router1 | pix1 | PC1 | RBB (backbone router) |
| Router2 | pix2 | PC2 | SW0 (backbone switch) |
| | | | SS (superserver) |

This equipment creates two standard Pods. Each Pod can accommodate one team consisting of one to four students.

### Task 2: Verifying the IOS Firewall Image on Pod Routers

**Step 1.** Power and test the router. If an IOS image upgrade is needed, the IOS software can be downloaded from Cisco.com. The download is available only to registered users.

| Platform | Release | Software Features |
|---|---|---|
| 2610XM-2611XM | 12.2.8T5 | IP/FW/IDS Plus IPSec 56 (or 3DES) |

Minimum Recommended Memory to download image: 16 MB Flash and 64 MB RAM.

| Filename | Description | Size in Bytes |
|---|---|---|
| c2600-ik8o3s-mz.122-8.T5.bin | IP/FW/IDS PLUS IPSEC 56 | 14341412 |

### Task 3: Loading Default Configurations on Pod Routers

**Step 1.** Reload, configure, and verify Pod routers. On the respective router, load the following configuration:

```
hostname Router1
!
no logging console
enable password cisco
!
interface Fa0/0
 description inside
 ip address 10.0.1.2 255.255.255.0
 no shut
!
interface Fa0/1
 description outside
 ip address 172.30.1.2 255.255.255.0
 no shut
!
router eigrp 1
 network 10.0.0.0
 network 172.30.0.0
 no auto-summary
!
ip classless
no ip http server
!
line vty 0 4
 password cisco
 login
!
end
```

```
hostname Router2
!
no logging console
enable password cisco
!
interface Fa0/0
 description inside
 ip address 10.0.2.2 255.255.255.0
 no shut
!
interface Fa0/1
 description outside
 ip address 172.30.2.2 255.255.255.0
 no shut
!
router eigrp 1
 network 10.0.0.0
 network 172.30.0.0
 no auto-summary
!
ip classless
no ip http server
!
line vty 0 4
 password cisco
 login
!
end
```

**Step 2.** Verify the configuration and save to flash. Notice the **P** value depends on which Pod router is being configured:

```
RouterP> show run
RouterP> copy run star
```

**Step 3.** The instructor configures and verifies RBB, SW0.

**Task 4: Configuring Student PCs (PC1 and PC2)**

**Step 1.** On the student PCs, log in as administrator. Verify the following list of installer software packages is located on the PC as directed by the instructor:

- Cisco Secure ACS 3.2
- Syslog Server: Kiwi or equivalent
- SSH Client: Putty.exe or equivalent
- TFPT Server: SolarWinds TFTP Server or equivalent
- SNMP Application: SNMP Trap watcher or equivalent
- Other applications as directed by the instructor

List any other applications in the folder.

**Step 2.** Verify that the i386 folder is located on the root drive C:\, as shown in Figure 1-5.

**Figure 1-5 Verifying the Directory Path of i386**

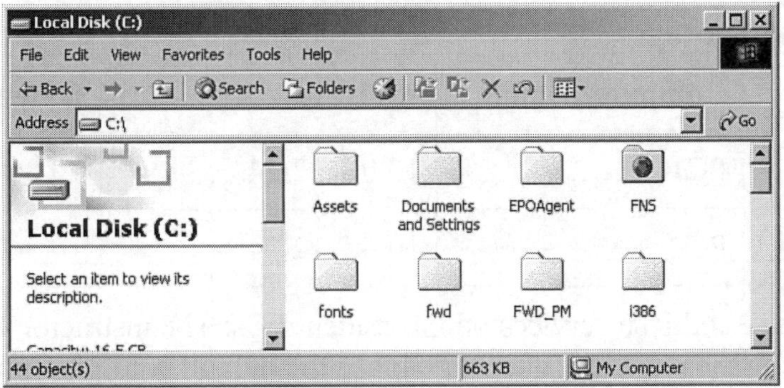


**Step 3.** Verify HyperTerminal is installed, as shown in Figure 1-6.

**Step 4.** Configure the student PCs' IP settings and services, as shown in Table 1-4. In general, these settings are used for Chapters 1–7.

**Figure 1-6 Verifying HyperTerminal Installation**

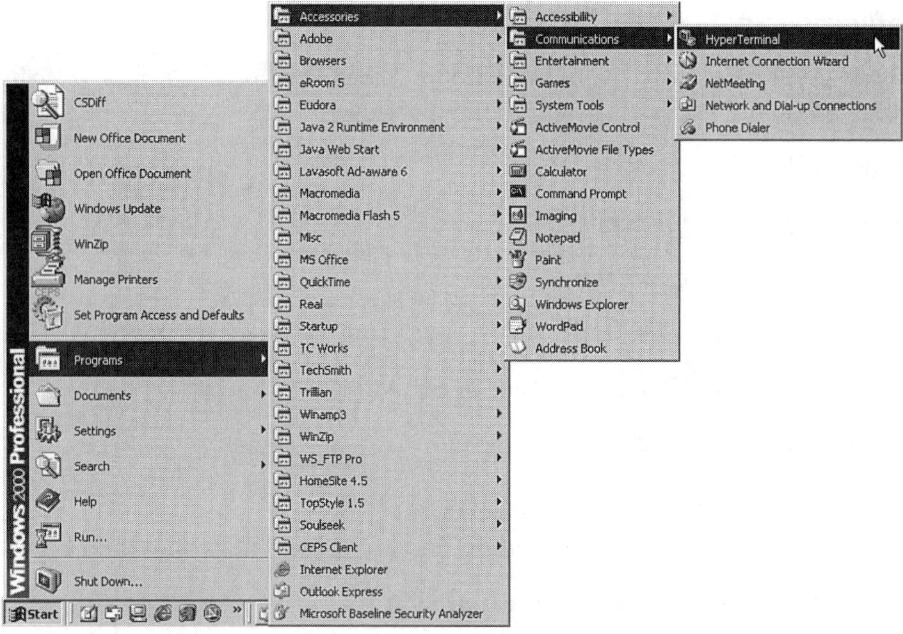


**Table 1-4 PC IP Settings**

| Label | Computer Name | Address | Gateway |
|---|---|---|---|
| PC1 | PC1 | 10.0.1.12/24 | 10.0.1.2 |
| PC2 | PC2 | 10.0.2.12/24 | 10.0.2.2 |

**Step 5.** Configure web and FTP services on the student PCs. The instructor will provide default web pages to install in the wwwroot directory. Place the default configuration of all Pod devices in the ftproot directory.

**Task 5: Verifying the Lab Topology Cabling**

**Step 1.** Figure 1-7 illustrates a port mapping of SW0 to cable or verify the physical connections.

**Figure 1-7 FNS Lab Topology: Physical Connections**

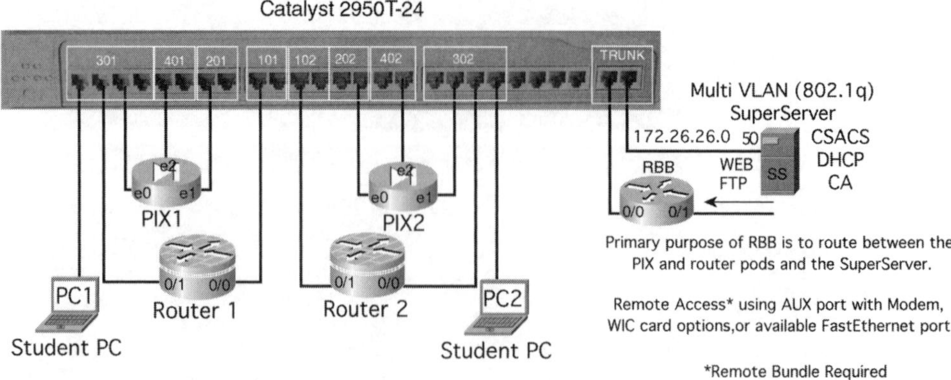


Figure 1-8 illustrates the logical FNS topology.

**Figure 1-8 FNS Lab Logical Topology**

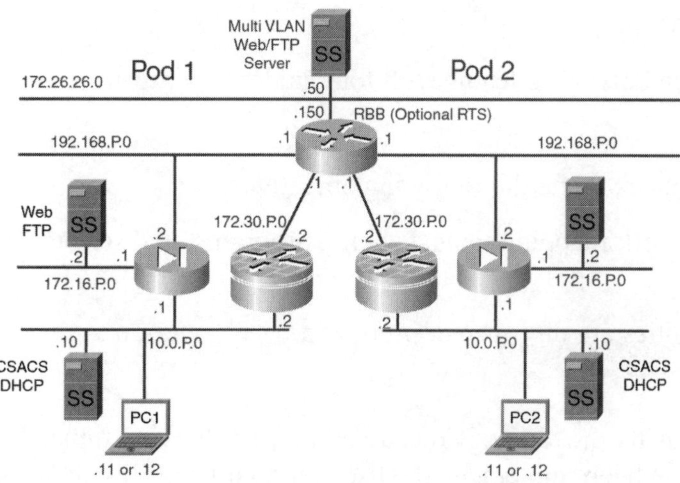


## Task 6: Testing Connectivity

**Step 1.** From the router, ping the peer router outside interface:

```
RouterP> ping 172.30.Q.2
RouterP> show ip interface
RouterP> show ip interface brief
RouterP> show interface
RouterP> show ip route
```

**Step 2.** From the PC, ping the peer inside PC:

```
C:\ ping 10.0.Q.12
```

**Step 3.** From a browser, access the web page of the peer PC:

```
http://10.0.Q.12
```

**Step 4.** From a browser, access the FTP page of the peer PC:

```
ftp://10.0.Q.12
```

# Lab 1.2.8: Vulnerabilities and Exploits

Estimated Time: 20 Minutes

Number of Team Members: Two teams with four students per team

## Objective

In this lab, the students examine the following objectives:

- Use common network mapping tools, hacking programs, and scripts on a LAN and across a WAN.
- Where vulnerabilities are discovered, propose a fix or solution to the problem.

## Overview

A small company is using the topology discussed in the following topic. Assume that minimal security measures have been implemented. Discover a vulnerability in any of the devices or software used in the network. This includes routers, switches, workstations, printer, server, hubs, and wiring. The students demonstrate this solution in the lab environment for observation by peers and the instructor.

Figure 1-9 illustrates the network environment students create.

**Figure 1-9 IOS Firewall Lab Visual Objective**

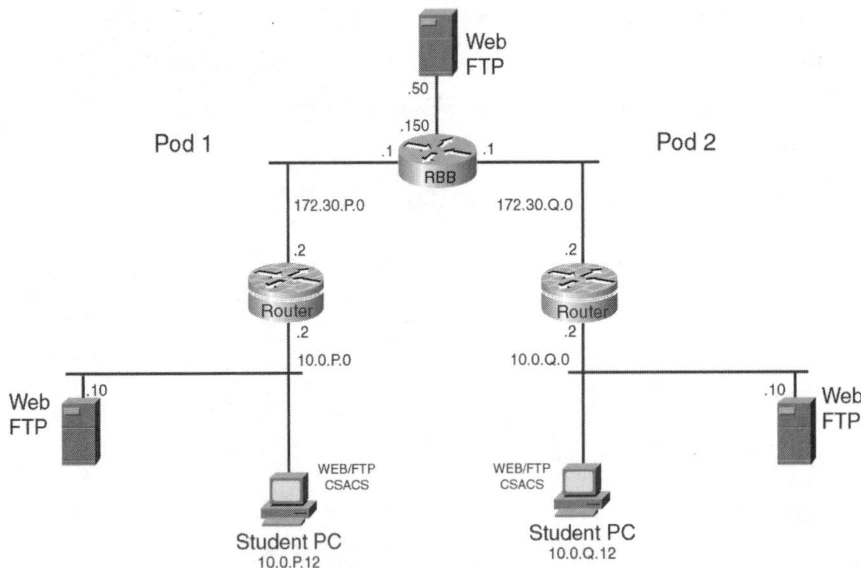


Use the standard lab topology and router configuration for POD P and POD Q. Configure the additional devices with the appropriate network address, gateway, and subnet mask, if required.

Students or small groups conduct a search for one known vulnerability or exploit. This lab can be repeated to allow students to experience each type of tool. Some of the common tools used are as follows:

- Reconnaissance
- Network/packet sniffers or port scanners

- Key loggers
- Simple Network Management Protocol (SNMP) or other network management/configuration tools
- Access
- Java, ActiveX, or cgi scripts
- Self-executing software
- Robots and control daemons
- SNMP or other network management/configuration tools
- Password tools such as brute force, dictionary, and so on
- Denial of service
- Ping of death
- SYN flood, User Datagram Protocol (UDP) bomb, and so on

When construction of the network is complete, verify connectivity between the LANs. Also verify that the workstations are configured correctly for the network in which they reside. For verification, use the following or any other relevant commands:

- **show ip route**
- **show interfaces**
- **show running-configuration**
- **ping**
- **telnet**
- **ipconfig**
- **winipcfg**
- **ifconfig**

For this lab, students can use any host PC or server for demonstration or implementation.

## Tools and Resources

To complete this lab, students should have access to the following equipment:

- Standard lab topology setup
- Network inspector, protocol analyzers, or sniffing software

## Additional Materials

The curriculum lists several excellent links that help the student understand the material presented in these labs. Other resources include the following:

- http://www.2600.com/
- http://www.cert.org
- *Hacking Exposed: Network Security Secrets & Solutions*, Third Edition, by Stuart McClure, Joel Scambray, and George Kurtz

## Safety

Students and instructors need to be careful not to violate any local, state, or federal laws or any network security policies. Be extremely cautious not to cause any permanent hardware damage to any device. Furthermore, it might be necessary to reimage or reload a workstation, device, or server operating system (OS) to completely eliminate any malicious code, virus, Trojan horse, or control daemon encountered in this lab.

### Task 1: Researching

**Step 1.** Research on the Internet or in a file the instructor designates one known exploit, script, or software tool for use in this task.

a. What is the filename, program name, and exploit name?

______________________________________________________________________

b. Obtain instructor approval, and install the file. Make sure that instructor approval has been obtained before downloading. What is the filename of the executable that has been downloaded?

______________________________________________________________________

c. How long did it take find the desired exploit, script, and software tool?

______________________________________________________________________

d. What was the source of the file, exploit, or vulnerability?

______________________________________________________________________

e. Describe the target device in terms of its name, model, OS, and function in the network.

______________________________________________________________________

______________________________________________________________________

f. What source device or operating system is required to implement this exploit or vulnerability?

______________________________________________________________________

g. Is this a known exploit? Who posted the advisory? Did the vendor acknowledge the problem? What are the recommended countermeasures?

______________________________________________________________________

______________________________________________________________________

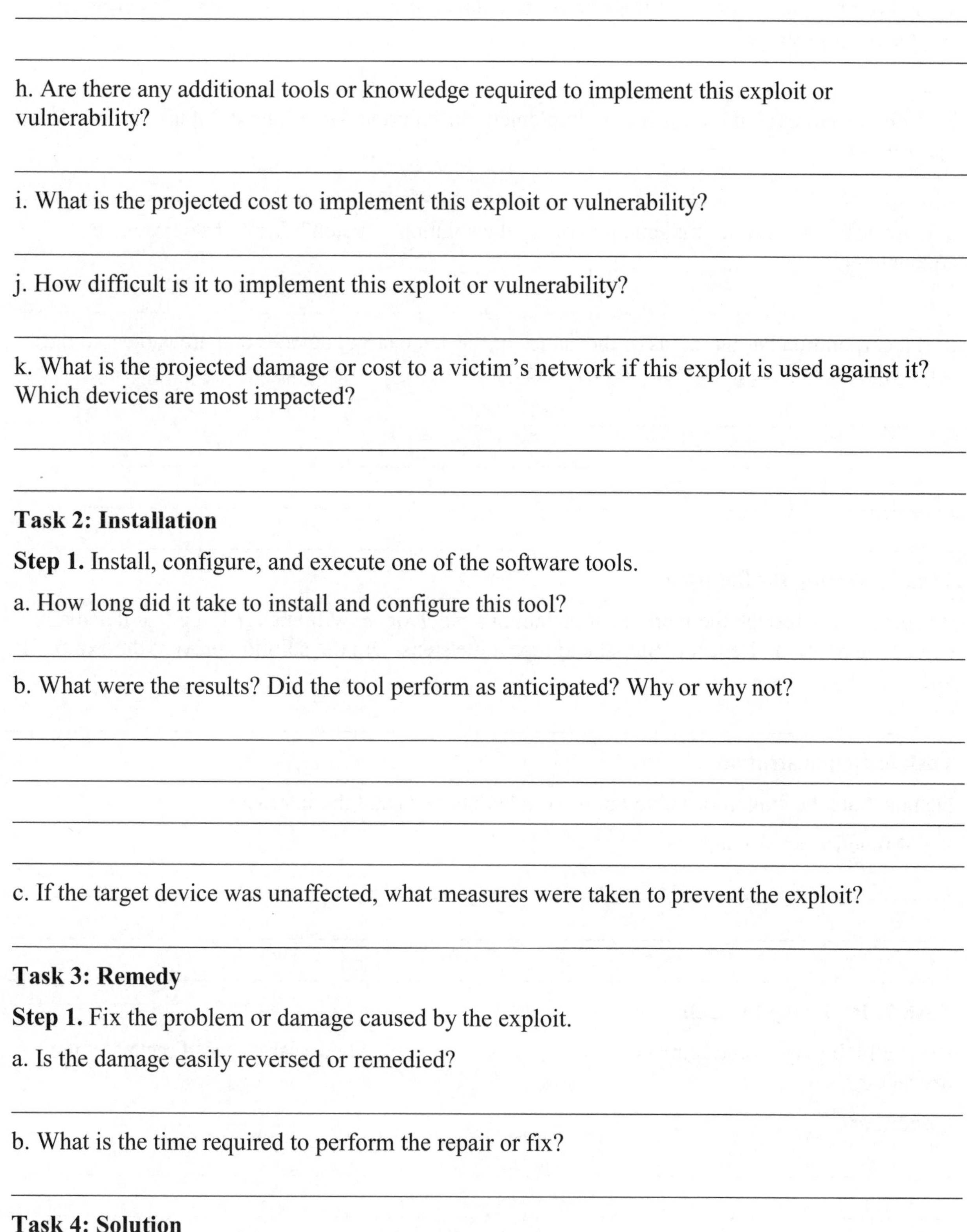

h. Are there any additional tools or knowledge required to implement this exploit or vulnerability?

i. What is the projected cost to implement this exploit or vulnerability?

j. How difficult is it to implement this exploit or vulnerability?

k. What is the projected damage or cost to a victim's network if this exploit is used against it? Which devices are most impacted?

**Task 2: Installation**

**Step 1.** Install, configure, and execute one of the software tools.

a. How long did it take to install and configure this tool?

b. What were the results? Did the tool perform as anticipated? Why or why not?

c. If the target device was unaffected, what measures were taken to prevent the exploit?

**Task 3: Remedy**

**Step 1.** Fix the problem or damage caused by the exploit.

a. Is the damage easily reversed or remedied?

b. What is the time required to perform the repair or fix?

**Task 4: Solution**

**Step 1.** Implement a solution to prevent recurrence of the exploit.

a. Find or propose a solution to this exploit or vulnerability. Describe the proposed permanent solution or prevention.

_______________

b. With the approval of the instructor, implement the solution. How long did it take to implement the solution?

_______________

c. How difficult was it to implement or apply the solution or patch? What obstacles were encountered?

_______________

d. If a corporation has hundreds or thousands of the same target devices that are subject to the same exploit, how could a solution be implemented?

_______________

_______________

_______________

_______________

**Task 5: Testing the Solution**

It is easy to go through the motions of installing a patch or fix without verifying that it actually solved the problem. Return to Step 2 and repeat the steps. Did the solution prevent the exploit or vulnerability?

_______________

**Task 6: Demonstration**

Demonstrate the exploit or vulnerability to other students and the instructor.

Did it function as planned?

_______________

_______________

_______________

**Task 7: Restoring the Lab**

Reset all lab devices and reimage the computers or devices if necessary, or as directed by the instructor.

**Comments**

_______________

_______________

_______________

_______________

# Lab 1.3.3: Designing a Security Plan

Estimated Time: 30 Minutes

Number of Team Members: Work individually or in teams of two

## Objective

In this lab, students analyze, offer recommendations, and help improve the security infrastructure of a fictitious business. Students are asked to perform the following tasks:

- Analyze business application requirements.
- Analyze security risks.
- Identify network assets.
- Analyze security requirements and tradeoffs.

## Overview

Widget Warehouse is a medium sized e-commerce company that supports 200 customers daily. The student has been hired to assist in the development of a new security policy. An assignment has been received to analyze the current network of Widget Warehouse. The Widget Warehouse network is comprised of an intranet with 200 users and a public web server that processes the company's e-commerce traffic. The internal network is logically divided into an information technology (IT) department branch, an accounting branch, a customer service branch, a sales branch, and an inventory branch.

To complete this lab, the students should have a firm understanding of the various security exploits that pose a risk to companies. Students should review the topics covered in Chapter 1 of the *Fundamentals of Network Security Companion Guide* prior to beginning this lab.

## Tools and Resources

The curriculum lists a number of excellent links that help the student understand the material presented in these labs, including the following:

- Carnegie Mellon Software Engineering Institute (CERT) at http://www.cert.org
- National Institute of Standards and Technology Security Division (NIST) at http://csrc.nist.gov/

### Task 1: Explaining Security Threats to the IT Department

The IT department for Widget Warehouse has a general understanding of security, but it is inexperienced with the various attacks an intruder can use to exploit their network resources. Create a list of various attacks intruders can use maliciously against the Widget Warehouse network. Also, in Table 1-5, provide a brief description of possible attacks, including their purpose(s).

**Table 1-5 Possible Attacks and Descriptions**

| Attack Name | Attack Description |
|---|---|
| | |
| | |
| | |
| | |
| | |
| | |
| | |
| | |
| | |

## Task 2: Gathering Security Related Information

One of the first steps in creating a security policy is gathering the requirements for the company. Create a list of questions to ask the Widget Warehouse executives to better understand their security requirements and business goals.

**Widget Warehouse Requirements**

1. ____________________________________________________________

______________________________________________________________

2. ______________________________________________________________

______________________________________________________________

3. ______________________________________________________________

______________________________________________________________

4. ______________________________________________________________

______________________________________________________________

5. ______________________________________________________________

______________________________________________________________

6. ______________________________________________________________

______________________________________________________________

7. ______________________________________________________________

______________________________________________________________

### Task 3: Determining the Security Implementation

Based on the questions, it is discovered that mission-critical information is passed between remote departments in the company over the LAN and the Internet. What security implementation could be used to keep this information out of unauthorized hands? Provide a brief explanation with each answer.

______________________________________________________________

______________________________________________________________

______________________________________________________________

______________________________________________________________

### Task 4: Describing the Security Wheel

The Widget Warehouse executives do not completely understand the continual process of security. They appear to be under the impression that once a security policy is in place, it is sufficient for an extended period of time. Create a description of the security wheel and discuss the benefits of such a model.

The security wheel is comprised of four steps. List them in Table 1-6.

**Table 1-6 Security Wheel Steps**

| Step Name | Step Description |
|---|---|
| 1. | |
| 2. | |
| 3. | |
| 4. | |

**Task 5: Determining the Security Monitoring Scheme**

The management of Widget Warehouse wants to see some of the available options in security monitoring. As the consultant, suggest that a passive monitoring scheme might be an option it should pursue. Write a description of passive monitoring for Widget Warehouse management.

**Task 6: Explaining Using a Security Policy**

Explain to the IT department how using a security policy can provide advantages to the company as a way to secure sensitive information.

**Comments**

## Review Questions

1. Name and describe the three goals of network security.

2. Name the three primary network security weaknesses and explain security vulnerabilities of each.

3. List some common ways employees misuse network resources.

4. List a vulnerability or attack for each layer of the OSI model.

5. Describe the three hacking methods covered in Chapter 1.

## Chapter 1 Quiz Questions

1. Which of the following is *not* an example of a technology weakness?

    A. TCP/IP protocol weaknesses

    B. Operating system vulnerabilities

    C. Unsecured user accounts

    D. Network equipment weaknesses

2. Which of the following represents the greatest potential threat to most networks?

    A. External threats

    B. Internal threats

3. The group of hackers who consider themselves "true hackers" and think theirs is a noble profession are known as

    A. Black hats

    B. Script kiddies

    C. White hats

    D. Red marauders

4. Most businesses' losses can be attributed to

    A. Stolen business secrets as a result of a successful hacking attempt

    B. Lost productivity and bandwidth as a result of worker misuse of network resources

    C. Damaged equipment as a result of viruses and worms introduced by hackers

    D. Data corruption as a result of external access

5. The unauthorized discovery and mapping of systems, services, or vulnerabilities is known as

    A. Denial of service

    B. Reconnaissance

    C. Script hacking

    D. Access

6. Which of the following is *not* a step in using the security wheel to implement network security?

    A. Secure

    B. Monitor

    C. Upgrade

    D. Improve

7. The section of your security policy that defines the responsibilities of users, operations staff, and management is called:

   A. Authentication

   B. Access

   C. Accountability

   D. Technology purchase

8. The key elements of a security solution are

   A. Identity, perimeter security, data privacy, security monitoring, and policy management

   B. System analysis, software configuration, role definition, and hardware inventory

   C. Secure, monitor, test, and improve

   D. Structured, unstructured, internal, and external

9. Which of the following is *not* one of the three types of networks considered when implementing network security?

   A. Trusted

   B. Untrusted

   C. Unknown

   D. Known

10. When implementing network security, you must balance:

   A. Cost and time

   B. Bandwidth and access

   C. Access and security

   D. Expertise and technology

# Chapter 2

## Basic Router and Switch Security

Building on the knowledge learned in Chapter 1, "Overview of Network Security," this chapter shows you how to protect the routers and switches in your network from attacks. In addition, this chapter discusses general router security that applies to all the routers, internal and perimeter. These techniques help improve the security of the network.

Disabling unneeded services on the router not only makes it less vulnerable to attacks, but it also has the benefit of improved performance because the router uses fewer resources. The decision to turn off services is based on the organization's needs and where the router is located.

Securing the perimeter router is important because it is the entrance and exit to your network. Special consideration should be given to the configuration of this device to provide the proper ingress and egress filtering and the thoughtful utilization of IP addresses.

To help you understand the management of the routers and switches, logging and Secure Shell (SSH) server are discussed. These tools track what is happening to the equipment and offer a more secure way to access the routers.

Finally, virtual LANs (VLANs) and port security are discussed as a means to increase security in the network by using switches.

**Vocabulary Exercise**

NAT

PAT

Syslog server

logging

MD5

______________________________________________________________________

______________________________________________________________________

______________________________________________________________________

NTP

______________________________________________________________________

______________________________________________________________________

______________________________________________________________________

authentication proxy

______________________________________________________________________

______________________________________________________________________

______________________________________________________________________

SSH

______________________________________________________________________

______________________________________________________________________

______________________________________________________________________

## Lab Activities

The topology figures and lab examples contain **P** and **Q** values. The **P** value in the addressing and naming scheme refers to *your* assigned Pod number.

The following are examples of determining P values:

- Pod2 is looking at a topology figure and is trying to determine the P values in the figure. In this scenario the **P** values would equal **2**. 10.0.**P**.12 would become 10.0.**2**.12, 172.30.**P**.2 would become 172.30.**2**.2, and so on.
- Pod1 is looking at a topology figure and is trying to determine the P values in the figure. In this scenario the **P** values would equal **1**. 10.0.**P**.12 would become 10.0.**1**.12, 172.30.**P**.2 would become 172.30.**1**.2, and so on.

In both examples, the P values are directly related to the Pod number of the team.

The **Q** value in the naming and addressing scheme is used when testing the security or connectivity with the peer team.

The following are examples of determining Q values:

- In a lab, Pod2 has been asked to test connectivity to their peer inside host at IP address 10.0.Q.12. In this scenario, 10.0.Q.12 would equal 10.0.1.12.
- In a lab, Pod1 has been asked to test connectivity to their peer inside host at IP address 10.0.Q.12. In this scenario, 10.0.Q.12 would equal 10.0.2.12.

In both examples, the Q value is directly related to the peer Pod number.

# Lab 2.1.6: Configure General Router Security

Estimated Time: 15 Minutes

Number of Team Members: Two teams with four students per team

## Objective

In this lab, students cover the following objectives:

- Use no-cost router features to enhance security.
- Set passwords.
- Encrypt passwords.
- Set privileges.
- Define user privileges.
- Verify privilege level settings.

## Overview

Many overlooked security features of the router come at no additional expense whatsoever. These features are often misconfigured or overlooked because they are not traditional security features. Passwords are the primary defense against unauthorized access to the router.

Leaving a console unattended can cause serious problems, especially if the user is logged in as a privileged user. The use of console timeouts can control how long the console will remain logged in after a period of inactivity.

This lab also covers the commands used to establish password protection and configure privilege levels. Password protection allows a network security administrator to restrict access to a network or a network device. Privilege levels allow a security administrator to define what commands various users can issue after they have logged in to a network device. This is very important in larger networks where the IT staff needs access to network devices with different levels of access.

In some jurisdictions, civil or criminal prosecution of hackers who break into the systems are made much easier if a banner message informing unauthorized users that their use is, in fact, unauthorized.

Figure 2-1 illustrates the network environment for this lab.

## Preparation

Begin with the standard lab topology and verify the standard router configuration on the Pod routers. Test the connectivity between the Pod routers. Access the perimeter router console port using the terminal emulator on the Windows 2000 server. If desired, save the router configuration to a text file for later analysis. Refer to the *Student Lab Orientation* if you need more help.

**Figure 2-1 Lab 2.1.6 Network Topology**

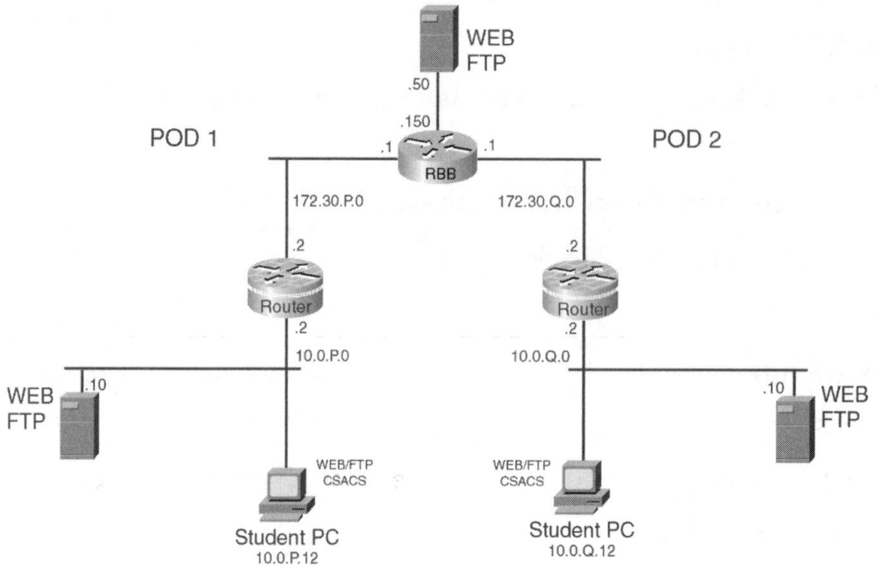

## Tools and Resources

To complete the lab, the standard lab topology is required:

- Two Pod routers
- Two student PCs
- Two servers
- Backbone switch and router
- Two console cables and HyperTerminal

## Additional Materials

Further information regarding the objectives covered in this lab can be found at the following websites:

- http://www.cisco.com/en/US/products/sw/iosswrel/ps1835/products_command_reference_chapter09186a00800ca7cd.html
- http://www.cisco.com/en/US/products/sw/iosswrel/ps1831/products_configuration_guide_chapter09186a00800d984e.html
- http://www.cisco.com/en/US/products/sw/iosswrel/ps1828/products_command_summary_chapter09186a00800eeadc.html

## Command List

This lab uses the commands listed in Table 2-1. Refer to this list if you need help during the lab.

**Table 2-1 Lab 2.1.6 Command List**

| Command | Description |
|---|---|
| **exec-timeout** | Sets the interval that the EXEC command interpreter waits until user input is detected |
| **enable** | Enters privileged EXEC mode |
| **enable password** *password* | Sets a local password to control access to various privilege levels |
| **enable secret** *password* | Specifies an additional layer of security over the enable password command |
| **enable secret level** *level password* | Sets a password for the privilege level |
| **login local** | Defines a login authentication mechanism for the lines<br>The authentication method must utilize a username and password. |
| **privilege level** *level* | Configures a new privilege level for users and associates commands with that privilege level<br>*level* is the privilege level associated with the specified line. |
| **privilege** *mode* {**level** *level* \| **reset**} *command-string* | *mode* is the configuration mode for the specified command.<br>**level** *level* specifies the privilege level configured for the specified command or commands. The level argument must be a number from 0 to 15.<br>**reset** resets the privilege level of the specified command or commands to the default and removes the privilege level configuration from the running-config file.<br>*Note:* If the **no** form of this command is used to reset the privilege level to the default, the default form of this command still appears in the configuration file. To completely remove a privilege configuration, use the reset keyword.<br>*command-string* is the command associated with the specified privilege level. If the all keyword is used, it specifies the command and subcommands associated with the privilege level. |

| Command | Description |
|---|---|
| **service password-encryption** | Encrypts all passwords in the configuration files |
| **show privilege** | Displays the current level of privilege |
| **transport input** | Defines which protocols to use to connect to a specific line of the router |

**Task 1: Setting Enable Passwords**

**Step 1.** Defining an enable password.

The enable password should always be set in any production environment. Setting the enable password authenticates the user when he or she tries to enter the privileged EXEC mode (RouterP#). Defining an enable password helps prevent unauthorized access to the various router configuration modes.

To define an enable password, use the **enable password** *password* command:

```
RouterP(config)# enable password cisco
```

This command sets the enable password to **cisco**.

**Step 2.** Verifying the enable password.

To verify the enable password, exit out of the router completely using the **exit** command. After logging out, reconnect to the user level (RouterP>). Then, enter the **enable** command. A prompt appears asking for a password. Enter the enable password that was configured. If the password is entered correctly, access is granted to the privileged EXEC mode (RouterP#).

**Step 3.** View the enable password.

To view the enable password, use the **show running-config** command in the privileged EXEC mode.

a. Is the enable password in the output? If so, write the output line that it is included.

Yes, enable password cisco
_______________________________________________

b. Is the password displayed in plain text or is it encrypted?

Plain text
_______________________________________________

**Task 2: Enabling Secret Password**

As shown in Task 1, the enable password is displayed in plain text in the running configuration file.

It is also displayed in the startup configuration file if the **copy running-config startup-config** command is used.

However, defining the enable password using the **enable password** command can be a security risk.

Why would setting the enable password using the **enable password** command be a possible security risk? it is in clear text

**Step 1.** Setting the enable secret password.

In the global configuration mode, use the **enable secret password** command to set an enable secret password. Set the password to **class** using the following command:

```
RouterP(config)# enable secret class
```

**Step 2.** View the encrypted password.

To view the encrypted enable password, view the running configuration:

```
RouterP#show run       *(abbreviated show running-config command)
```

a. Is the enable password encrypted?

no

b. Is the enable secret password encrypted?

yes

c. How is the enable secret password displayed?

enable secret 5

After setting a password using the **enable secret** command, a password set using the **enable password** command works only if the **enable secret** is disabled or an older version of Cisco IOS Software is being used, such as when running an older rxboot image.

**Task 3: Service Password Encryption**

**Step 1.** Service password encryption.

From the previous tasks, both an **enable** password and an **enable secret** command were set. The different output generated by each command was viewed. Remember that the **enable password** command is unencrypted and the **enable secret** command generates encrypted output in the configuration file. The **service password-encryption** command encrypts all passwords in the configuration files.

View the running configuration again and look for the line "no service password-encryption." This means that the password encryption service is disabled and that this is the default setting.

Enable the password encryption service by entering the **service password-encryption** command:

```
RouterP(config)# service password-encryption
```

**Step 2.** View the running configuration file.

View the running configuration file using the **show running-config** command:

```
RouterP# show run
```

Are both the `enable password` and `enable secret` passwords encrypted?

yes

**Task 4: Configuring vty for Telnet**

Protect the vty connections that are made through the router. These connections are commonly established through Telnet, but can use other protocols as well. To control the protocols that will be accepted on the vty, use the **transport input** *protocol* command. Check to see what transport protocols are available.

a. What command displays the available transport protocols?

transport input ?

b. What are the protocols?

pad, Rlogin, telnet, uDptn

c. Now allow Telnet on the vty using the **transport input** Telnet command to enable it. What is the configuration mode required to configure this feature?

config line vty 0 15

**Task 5: Controlling Telnet Access**

The **access-class** *ACL number* command can direct the router to accept virtual connections from only certain IP addresses. To use this command, the host(s) or network(s) must be defined to accept virtual connections. A standard or extended access control list (ACL) defines this list.

Define a standard ACL that directs the router to accept virtual connections from the inside host. Remember that the command to create a standard access list for a single host is **access-list** *number* **permit host** *host-ip*.

Use this access list to define the access class for the vty connections. Set the access class to the vty lines (0–4) for inbound connections.

a. Try to Telnet to the router from the inside host. Is the connection successful?

no

b. Try to Telnet to the peer router from the inside host. Is the connection successful to the peer router? Why or why not?

no, no password was set

Further restrict Telnet access based on local username and password pairs. The vty lines should be configured to use local authentication with the **login local** command at line configuration mode.

A username and password pair must be configured in global configuration mode. Configure the username bob to be used with password cisco4me.

c. Try to Telnet to the router. Did the router prompt for a username and password?

yes

d. Use the correct username and password. Was it successful?

yes

e. Exit Telnet and connect again. Try to access the router by using another username or another password. What was the error message?

% Login invalid

---

**Task 6: Controling Console Timeout**

Change the console timeout to log out after a period of inactivity of 2 minutes, 30 seconds. Remember to use the **exec-timeout** *mm ss* command in line configuration mode to change the default value.

What is the maximum amount in minutes? What command will display the new changes?

35791 , show run

---

**Task 7: Setting Privilege Levels**

By default, the Cisco IOS Software has two modes of password security: user mode (EXEC) and privilege mode (enable). Sixteen hierarchical levels of commands for each mode can be defined. By configuring multiple passwords, different sets of users are allowed access to specified commands.

The command to assign allowed commands to privilege mode is **privilege level level**. In this task, assign an **enable secret** password for privilege level 10 for system operators, and make specific **debug** commands available to anyone with that privilege level enabled.

Begin by entering global configuration mode, RouterP(config)#, and complete the following steps.

**Step 1.** Assign privilege level passwords.

It is recommended to assign a password to each privilege level that is defined. To set a privilege level password, use the **enable secret level** *level password* command.

Define an enable secret of pswd10 for level 10 by entering the following command:

```
RouterP(config)# enable secret level 10 pswd10
```

What are the available arguments for the **enable secret level 10** command?

0, 5, Line

---

**Step 2.** Defining privilege level rights.

Assign specific commands to be used in privilege level 10. To configure a new privilege level for users and associate commands to that privilege level, use the **privilege** command. The syntax for the privilege command is **privilege mode {level** *level* | **reset}** *command-string*. Enter the following commands to assign specific commands to privilege level 10:

```
RouterP(config)# privilege exec level 10 debug ppp auth
RouterP(config)# privilege exec level 10 debug ppp error
RouterP(config)# privilege exec level 10 debug ppp negotiation
```

In the preceding commands, specific **debug** commands were allowed for anyone logging in with privilege level 10.

**Step 3.** Displaying current privilege level.

To verify the current privilege level, enter the show **privilege** command.

What privilege level is shown?

15

**Step 4.** Log in to privilege level 10.

To enter into a specific privilege level, use the **enable *level*** command. Exit out of the router and then reconnect. Enter the following commands to enter privilege level 10:

```
RouterP> enable 10
Password:pswd10
RouterP#
```

How can current privilege level be displayed? What is the current privilege level?

show privilgo , 10

**Step 5.** Verify privilege level commands.

After the current privilege level of 10 is confirmed, verify the previously configured privilege level 10 commands. Enter the following commands to verify the defined privileges:

```
RouterP#debug ?
RouterP#debug ppp ?
```

a. What are the available parameters for the **debug ?** command?

(authentication, error, negoation) ppp, ion

b. What are the available parameters for the **debug ppp ?** command?

**Step 6.** Compare privilege levels.

Log back into the router with privilege level 15. Then, compare the **debug ?** and **debug ppp ?** command output to that of privilege level 10.

a. What is the difference, if any?

yes, alot more options (examples?)

b. By default, what is the privilege level when logging in with the **enable** command without specifying a level?

15

**Task 8: Setting a Banner Message**

Another security feature that is useful to configure on the router is a warning message that each user sees when logging into the router. This message is configured using the **banner motd** command.

Create a warning message that says, "This router is not to be used by unauthorized personnel!" The command syntax to create this banner is **banner motd** *<delimiting character> <message> <delimiting character>*.

a. Exit the router and log back in. Is the warning displayed?

yes

b. Telnet to the router from the allowed workstation. Is the warning displayed?

yes
___

## Lab 2.2.1: Controlling TCP/IP Services

Estimated Time: 15 Minutes

Number of Team Members: Two teams with four students per team

### Objective

In this lab, students complete the following objectives:

- Begin the process of implementing a secure perimeter router.
- Explicitly deny common TCP/IP services.
- Verify TCP/IP services have been disabled.

### Overview

The XYZ Company is in the process of installing a perimeter router to defend their network against various security threats. It is the responsibility of the network security administrator to implement a secure perimeter router based on the security policy. The first configuration task is to disable common TCP/IP services that can pose a risk to the internal network. Remember that TCP/IP was designed to provide connectivity and services, not security. Many standards have been implemented to help secure TCP/IP. Fortunately, the new IPv6 standard addresses many of the security issues and vulnerabilities of the current TCP/IP, which is also called IPv4. Until then, the security administrator must secure the system with the available tools and methods.

Telnet, Simple Network Management Protocol (SNMP), and HTTP access to the router should be secured or disabled. One way to secure Telnet access is to limit the IP addresses that might Telnet to the router. HTTP can be limited using access lists and/or authentication. Securing SNMP is covered in Chapter 5, "Router Intrusion Detection, Monitoring, and Management."

The TCP and User Datagram Protocol (UDP) protocol standard includes a recommended list of simple services that hosts should provide. When theses services are enabled, they can leave the router vulnerable to TCP and UDP diagnostic port attacks. Many routers offer the small services, echo, Character generation (chargen), and discard, by default. These services, especially their UDP versions, are infrequently used for legitimate purposes, but can be used to launch denial of service (DoS) and other attacks that would otherwise be prevented by packet filtering.

Figure 2-2 illustrates the network environment for this lab.

### Preparation

Begin with the standard lab topology and verify the standard router configuration on the Pod routers. Test the connectivity between the Pod routers. Access the perimeter router console port using the terminal emulator on the Windows 2000 server. If desired, save the router configuration to a text file for later analysis. Refer to the *Student Lab Orientation* (Lab 1.1.5) if you need more help.

**Figure 2-2 Lab 2.2.1 Network Topology**

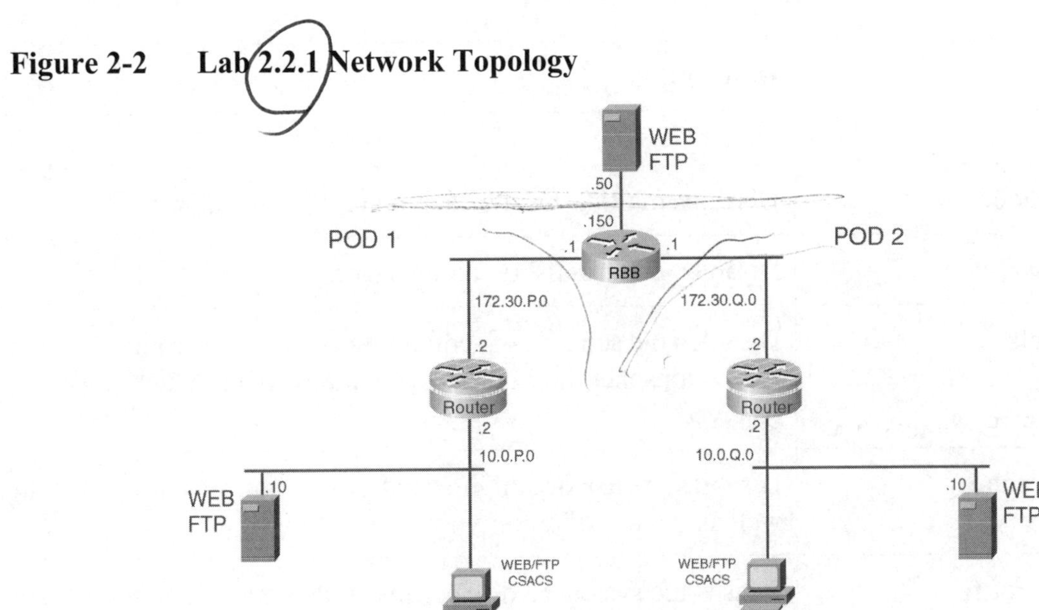


## Tools and Resources

To complete the lab, the standard lab topology is required:

- Two Pod routers
- Two student PCs
- Two servers
- Backbone switch and router
- Two console cables and HyperTerminal

## Additional Materials

Further information about the objectives covered in this lab can be found at this website:

- http://www.cisco.com/en/US/products/sw/iosswrel/ps1828/products_configuration_guide_chapter09186a00800b3dda.html.

## Command List

This lab uses the commands listed in Table 2-2. Refer to this list if you need any assistance or help during the lab.

**Table 2-2 Lab 2.2.1 Command List**

| **Command** | **Description** |
|---|---|
| **no cdp enable** | Disables Cisco Discovery Protocol on an interface |
| **no cdp run** | Disables Cisco Discovery Protocol globally |
| **no ip mask-reply** | Disables the Cisco IOS Software response to the Internet Control Message Protocol (ICMP) mask requests by sending ICMP mask |

| Command | Description |
|---|---|
| | reply messages |
| **no mroute-cache** | Disables multicast route caching on the outside interface |
| **no ip proxy-arp** | Disables proxy ARP on an interface |
| **no ip redirects** | Disables the sending of redirect messages if the router is forced to resend a packet through the same interface on which it was received |
| **no ip route-cache** | Disables the use of a high-speed switching cache for IP routing as well as the use of autonomous switching |
| **no ip source-route** | Causes the system to discard any IP datagram containing a source-route option |
| **no ip unreachables** | Enables the generation of ICMP unreachable messages on a specified interface |
| **no service finger** | To disallow finger protocol requests, defined in RFC 742, to be made of the network server, use the **no service finger** global configuration command. This service is equivalent to issuing remote **show users** command. |
| **no ntp** | Turns off the Network Time Protocol that is used for the synchronization of clocks on devices in a network; defined in RFC-1305 |
| **no service tcp-small-servers** | Denies access to minor TCP/IP services available from hosts on the network |
| **no service udp-small-servers** | Denies access to minor UDP services available from hosts on the network. |

**Task 1: Disabling ICMP Messages on Ethernet 0**

**Step 1.** Enter interface configuration mode for Fast Ethernet 0/1 or the outside interface on the perimeter router. In many production environments, this is a serial port such as Serial0/0 or Serial0/1. In this lab, enter the command **interface fa 0/1** at global configuration mode. This might vary depending on the router model.

How is the prompt displayed after entering interface configuration mode?

Router(config-if)#
_______________________________________________

**Step 2.** Disable the automatic generation of ICMP or ping messages to untrusted or public networks. By default, ICMP automatically generates Redirect, Host Unreachable, and Mask

Reply message. Intruders can intercept these messages and expose the network topology. Enter the following commands to disable these ICMP messages:

- To disable ICMP Redirect messages on the interface, enter the command **no ip redirects**.
- To disable ICMP Unreachable messages on the interface, enter the command **no ip unreachables**.
- To disable ICMP Mask Reply messages on the interface, enter the command **no ip mask-reply**.

ICMP messages are sent in response to certain IP packets; what information could an intruder gather if this information is not blocked?

machine is available and alive
___

Refer to Table 2-2 for help configuring this security policy.

**Task 2: Disabling Multicast Route Caching**

Disable multicast route caching on the outside interface by entering the following command:

```
no ip mroute-cache
```

Refer to Table 2-2 for help configuring this security policy.

**Task 3: Disabling Cisco Discovery Protocol**

Disable the Cisco Discovery Protocol (CDP) on the outside interface. Enter the following command to disable CDP on an interface:

```
no cdp enable
```

What command globally disables CDP?

no CDP Run
___

Refer to the Table 2-2 for help configuring this security policy.

**Task 4: Controlling HTTP and SNMP Access**

Control the hosts that are allowed to create HTTP connections to the router. In this lab, accept HTTP connections from the inside host, but not from the peer inside host.

a. What ACL will define a permit for the inside host?

___

Apply this new ACL to HTTP connections using the **ip http access-class** *acl* command. Remember to use the newly defined ACL number. Test this connection from the inside host.

b. Was the connection successful?

yes
___

c. Try to connect to the HTTP server of the peer router. Was the connection successful? What was the error message?

not found
___

d. To disable HTTP access, use the **no ip http-server** command. Test this connection from the inside host. Was the connection successful?

no

e. To disable SNMP access, use the **no snmp-server** command. Use the **show snmp** and **show run** commands to verify that the service is shut down. Was there a response? Notice that a **show run** will not display the snmp service as disabled.

no, it shows no activity

**Task 5: Disabling Small Services**

Most routers support a multitude of small services that might or might not be needed or used by an organization. These small services should be disabled, unless specifically needed.

Disable each of the following services, using the **no** form of the commands:

- **no service tcp-small-servers**
- **no service udp-small-servers**
- **no service finger**
- **no ntp**
- **no cdp run**

Show the running configuration. Do these services show up?

no

**Task 6: Verifying Configurations**

**Step 1.** Exit interface configuration mode and return to the privileged EXEC mode (RouterP#). Verify the configuration by entering the **show running-configuration** command.

Verify the configurations displayed under "interface FastEthernet0/1" or the outside interface. Document the configuration here.

IP address 172.16.26.50 255.255.255.0, no ip redirects, no IP unreachables, no IP m-route cache, speed auto, no cdp enable

**Step 2.** Verify the CDP information. Enter the command **show cdp**.

What information is displayed? In the earlier CDP, why does the output show differently?

CDP global info, It is disabled

**Step 3.** Verify that Cisco Discover Information has been disabled on the outside interface. Enter the command **show cdp interface** to display CDP information specific to the interfaces.

Does the output display CDP information for the outside port? Why or why not?

no, it was globally disabled

## Sample Perimeter Router Configuration

The following sample configuration for the Pod 1 perimeter router is one possible outcome of this lab. Other configurations might vary according to available router features and interfaces:

```
Current configuration:
!version 12.0
service timestamps debug datetime msec localtime show-timezone
service timestamps log datetime msec localtime show-timezone
no service password-encryption
!
hostname Router1
!
logging buffered 4096 debugging
no logging console
!
username student password 0 cisco
memory-size iomem 25
clock timezone PST -8
clock summer-time zone recurring
ip subnet-zero
no ip source-route
no ip finger
ip tcp selective-ack
ip tcp path-mtu-discovery
no ip domain-lookup
no ip bootp server
!
interface FastEthernet0/0
description inside
ip address 10.0.1.2 255.255.255.0
ip access-group 102 in
!
interface FastEthernet 0/1
description outside
ip address 172.30.1.2 255.255.255.0
no ip directed-broadcast
no ip redirects
no ip unreachables
no ip directed-broadcast
no ip proxy-arp
no ip route-cache
no ip mroute-cache
!
ip classless
ip route 0.0.0.0 0.0.0.0 172.16.1.2
no ip http server
!
logging trap debugging
logging source-interface FastEthernet0
logging 192.168.1.10
access-list 1 permit 192.168.1.10
access-list 101 deny ip 127.0.0.0 0.255.255.255 any log
access-list 101 deny ip 255.0.0.0 0.255.255.255 any log
access-list 101 deny ip 224.0.0.0 7.255.255.255 any log
access-list 101 deny ip host 0.0.0.0 any log
access-list 101 deny ip 192.168.1.0 0.0.0.255 any log
access-list 101 deny ip 10.0.0.0 0.255.255.255 any log
access-list 101 deny udp any any eq snmp
access-list 101 permit tcp any 192.168.1.0 0.0.0.255 established
access-list 101 permit tcp any host 192.168.1.3 eq smtp
access-list 101 permit tcp any host 192.168.1.3 eq www
access-list 101 permit tcp any host 192.168.1.3 eq 443
access-list 101 permit tcp any host 192.168.1.3 eq ftp
access-list 101 permit tcp any host 192.168.1.3 gt 1023
access-list 101 permit icmp any 192.168.1.0 0.0.0.255 echo-reply
access-list 101 permit icmp any host 172.16.1.1 echo-reply
access-list 101 permit icmp host 192.168.255.2 host 172.16.1.1 echo
access-list 101 permit udp any host 192.168.1.3 eq domain
access-list 101 permit tcp host 192.168.255.2 host 192.168.1.3 eq nntp
access-list 101 permit udp host 192.168.255.2 host 192.168.1.3 eq ntp
access-list 101 deny icmp any host 192.168.1.1 echo log
access-list 101 deny tcp any host 192.168.1.1 eq telnet log
access-list 101 deny tcp any host 172.16.1.1 eq telnet log
access-list 101 deny tcp any host 192.168.1.2 eq telnet log
access-list 101 deny ip any any log
access-list 102 permit ip 192.168.1.0 0.0.0.255 any
access-list 102 deny ip any any log
```

```
no cdp run
!
line con 0
exec-timeout 0 0
logging synchronous
login local
transport input none
line aux 0
no exec
login local
line vty 0 4
access-class 1 in
login local
!
end
```

## Lab 2.3.2: Configure NAT/PAT

Estimated Time: 15 Minutes

Number of Team Members: Two teams with four students per team

### Objective

In this lab, students use Network Address Translation (NAT) and port address translation (PAT) to hide internal addresses.

### Overview

In a secure network, it is important that internal network IP addresses remain hidden from the outside so that potential attackers are not able to gain an understanding of the network topology and design. NAT can hide these addresses, which makes it more difficult for a potential attacker to gain an understanding of the network architecture and to subsequently exploit it.

Figure 2-3 illustrates the network environment for this lab.

**Figure 2-3 Lab 2.3.2 Network Topology**

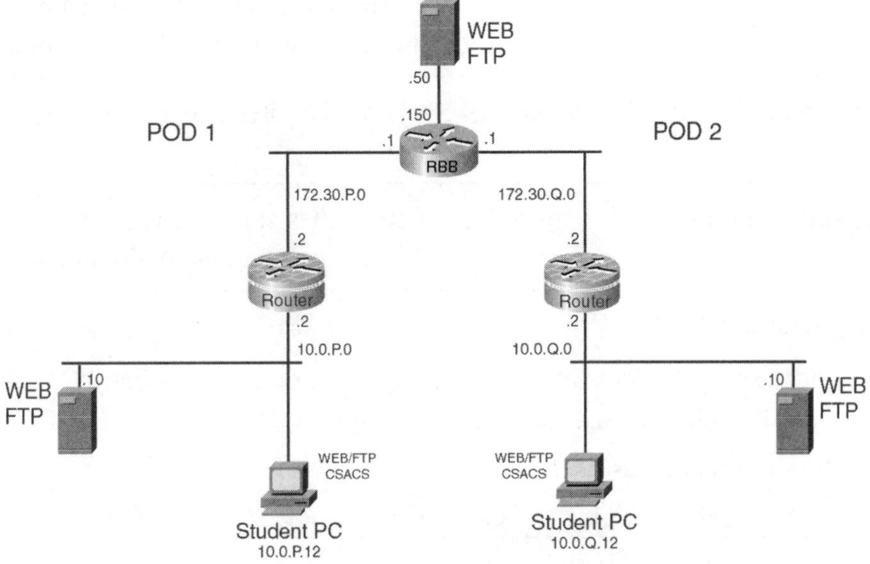


### Preparation

Begin with the standard lab topology and verify the standard router configuration on the Pod routers. Test the connectivity between the Pod routers. Access the perimeter router console port using the terminal emulator on the Windows 2000 server. If desired, save the router configuration to a text file for later analysis. Refer to the *Student Lab Orientation (Lab 1.1.5)* if you need more help.

### Tools and Resources

To complete the lab, the standard lab topology is required:

- Two Pod routers
- Two student PCs

- Two servers
- Backbone switch and router
- Two console cables and HyperTerminal

## Additional Materials

You can find further information about the objectives covered in this lab at this website:

- http://www.cisco.com/en/US/products/sw/iosswrel/ps1835/products_command_reference_chapter09186a0080087387.html#1053499

## Command List

This lab uses the commands listed in Table 2-3. Refer to this list if you need any assistance or help during the lab.

**Table 2-3 Lab 2.3.2 Command List**

| Command | Description |
|---|---|
| **access-list** | Defines a standard access list permitting those addresses that are to be translated |
| **ip nat** {**inside** \| **outside**} \| **log** {**translations syslog**} | Marks the interface as connected to the inside or outside |
| **ip nat inside source static** *local-ip global-ip* | Establishes static translation between an inside local address and an inside global address |

### Task 1: Configuring PAT

**Step 1.** Define addresses to be translated by creating a standard access list:

```
RouterP(config)# access-list 1 permit 10.0.P.0 0.0.0.255
```

What is the purpose of this access list?

List of addresses allowed for pat
_______________________________________________

**Step 2.** Verify the access list created:

```
RouterP# show access-list
```

**Step 3.** Now, connect the access list to a NAT statement:

```
RouterP(config)#ip nat inside source list 1 interface Fa0/1 overload
```

What is meant by NAT overloading?

to enable nat to have more than one conn on an int
_______________________________________________

**Step 4.** Use the **ip nat** command to indicate which router interface is connected to the inside network and which interface is connected to the outside:

```
RouterP(config)#interface Fa 0/0
RouterP(config-if)#ip nat inside

RouterP(config)#interface Fa 0/1
RouterP(config-if)#ip nat outside
```

a. Why is it important for the router to know which interface is connected to the inside network and which is connected to the outside network?

to ensure that routing is correct

b. What timeout values, in seconds, can be set for NAT?

0 - 2147483647 and never

```
RouterP(config)# ip nat translation ?
```

**Step 5.** Configure timeout values in seconds:

```
RouterP(config)# ip nat translation udp-timeout 120
RouterP(config)# ip nat translation dns-timeout 60
RouterP(config)# ip nat translation tcp-timeout 120
RouterP(config)# ip nat translation icmp-timeout 120
```

Name a reason when you might want to give more or less time than the Cisco default timeout.

excess fragmentation

**Task 2: Testing**

**Step 1.** Verify the routers address translation:

```
RouterP# show ip nat translations
```

a. With what information did the router respond?

protocol, Inside global, Inside local, Outside local and global

```
RouterP# show ip nat translations verbose
```

b. With what additional information did the router respond?

creation time, l enth, and flags

```
RouterP# show ip nat statistics
```

c. With what information did the router respond?

Interfaces, Hits and misses, and mappings

```
RouterP# clear ip nat translation *
RouterP# show ip nat translations
```

d. With what additional information did the router respond?

none

**Step 2.** From a workstation on the inside network, ping the peer inside host address at 10.0.Q.12. Was it successful?

~~No~~ yes

**Task 3: Allowing Access to the Student PC**

Many times, it is necessary to allow access to an internal device such as a web, e-mail, or file server. To allow access, a static translation must be established between the inside server address and an inside global address that allows the traffic.

**Step 1.** Configure access to the student PC at 10.0.P.12. Many times, when making configuration changes to NAT, the router interface might need to be shut down to make changes. Also, a reload might be required to assure proper operation:

```
RouterP(config)# ip nat inside source static tcp 10.0.P.12 80 172.30.P.12 80
```

Now, verify the router's address translation after the change:

```
RouterP#show ip nat translations
```

With what information did the router respond?

the new map
___

Load the default FNS configuration on the routers before proceeding to the next lab.

## Lab 2.3.3: Configure Routing Authentication and Filtering

Estimated Time: 15 Minutes

Number of Team Members: Two teams with four students per team

### Objective

In this lab, students demonstrate the use of authentication and filters to control route updates from peer routers.

### Overview

Routing protocols are vulnerable to eavesdropping and spoofing of routing updates. Cisco IOS Software supports authentication of routing protocol updates to prevent the introduction of unauthorized or false routing messages from unknown sources. Routing protocol authentication is also known as neighbor authentication.

Filtering networks in routing updates sent from the private network to external routers helps secure networks by hiding the details of networks that should not be accessed by external users. If a network is not advertised, no apparent route exists to that network, and intruders will have more trouble getting there.

Incoming routing updates can be filtered to provide protection against receiving false information in routing updates because of improper configuration or intentional activity that could cause routing problems. Suppressing networks listed in updates keeps a router from using routes that might be spurious. This helps prevent route spoofing.

Figure 2-4 illustrates the network environment for this lab.

**Figure 2-4 Lab 2.3.3 Network Topology**

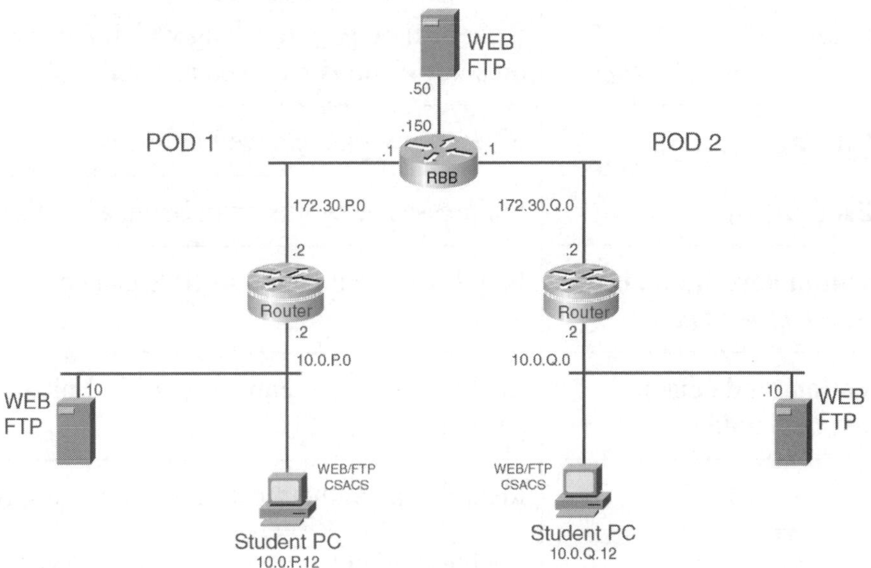


### Preparation

Begin with the standard lab topology and verify the standard router configuration on the Pod routers. Test the connectivity between the Pod routers. Access the perimeter router console port using the terminal emulator on the Windows 2000 server. If desired, save the router configuration to a text file for later analysis. Refer to the *Student Lab Orientation (Lab 1.1.5)* if you need more help.

## Tools and Resources

To complete the lab, the standard lab topology is required:

Two Pod routers

Two student PCs

Two servers

Backbone switch and router

Two console cables and HyperTerminal

## Additional Materials

Further information about the objectives covered in this lab can be found at this website:

- http://www.cisco.com/en/US/products/sw/iosswrel/ps1835/products_configuration_guide_chapter09186a00800ca762.html

## Command List

This lab uses the commands listed in Table 2-4. Refer to this list if you need any assistance or help during the lab.

**Table 2-4 Lab 2.3.3 Command List**

| Command | Description |
|---|---|
| **accept-lifetime** | Sets the time period during which the authentication key on a key chain is received as valid |
| **distribute-list (in)** | Filters networks received in updates |
| **distribute-list (out)** | Suppresses networks from being advertised in updates |
| **ip authentication key-chain eigrp** *autonomous-system key-chain* | Enables authentication of IP Enhanced IGRP packets |
| **ip authentication mode eigrp** *autonomous-system* **md5** | Enables MD5 authentication in IP Enhanced IGRP packets |
| **key** | Identifies an authentication key on a key chain |
| **key chain** | Enables authentication for routing protocols and identifies a group of authentication keys |
| **key-string** | Specifies the authentication string for a key |

| Command | Description |
|---|---|
| **passive-interface** | Prevents other routers on the network from learning about routes dynamically |
| **send-lifetime** | Sets the time period during which an authentication key on a key chain is valid to be sent |

**Task 1: Enabling MD5 Authentication**

On the outside interface, enable Message Digest 5 (MD5) authentication for autonomous system 1. MD5 is a security technology, which is similar to a frame cyclic redundancy check (CRC). MD5 is covered in depth later in the course. Remember that the command syntax is **ip authentication mode eigrp** *autonomous-system* **md5**.

Did the prompt change?

Now, configure the key chain mykeychain to be used in this authentication scheme. Remember that the syntax for this command is **ip authentication key-chain eigrp** *autonomous-system key-chain* in interface configuration mode. Remember to use the correct autonomous system number.

**Task 2: Configuring the Key Chain**

Configure the parameters of the key chain identified in the previous task. The key number, key string, and accept and send characteristics of the key chain must be configured.

From global configuration mode, configure the parameters of mykeychain by using the **key chain** *nameofchain* command. Replace *nameofchain* with *mykeychain*, which is the key chain identified earlier.

a. Did the prompt change? If so, how does the prompt appear?

This key chain can have a number of keys. Configure key 1. The command syntax is **key** *number*.

b. Did the prompt change? If so, how does the prompt appear?

For key 1, configure the key string text of 123456789. Remember that the command syntax is **key-string** *text.* Save the configuration.

The *accept-lifetime* and *send-lifetime* parameters are shown in the following configuration. Set these to the current time and timezone:

```
RouterP(config-keychain-key)#accept-lifetime ?
hh:mm:ss   Time to start
local      Specify time in local timezone
RouterP(config-keychain-key)#send-lifetime ?
hh:mm:ss   Time to start
local      Specify time in local timezone
```

To see authentication occurring, use the **debug eigrp packet** command. Notice that if the peer router is not authenticating, updates are ignored. When the peer router begins to authenticate, updates are processed.

To turn debugging off, use the **undebug all** command.

### Task 3: Controlling Outbound Route Advertisements

To control which networks the router advertises, a network security administrator can use a combination of an access list that defines the network and a distribution list. This combination ties that access list to the advertising interface. In this topology, direct the router to hide the details of the inside network, 10.0.P.0, because this network is internal.

Create a standard access list #10, which contains a deny statement for network 10.0.P.0 and a permit for all other networks.

Now, bind this access list to the correct autonomous system and advertising interface. First, go into router configuration mode using the **router eigrp 1** command. Then, use the **distribute-list** command for the FastEthernet 0/0 outbound interface. Remember that the command syntax is **distribute-list** *acl_num direction interface*.

### Task 4: Controlling Inbound Route Advertisements

To control from which networks the router will accept routing updates, use a combination of an access list and a distribute list applied in the inbound direction.

Create a standard access list #11 to permit only network 10.0.P.0 to send routing updates to the outside interface inbound. Then, use the **distribute-list** command to tie the access list to the interface in the correct direction.

Save the configuration. View the configuration. Where is the information about distribution lists contained?

---

### Task 5: Passive Interface

One other method of controlling router advertisements is the **passive-interface** command, which prevents other routers on the network from learning about routes dynamically. It can also be used to keep any unnecessary parties from learning about the existence of certain routes or routing protocols used.

Now, configure the inside interface to prevent broadcasting routing information:

```
RouterP(config)#router eigrp 1
RouterP(config-router)#passive-interface Fa0/0
```

### Sample Configuration

A sample configuration for configure routing authentication and filtering is as follows:

```
hostname Router1
!
key chain mykeychain
 key 1
  key-string 7 101F5B4A5142445C545D
!
interface FastEthernet0/0
 description inside
 ip address 10.0.1.1 255.255.255.0
 no ip directed-broadcast
!
```

```
interface FastEthernet0/1
 description outside
 ip address 172.30.1.1 255.255.0.0
 no ip directed-broadcast
 ip authentication mode eigrp 1 md5
 ip authentication key-chain eigrp 1 mykeychain
 no ip mroute-cache
!
!
router eigrp 1
 passive-interface FastEthernet0/0
 network 10.0.0.0
 network 172.30.0.0
 distribute-list 10 out FastEthernet0/0
 distribute-list 11 in FastEthernet0/1
 no auto-summary
!
access-list 10 deny   10.0.1.0 0.0.0.255
access-list 10 permit any
access-list 11 permit 10.0.1.0 0.0.0.255
```

## Lab 2.4.2: Configure Logging

Estimated Time: 15 Minutes

Number of Team Members: Two teams with four students per team

### Objective

In this lab, students use logging to monitor network events.

### Overview

A network security administrator should always log significant events on the router to the Syslog server. A Syslog server should be located on a secure internal network to ensure log integrity. The Syslog server can be a dedicated server or another server running Syslog services. In this lab, the Syslog server will be located at the network address **10.0.P.12**. Refer to the appendix to properly install the Syslog server software.

Figure 2-5 illustrates the network environment for this lab.

**Figure 2-5 Lab 2.4.2 Network Topology**

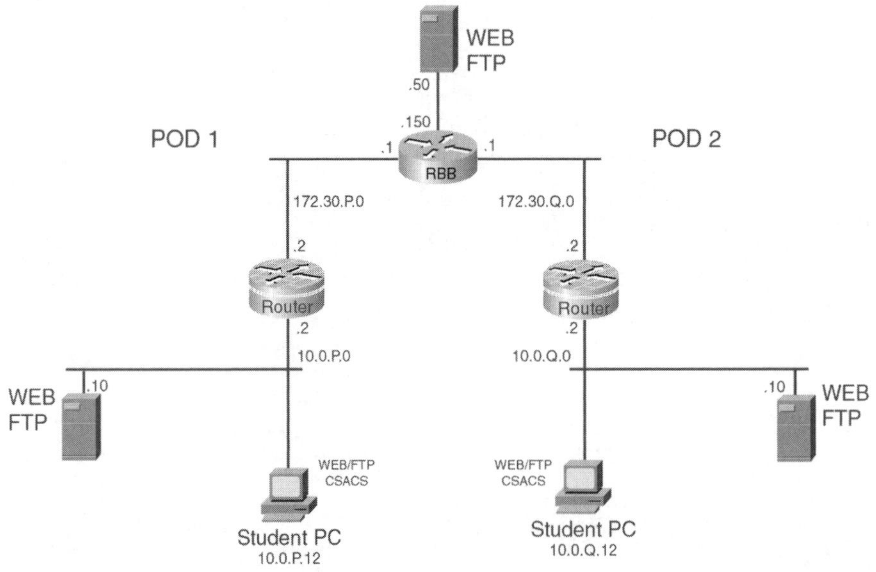


### Preparation

Begin with the standard lab topology and verify the standard router configuration on the Pod routers. Test the connectivity between the Pod routers. Access the perimeter router console port using the terminal emulator on the student PC. If desired, save the router configuration to a text file for later analysis. Refer to the *Student Lab Orientation (Lab 1.1.5)* if you need more help.

### Tools and Resources

To complete the lab, the standard lab topology is required:

- Two Pod routers
- Two student PCs

- Two servers
- Backbone switch and router
- Two console cables and HyperTerminal
- Syslog Server application

## Additional Materials

To download Kiwi Syslog Server, visit http://www.kiwisyslog.com.

Further information about the objectives covered in this lab can be found at the following websites:

- http://www.cisco.com/en/US/products/sw/iosswrel/ps1831/products_command_reference_chapter09186a00800ee834.html
- http://www.cisco.com/en/US/products/sw/iosswrel/ps1831/products_command_reference_chapter09186a00800d9840.html#1017942

## Command List

This lab uses the commands listed in Table 2-5. Refer to this list if you need any assistance or help during the lab.

**Table 2-5 Lab 2.4.2 Command List**

| Command | Description |
|---|---|
| **clear logging** | Clears the contents of the logging buffer |
| **logging buffered** | Stores messages in the internal buffer |
| **logging on** | Enables logging |
| **logging (hostname or IP address)** | Specifies the destination when sending syslog messages |
| **show logging** | Displays the contents of the logging parameters |

### Task 1: Installing a Syslog Server

**Step 1.** First, verify that the computer has a syslog server installed. If the computer already has a syslog server installed, continue onto Task 2. If not, continue onto Step 2.

**Step 2.** Numerous Syslog servers are available on the Internet. This lab assumes Kiwi Syslog Daemon is used. This is a freeware utility that can be downloaded from http://www.kiwisyslog.com. Download the syslog server and install the executable file.

### Task 2: Viewing Logging Configuration

Access the router and view the current logging configuration. Use the **show logging** command from privilege mode to show the current logging configuration.

a. What logging services are enabled on the router?

console, monitor, Buffer

b. How many messages have been logged to the console?

many

**Task 3: Enabling Logging**

Enable logging with the **logging on** command:

```
RouterP(config)# logging on
```

The **logging buffered** command copies logging messages to an internal buffer. The buffer works in a circular fashion. When the buffer becomes full, the latest messages overwrite the oldest messages. You can then enable the internal buffer on the router.

Generate some system messages by issuing a **shutdown** command on the serial interface from interface configuration mode. After the interface is disabled, reenable the serial interface by using the **no shutdown** command.

To display the messages that are logged in the buffer, use the **show logging** command. The first message displayed is the oldest message in the buffer.

What, if any, messages appeared in the buffer?

the buffer

To clear the current contents of the buffer, use the **clear logging** privileged command.

**Task 4: Enabling Logging to Syslog Server**

The **logging** command identifies a Syslog server host to receive logging messages. The argument host is the name or Internet address of the host. By issuing this command more than once, a list of Syslog servers that receive logging messages is built. Identify the Syslog server at 10.0.P.12 as a Syslog host using the **logging 10.0.P.12** command.

Use the **show logging** command to view the new configuration. How has the output changed?

It now goes to a syslog

**Task 5: Setting Logging Levels**

The **logging console**, **logging monitor**, **logging buffered**, and **logging trap** commands can all be used with the level parameter to set the severity level of the messages that are logged.

Type the **logging buffered** command followed by the **?** to see the available levels. List those levels here.

0 ~ 7, with names

Set the syslog server logging level using the **logging trap** command to debug messages:

```
RouterP(config)# logging trap debugging
```

**Task 6: Sending Logging Messages to a Syslog Server**

Trigger debug messages by entering the **debug ip packet** command in the privileged EXEC mode:

```
RouterP# debug ip packet
```

This command trigger IP packet debugging messages. These messages are currently being sent to 10.0.P.12.

Open the Syslog server on the inside host PC. The IP debugging messages should appear on the Syslog server.

Are the Syslog server logging debugging messages from the router at 10.0.P.2?

Yes
___

The Syslog server message should look similar to the following output:

```
12-19-2002    12:44:17    Local7.Debug    10.0.1.2    4974: 1d23h:
IP: s=172.30.1.2 (local), d=10.0.2.12 (Ethernet0/1), len 56, sending
12-19-2002    12:44:17    Local7.Debug    10.0.1.2    4973: 1d23h:

IP: s=10.0.2.12 (Ethernet0/1), d=10.0.1.2, len 78, rcvd 4
```

## Lab 2.4.3: Setting the Time and the Network Time Protocol

Estimated Time: 15 Minutes

Number of Team Members: Two teams with four students per team

### Objective

In this lab, students learns the following objectives:

Setting the time manually

Configuring NTP

Monitoring time services

### Overview

All Cisco routers provide an array of time-of-day services. These services enable the products to accurately keep track of the current time and date, to synchronize multiple products to the same time, and to provide time services to other systems.

Figure 2-6 illustrates the network environment for this lab.

**Figure 2-6 Lab 2.4.3 Network Topology**

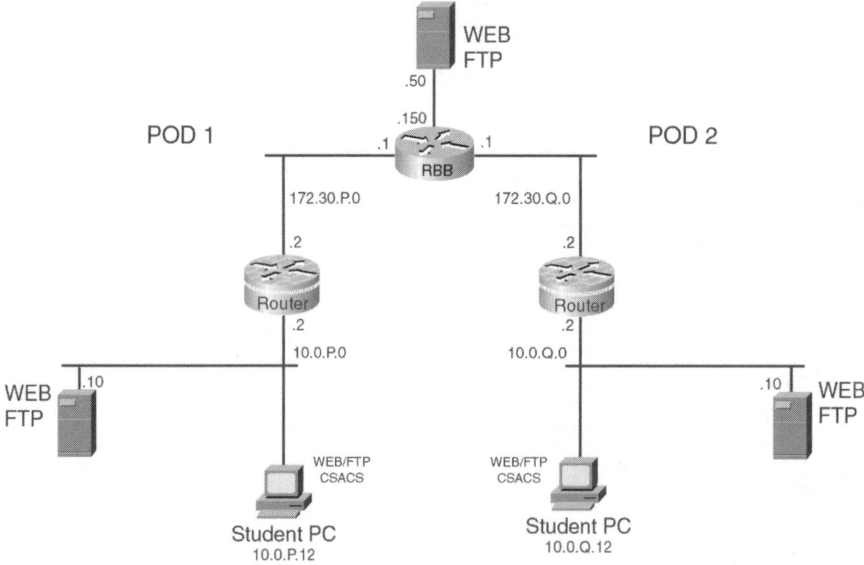


### Preparation

Begin with the standard lab topology and verify the standard router configuration on the Pod routers. Test the connectivity between the Pod routers. Access the perimeter router console port using the terminal emulator on the Windows 2000 server. If desired, save the router configuration to a text file for later analysis. Refer to the *Student Lab Orientation (Lab 1.1.5)* if you need more help.

## Tools and Resources or Equipment

To complete the lab, the standard lab topology is required:

Two Pod routers

Two student PCs

Two servers

Backbone switch and router

Two console cables and HyperTerminal

### Additional Materials

Further information about the objectives covered in this lab can be found at the following websites:

- http://www.cisco.com/en/US/products/hw/routers/ps368/products_configuration_guide_chapter09186a008007daed.html
- http://www.cisco.com/en/US/products/sw/iosswrel/ps1831/products_configuration_guide_chapter09186a00800ca66f.html#xtocid16

### Command List

This lab uses the commands listed in Table 2-6. Refer to this list if you need any assistance or help during the lab.

**Table 2-6 Lab 2.4.3 Command List**

| **Command** | **Description** |
|---|---|
| **clock set** *hh: mm: ss month date year* | Sets the system clock. |
| **clock summer-time** *zone*<br>**recurring** [*week day month hh***:***mm week day month hh***:***mm* [*offset*]] | Configures summer time. |
| **clock timezone** *zone*<br>*hours-offset* [*minutes-offset*] | Sets the timezone. The zone argument is the name of the timezone, typically a standard acronym. The hours-offset argument is the number of hours the timezone is different from Coordinated Universal Time (UTC). The minutes-offset argument is the number of minutes the timezone is different from UTC. |
| **ntp authenticate** | Enables the NTP authentication feature. |
| **ntp authentication-key** *number* **md5** *value* | Defines the authentication keys. |
| **ntp master** [*stratum*] | Makes the system an authoritative NTP server. |

| Command | Description |
| --- | --- |
| **ntp server ip-address** | Forms a server association with another system. |
| **ntp trusted-key** *key-number* | Defines trusted authentication keys. |

### Task 1: Setting the Time Manually

**Step 1.** Configure a time zone.

Use the following command in global configuration mode to manually configure the time zone:

```
RouterP(config)# clock timezone GTM -6 00
```

**Step 2.** Configure daylight savings time.

Use the following command in global configuration mode to configure summer time or daylight savings time in areas where it starts and ends on a particular day of the week each year:

```
RouterP(config)# clock summer-time GMT recurring first sunday april 02:00 last sunday october
  02:00
```

Check the current time on the router with the **show clock** command.

**Step 3.** Set time manually.

Set the system clock manually by using the **clock set** *hh:mm:ss month day year* command shown in the following example. *Note:* Set the wrong time on purpose:

```
RouterP# clock set 12:00:00 October 22 1999
```

The time remains accurate until the next system restart.

Check the time again; has the time changed?

Yes

---

### Task 2: Configuring NTP

NTP synchronizes timekeeping among a set of distributed time servers and clients. This synchronization enables events to be correlated when system logs are created and other time-specific events occur.

**Step 1.** Enable authentication.

To authenticate the associations with other systems for security purposes, use the following command to enable the NTP authentication feature:

```
RouterP(config)# ntp authenticate
```

**Step 2.** Define authentication keys.

Define each of the authentication keys by using the **ntp authentication-key** *number* **md5** *value* command, as follows:

```
RouterP(config)# ntp authentication-key 357159 md5 PEER
```

**Step 3.** Define trusted keys.

A list of trusted authentication keys is then defined. If a key is trusted, this system will be ready to synchronize to a system that uses this key in its NTP packets. Use the **ntp trusted-key** *key-number* command to specify trusted keys, as follows:

```
RouterP(config)# ntp trusted-key 159357
```

**Step 4.** Create a server association.

An NTP association can be a peer association. This means that the system is willing to synchronize to the other system or to allow the other system to synchronize to it. An NTP can also be a server association. This means that only this system will synchronize to the other system, and not the other way around. Use the **ntp server** ***ip-address*** command to form server associations with the other systems.

```
RouterP(config)# ntp server 172.30.P.1
```

Use the **show clock** command again to check the time. If the time is not changed, wait about 30 to 60 seconds for it to update, and try again.

Will the time remain accurate after a restart?

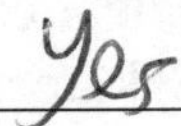


### Task 3: Monitoring Time Services

To monitor clock and NTP EXEC services, use any of the following commands in EXEC mode.

The **show ntp associations** command shows the status of NTP associations:

```
RouterP# show ntp associations
address       ref clock      st  when  poll reach  delay  offset    disp
*~172.30.3.1  127.127.7.1    2   55     64   377    3.3    0.14      0.1
* master(synced),# master(unsynced),+selected,- candidate,~ configured
```

The **show ntp status** command shows the status of NTP:

```
RouterP(config)# show ntp status
Clock is synchronized, stratum 3, reference is 172.30.3.1
nominal freq is 250.0000 Hz,actual freq is 250.0000 Hz,precision is 2**18
reference time is C1B693F2.EFF77563 (02:55:14.937 GTM Fri Dec 27 2002)
clock offset is 0.1731 msec, root delay is 3.33 msec
root dispersion is 0.23 msec, peer dispersion is 0.03 msec
```

### Task 4: Securing Time Services

NTP access lists can be used to impose fine-grained access control on NTP servers, clients, and peers.

**Step 1.** Use the following commands to secure the NTP connection:

```
RouterP(config)# ntp server 172.30.P.1 source fa 0/1
RouterP(config)# access-list 21 permit host 172.30.P.1
RouterP(config)# access-list 21 deny any
RouterP(config)# ntp access-group peer 21
```

Students should disable NTP on all external interfaces, unless the network is responsible for providing time service to other networks.

**Step 2.** Now, disable NTP server facilities on the inside interface:

```
RouterP(config)# interface fa 0/0
RouterP(config-if)# ntp disable
```

When this command is issued, the router does not receive updates on this interface.

# Lab 2.4.5: Configure SSH

Estimated Time: 20 Minutes

Number of Team Members: Two teams with four students per team

## Objective

In this lab, the student learns the following objectives:

- Configure a router as an SSH server.
- Establish an SSH connection between a PC and a router.
- Use show and debug commands to troubleshoot SSH.

## Overview

SSH is a program, similar to Telnet, that enables a network administrator to log into another computer over a network. SSH enables an administrator to execute commands in a remote machine and to move files from one machine to another. It provides strong authentication and secure communications over insecure networks. Currently, two versions of SSH are available: SSH version 1 and SSH version 2. Only SSH version 1 is implemented in the Cisco IOS Software.

Figure 2-7 illustrates the network environment for this lab.

**Figure 2-7 Lab 2.4.5 Network Topology**

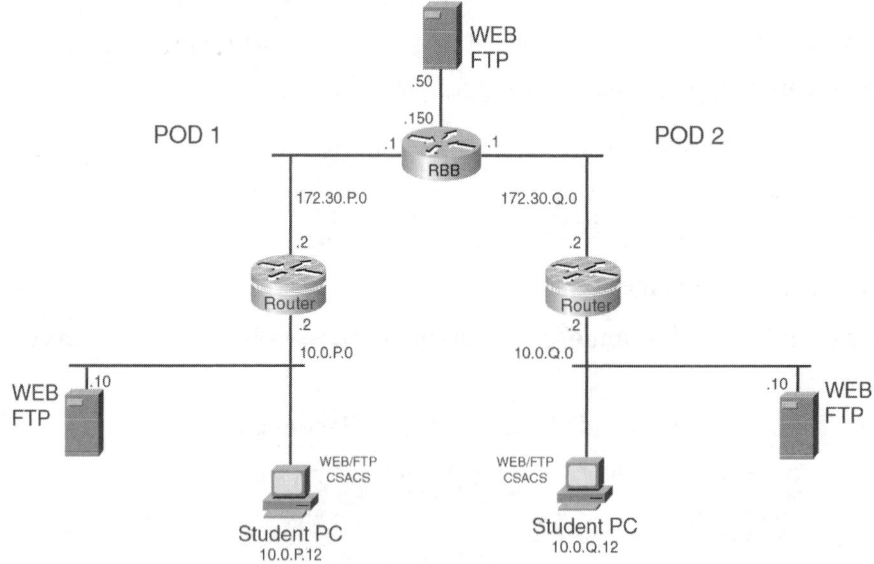


## Preparation

Begin with the standard lab topology and verify the standard router configuration on the Pod routers. Test the connectivity between the Pod routers. Access the perimeter router console port using the terminal emulator on the student PC. If desired, save the router configuration to a text file for later analysis. Refer to the *Student Lab Orientation (Lab 1.1.5)* if you need more help.

Prior to starting the lab, ensure that each host PC is loaded with a SSH client. Numerous SSH clients are available for free on the Internet. The lab was developed using the PuTTY SSH client.

## Tools and Resources

To complete the lab, the standard lab topology is required:

Two Pod routers

Two student PCs

Two servers

Backbone switch and router

Two console cables and HyperTerminal

SSH client

## Additional Materials

Further information about the objectives covered in this lab can be found at the following websites:

- http://www.cisco.com/en/US/products/sw/iosswrel/ps1835/products_configuration_guide_chapter09186a00800ca7d5.html
- http://www.chiark.greenend.org.uk/~sgtatham/putty/

## Command List

This lab uses the commands listed in Table 2-7. Refer to this list if you need any assistance or help during the lab.

**Table 2-7 Lab 2.4.5 Command List**

| Command | Description |
|---|---|
| **crypto key generate rsa** | Generates Rivest, Shamir, and Adleman (RSA) key pairs |
| **hostname** | Changes the router's hostname |
| **ip domain-name** | Defines a default domain name that the Cisco IOS Software uses to complete unqualified host names |
| **ip ssh** | Configures SSH control parameters on the router |
| **transport input** | Defines which protocols to use to connect to a specific line of the router |

### Task 1: Configuring SSH on a Router

To enable SSH on the router, the following parameters need to be configured:

Hostname

Domain-name

Asymmetrical keys

SSH timeouts

Local authentication

**Step 1.** Set router parameters.

To configure the router hostname, use the **hostname** *hostname* command in configuration mode. In this lab, the hostname has been configured to RouterP, where P is the Pod number. For example, if the team has been assigned to Pod5, the hostname would be Router5#:

```
RouterP(config)# hostname RouterP
```

After the hostname is set, the active CLI dynamically changes.

To configure the router IP domain-name, use the **ip domain-name domain name** command in configuration mode:

```
RouterP(config)# ip domain-name cisco.com
```

What command can view both the hostname and IP domain name?

show run

### Task 2: Generating Asymmetric Keys

**Step 1.** Generate RSA keys.

Enter the following command in configuration mode:

```
RouterP(config)# crypto key generate rsa ?
```

What are the available help options for this command?

general and usage keys

**Step 2.** Generate RSA keys (continued).

To enable SSH for local and remote authentication on the router, enter the command **crypto key generate rsa** and press **Enter**. The router responds with a message showing the naming convention for the keys.

What is the default size, in bits, of the key modulus?

512

Press **Enter** to accept the default key size and continue.

### Task 3: Configuring SSH Timeouts

Configuring SSH timeouts and authentication retries is a way of providing additional security for the connection. Use the command **ip ssh** {[**time-out** *seconds*]} {**authentication-retries** *integer*} to enable timeouts and authentication retries. Set the SSH timeout to 15 seconds and the amount of retries to 3 by entering the following commands:

```
RouterP(config)# ip ssh time-out 15
RouterP(config)# ip ssh authentication-retries 3
```

What is the maximum timeout value allowed? What is the maximum amount of authentication retries allowed?

120, 5

### Task 4: Configuring Local Authentication and vty

Use the following commands to define a local user and assign SSH communication to the vty lines:

```
RouterP(config)# username cisco password student
RouterP(config)# line vty 0 4
RouterP(config-line)# transport input ssh
RouterP(config-line)# login local
```

What are the available parameters `for the` **`transport input`** command?

all, lapb, mop, none, pad, Rlogin, ssh, telnet, udptn, v120

### Task 5: Communicating Between a SSH PC (Client) and a Router (Server)

The basic settings to enable a PC and a router to establish a SSH session is now configured. To establish a SSH session, launch the SSH client from the student PC.

The configurations vary among the different SSH clients. If PuTTY is being used as the SSH client, following these instructions: Launch the PuTTY.exe file and a pane with various configuration options opens (see Figure 2-8).

**Figure 2-8 PuTTY Configuration Dialog Box**

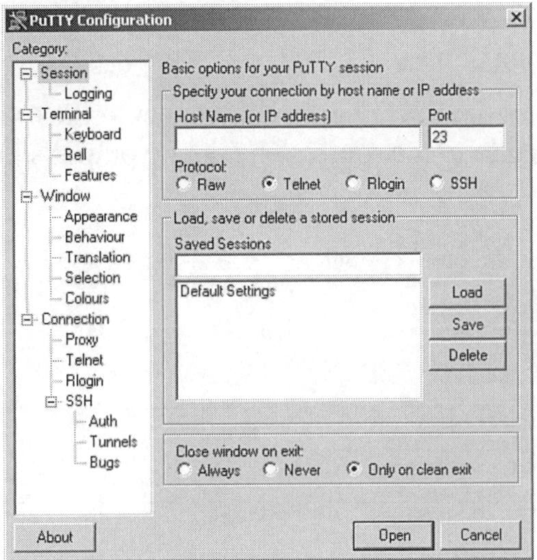

In the "Host Name (or IP address)" input box, enter the IP address of the Pod router. Next, change the protocol to SSH. These two values must be set to establish the SSH. To test the connection, click the **Open** command button at the bottom of the window.

The SSH client prompts for the local username and password that was previously set on the Pod router (see Figure 2-9). Enter **cisco** for the username and **student** for the password.

**Figure 2-9 PuTTY Login**

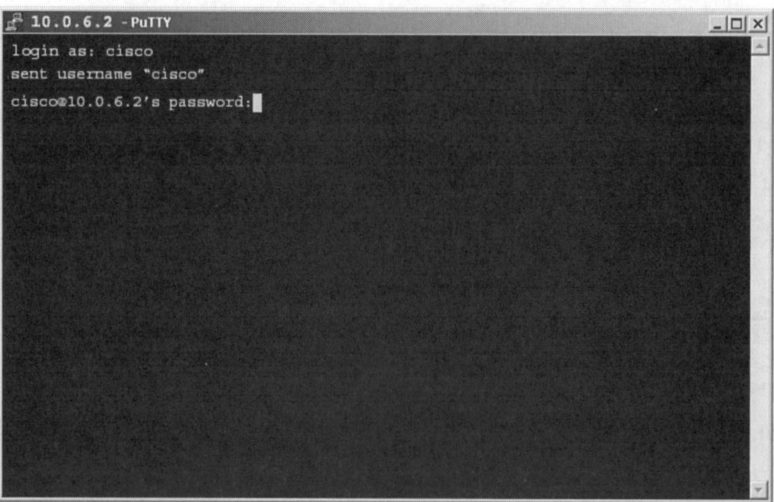


Was the SSH connection successful? If so, how is the prompt displayed?

Router1>

## Task 6: Debugging and Verifying SSH

**Step 1.** Enable debugging.

Enable debugging of SSH by entering the following commands:

```
RouterP# terminal monitor
RouterP(config)# logging console
RouterP# debug ip ssh
```

**Step 2.** Display the SSH debug output.

Next, open another instance of the SSH client and connect to the router. Use the correct username and password to log in to the router. The debug output should be similar to the following output:

```
03:45:37: SSH1: starting SSH control process
03:45:37: SSH1: sent protocol version id SSH-1.5-Cisco-1.25
03:45:37: SSH1: protocol version id is - SSH-1.5-PuTTY-Release-0.53b
03:45:37: SSH1: SSH_SMSG_PUBLIC_KEY msg
03:45:38: SSH1: SSH_CMSG_SESSION_KEY msg - length 112, type 0x03
03:45:38: SSH: RSA decrypt started
03:45:39: SSH: RSA decrypt finished
03:45:39: SSH: RSA decrypt started
03:45:39: SSH: RSA decrypt finished
03:45:39: SSH1: sending encryption confirmation
03:45:39: SSH1: keys exchanged and encryption on
03:45:41: SSH1: SSH_CMSG_USER message received
03:45:41: SSH1: authentication request for userid cisco
03:45:41: SSH1: SSH_SMSG_FAILURE message sent
03:45:44: SSH1: SSH_CMSG_AUTH_PASSWORD message received
03:45:44: SSH1: authentication successful for cisco
03:45:44: SSH1: requesting TTY
```

```
03:45:44: SSH1: setting TTY - requested: length 24, width 80; set: length 24, width 80
03:45:44: SSH1: SSH_CMSG_EXEC_SHELL message received
03:45:44: SSH1: starting shell for vty03:45:37: SSH1: starting SSH control process
```

To get an idea of the debugging process and the debugging message, open another instance of the SSH client and intentionally enter the wrong username or password. View the debugging output for failed authentication.

**Step 3.** View SSH sessions.

Use the **show ssh** command to view the active SSH sessions.

Fill in the appropriate values in Table 2-8, based on the output of the show ssh command.

**Table 2-8 SSH Session Information**

| Connection | Version | Encryption | State | Username |
|---|---|---|---|---|
| 0 | 2.0 | aes(256) | session started | cisco |

**Step 4.** View SSH parameters.

To display the version information and SSH parameters, use the **show ip ssh** command.

Is the output displayed exactly like the following output? If not, what are the differences?

no, ssh is 1.99

```
RouterP> show ip ssh
SSH Enabled - version 1.5
Authentication timeout: 15 secs; Authentication retries: 3
```

## Task 7: Router to Router SSH Connection

**Step 1.** Confirm peer SSH configurations.

Verbally communicate with the peer team to ensure the peer router Q has been configured to accept a SSH connection. The settings configured in Task 1 through Task 6 are needed to enable a SSH connection between two routers. Only this time, instead of using a SSH client running on a host computer, the router will be the SSH client and will establish a connection to the peer router. By default, the Cisco IOS acts as both a SSH server and SSH client.

**Step 1.** Test Telnet.

When the peer group is ready, enter the **telnet** command and establish connectivity with the peer router:

```
RouterP# telnet 172.30.Q.2   (where Q is the peer team router)
```

Was the Telnet connection successful? Why or why not?

no, no pass enabled

**Step 2.** Establish an SSH connection.

Enter the following commands to establish an SSH connection to the peer router:

```
RouterP(config)# ssh ?
```

a. What are the additional arguments of the **ssh** command?

-v, -c, -l, -m, -o, p, IP

b. What encryption algorithms are available?

**Step 3.** Establish a router to router SSH connection.

Enter the following command to establish a SSH connection to the peer router:

```
RouterP> ssh -c des -l cisco 172.30.Q.2
```

This command makes a SSH connection to a peer router with an address of 172.30.Q.2, DES as the encryption, and cisco as the login username.

Was the SSH connection successful?

3des, aes 128, aes 192, aes 256

Step 4. Verify SSH.

no, bad encryptón

Enter the following command to verify the SSH connection:

```
RouterP# show ip ssh
RouterP# show ssh
```

What other commands might be useful to verify and troubleshoot SSH connections?

debug ssh

## Review Questions

1. What is the difference between using the **enable password** and the **enable secret** commands?

2. What is an anti-spoofing access list?

3. What would be one user-addressing option for an organization if it had only two public IP addresses and needed to statically map one of those to its web server?

4. How can NAT add to network security?

________________________________________

________________________________________

________________________________________

5. How can the use of static routes enhance network security?

________________________________________

________________________________________

________________________________________

## Chapter 2 Quiz Questions

1. Which of the following is *not* one of the identity technologies used in AAA?

   A. Authorization

   B. Access

   C. Authentication

   D. Accounting

2. Which of the following correctly describes one of the primary differences between PAP and CHAP authentication?

   A. CHAP uses a 2-way handshake, whereas PAP uses a 3-way handshake.

   B. CHAP uses passwords agreed upon and shared out-of-band.

   C. PAP sends encrypted passwords over the wire.

   D. PAP provides protection from replay attacks.

3. Which port is used by TACACS servers?

   A. 41

   B. 47

   C. 49

   D. 52

4. Which of the following is *not* true about TACACS+ and RADIUS servers?

   A. Transactions between the client and RADIUS server are authenticated through the use of a shared secret, which is sent over the network.

   B. TACACS+ provides separation of authentication, authorization, and accounting.

   C. RADIUS is a client/server protocol.

   D. TACACS+ encrypts all traffic between the TACACS+ client and the TACACS+ server daemon.

5. When a certificate becomes invalid before the expiration of the validity period, to what list is it added?

   A. CA Certification Release List

   B. CA Canceled Rights List

   C. CA Certification Revocation List

   D. CA Certificate Revocation List

6. Public key/private key is an example of what kind of encryption system?

   A. Symmetric

   B. Asymmetric

   C. Kerberized

   D. SNMP security

7. How much stronger is 3DES than DES?

   A. Five times stronger

   B. Four times stronger

   C. Three times stronger

   D. Two times stronger

8. Which of the following is a public-key cryptography protocol that enables two parties to establish a shared secret key used by encryption algorithms?

   A. DES

   B. 3DES

   C. MD5

   D. DH

9. Which of the following is *not* one of the protocols used in the Secure Socket Layer (SSL) process?

   A. Handshake

   B. Transport

   C. Record

   D. Alert

10. Which of the following refers to the real-time monitoring of network activity and the analyzing of data for potential vulnerabilities and attacks in progress?

   A. SNMP

   B. Remote Monitoring MIB

   C. Intrusion detection

   D. Syslog management

# Chapter 3

## Router ACLs and CBAC

Chapter 2, "Basic Router and Switch Security," discussed general router and switch security for improving overall network security. The methods discussed generally applied to everyone on the network. In this chapter, specific methods are applied, which gives students the ability to tune the network's security.

This chapter discusses different types of access control lists (ACLs) and shows students how to permit or deny traffic based on location, content, or time. Remember that ACLs are used to filter traffic, and in filtering out unwanted traffic, the security of the network is increased. One particular type of ACL, Context-Based Access Control (CBAC), provides a greater level of security by being able to filter on Layer 3 and above.

By using CBAC on the router, temporary openings can be created based on parameters specified by the student. These parameters permit traffic based on the internal request and deny other traffic.

**Vocabulary Exercise**

applet

__________________________________________________________

__________________________________________________________

__________________________________________________________

CBAC

__________________________________________________________

__________________________________________________________

__________________________________________________________

half-open connection

__________________________________________________________

__________________________________________________________

__________________________________________________________

PAM

__________________________________________________________

__________________________________________________________

__________________________________________________________

RPC

state table

**Lab Activities**

The topology figures and lab examples contain **P** and **Q** values. The **P** value in the addressing and naming scheme refers to *your* assigned Pod number.

The following are examples of determining P values:

- Pod2 is looking at a topology figure and is trying to determine the P values in the figure. In this scenario, the **P** values would equal **2**. 10.0.**P**.12 would become 10.0.**2**.12, 172.30.**P**.2 would become 172.30.**2**.2, and so on.
- Pod1 is looking at a topology figure and is trying to determine the P values in the figure. In this scenario, the **P** values would equal **1**. 10.0.**P**.12 would become 10.0.**1**.12, 172.30.**P**.2 would become 172.30.**1**.2, and so on.

In both examples, the P values are directly related to the Pod number of the team.

The **Q** value in the naming and addressing scheme is used when testing the security or connectivity with the peer team

The following are examples of determining Q values:

- In a lab, Pod2 has been asked to test connectivity to their peer inside host at IP address 10.0.Q.12. In this scenario, 10.0.**Q**.12 would equal 10.0.**1**.12.
- In a lab, Pod1 has been asked to test connectivity to their peer inside host at IP address 10.0.Q.12. In this scenario, 10.0.**Q**.12 would equal 10.0.**2**.12.

In both examples, the Q value is the directly related to the peer Pod number.

# Lab 3.2.4: Standard, Extended, Named, and Commented ACLs

Estimated Time: 30 Minutes

Number of Team Members: Two teams with four students per team

## Objective

In this lab, students learn the following objectives:

- Define a standard access list.
- Define an extended access list.
- Define a named access list.
- Comment within an access list.
- Apply an access list.
- Verify an access list.

## Overview

In this lab, students configure various access lists. The ability to configure an access list is important to securing network resources. This lab also presents a few of the available options in securing network resources. This lab covers standard, extended, named, and commented ACLs.

Figure 3-1 illustrates the network environment students create for this lab.

**Figure 3-1 Lab 3.2.4 Network Topology**

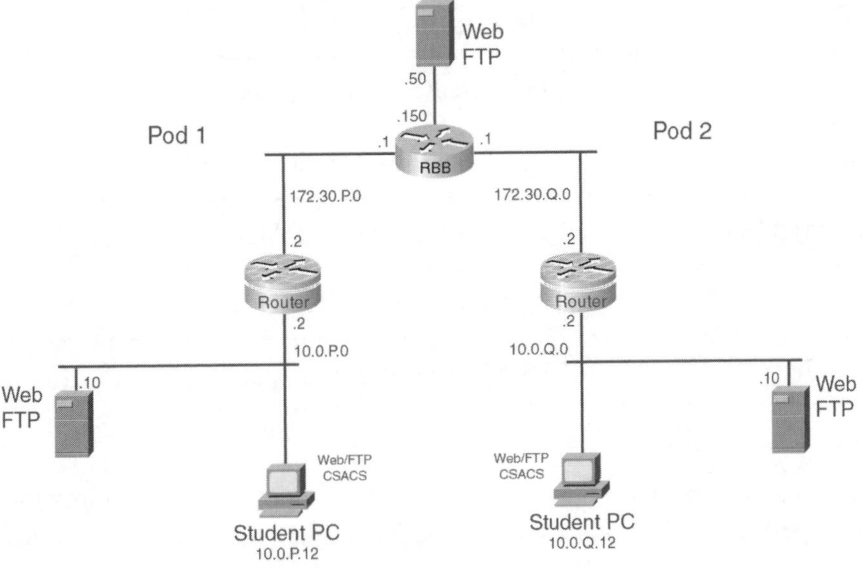


## Preparation

Begin with the standard lab topology and verify the standard router configuration on the Pod routers. Test the connectivity between the Pod routers. Access the perimeter router console port using the terminal emulator on the student PC. If desired, save the router configuration to a text file for later analysis. Refer to the *Student Lab Orientation (Lab 1.1.5)* if you need more help.

## Tools and Resources

To complete the lab, the standard lab topology is required:

- Two Pod routers
- Two student PCs
- Two servers
- Backbone switch and router
- Two console cables and HyperTerminal

## Additional Materials

Further information about the objectives covered in this lab can be found at the following websites:

- http://www.cisco.com/en/US/products/sw/iosswrel/ps1831/products_configuration_guide_chapter09186a00800d9816.html
- http://www.cisco.com/en/US/products/sw/iosswrel/ps1835/products_command_reference_chapter09186a00800873c8.html

## Command List

Table 3-1 lists the commands used throughout this lab. Students should be familiar with these commands.

**Table 3-1 Lab 3.2.4 Command List**

| Command | Description |
|---|---|
| **access-list** | Defines ACL parameters |
| **ip access-group** | Assigns an ACL to an interface |
| **ip access-list extended** | Defines an extended ACL |
| **remark** | Comments an ACL |
| **show ip access-list** | Displays configured ACLs |

**Task 1: Standard Access List**

**Step 1.** A standard access list uses numbers 1–99 and provides system administrators with the ability to deny or permit traffic from a set of IP addresses or a specific IP address.

**Step 2.** To get acquainted with the **access-list** command, enter global configuration mode and enter **access-list?**

What parameters are available?

the diffrant ACL nums

**Step 3.** Create a standard access list that, when applied, will deny outbound traffic from host 10.0.P.12. Define the access list as 77.

What is the syntax for access list 77?

acess-List 77 deny 10.0.P.12 0.0.0.0 <CR>

**Step 4.** Before applying the access list to the interface, test the network connectivity by pinging the inside host at IP address 10.0.Q.12 from the inside host at IP address 10.0.P.12.

Was the ping successful?

yes

**Step 5.** For an access list to be active, it must be applied to an interface. When an access list is applied to an interface, the direction of traffic must be specified. Use the following commands to assign standard access list 77 to the outside interface for outbound traffic:

```
RouterP(config)# int e 0/1
RouterP(config-if)# ip access-group 77 out
```

This scenario prevents host 10.0.P.12 from reaching the outside network.

**Step 6.** Test the access list by issuing a ping to the peer's inside host. The ping should be sent from the Pod inside the host.

Was the ping successful?

no

**Step 7.** Remove the access list from the outside interface by using the **no** form of the **ip access-group** command.

### Task 2: Extended Access List

**Step 1.** An extended access list gives administrators greater control of network traffic. An extended access list enables both the destination address and the source address to be defined as criteria for traffic. Standard access lists are restricted to either a source or destination IP address. Extended access lists also enable filtering based on protocol and port numbers.

Create an extended access list that has the following parameters:

- Deny Telnet traffic from host 10.0.P.12 to 172.26.26.50
- Deny Internet Control Message Protocol (ICMP) traffic from host 10.0.P.12 10.0.Q.12
- Permit Enhanced Interior Gateway Routing Protocol (EIGRP) packets from any source to any destination
- Permit all other TCP traffic
- Permit all other IP traffic

Define this access list as 101.

The extended access list should look similar to the following:

```
RouterP(config)# access-list 101 deny tcp host 10.0.1.12 host 172.26.26.50 eq telnet
RouterP(config)# access-list 101 deny icmp host 10.0.1.12 host 10.0.2.12
RouterP(config)# access-list 101 permit eigrp any any
RouterP(config)# access-list 101 permit tcp any any
RouterP(config)# access-list 101 permit ip any any
```

**Step 2.** Before applying the access list 101 to the outside interface, verify connectivity to the peer by pinging the inside host. After this is complete, Telnet to the outside server.

a. Was the ping to the peer inside host successful?

yes

b. Was the Telnet to the outside server successful?

Yes

**Step 3.** Apply access list 101 to the outside interface for outbound traffic.

From global configuration mode, what commands are required to apply the access list to the outside interface?

int e0/1 access group 101 out

**Step 4.** After the access list is applied to the interface, initiate a ping to the peer's inside host at 10.0.Q.12.

a. Was the ping successful? Why or why not?

no, it was blocked

b. Next, initiate a Telnet session to the outside server at 172.26.26.50.

Was the Telnet successful? Why or why not?

no, it was blocked

c. Verify the access list by using the privileged EXEC mode **show ip access-lists 101** command.

Does the output of the **show ip access-lists 101** command indicate when the access list has been used?

yes

## Task 3: Named IP Access List

**Step 1.** Standard and extended access lists can also be named. The command to name an access list is **ip access-list {standard | extended}** ***name*** in the global configuration mode.

Create an extended access list named NOPING.

What is the syntax of the extended access list?

ip access-list extended noping

**Step 2.** Define the following parameters for the extended named ACL:

- Deny icmp traffic from host 10.0.P.12 to 10.0.P.2
- Permit all other TCP traffic
- Permit all other IP traffic

What commands define the preceding parameters?

access-list noping deny ICMP host 10.0.P.12 host 10.0.P.2

**Step 3.** Apply the access list to the inside inbound interface. Verify the configuration by using **show ip access-list NOPING.**

**Step 4.** Test the access list by pinging the inside interface from the inside host.

Was the ping successful? Why or why not?

no it was blocked

---

**Task 4: Commenting Access List**

**Step 1.** The **remark** command comments an access list. Comment the extended access list NOPING with the following description:

"This access list denies ICMP from the inside host."

a. What is this syntax for this command?

access-list no ping remark " "

---

b. What command verifies the **remark** command settings?

~~access-list noping remark~~

show access-list noping

# Lab 3.2.5: Lock-and-Key ACLs

Estimated Time: 30 Minutes

Number of Team Members: Two teams with four students per team

## Objective

In this lab, students configure a dynamic access list for lock-and-key security.

## Overview

In this lab, students configure a lock-and-key ACL to enable a Telnet session from the peer's inside host (10.0.Q.12) to their internal network. The student's Pod router acts as a firewall in this scenario. The dynamic access list is applied to the student's router's outside interface.

Figure 3-2 illustrates the network environment students create for this lab.

**Figure 3-2 Lab 3.2.5 Network Topology**

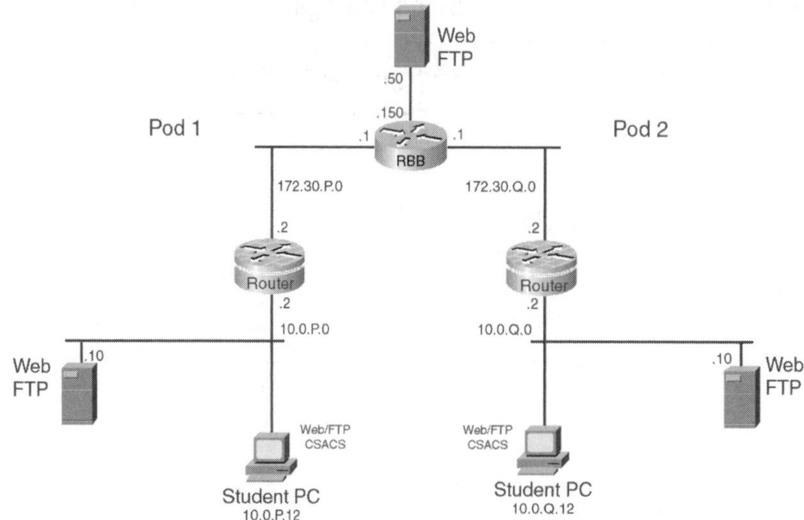


## Preparation

Begin with the standard lab topology and verify the standard router configuration on the Pod routers. Test the connectivity between the Pod routers. Access the perimeter router console port using the terminal emulator on the student PC. If desired, save the router configuration to a text file for later analysis. Refer to the *Student Lab Orientation (Lab 1.1.5)* if you need more help.

## Tools and Resources

To complete the lab, the standard lab topology is required:

- Two Pod routers
- Two student PCs
- Two servers
- Backbone switch and router
- Two console cables and HyperTerminal

## Additional Materials

Further information about the objectives covered in this lab can be found at the following websites:

- http://www.cisco.com/warp/public/69/13.html
- http://www.cisco.com/en/US/products/sw/iosswrel/ps1839/products_command_reference_chapter09186a008010a7c0.html

## Command List

Table 3-2 lists the commands that are used throughout this lab. Students should be familiar with these commands.

**Table 3-2 Lab 3.2.5 Command List**

| Command | Description |
|---|---|
| **access-list** | Defines an ACL |
| **autocommand access-enable host timeout 2** | Automatically creates a temporary ACL |
| **ip access-group** | Assigns an ACL to an interface |
| **line vty 0 4** | Configures vty lines 0 through 4 |
| **login local** | Authenticates users against the local database |
| **show ip access-lists** | Displays the configured ACLs |
| **show ip route** | Shows routing information |
| **username** *username* **password** *password* | Defines a username/password combination in the local database |

### Task 1: Building and Configuring the Network According to the Diagram

Use the Enhanced Interior Gateway Routing Protocol (EIGRP) as the routing protocol. Be sure to enter the correct network statements.

Use ping and **show ip route** to test connectivity among all interfaces. Each router should have a complete routing table.

### Task 2: Configuring Lock-and-Key

**Step 1.** Students can assume their Pod routers have a comprehensive access list defined on the outside interface. However, for the purposes of this lab, students need to configure only the portions of the list relevant to lock-and-key.

In this lab, the lock-and-key access list uses the following logic:

- Students configure a dynamic ACL, LETMEIN, for the peer's inside host to the Pod inside host, which is on a secure network.
- The peer's inside host, on the 10.0.Q.0 network, authenticates a Telnet session to the student's outside interface, which is 172.30.P.2.
- After local authentication occurs for the Telnet session, the connection is immediately disconnected. This triggers the dynamic access list to become active.
- When the dynamic access list is active, the peer is able to Telnet and ping the inside host.
- In addition, the router needs to exchange routing updates with the peer routers, so the students must be sure to permit EIGRP. To do so, they need to enter the following commands on the router:

```
RouterP(config)# access-list 101 permit tcp 10.0.Q.0 0.0.0.255 host 172.30.P.2 eq telnet
RouterP(config)# access-list 101 permit eigrp any any
RouterP(config)# access-list 101 dynamic LETMEIN timeout 90 permit ip 10.0.Q.0 0.0.0.255 10.0.P.0
  0.0.0.255
RouterP(config)# username ernie password bert
RouterP(config)# interface ethernet 0/1
RouterP(config-if)# ip access-group 101 in
RouterP(config-if)# line vty 0 4
RouterP(config-line)# login local
RouterP(config-line)# autocommand access-enable host timeout 2
```

The dynamic access list statement contains the option timeout 90, which places an absolute limit on the amount of time that the temporary hole in the firewall can exist. After 90 minutes, users have to authenticate again, even if the users kept the connection busy with traffic.

The **autocommand** configuration automates the process of creating a temporary access list entry. Upon authentication, the inside host executes the **access-enable** command and creates a temporary entry for the peer's individual IP address. The **host** keyword prevents this temporary entry from including other members of the subnet. Finally, the **timeout 2** option configures the idle timeout to 2 minutes. Users must authenticate again if the connection is idle for more than 2 minutes.

**Task 3: Verifying the Dynamic Access List**

**Step 1.** To verify that the dynamic access list is working, students need to work closely with their peer group. Verbally communicate with the peer group and have them ping their peer inside host.

a. Were they successful? Why or why not?

Yes, they got in through lock and key
_______________________________________________

b. Have the peer group Telnet to their peer inside host at IP address 10.0.Q.12. Were they successful? Why or why not?

no, acL is working
_______________________________________________

If the answer to the preceding questions is "no," this means that the dynamic ACL has been configured correctly and the group can proceed to Step 2. If the peer Pod can ping and Telnet to the inside host at IP address 10.0.Q.12, the access list is not working. Troubleshoot the access list and have the peer group try again.

**Step 2.** After students verify their dynamic access list is working, have the peer group Telnet to the outside interface at 172.30.Q.2. This will be their neighboring router. The peer group is prompted for a username and password, which is set to username **ernie** and the password **bert**.

a. Were they able to Telnet to the outside interface?

yes

b. Was the connection lost after authentication?

yes

If the answers to the preceding questions are "yes," the dynamic access list has been properly configured. Congratulations! Proceed to Step 3. If not, troubleshoot the dynamic access list.

**Step 3.** After the Telnet to the inside host is successful, use the **show ip access-list** command to confirm the active dynamic access list.

a. Is a dynamic access list displayed? How much time is left until the idle timeout value expires?

2 min

b. How is the dynamic access list displayed?

dynamic 101 Lethneir

**Step 4.** Communicate with the peer group and instruct them to leave the Telnet inactive for at least 2 minutes. Continue to monitor the timeout value with the **show ip access-list** command. Notice the timeout value decreasing until it expires. After the timeout value expires, ask the peer group to ping the inside host at IP address 10.0.Q.12. This will be their neighboring inside host.

Was the peer group successful? Why or why not?

no, the acl has expired

**Task 4: Real-World Implications**

What is a real-life scenario where using a dynamic access list would be beneficial to implement?

during remote maintiance

# Lab 3.2.7: Time-Based ACLs

Estimated Time: 20 Minutes

Number of Team Members: Two teams with four students per team

## Objective

In this lab, students learn the following objectives:

- Apply time ranges to ACLs.
- Apply ACLs to interfaces.
- Define a time range.
- Verify a time range.

## Overview

Time-based access lists enable administrators to control when users are permitted or denied access to network resources. In this lab, students control Telnet access based on the time of day.

Figure 3-3 illustrates the network environment students create for this lab.

**Figure 3-3 Lab 3.2.7 Network Topology**

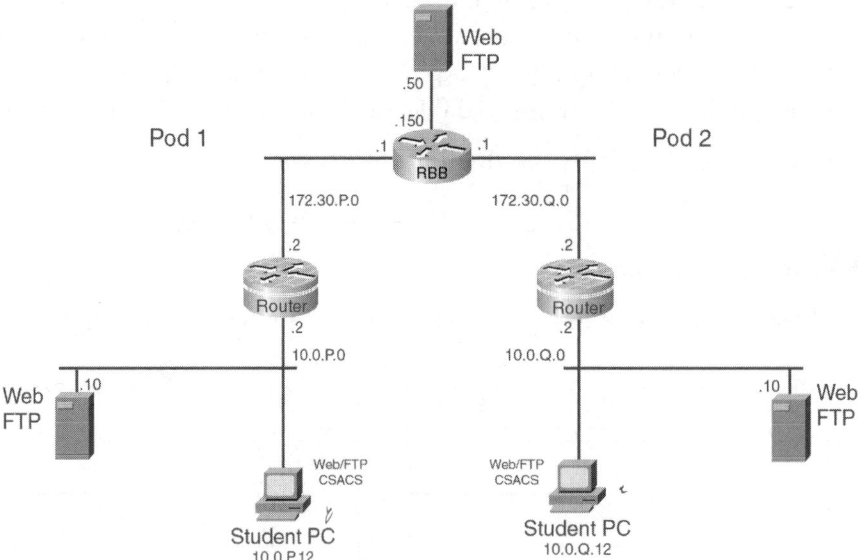


## Preparation

In preparation for this lab, verify the network configuration is consistent with the lab topology. This lab requires Telnet services be installed and configured with a username and password on the inside hosts.

Begin with the standard lab topology and verify the standard router configuration on the Pod routers. Test the connectivity between the Pod routers. Access the perimeter router console port using the terminal emulator on the student PC. If desired, save the router configuration to a text file for later analysis. Refer to the *Student Lab Orientation (Lab 1.1.5)* if you need more help.

## Tools and Resources

To complete the lab, the standard lab topology is required:

- Two Pod routers
- Two student PCs
- Two servers
- Backbone switch and router
- Two console cables and HyperTerminal

## Additional Materials

Further information about the objectives covered in this lab can be found at the following websites:

- http://www.cisco.com/en/US/products/sw/secursw/ps1018/products_tech_note09186a00800a5b9a.shtml
- http://www.cisco.com/en/US/products/sw/iosswrel/ps1839/products_feature_guide_chapter09186a0080110dc7.html

## Command List

Table 3-3 lists the commands used throughout this lab. Students should be familiar with these commands.

**Table 3-3 Lab 3.2.7 Command List**

| Command | Description |
|---|---|
| **access-list** | Configures ACL parameters |
| **ip access-group** | Assigns an ACL to an interface |
| **ip access-list extended** | Defines an extended ACL |
| **show clock** | Displays the current system time |
| **show time-range** | Displays time-range parameters |
| **time-range** | Defines a time-range |

**Task 1: Testing Connectivity**

a. Connect to the inside host computer and open MS-DOS. Ping the peer's inside host at 10.0.Q.12.

Was the ping successful?

Yes, basic allows it to get thr
_______________________________________________

b. Telnet to the peer's inside host at 10.0.Q.12.

Was the Telnet successful?

no, no telnet its running

Move on to Task 2 only if the ping and Telnet were successful. If not, troubleshoot the connectivity between the two inside hosts.

**Task 2: Defining the Time-Based ACL**

**Step 1.** Enter global configuration mode. Then, configure an extended access list with the following parameters:

- ACL number = 101
- Permit Telnet packet from the peer's inside host (10.0.Q.12) to the inside host at IP address 10.0.P.12
- Name the time range "allow telnet"

What is the syntax for this access list?

This extended access list enables a Telnet session from the peer's inside host to the inside host at IP address 10.0.P.12. This access list is active only when the time range **allowtelnet** parameters have been met. If the time range parameters are not met, the access list is inactive. Later, the time range parameters will be defined for this access list.

**Step 1.** Configure an extended access list with the following parameters:

- ACL number = 101
- Deny Telnet from any source to any destination

What is the syntax for this access list?

**Task 3: Applying the ACL to the Interface**

**Step 1.** Apply the extended access list 101 to the inside interface for outbound traffic.

What command is applied to access list 101 to the inside interface?

**Step 2.** Communicate verbally with the peer group and verify it has applied access list 101 to their inside interface. After this is confirmed, Telnet to the peer's inside host.

Was the Telnet successful? Why or why not?

**Task 4: Defining the Time Range**

**Step 1.** For future purposes, obtain the current system time by using the **show clock** command in privileged EXEC mode.

What is the current system time?

_______________________________________________

**Step 2.** In global configuration mode, use the **time-range** *name* command to define the time range parameters for access list 101.

a. What is the syntax for the command?

_______________________________________________

b. How is the command prompt displayed?

_______________________________________________

c. What options are available in this new configuration mode?

_______________________________________________

**Step 3.** Define a time range with the following parameters:

- Periodic.
- Start date is today. Students need to know the current system time.
- Start time is 3 minutes from now. Students need to know current system time.
- End date is today.
- End time is 8 minutes from now.

The command syntax looks similar to the following:

```
RouterP(config-time-range)# periodic wednesday 11:33 to wednesday 11:35
```

**Step 4.** Exit Time Range Configuration mode and enter privileged EXEC mode.

**Task 5: Verifying the Time Range**

Verify the time range allow telnet by using the **show time-range** *name* command.

What is displayed in parenthesis ( )? What does this indicate?

_______________________________________________

**Task 6: Testing the Time Range**

**Step 1.** In Task 4, the time range was configured to start in 3 minutes. To test the time range, students need to wait for these 3 minutes to elapse. Students can use the **show clock** command to see the current system time. Use the **show time-range** command to verify the time range parameters when the 3 minutes have elapsed.

What is displayed in parentheses ( )? What does this indicate?

_______________________________________________

If active is not displayed in the output of the **show time-range** command, verify that enough time has elapsed and that the proper time range parameters have been configured. Troubleshoot these by using the **show clock** and **show time-range** commands.

If active is displayed in the **show time-range** command, proceed to Step 2.

**Step 2.** When active is in the **show time-range** output, inform the peer group that they can attempt another Telnet session.

After a few moments, ask the peer group if they were able to establish a Telnet session.

Were they successful? Why or why not?

_______________________________________________________________________________

**Task 7: Real-World Implications**

What would be a real-world scenario where time-based ACLs would be beneficial to implement?

_______________________________________________________________________________

_______________________________________________________________________________

# Lab 3.8.3: Configure Cisco IOS Firewall CBAC on a Cisco Router

Estimated Time: 35 Minutes

Number of Team Members: Two teams with four students per team

## Objective

In this lab exercise, students complete the following tasks:

- Configure logging and audit trails
- Define and apply inspection rules to ACLs
- Test and verify CBAC

## Overview

The task in this exercise is to configure CBAC on a Cisco router. Work in a group to perform the following steps in this lab exercise:

**Task 1:** Configuring logging and audit trails

**Task 2:** Defining and applying inspection rules for ACLs

**Task 3:** Testing and verifying CBAC

Figure 3-4 illustrates the network environment students create for this lab.

**Figure 3-4 Lab 3.8.3 Network Topology**

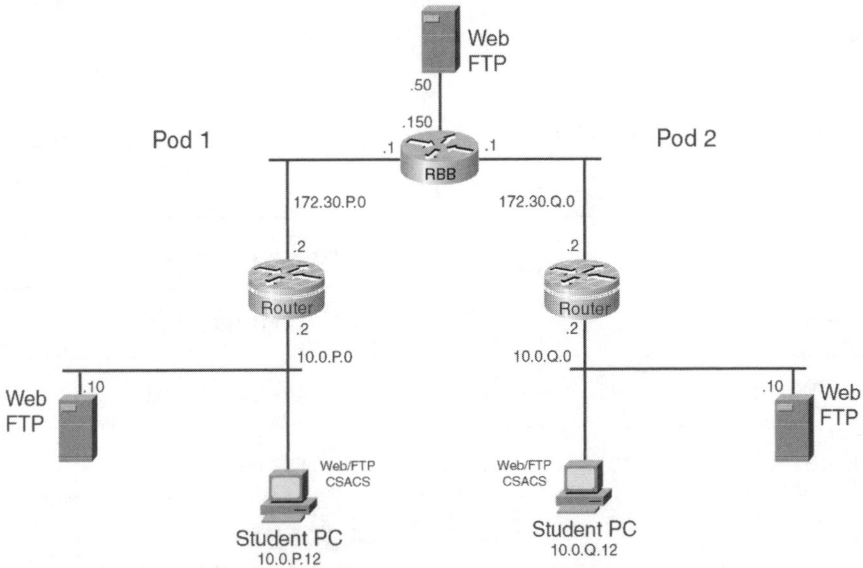


## Preparation

Begin with the standard lab topology and verify the standard router configuration on the Pod routers. Test the connectivity between the Pod routers. Access the perimeter router console port using the terminal emulator on the student PC. If desired, save the router configuration to a text file for later analysis. Refer to the *Student Lab Orientation (Lab 1.1.5)* if you need more help.

## Tools and Resources

To complete this lab, the following resources are required:

- Two Pod routers
- One backbone router
- Two inside hosts
- One outside server
- One switch
- Assorted cabling

## Additional Materials

Further information about the objectives covered in this lab can be found at the following websites:

- http://www.cisco.com/en/US/products/sw/iosswrel/ps1831/products_configuration_guide_chapter09186a00800d981a.html
- http://www.cisco.com/en/US/products/sw/secursw/ps1018/products_tech_note09186a0080094112.shtml
- http://www.cisco.com/warp/public/110/32.html

## Command List

Table 3-4 lists the commands that are used throughout this lab. Students should be familiar with these commands.

**Table 3-4 Lab 3.8.3 Command List**

| Command | Description |
|---|---|
| **access-list** | Configures an ACL |
| **ip access-group** | Assigns an ACL to an interface |
| **ip inspect audit-trail** | Configures a CBAC audit trail. |
| **ip inspect name** | Defines a CBAC rule |
| **logging** | Enables logging |
| **show access-lists** | Displays configured access lists |
| **show ip inspect** | Verifies CBAC operation |
| **write memory** | Saves the running configuration to the startup configuration |

## Task 1: Configuring Logging and Audit Trails

To configure logging and audit trails, complete the following steps:

**Step 1.** Enable logging to the console and the Syslog server:

```
RouterP(config)# logging on
RouterP(config)# logging 10.0.P.12
```

**Step 2.** Enable the audit trail:

```
Router(config)# ip inspect audit-trail
```

**Step 3.** Save the configuration and return to global configuration mode:

```
RouterP(config)# end
RouterP# write memory
```

a. What command shows detailed logging information?

Debug —
___

b. What command erases the entries in the logging buffer?

___

## Task 2: Defining and Applying Inspection Rules for ACLs

**Step 1.** Define a CBAC rule to inspect all TCP and FTP traffic:

```
RouterP(config)# ip inspect name FWRULE tcp timeout 300
RouterP(config)# ip inspect name FWRULE ftp timeout 300
```

**Step 2.** Define the ACLs to enable outbound ICMP traffic and CBAC traffic such as FTP and WWW. Block all other inside initiated traffic:

```
RouterP(config)# access-list 101 permit icmp any any
RouterP(config)# access-list 101 permit tcp 10.0.P.0 0.0.0.255 any eq ftp
RouterP(config)# access-list 101 permit tcp 10.0.P.0 0.0.0.255 any eq www
RouterP(config)# access-list 101 deny ip any any
```

**Step 3.** Define ACLs to enable inbound ICMP traffic and CBAC traffic such as FTP and WWW to the inside web or FTP server. Block all other outside initiated traffic:

```
RouterP(config)# access-list 102 permit eigrp any any
RouterP(config)# access-list 102 permit icmp any any
RouterP(config)# access-list 102 permit tcp any host 10.0.P.12 eq ftp
RouterP(config)# access-list 102 permit tcp any host 10.0.P.12 eq www
RouterP(config)# access-list 102 deny ip any any
```

**Step 4.** Apply the inspection rule and the ACL to the inside interface:

```
RouterP(config)# interface ethernet 0/0
RouterP(config-if)# ip inspect FWRULE in
RouterP(config-if)# ip access-group 101 in
```

**Step 5.** Apply the ACL to the outside interface:

```
RouterP(config-if)# interface ethernet 0/1
RouterP(config-if)# ip access-group 102 in
```

**Step 6.** Save the configuration and return to global configuration mode:

```
Router(config-if)# end
Router# write memory
```

## Task 3: Testing and Verifying CBAC

Complete the following steps to test and verify CBAC.

**Step 1.** Check the ACLs:

```
Router# show access-lists
```

In the output for the **show access-lists** command, how many matches for EIGRP packets are in access list 102?

---

**Step 2.** From the MS command prompt, ping the backbone server:

```
C:\> ping 172.26.25.50
Pinging 172.26.26.50 with 32 bytes of data:
Reply from 172.26.26.50: bytes=32 time=34ms TTL=125
Reply from 172.26.26.50: bytes=32 time=34ms TTL=125
Reply from 172.26.26.50: bytes=32 time=34ms TTL=125
Reply from 172.26.26.50: bytes=32 time=36ms TTL=125
```

**Step 3.** Use your web browser to connect to the backbone web server:

Enter **http://172.26.26.50** in the URL field.

**Step 4.** Connect to the backbone FTP server using anonymous FTP:

```
C:\> ftp 172.26.26.50
...
User (10.0.0.12:(none)): anonymous
...
Password: user@
```

**Step 5.** Do a directory listing to verify data channel connectivity:

```
ftp> ls
```

**Step 6.** Use the **show access-lists** command to view the new dynamic ACL entry added by the **ip inspect** statement in Task 2, Step 1:

```
Router# show access-lists
```

**Step 7.** Use the following **show** commands to verify CBAC operation:

```
RouterP# show ip inspect name FWRULE
RouterP# show ip inspect config
RouterP# show ip inspect interfaces
RouterP# show ip inspect sessions
RouterP# show ip inspect sessions detail
RouterP# show ip inspect all
```

**Step 8.** From the MS command prompt, ping the inside host/server of the neighboring Pod:

```
C:\> ping 10.0.Q.12
Pinging 10.0.1.3 with 32 bytes of data:
Reply from 10.0.1.3: bytes=32 time=34ms TTL=125
Reply from 10.0.1.3: bytes=32 time=34ms TTL=125
Reply from 10.0.1.3: bytes=32 time=34ms TTL=125
Reply from 10.0.1.3: bytes=32 time=36ms TTL=125
```

**Step 9.** Use your web browser to connect to the inside server of the neighboring peer:

Enter **http://10.0.Q.12** in the URL field.

**Step 10.** Connect to the neighboring peer FTP server by using an anonymous FTP:

```
C:\> ftp 10.0.Q.12
...
User (10.0.P.12:(none)): anonymous
...
Password: user@
```

**Step 11.** Use the following **show** commands to verify CBAC operation:

```
RouterP# show ip inspect name FWRULE
RouterP# show ip inspect config
```

```
RouterP# show ip inspect interfaces
RouterP# show ip inspect sessions
RouterP# show ip inspect sessions detail
RouterP# show ip inspect all
```

## Review Questions

1. Describe why the order of ACLs is important.

_______________________________________________

_______________________________________________

_______________________________________________

2. How does one go about logging ACLs?

_______________________________________________

_______________________________________________

_______________________________________________

3. Describe lock-and-key ACLs.

_______________________________________________

_______________________________________________

_______________________________________________

4. Describe the difference between lock-and-key ACLs and authentication proxy.

_______________________________________________

_______________________________________________

_______________________________________________

5. Describe CBAC.

_______________________________________________

_______________________________________________

_______________________________________________

## Chapter 3 Quiz Questions

1. Which of the following could be classified as a dedicated firewall device?

   A. Packet Internet Exchange (PIX) Firewall

   B. Cisco IOS router

   C. Cisco Secure ACS

   D. Certificate Authority

2. Which of the following is *not* a type of access list mentioned for use by Cisco IOS routers using the firewall feature set?

   A. Reflexive

   B. Automatic

   C. Time-based

   D. Commented

3. Which of the following is *not* a feature of a Cisco IOS router with firewall features?

   A. Context-based access control

   B. Network Address Translation (NAT)

   C. IPSec

   D. Virus detection

4. Which of the following is the most commonly used point product for network security?

   A. Intrusion detection system (IDS)

   B. Firewall

   C. Router

   D. AAA server

5. What graphically depicts the dynamic approach to security management?

   A. Networking device icons

   B. A closed loop circle

   C. A security wheel

   D. An implementation outline

6. Which of the following is not a characteristic of a strong user password?

   A. Can be checked against a dictionary for correct spelling

   B. Has a mixture of upper and lowercase letters

   C. Includes non-alphabetic characters

   D. Can consist of multiword phrases

7. When should the Cisco Secure Scanner software run security tests?

   A. When network traffic is low

   B. At various times of the day and days of the week

   C. After the network has been secured

   D. All of the above

8. In the network mapping phase of a network scan using the Cisco Secure Scanner software, which hosts are scanned?

   A. All hosts

   B. All hosts on a network segment

   C. One host for each run

   D. Live hosts

9. What is the NSDB?

   A. Network Security Database

   B. Network Scanning Daemon

   C. Non Secure Detection Bridge

   D. Network Source Default Broadcast

10. Which of the following is *not* a feature of personal firewalls?

    A. Can be used to interconnect multiple PCs that are connected to the Internet via dialup or other connections

    B. Server-based software makes updates easy to implement.

    C. May prevent the PC from making LAN connections

    D. Resides on the user's PC

# Chapter 4

## Router AAA Security

This chapter introduces the student to authentication, authorization, and accounting (AAA) security on the router. When using AAA in the network, security can be increased even further. By providing a way to authenticate all remote user access, the administrator can authorize different access to resources and keep track of what resources have been accessed.

There are several different ways for the remote user to authenticate to the network. By providing a means to authenticate either locally or through a Network Access Server (NAS) or an AAA server, the administrator has flexibility to adapt to the changing requirements of the organization. The chapter also covers how Cisco Secure ACS works with AAA servers.

The chapter then introduces TACACS+ and RADIUS AAA servers. Both protocols are discussed and compared to give the student the ability to choose the best authentication method based on the organization's needs.

**Vocabulary Exercise**

3DES

_______________________________________________

_______________________________________________

ACEs

_______________________________________________

_______________________________________________

Data Encryption Standard (DES)

_______________________________________________

_______________________________________________

rcp

_______________________________________________

_______________________________________________

rlogin

_______________________________________________

_______________________________________________

rsh

_______________________________________________

_______________________________________________

Network Access Server

---

---

**Lab Activities**

The topology figures and lab examples contain **P** and **Q** values. The **P** value in the addressing and naming scheme refers to *your* assigned Pod number.

The following are examples of determining P values:

- Pod2 is looking at a topology figure and is trying to determine the P values in the figure. In this scenario, the **P** values would equal **2**. 10.0.**P**.12 would become 10.0.**2**.12, 172.30.**P**.2 would become 172.30.**2**.2, and so on.
- Pod1 is looking at a topology figure and is trying to determine the P values in the figure. In this scenario, the **P** values would equal **1**. 10.0.**P**.12 would become 10.0.**1**.12, 172.30.**P**.2 would become 172.30.**1**.2, and so on.

In both examples, the P values are directly related to the Pod number of the team.

The **Q** value in the naming and addressing scheme is used when testing the security or connectivity with the peer team.

The following are examples of determining Q values:

- In a lab, Pod2 has been asked to test connectivity to their peer inside host at IP address 10.0.Q.12. In this scenario, 10.0.**Q**.12 would equal 10.0.**1**.12.
- In a lab, Pod1 has been asked to test connectivity to their peer inside host at IP address 10.0.Q.12. In this scenario, 10.0.**Q**.12 would equal 10.0.**2**.12.

In both examples, the Q value is the directly related to the peer Pod number.

# Lab 4.2.3: Configure AAA on Cisco Router

Estimated Time: 20 Minutes

Number of Team Members: Two teams with four students per team

## Objective

In this exercise, students protect the NAS, or Pod router, by securing access using simple passwords without AAA. Then students configure the NAS to perform AAA authentication functions against the server local security database. In this lab, students complete the following tasks:

- Secure and test access to the privileged EXEC, vty, and console.
- Configure local database authentication using AAA.
- Create a sample configuration for the NAS for a completed lab.

## Overview

Access control is a means that network administrators can use to control the individuals allowed access to the network server and what services they are allowed to use after they have access. AAA network security services provide the primary framework through which network administrators can set up access control.

Figure 4-1 illustrates the network environment students create for this lab.

**Figure 4-1 Lab 4.2.3 Network Topology**

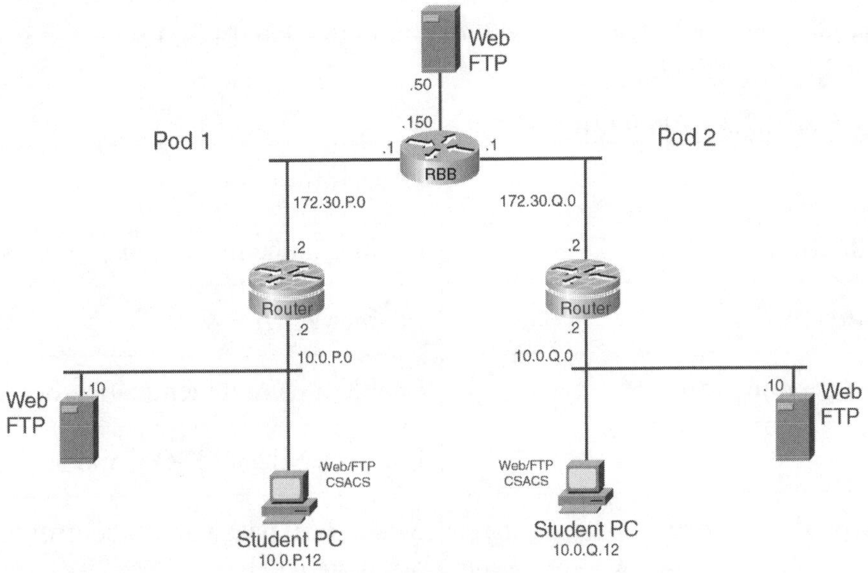


## Preparation

Begin with the standard lab topology and verify the standard router configuration on the Pod routers. Test the connectivity between the Pod routers. Access the perimeter router console port using the terminal emulator on the student PC. If desired, save the router configuration to a text file for later analysis. Refer to the *Student Lab Orientation (Lab 1.1.5)* if you need more help.

## Tools and Resources

To complete the lab, the standard lab topology is required:

- Two Pod routers
- Two student PCs
- Two servers
- Backbone switch and router
- Two console cables and HyperTerminal

**Additional Materials**

The following websites provide additional information on AAA:

- http://www.cisco.com/en/US/products/sw/iosswrel/ps1831/products_configuration_guide_chapter09186a00800d980f.html
- http://www.cisco.com/en/US/products/sw/iosswrel/ps1831/products_configuration_guide_chapter09186a00800d9811.html
- http://www.cisco.com/en/US/products/sw/iosswrel/ps1831/products_configuration_guide_chapter09186a00800d9810.html
- http://www.cisco.com/en/US/products/sw/iosswrel/ps1831/products_configuration_guide_chapter09186a00800d9813.html

## Command List

Table 4-1 lists the commands that are used throughout this lab. Refer to this list if you need any assistance or help during the lab.

**Table 4-1 Lab 4.2.3 Command List**

| Command | Description |
|---|---|
| **aaa authentication** | Defines authentication parameters |
| **aaa new-model** | Enables AAA |
| **debug aaa authentication** | Enables AAA authentication debugging |
| **enable** | Enters privileged EXEC mode. |
| **enable password** *password* | Sets a local password to control access to various privilege levels |
| **enable secret** *password* | Specifies an additional layer of security over the **enable password** command |
| **enable secret level** *level* **password** | Sets a password for the privilege level |

| Command | Description |
|---|---|
| **privilege level** *level* | Configures a new privilege level for users and associate commands with that privilege level<br>*level* is the privilege level associated with the specified line. |
| **privilege** *mode* {**level** *level* \| **reset**} *command-string* | *mode* is the configuration mode for the specified command.<br>**level** *level* specifies the privilege level configured for the specified command or commands. The level argument must be a number from 0 to 15.<br>**reset** resets the privilege level of the specified command or commands to the default and removes the privilege-level configuration from the running-config file.<br>*Note:* If the **no** form of this command is used to reset the privilege level to the default, the default form of this command still appears in the configuration file. To completely remove a privilege configuration, use the **reset** keyword.<br>*command-string* is associated with the specified privilege level. If the **all** keyword is used, it specifies the command and subcommands associated with the privilege level. |
| **service password-encryption** | Encrypts all passwords in the configuration files |
| **show privilege** | Displays the current level of privilege |
| **username** *username* **password** *password* | Defines a local user and password combination |

## Task 1: Securing and Testing Access to Privileged EXEC, vty, and Console

The router currently has no password protection. Begin by protecting access points into the router with passwords. Complete the following steps on the Pod router:

**Step 1.** Secure privileged EXEC mode by configuring an enable password of **bravo1**.

**Step 2.** Continue to set the security of the privileged EXEC mode by configuring an enable secret password of **rouge7fox**.

**Step 3.** Configure the vty password of all vtys of **echo9**, and enable password checking.

**Step 4.** Configure a console password of **front door**, and enable password checking. Yes, there is a space in the password.

**Step 5.** Test the vty, console, and enable passwords. Verify that access to the privileged EXEC can be established after Telneting.

**Step 6.** Look at the running configuration. Note that all passwords except "enable secret" are clear text. Use the **service password-encryption** command to correct this.

Show the running configuration again to ensure all passwords are now encrypted.

What happens to the passwords when the **no service password-encryption** command is used?

---

**Task 2:Configuring Local Database Authentication Using AAA**

In this section, configure the local database authentication using AAA for the enable, line, and local methods.

Now that the NAS access points are protected, use the AAA commands to prepare for migration to a Cisco Secure Access Control Server (CSACS) environment. The goal of this task is to illustrate that each router access point can be secured using unique methods.

In this lab, there are two access points or lines to protect: vty and console.

Complete the following steps to configure a unique method login authentication on all access points.

**Step 1.** Turn on AAA features. Note that on command examples, spaces are added at times for readability only:

```
RouterP(config)# aaa new-model
```

**Step 2.** Configure the login authentication to use the enable password using the default list:

```
RouterP(config)# aaa authentication login default enable
```

This protects all logins access instantly.

**Step 3.** Add variations and put in controls specific to the needs of the user.

**Step 4.** Test the model. Exit from the privilege mode and then exit from user mode. Then try to access the router on the console port. A password prompt appears. Which password will be valid, **front door** or **rouge7fox**? Why?

---

**Step 5.** Protect the console specifically. Enter the following commands so that the IS group can access the console. Be aware that some passwords contain spaces:

```
RouterP(config)# username admin password back door
RouterP(config)# aaa authentication login console-in local
RouterP(config)# line con 0
RouterP(config-line)# login authentication console-in
```

Using the local database, students have just given the console a different login method from all the others. Cisco recommends never using `admin` as a username because it is too easy to guess.

**Step 6.** Exit the config, enable, and user modes, and test the method.

**Step 7.** Secure the vty access for the IS personnel by using the following commands:

```
RouterP(config)# username isgroup password other door
RouterP(config)# aaa authentication login is-in local
RouterP(config)# line vty 0 4
RouterP(config-line)# login authentication is-in
```

This is the same idea as the console protection, but on the Telnet access via the vty ports. Test by Telneting into the NAS from the student PC.

What is prompted for at the beginning of the Telnet session?

---

*Note*: Do not use any of the Telnet icons on the desktop. They might be mapped to a specific server. Instead, use the Telnet applet from MS-DOS.

**Task 3: Testing the Connection with Debug**

In this task, use **debug** to look at the indicators for successful and unsuccessful authentication attempts. Before beginning this section, ensure that all Telnet sessions are disconnected, except for the console session. It is important in debugging to ensure the proper time is set to reference messages, especially if you are logging multiple devices to a central logging system.

Check the NAS clock by logging in to user mode and typing **show clock**. If the time and date are incorrect, enter the following command: **clock set *HH:MM:SS DD month YYYY***. For example, **clock set 10:00:00 15 January 2004**.

To look at the indicators for successful and unsuccessful authentication attempts, complete the following steps.

**Step 1.** Log in to privilege mode and use the following command to verify the correct timestamp information for the debug output:

```
RouterP(config)# service timestamps debug datetime msec
RouterP(config)# exit
```

**Step 2.** Turn on debugging for AAA authentication:

```
RouterP# debug aaa authentication
```

**Step 3.** Trigger an AAA authentication event by exiting the console connection and then logging in using **`admin back door`** as the username and password.

**Step 4.** After logging in and being presented the user mode prompt, continue with privileged mode. The debug should be similar to the following:

```
Username:
Mar 21 17:05:00.461: AAA/AUTHEN/LOGIN (00000053): Pick method list 'console-in'
Username: admin
Password:
RouterP>enable
Password:
Mar 21 17:05:11.656: AAA: parse name=tty0 idb type=-1 tty=-1
Mar 21 17:05:11.656: AAA: name=tty0 flags=0x11 type=4 shelf=0 slot=0 adapter=0 port=0 channel=0
Mar 21 17:05:11.656: AAA/MEMORY: create_user (0x82B2138C) user='admin' ruser='NU
LL' ds0=0 port='tty0' rem_addr='async' authen_type=ASCII service=ENABLE priv=15
initial_task_id='0'
Mar 21 17:05:11.656: AAA/AUTHEN/START (3254755694): port='tty0' list='' action=LOGIN
service=ENABLE
Mar 21 17:05:11.656: AAA/AUTHEN/START (3254755694): console enable - default to enable password
(if any)
Mar 21 17:05:11.656: AAA/AUTHEN/START (3254755694): Method=ENABLE
Mar 21 17:05:11.660: AAA/AUTHEN(3254755694): Status=GETPASS
RouterP#
Mar 21 17:05:18.671: AAA/AUTHEN/CONT (3254755694): continue_login (user='(undef)')
Mar 21 17:05:18.671: AAA/AUTHEN(3254755694): Status=GETPASS
Mar 21 17:05:18.671: AAA/AUTHEN/CONT (3254755694): Method=ENABLE
Mar 21 17:05:18.755: AAA/AUTHEN(3254755694): Status=PASS
Mar 21 17:05:18.755: AAA/MEMORY: free_user (0x82B2138C) user='NULL' ruser='NULL'
port='tty0' rem_addr='async' authen_type=ASCII service=ENABLE priv=15
RouterP#
```

**Step 5.** Log out of the router before continuing.

**Step 6.** Log in to the router and enter an invalid password:

```
Username:
Mar 21 17:07:40.612: AAA/AUTHEN/LOGIN (00000054): Pick method list 'console-in'
Username: admin
Password:
RouterP>enable
Password:
Mar 21 17:07:52.103: AAA: parse name=tty0 idb type=-1 tty=-1
Mar 21 17:07:52.103: AAA: name=tty0 flags=0x11 type=4 shelf=0 slot=0 adapter=0 p ort=0 channel=0
Mar 21 17:07:52.107: AAA/MEMORY: create_user (0x82CE62E0) user='admin' ruser='NULL' ds0=0
  port='tty0' rem_addr='async' authen_type=ASCII service=ENABLE priv=15 initial_task_id='0'
Mar 21 17:07:52.107: AAA/AUTHEN/START (2358711356): port='tty0' list='' action=LOGIN
  service=ENABLE
Mar 21 17:07:52.107: AAA/AUTHEN/START (2358711356): console enable - default to enable password
  (if any)
Mar 21 17:07:52.107: AAA/AUTHEN/START (2358711356): Method=ENABLE
Mar 21 17:07:52.107: AAA/AUTHEN(2358711356): Status=GETPASS
% Access denied
RouterP>
Mar 21 17:07:55.180: AAA/AUTHEN/CONT (2358711356): continue_login (user='(undef)')
Mar 21 17:07:55.180: AAA/AUTHEN(2358711356): Status=GETPASS
Mar 21 17:07:55.180: AAA/AUTHEN/CONT (2358711356): Method=ENABLE
Mar 21 17:07:55.260: AAA/AUTHEN(2358711356): password incorrect
Mar 21 17:07:55.260: AAA/AUTHEN(2358711356): Status=FAIL
Mar 21 17:07:55.260: AAA/MEMORY: free_user (0x82CE62E0) user='NULL' ruser='NULL'
port='tty0' rem_addr='async' authen_type=ASCII service=ENABLE priv=15
RouterP>
```

## Task 4: Testing Telnet Authentication

**Step 1.** Telnet from the student PC to the NAS and enter a username and password. After a successful Telnet authentication, enter the privileged EXEC mode. You should use the following passwords:

- Telnet username: **isgroup**
- Telnet password: **other door**
- Enable password: **rouge7fox**

The **debug aaa authentication** and **debug aaa authorization** output should be similar to the following output:

```
RouterP#
*Mar  1 21:42:18.065: AAA/AUTHEN/LOGIN (00000011): Pick method list 'is-in'
*Mar  1 21:42:25.890: AAA/AUTHOR (00000011): Method list id=0 not configured. Sk ip author
*Mar  1 21:42:29.817: AAA: parse name=tty67 idb type=-1 tty=-1
*Mar  1 21:42:29.817: AAA: name=tty67 flags=0x11 type=5 shelf=0 slot=0 adapter=0  port=67
channel=0
*Mar  1 21:42:29.817: AAA/MEMORY: create_user (0x82D1B690) user='isgroup' ruser=
'NULL' ds0=0 port='tty67' rem_addr='10.0.1.12' authen_type=ASCII service=ENABLE priv=15
initial_task_id='0'
*Mar  1 21:42:29.817: AAA/AUTHEN/START (3905120739): port='tty67' list='' action=LOGIN
service=ENABLE
*Mar  1 21:42:29.821: AAA/AUTHEN/START (3905120739): non-console enable - default to enable
password
*Mar  1 21:42:29.821: AAA/AUTHEN/START (3905120739): Method=ENABLE
*Mar  1 21:42:29.821: AAA/AUTHEN(3905120739): Status=GETPASS
*Mar  1 21:42:34.064: AAA/AUTHEN/CONT (3905120739): continue_login (user='(undef)')
*Mar  1 21:42:34.068: AAA/AUTHEN(3905120739): Status=GETPASS
*Mar  1 21:42:34.068: AAA/AUTHEN/CONT (3905120739): Method=ENABLE
*Mar  1 21:42:34.152: AAA/AUTHEN(3905120739): Status=PASS
*Mar  1 21:42:34.152: AAA/MEMORY: free_user (0x82D1B690) user='NULL' ruser='NULL
' port='tty67' rem_addr='10.0.1.12' authen_type=ASCII service=ENABLE priv=15
```

**Step 2.** Telnet from the student PC to the Pod router, but enter a wrong enable password. The **debug aaa authentication** and **debug aaa authorization** output should be similar to the following output:

```
RouterP#
*Mar  1 21:43:56.639: AAA/AUTHEN/LOGIN (00000012): Pick method list 'is-in'
*Mar  1 21:44:05.129: AAA/AUTHOR (00000012): Method list id=0 not configured. Sk ip author
*Mar  1 21:44:08.090: AAA: parse name=tty67 idb type=-1 tty=-1
*Mar  1 21:44:08.090: AAA: name=tty67 flags=0x11 type=5 shelf=0 slot=0 adapter=0  port=67
  channel=0
*Mar  1 21:44:08.090: AAA/MEMORY: create_user (0x82D1BE74) user='isgroup' ruser=
'NULL' ds0=0 port='tty67' rem_addr='10.0.1.12' authen_type=ASCII service=ENABLE priv=15
  initial_task_id='0'
*Mar  1 21:44:08.090: AAA/AUTHEN/START (3951678639): port='tty67' list='' action=LOGIN
  service=ENABLE
*Mar  1 21:44:08.094: AAA/AUTHEN/START (3951678639): non-console enable - default to enable
  password
*Mar  1 21:44:08.094: AAA/AUTHEN/START (3951678639): Method=ENABLE
*Mar  1 21:44:08.094: AAA/AUTHEN(3951678639): Status=GETPASS
*Mar  1 21:44:12.886: AAA/AUTHEN/CONT (3951678639): continue_login (user='(undef)')
*Mar  1 21:44:12.890: AAA/AUTHEN(3951678639): Status=GETPASS
*Mar  1 21:44:12.890: AAA/AUTHEN/CONT (3951678639): Method=ENABLE
*Mar  1 21:44:12.974: AAA/AUTHEN(3951678639): password incorrect
*Mar  1 21:44:12.974: AAA/AUTHEN(3951678639): Status=FAIL
*Mar  1 21:44:12.974: AAA/MEMORY: free_user (0x82D1BE74) user='NULL' ruser='NULL
' port='tty67' rem_addr='10.0.1.12' authen_type=ASCII service=ENABLE priv=15
```

What syntax indicates the authentication was unsuccessful?

---

## Task 5: Viewing a Sample Configuration for the NAS

At this point, the NAS configuration should look like the one shown in this task.

**Step 1.** To view the configuration, log in to privilege mode and type **show running config**:

```
Router1# show running-config
Building configuration...
Current configuration : 1165 bytes
!
version 12.2
service timestamps debug uptime
service timestamps log uptime
no service password-encryption
!
hostname Router1
!
no logging console
aaa new-model
!
aaa authentication login default enable
aaa authentication login console-in local
aaa authentication login is-in local
aaa session-id common
enable secret 5 $1$xQw7$onU.pB6fCpSGuEJonLiiC/
enable password bravo1
!
username admin password 0 back door
username isgroup password 0 other door
memory-size iomem 15
ip subnet-zero
!
no ip domain-lookup
!
ip audit notify log
ip audit po max-events 100
!
interface FastEthernet0/0
 description inside
 ip address 10.0.P.2 255.255.255.0
!
interface FastEthernet0/1
 description outside
 ip address 172.30.P.2 255.255.255.0
```

```
!
router eigrp 1
 network 10.0.0.0
 network 172.30.0.0
 no auto-summary
 no eigrp log-neighbor-changes
!
ip classless
no ip http server
ip pim bidir-enable
!
line con 0
 password front door
 login authentication console-in
line aux 0
line vty 0 4
 password echo9
 login authentication is-in
!
!
end
```

## Lab 4.3.1: Install and Configure CSACS 3.0 for Windows

Estimated Time: 30 Minutes

Number of Team Members: Two teams with four students per team

### Objective

In this lab, students complete the following objectives:

- Install CSACS for Windows 2000.
- Take a grand tour of CSACS for Windows.

### Overview

CSACS for Windows 2000/NT Servers network security software helps administrators authenticate users by controlling dialin access to an NAS device, an access server, a Cisco PIX Firewall, a switch, a wireless access point, or a router. CSACS operates as a Windows NT or Windows 2000 service and controls the AAA of users accessing networks.

### Preparation

Begin with the standard lab topology and verify the standard router configuration on the Pod routers. Test the connectivity between the Pod routers. Access the perimeter router console port using the terminal emulator on the student PC. If desired, save the router configuration to a text file for later analysis. Refer to the *Student Lab Orientation* if you need more help.

### Tools and Resources

To complete the lab, the standard lab topology is required:

- Two Pod routers
- Two student PCs
- Two servers
- Backbone switch and router
- Two console cables and HyperTerminal

### Additional Materials

The following websites provide additional information on CSACS:

- http://www.cisco.com/en/US/products/sw/secursw/ps2086/products_qanda_item09186a0080094bac.shtml
- http://www.cisco.com/en/US/products/sw/secursw/ps2086/products_white_paper09186a0080115464.shtml
- http://www.cisco.com/en/US/products/sw/secursw/ps2086/prod_configuration_examples_list.html

**Task 1: Installing CSACS 3.0 for Windows 2000**

Complete the following steps to install CSACS on the Windows 2000 server. This procedure assumes that the Windows 2000 server is operational.

**Step 1.** Log in to Windows 2000 server using the administrator account. The instructor will provide the correct username and password combination for the administrator account.

**Step 2.** Open the CSACS folder on the PC. Begin the CSACS installation by double-clicking the **Setup.exe** file. The CSACS for Windows NT/2000 installation wizard starts. Ignore any warning messages concerning memory requirements.

**Step 3.** Click **Accept** to acknowledge the terms of the CSACS license agreement. Click **Next** to close the Welcome window. Check all items listed in the Before You Begin window and click **Next**. Click **Next** to accept the default settings in the Choose Destination Location window.

**Step 4.** Complete the following substeps within the Authentication Database Configuration window:

a. Select the Also check the Windows 2000/NT User Database option.

b. Select the **Yes, refer to "Grant dialin permission" to user setting** checkbox.

*Note*: The **Yes, refer to "Grant dialin permission to user" setting** checkbox applies to all forms of access controlled by Cisco Secure ACS, not just dialin access. For example, a user accessing the network through a VPN tunnel is not dialing into a network access server; however, if the **Yes, refer to "Grant dialin permission to user" setting** checkbox is selected, Cisco Secure ACS applies the Windows user dialin permissions to determine whether to grant the user access to your network.

c. Click **Next**.

**Step 5.** Complete the following substeps within the CSACS Network Access Server Details window:

a. Select TACACS+ (Cisco IOS) from the Authenticate Users Using scroll box.

b. Type the name of the NAS in the Access Server Name box. For example, NAS1, NAS2, and so on.

c. Type the IP address of the NAS in the Access Server IP Address box.

d. Ensure that the IP address of the CSACS server is entered in the Windows Server IP Address box.

e. Type **ciscosecure** (one word and all lowercase) in the TACACS+ or RADIUS key box.

f. Click **Next**. Setup starts to install files to this Windows 2000 CSACS laptop PC.

**Step 6.** Check all the options within the Advanced Options window and click **Next**. This list determines what ACS options can be configured later.

**Step 7.** Accept the default settings within the Active Service Monitoring window by clicking **Next**. Accept the default settings within the Network Access Server Configuration window by clicking **Next**.

**Step 8.** Accept the default setting with no password specified in the Enable Secret Password window by clicking **Next**. Accept the default settings within the Access Server Configuration window by clicking **Next**.

**Step 9.** Complete the following substeps within the NAS Configuration window:

a. Use the scroll bar to view all the parameters in the command box. These parameters are created during the installation process of the CSACS software.

b. Do not use the Telnet Now? function at this time. This function enables Telnet to the NAS. If this option is selected, the CSACS setup program opens a Telnet window. The user can then log into the NAS and copy and paste these parameters into the NAS, saving time in the NAS setup process.

**Step 10.** Accept the default settings within the Cisco Secure ACS Initiation window by clicking **Next**. Click **Finish** to close the Setup Complete window. Review the contents of the Read Me file and close the associated window. Ensure that an Internet Explorer window containing the CSACS Main Window opens.

**Step 11.** Using Windows Task Manager (**Ctrl-Alt-Delete** > **Task Manager**), check whether the following services are now running on the Windows 2000 server PC:

- CSAdmin
- CSAuth
- CSDbSync
- CSLog
- CSMon
- CSRadius
- CSTacacs

If these services are not listed as running, restart the Windows 2000 server l PC and repeat this step.

If all the tasks are running, CSACS 3.0 for Windows 2000 has been successfully installed.

**Task 2: Taking a Grand Tour of CSACS for Windows**

Complete the following steps to become familiar with the CSACS for Windows administration interface and to change some global settings:

**Step 1.** Start the ACS configuration manager by double-clicking the **ACS Admin** desktop icon.

**Step 2.** Select the **Cisco Systems** icon at the top of the left frame.

What is displayed in the right frame? What is the release version?

_______________________________________________

**Step 3.** Examine the user setup functions by completing the following substeps:

Select **User Setup** in the left frame.

Select the **List All Users** button.

How many users are configured?

_______________________________________________

**Step 4.** Examine the group setup functions by completing the following substeps:

a. Select **Group Setup** in the left frame.

What group is shown in the Group window?

---

b. Select the **Users in Group** button in the left frame.

How many users are in the group?

---

**Step 5.** Select Network Configuration in the left frame:

How many NAS are configured?

---

**Step 6.** Examine the system configuration functions by completing the following substeps:

a. Select **System Configuration** in the left frame.

b. Select the **Service Control** blue text in the System Configuration window, answer the following question, and then select **Cancel** to return to the select list.

What is the status of the Cisco Secure service, the level of detail for logging, and the frequency of the new file generation?

---

c. Select the **Logging** blue text in the System Configuration window, answer the following question, and then select **Cancel** to return to the select list.

What log targets are enabled?

---

d. Select the **Password Validation** blue text in the System Configuration window, answer the following question, and then select **Cancel** to return to the select list.

What is the purpose of the password validation options?

---

e. Select the **Cisco Secure Database Replication** blue text in the System Configuration window, answer the following question, and then select **Cancel** to return to the select list.

What is the purpose of **Cisco Secure** Replication Setup?

---

f. Select the **ACS Backup** blue text in the System Configuration window, answer the following question, and then select **Cancel** to return to the select list.

Where can the ACS user and group databases be backed up?

---

g. Select the **ACS Restore** blue text in the System Configuration window, answer the following question, and then select **Cancel** to return to the select list.

What components can be backed up and restored?

---

h. Select the **ACS Service Management** blue text in the System Configuration window, answer the following question, and then select **Cancel** to return to the select list.

How can a system administrator be notified of events that are logged?

---

**Step 7.** Examine the interface configuration functions by completing the following substeps:

a. Select **Interface Configuration** in the left frame.

b. Select the **User Data Configuration** blue text in the Interface Configuration window, answer the following question, and then select **Cancel** to return to the select list.

How are user-defined fields useful?

---

c. Select the **Advanced Option** blue text in the Interface Configuration window, perform Step d, and answer the following question.

d. Ensure that all options are checked.

What is the purpose of selecting advanced options?

---

e. Select **Submit** to return to the select list.

f. Select the **TACACS+ (Cisco)** blue text in the Interface Configuration window, perform Steps g through i, and answer the following question.

g. In the TACACS+ Services window, ensure that PPP IP, PPP LCP, PPP Multilink, and Shell (exec) are selected for both the user and group columns.

h. In the Advanced Configuration Options window, ensure that all four boxes are checked.

i. Select **Submit** to return to the select list.

Where are the TACACS+ services and advanced configuration objects applied in this window?

---

**Step 8.** Select **Administration Control** in the left frame.

a. What administrator accounts are configured?

---

b. What is the purpose of administrator control?

---

**Step 9.** Examine the external user database functions by completing the following substeps:

a. Select External User Databases in the left frame.

b. Select the **Unknown User Policy** blue text in the External User Databases window, answer the following question, and then select **Cancel** to return to the select list.

What two options are available if a user is not found in the Cisco Secure database?

______________________________________________________________________________

Which one is the default?

______________________________________________________________________________

What external databases can be checked for the unknown user?

______________________________________________________________________________

c. Select the **Database Group Mappings** blue text in the External User Databases window. Scroll down through the Unknown Users Group Mappings windows to answer the following question, and then select **Cancel to return** back to the select list.

d. Select the **Database Configuration** blue text in the External User Databases window, answer the following question, and then select **Cancel** to return to the select list.

What can be configured in the External User Database Configuration window?

______________________________________________________________________________

**Step 10.** Examine the reports and activity functions by completing the following substeps:

a. Select **Reports and Activity** in the left frame.

b. Select the **Administration Audit** blue text in the Reports and Activity window, and answer the following question.

What appears in the Administration Audit.csv file?

______________________________________________________________________________

**Step 11.** Select **Online Documentation** in the left frame.

Take a moment to browse the new features, software requirements, and troubleshooting sections of the online documentation.

# Lab 4.5.2: Configuring Authentication Proxy

Estimated Time: 30 Minutes

Number of Team Members: Two teams with four students per team

## Objective

In this lab, students complete the following tasks:

- Configure CSACS for Windows 2000.
- Configure AAA.
- Configure an authentication proxy.
- Test and verify an authentication proxy.

## Scenario

With the authentication proxy feature, users can log into the network or access the Internet through HTTP. The user's specific access profiles are automatically retrieved and applied from a CSACS. The user profiles are active only when there is active traffic from the authenticated users. In this lab, students configure authentication proxy on a Cisco router with the following steps:

**Step 1.** Configure CSACS for Windows 2000.

**Step 2.** Configure AAA.

**Step 3.** Configure ACLs.

**Step 4.** Configure an authentication proxy.

**Step 5.** Test and verify an authentication proxy.

**Step 6.** Clear the authentication proxy cache.

## Topology

Figure 4-2 illustrates the network environment students create for this lab.

## Preparation

Begin with the standard lab topology and verify the standard router configuration on the Pod routers. Test the connectivity between the Pod routers. Access the perimeter router console port using the terminal emulator on the Windows 2000 server. If desired, save the router configuration to a text file for later analysis. Refer to the *Student Lab Orientation* if you need more help.

In preparation for this lab, CSACS should be configured with a user in the default group, with a username of aaauser and a password of aaapass.

**Figure 4-2 Lab 4.5.2 Network Topology**

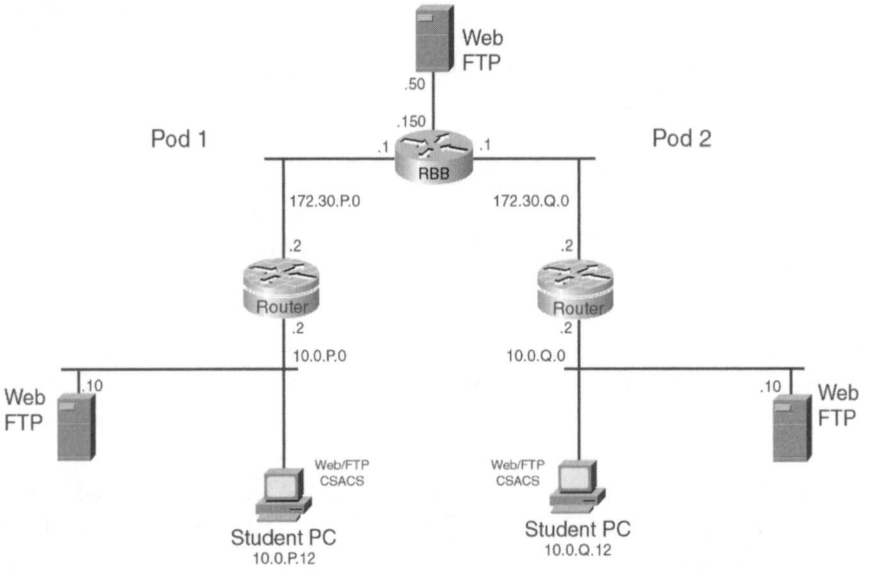

Web
FTP
.50
.150
Pod 1
.1
RBB
.1
Pod 2
172.30.P.0
172.30.Q.0
.2
.2
Router
Router
.2
.2
10.0.P.0
10.0.Q.0
.10
.10
Web
FTP
Web
FTP
Web/FTP
CSACS
Web/FTP
CSACS
Student PC
10.0.P.12
Student PC
10.0.Q.12

## Tools and Resources

To complete the lab, the standard lab topology is required:

- Two Pod routers
- Two student PCs
- One SuperServer
- Backbone switch and one backbone router
- Two console cables
- HyperTerminal

## Additional Materials

Further information about the objectives covered in this lab can be found at the following websites:

- http://www.cisco.com/en/US/products/sw/iosswrel/ps1831/products_configuration_guide_chapter09186a00800d981d.html
- http://www.cisco.com/en/US/products/sw/iosswrel/ps1831/products_command_reference_chapter09186a00800d9807.html

## Command List

Table 4-2 lists the commands that are used throughout this lab. Refer to this list if you need any assistance or help during the lab.

**Table 4-2 Lab 4.5.2 Command List**

| Command | Description |
|---|---|
| **aaa authentication** | Defines AAA authentication parameters |
| **aaa authorization** | Defines AAA authorization parameters |
| **aaa new-model** | Enables AAA |
| **debug aaa authentication** | Enables AAA authentication debugging |
| **ip auth-proxy** | Defines authentication proxy rules |
| **ip http** | Defines HTTP settings |
| **tacacs-server** | Defines TACACS server settings |

## Task 1: Configuring CS ACS for Windows 2000

**Step 1.** On the workstation, open Cisco Secure ACS from the desktop.

**Step 2.** Click **Interface Configuration** on the far left column of CSACS to go to the Interface Configuration window.

**Step 3.** Click **TACACS+ (Cisco)** to configure this option. Scroll to the New Services frame.

**Step 4.** Select the first line under New Service and enter **auth-proxy** under service. Check the group checkbox. Check the box closest to auth-proxy service field. Choose **Advanced TACACS+ features**.

**Step 5.** Click **Submit** to submit the changes.

**Step 6.** Click **Group Setup** to open the Group Setup window. Select **Default Group (1 user)** under the Group drop-down menu. Click **Edit Settings** to go to the Group Setup for this group.

**Step 7.** Scroll down to the auth-proxy checkbox followed by the Custom attributes checkbox. Check both the **auth-proxy** checkbox and the **Custom attributes** checkbox.

**Step 8.** Enter the following in the Custom attributes box:

```
proxyacl#1=permit tcp any any
priv-lvl=15
```

**Step 9.** Click **Submit + Restart** to submit the changes and restart CSACS. Wait for the interface to return to the Group Setup main window.

Did CSACS restart successfully?

_______________________________________________

## Task 2: Configuring AAA

To configure AAA, complete the following steps.

**Step 1.** On the router, enter global configuration mode.

```
RouterP# configure terminal
```

**Step 2.** Enable AAA:

```
RouterP(config)# aaa new-model
```

The **aaa ?** command provides what options?

_______________________________________________________________________________

_______________________________________________________________________________

**Step 3.** Specify the authentication protocol:

```
RouterP(config)# aaa authentication login default group tacacs+
```

**Step 4.** Specify the authorization protocol:

```
RouterP(config)# aaa authorization auth-proxy default group tacacs+
```

**Step 5.** Define the TACACS+ server and its key:

```
RouterP(config)# tacacs-server host 10.0.P.12
RouterP(config)# tacacs-server key secretkey
```

### Task 3: Defining the ACLs to Allow TACACS+ Traffic

**Step 1.** Define the ACLs to allow TACACS+ traffic to the inside interface from the AAA server. Also allow outbound Internet Control Message Protocol (ICMP) traffic and Context-based Access Control (CBAC) traffic, such as FTP and WWW. Block all other inside initiated traffic:

```
RouterP(config)# access-list 101 permit tcp host 10.0.P.12 eq tacacs host 10.0.P.2
RouterP(config)# access-list 101 permit icmp any any
RouterP(config)# access-list 101 permit tcp 10.0.P.0 0.0.0.255 any eq ftp
RouterP(config)# access-list 101 permit tcp 10.0.P.0 0.0.0.255 any eq www
RouterP(config)# access-list 101 deny ip any any
```

**Step 2.** Define the ACLs to allow inbound ICMP traffic and CBAC traffic, such as FTP and WWW, to the inside web or FTP server. Block all other outside initiated traffic:

```
RouterP(config)# access-list 102 permit eigrp any any
RouterP(config)# access-list 102 permit icmp any any
RouterP(config)# access-list 102 permit tcp any host 10.0.P.12 eq ftp
RouterP(config)# access-list 102 permit tcp any host 10.0.P.12 eq www
RouterP(config)# access-list 102 deny ip any any
```

**Step 3.** Enable the router HTTP server for AAA:

```
RouterP(config)# ip http server
RouterP(config)# ip http authentication aaa
```

What options are available with the **ip http ? help** command?

_______________________________________________________________________________

_______________________________________________________________________________

### Task 4: Configuring an Authentication Proxy

Complete the following steps to configure authentication proxy.

**Step 1.** Define an authentication proxy rule:

```
RouterP(config)# ip auth-proxy name APRULE http auth-cache-time 5
```

**Step 2.** Apply the authentication proxy rule to the inside interface:

```
RouterP(config)# interface fastethernet 0/0
RouterP(config-if)# ip auth-proxy APRULE
RouterP(config-if)# ip access-group 101 in
RouterP(config-if)# exit
```

**Step 3.** Apply the ACL to the outside interface:

```
RouterP(config-if)# interface fastethernet 0/1
RouterP(config-if)# ip access-group 102 in
```

## Task 5: Testing and Verifying an Authentication Proxy

Complete the following steps to test and verify authentication proxy.

**Step 1.** On the router, use the **show access-list** command to check the access lists. Fill in the following blanks using the output from this command:

```
RouterP# show access-list
```

a. Extended IP access list 101.

________________________________________________________________

________________________________________________________________

________________________________________________________________

________________________________________________________________

b. Extended IP access list 102.

________________________________________________________________

________________________________________________________________

________________________________________________________________

________________________________________________________________

**Step 2.** Use the **show ip auth-proxy configuration** command to verify the authorization proxy configuration. Fill in the following blanks using the output from this command:

```
RouterP# show ip auth-proxy configuration
```

a. Authentication global cache time is _____ minutes.

b. Auth-proxy name is ____________.

c. The idle timeout value for this named rule is _____ minutes.

**Step 3.** Use the **show ip auth-proxy cache** command to verify the authorization proxy configuration. Fill in the following blanks using the output from this command:

```
RouterP# show ip auth-proxy cache
```

________________________________________________________________

**Step 4.** From the workstation command prompt, ping the backbone server:

```
C:\> ping 172.26.26.50
Pinging 172.26.26.50 with 32 bytes of data:

Reply from 172.26.26.50: bytes=32 time=34ms TTL=125

Reply from 172.26.26.50: bytes=32 time=34ms TTL=125

Reply from 172.26.26.50: bytes=32 time=34ms TTL=125

Reply from 172.26.26.50: bytes=32 time=36ms TTL=125
```

**Step 5.** Use the web browser to connect to the backbone web server.

**Step 6.** In the URL field, enter **http://172.26.26.50.**

**Step 7.** Enter the following when the web browser prompts for a username and password:

```
Username: aaauser
Password: aaapass
```

**Step 8.** Use the **show access-list** command to check the ACLs. Fill in the following blanks using the output from this command:

```
RouterP# show access-list
```

a. Extended IP access list 101.

_______________________________________________

_______________________________________________

_______________________________________________

_______________________________________________

b. Extended IP access list 102.

_______________________________________________

_______________________________________________

_______________________________________________

_______________________________________________

**Step 9.** On the router, use the **show ip inspect all** command to see the CBAC parameters:

```
RouterP# show ip inspect all
```

CBAC parameters

_______________________________________________

_______________________________________________

_______________________________________________

_______________________________________________

**Step 10.** Use the **show ip auth-proxy cache** command to verify the authorization proxy configuration. Fill in the following blanks using the output from this command:

```
RouterP#show ip auth-proxy cache
```

Authorization proxy configuration

_______________________________________________

_______________________________________________

_______________________________________________

_______________________________________________

### Task 6: Testing and Verifying Authentication Proxy

Complete the following steps to test and verify authentication proxy a second time.

**Step 1.** Use the web browser to connect to the backbone web server.

**Step 2.** In the URL field, type **http://172.26.26.50**.

*Note*: Use a "." at the end of the IP address to download a new copy of the web page. Otherwise, the browser might display a cached copy.

Was it necessary to authenticate again? Why?

_______________________________________________

_______________________________________________

_______________________________________________

_______________________________________________

**Step 3.** Use the **clear ip auth-proxy cache** * command to clear the authorization proxy cache:

```
RouterP# clear ip auth-proxy cache *
```

Why is it necessary to clear the cache?

_______________________________________________

_______________________________________________

**Step 4.** Use the **show ip auth-proxy cache** command to verify the authorization proxy configuration. Fill in the following blanks using the output from this command:

```
RouterP# show ip auth-proxy cache
```

Authorization proxy configuration verification output

_______________________________________________

_______________________________________________

## Review Questions

1. What is the advantage of using server-based AAA over local AAA?

_______________________________________________

_______________________________________________

_______________________________________________

_______________________________________________

2. What are the primary objectives of AAA?

_______________________________________________

_______________________________________________

_______________________________________________

_______________________________________________

3. What is one way to give yourself an emergency "backdoor" into the router when configuring AAA to ensure that you don't get locked out during configuration changes?

_______________________________________________

_______________________________________________

4. What happens to your network security if you add the "none" method at the end of the list of authentication methods?

5. What is the TACACS server key?

## Chapter 4 Quiz Questions

1. Which of the following commands would set the console inactivity timeout value to 2 minutes?

   A. **exec-timeout 2**

   B. **exec idle-timeout 2**

   C. **exec-timeout 120**

   D. **exec idle-timeout 120**

2. What does the command **transport input telnet** entered at the vty line configuration prompt tell the router?

   A. The line should block all Telnet sessions.

   B. The line should log all Telnet session activity.

   C. The line should give priority to Telnet sessions.

   D. The line is expected to receive only Telnet sessions.

3. Why would you use a **distribute-list** command as part of your routing protocol configuration?

   A. To control which routing updates your router accepted

   B. To control advertisement of your internal networks

   C. To ensure that all internal networks were advertised externally

   D. To direct the router to advertise all known external routes

4. Which statement about network perimeters is *not* true?

   A. Perimeter security is traditionally provided by a firewall.

   B. Perimeters most commonly exist at points where private networks meet public ones.

   C. Perimeter security involves filtering only inbound traffic.

   D. The perimeter router is usually a general-purpose router with a serial connection to the Internet and an Ethernet connection to an inside network.

5. Which kind of access-lists are used to define reflexive access-lists?

   A. IP standard

   B. IP extended

   C. IP extended named

   D. IP standard named

6. Anti-spoofing filters should be built with what kind of access lists?

   A. Loopback

   B. Input

   C. Standard

   D. Output

7. When viewing event logs, what is the range of possible values?

   A. From 7=Debugging to 0=Emergencies

   B. From 10=Informational to 0=Unstable

   C. From 0=Debugging to 7=Emergencies

   D. From 1=Informational to 10=Emergencies

8. The process in which private internal addresses are mapped one-to-one with public external addresses is called:

   A. Static NAT

   B. Dynamic NAT

   C. Port Address Translation

   D. Extended NAT

9. TCP Intercept was designed to combat which kind of attack?

   A. Reconnaissance

   B. Access

   C. Denial of service

   D. Spoofing

10. What command is used to limit the number of MAC addresses allowable on a port to 6?

    A. **port enable count 6**

    B. **port security set stations 6**

    C. **port security max-mac-count 6**

    D. **port security 6**

# Chapter 5

## Router Intrusion Detection, Monitoring, and Management

This chapter introduces and discusses intrusion detection capabilities of the Cisco IOS. The Cisco IDS IOS feature set detects about 100 of the more common attack signatures. This gives a perimeter router the capability to monitor packets as the packets enter the network and then act on these suspicious packets.

For a description of Cisco IOS Firewall IDS signatures, see the section, "Configuring Cisco IOS Firewall Intrusion Detection System" in the *Cisco IOS Security Configuration Guide* at www.cisco.com/application/pdf/en/us/guest/products/ps4032/c1069/ccmigration_09186a008011dff4.pdf.

You now have a chance to configure the router to act as an intrusion detection system (IDS) using the following labs. You can then test the configuration by using tools discussed in Chapter 1, "Overview of Network Security."

As mentioned, logging the alerts from suspicious packets is an important aspect of network security. This gives the administrator a way to determine what type of attack is happening and how best to prevent trouble. It does no good to collect log messages and then never look at them. By using a Syslog server to collect log messages, a central location is available to check the log messages. By logging only the most critical events, the administrator can quickly focus on only those critical events rather than all the log events.

To aid in the managing of the router, the Simple Network Management Protocol (SNMP) protocol is discussed and you are shown how to configure the router to use SNMP. Using SNMP to manage the network equipment can be a great time saver for the administrator. Although SNMP is a simplistic protocol and has no security, its use can be secured somewhat.

**Vocabulary Exercise**

MIB

_______________________________________________

_______________________________________________

_______________________________________________

RMON

_______________________________________________

_______________________________________________

_______________________________________________

SNMP

_______________________________________________

_______________________________________________

_______________________________________________

Timeserver

_______________________________________________

_______________________________________________

_______________________________________________

**Lab Activities**

The topology figures and lab examples contain **P** and **Q** values. The **P** value in the addressing and naming scheme refers to *your* assigned Pod number.

The following are examples of determining P values:

- Pod2 is looking at a topology figure and is trying to determine the P values in the figure. In this scenario, the **P** values would equal **2**. 10.0.**P**.12 would become 10.0.**2**.12, 172.30.**P**.2 would become 172.30.**2**.2, and so on.
- Pod1 is looking at a topology figure and is trying to determine the P values in the figure. In this scenario, the **P** values would equal **1**. 10.0.**P**.12 would become 10.0.**1**.12, 172.30.**P**.2 would become 172.30.**1**.2, and so on.

In both examples, the P values are directly related to the Pod number of the team.

The **Q** value in the naming and addressing scheme is used when testing the security or connectivity with the peer team

The following are examples of determining Q values:

- In a lab, Pod2 has been asked to test connectivity to their peer inside host at IP address 10.0.Q.12. In this scenario, 10.0.**Q**.12 would equal 10.0.**1**.12.
- In a lab, Pod1 has been asked to test connectivity to their peer inside host at IP address 10.0.Q.12. In this scenario, 10.0.**Q**.12 would equal 10.0.**2**.12.

In both examples, the **Q** value is directly related to the peer Pod number.

## Lab 5.2.5: Configure IOS Firewall IDS

Estimated Time: 15 Minutes

Number of Team Members: Two teams with four students per team

### Objective

In this lab, students learn the following objectives:

- Initialize IOS Firewall IDS on the router.
- Configure and apply audit rules.
- Verify the IDS router configuration.
- Test the IDS router configuration.
- Set and test protected addresses.

### Overview

IDS provides a level of protection beyond the firewall by protecting the network from internal and external attacks and threats. Cisco IOS Firewall IDS technology enhances perimeter firewall protection by taking appropriate action on packets and flows that violate the security policy or represent malicious network activity based on almost 100 predefined IDS signatures.

Figure 5-1 illustrates the network environment students create for this lab.

**Figure 5-1 Lab 5.2.5 Network Topology**

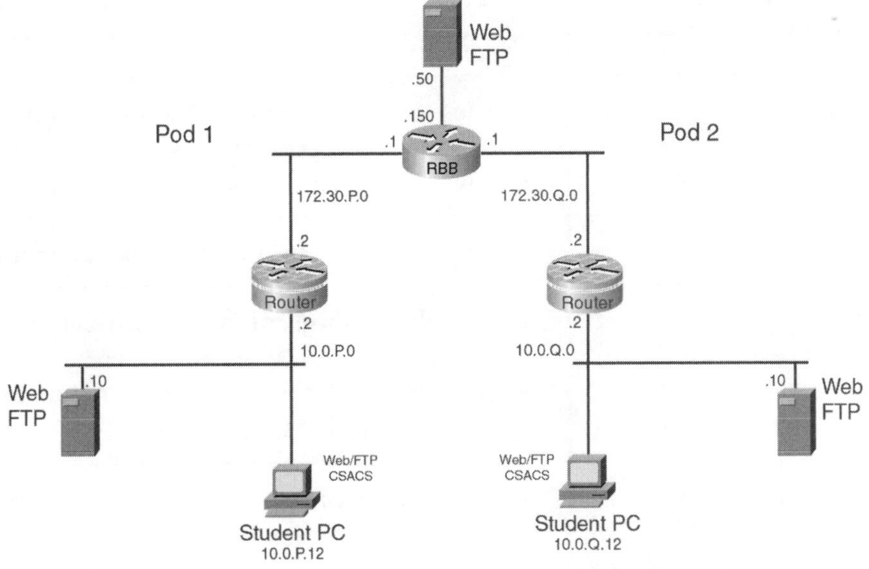


### Preparation

Begin with the standard lab topology and verify the standard router configuration on the Pod routers. Test the connectivity between the Pod routers. Access the perimeter router console port using the terminal emulator on the Windows 2000 server. If desired, save the router configuration to a text file for later analysis. Refer to the *Student Lab Orientation* (Lab 1.1.5) if you need more help.

## Tools and Resources or Equipment

In order to complete the lab, the standard lab topology is required:

- Two Pod routers
- Two student PCs
- Two servers
- Backbone switch and router
- Two console cables and HyperTerminal

## Additional Materials

Further information about the objectives covered in this lab can be found at the following websites:

- http://www.cisco.com/en/US/products/sw/iosswrel/ps1831/products_configuration_guide_chapter09186a00800d9819.html
- http://www.cisco.com/en/US/products/sw/iosswrel/ps1831/products_command_reference_chapter09186a00800d9808.html

## Command List

Table 5-1 lists the commands are used throughout this lab. Refer to this list if assistance or help is needed during the lab exercise.

**Table 5-1 Lab 5.2.5 Command List**

| Command | Description |
|---|---|
| **ip audit attack** | Specifies the default actions for attack signatures |
| **ip audit info** | Specifies the default actions for info signatures |
| **ip audit name** | Creates audit rules for info and attack signature types |
| **ip audit notify** | Specifies the methods of event notification |
| **ip audit po** | Specifies the local Post Office parameters used when sending event notifications |
| **ip audit po max-events** | Specifies the maximum number of event notifications that are placed in the router event cue |
| **ip audit signature** | Attaches a policy to a signature |
| **logging console info** | Sets the option of seeing the Syslog messages on the router console |

### Task 1: Initializing IOS Firewall IDS on the router

Complete the following lab steps to initialize IDS on the router.

**Step 1.** Use the **ip audit notify** command to specify the method of event notification:

```
RouterP(config)# ip audit notify log
```

What are the other methods of notification?

___

**Step 2.** Use the **ip audit po** command to specify the local Post Office when sending event notifications:

```
RouterP(config)# ip audit po local
```

**Step 3.** Use the **ip audit po max-events** command to specify the maximum number of event notifications that are placed in the router event cue:

```
RouterP(config)# ip audit po max-events 100
```

What is the maximum amount of events that can be set?

___

**Step 4.** Use the command **logging console info** to see the Syslog messages on the router console:

```
RouterP(config)# logging console info
```

**Step 5.** Configure logging to a Syslog server:

```
RouterP(config)# logging 10.0.P.12
RouterP(config)# logging on
```

**Step 6.** Set the protected network:

```
Router(config)# ip audit protected 10.0.P.20 to 10.0.P.254
```

**Step 7.** Save the configuration and reload:

```
RouterP# write memory
RouterP# reload
```

### Task 2: Configuring and Applying Audit Rules

Complete the following lab steps to configure and apply audit rules on the router.

**Step 1.** Globally disable signature 2004:

```
RouterP(config)# ip audit signature 2004 disable
```

**Step 2.** Use the **ip audit info** {**action** [**alarm**] [**drop**] [**reset**]} command to specify the default actions for info signatures:

```
RouterP(config)# ip audit info action alarm
```

**Step 3.** Use the **ip audit attack** {**action** [**alarm**] [**drop**] [**reset**]} command to specify the default actions for attack signatures:

```
RouterP(config)# ip audit attack action alarm drop reset
```

**Step 4.** Use the **ip audit name *audit name*** command to create audit rules for attack and info signatures, where *audit-name* is a user-defined name for an audit rule:

```
RouterP(config)# ip audit name AUDIT.1 info
RouterP(config)# ip audit name AUDIT.1 attack
```

*Note*: Use the same name when assigning attack and info type signatures.

**Step 5.** Apply the previously created rule to the outside interface using the `in` direction:

```
RouterP(config)# interface fa 0/1
RouterP(config)# ip audit AUDIT.1 in
```

What other direction can an audit rule be applied?

---

## Task 3: Verifying the IDS Router Configuration

**Step 1.** Display the IDS configuration:

```
RouterP# show ip audit configuration
```

Verify the parameters configured as well as several default settings.

**Step 2.** Display the IDS interface configuration:

```
RouterP# show ip audit interface
```

What are the parameters configured and the default settings?

---

**Step 3.** Display the IDS interface statistics:

```
RouterP# show ip audit statistics
```

## Task 4: Testing the IDS Router Configuration

Telnet to the peer Pod router, execute the subsequent operations, and answer the questions that follow:

```
RouterP# ping
Protocol [IP] <enter>
Target IP address: 10.0.P.2
Repeat count [5]: 20
Datagram size [100]: 2000
Timeout in seconds [2]: <enter>
Extended commands [n]: <enter>
Sweep range of size [n]: <enter>
```

The router now sends multiple packets to the peer router causing them to be discarded and causing audit rules to generate events in the statistics log.

a. What signature number is displayed in the console message?

---

Complete the next ping test:

```
RouterP# ping
Protocol [IP] <enter>
Target IP address: 10.0.P.2
Repeat count [5]: 20
Datagram size [100]: 1021
Timeout in seconds [2]: <enter>
Extended commands [n]: <enter>
Sweep range of size [n]: <enter>
```

b. What signature number is displayed in the console message?

---

End the Telnet session with the peer router.

Check to see the generated events by using the **show ip audit statistics** command:

```
RouterP# show ip audit statistics
```

c. What signatures show up in the log?

---

## Task 5: Setting and Testing Protected Addresses

Configure protected addresses by combining audit rules and access control lists (ACLs):

```
RouterP(config)# ip audit name AUDIT.1 attack list 90
RouterP(config)# access-list 90 deny host 172.30.P.2 (! use the peer neighbors router number)
RouterP(config)# access-list 90 permit any
```

*Note*: The ACL in the preceding example is not denying traffic from 172.30.P.2 host. This would be as expected if the ACL were applied to an interface. Instead, the hosts on that network are not filtered through the audit process because they are trusted hosts. On the other hand, all other hosts, as defined by **permit any**, are processed by the audit rule.

Telnet to the peer Pod router:

```
RouterP# ping
Protocol [IP] <enter>
Target IP address: 10.0.P.2
Repeat count [5]: 20
Datagram size [100]: 2000
Timeout in seconds [2]: <enter>
Extended commands [n]: <enter>
Sweep range of size [n]: <enter>
```

Were the packets successful?

---

## Lab 5.3.8: Configuring Syslog

Estimated Time: 30 Minutes

Number of Team Members: Two teams with four students per team

### Objective

In this lab, students learn the following objectives:

- Enable Syslog logging.
- Install a Syslog server.
- Configure Syslog servers.

### Overview

Syslog analysis allows a network security administrator to centrally log and track system error messages, exceptions, and other information, such as device configuration changes. The message data can be used to analyze router and network performance. Syslog analysis can be customized to produce the information and message reports important to the operation.

Figure 5-2 illustrates the network environment students create for this lab.

**Figure 5-2 Lab 5.3.8 Network Topology**

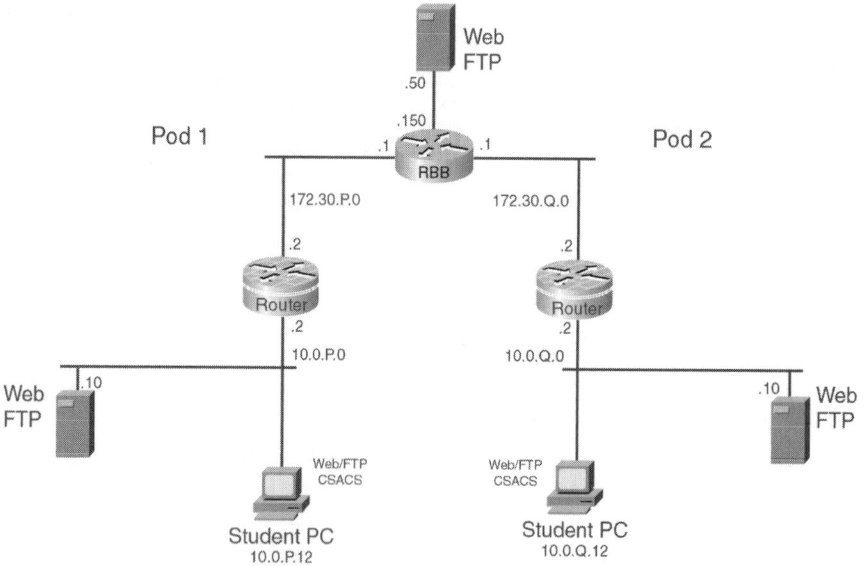


### Preparation

Begin with the standard lab topology and verify the standard router configuration on the Pod routers. Test the connectivity between the Pod routers. Access the perimeter router console port using the terminal emulator on the Windows 2000 server. If desired, save the router configuration to a text file for later analysis. Refer to the *Student Lab Orientation* (Lab 1.1.5) if you need more help.

## Tools and Resources or Equipment

In order to complete the lab, the standard lab topology is required:

- Two Pod routers
- Two student PCs
- Two servers
- Backbone switch and router
- Two console cables and HyperTerminal
- Kiwi Syslog Daemon

## Additional Materials

Further information about the objectives covered in this lab can be found at the following websites:

- http://www.kiwisyslog.com/software_downloads.htm
- http://www.cisco.com/en/US/products/sw/cscowork/ps2073/products_tech_note09186a00800a7275.shtml#task1

## Command List

Table 5-2 lists the commands are used throughout this lab. Refer to this list if you need any assistance during the lab.

**Table 5-2 Lab 5.3.8 Command List**

| **Command** | **Description** |
|---|---|
| **logging on** | Enables message logging |
| **logging** *hostname* \| *IP_address* | Enables logging to a sys server host |
| **logging trap** | Enables logging SNMP traps |
| **show logging** | Displays the addresses and levels associated with the current logging configuration, statistics, and buffer |
| **clear logging** | Clears the current logs contained in the buffer |

### Task 1: Enabling Syslog Logging

**Step 1.** Make sure logging is enabled by use the **logging on** command:

```
RouterP(config)# logging on
```

**Step 2.** Verify that logging is enabled:

```
RouterP# show logging
```

### Task 2: Installing a Syslog Server

Go to the following address to download the Kiwi Syslog Daemon:
http://www.kiwisyslog.com/software_downloads.htm

After downloading the application and installing it, run the application. Other freeware and retail packages that support Syslog are available.

Figure 5-3 shows the interface for the Kiwi Syslog Daemon.

**Figure 5-3 Kiwi Syslog Daemon GUI**

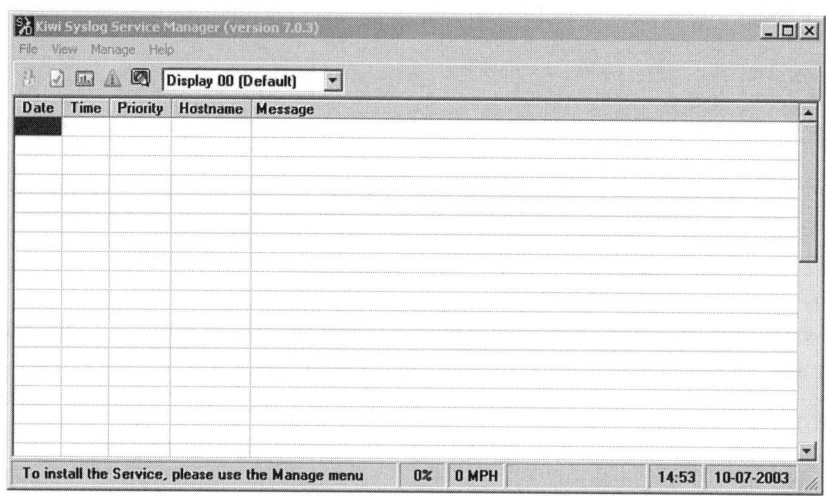


### Task 3: Configuring Syslog Servers

Specify the Syslog server that is to receive the router Syslog messages by using the **logging** *server ip* command, where *server ip* is the IP address of the Syslog server. Verify connectivity before configuration:

```
RouterP(config)#ping 10.0.P.12
RouterP(config)#logging 10.0.P.12
```

To limit the types of messages that can be logged to the Syslog server, set the appropriate logging trap level by using the **logging trap informational** command, where **informational** signifies severity level 6. This means all messages from level 0–5, from emergencies to notifications, will be logged to the Syslog server:

```
RouterP(config)# logging trap informational
```

What are other logging traps and their severity level? Provide these in Table 5-3.

**Table 5-3 Logging Traps and Severity Levels**

| **Logging Trap** | **Description** | **Severity Level** |
|---|---|---|
| | | |
| | | |
| | | |
| | | |
| | | |
| | | |
| | | |

Generate log entries in the Syslog server by making changes to the router. For example, shut down an interface using the **shutdown** command. Now check the log file on the router:

```
RouterP# show logging
```

Many times, it might be necessary to clear the log to get a better perspective of the current logs. Use the **clear logging** command to delete the logs in the buffer:

```
RouterP# clear logging
```

It should display the address to which the Syslog is located and other details.

## Lab 5.4.5: Configure SNMP

Estimated Time: 15 Minutes

Number of Team Members: Two teams with four students per team

### Objective

In this lab, students learn the following objectives:

- Install SNMP Trap Watcher.
- Enable SNMP community string.
- Establish the contact and location of the SNMP Agent.
- Test the configuration.
- Limit SNMP to inside server.
- Disable SNMP traps.
- Disable SNMP and associated access list.

### Overview

SNMP is an application layer protocol that facilitates the exchange of management information between network devices. It is part of the TCP/IP protocol suite. The SNMP enables network administrators to manage network performance, find and solve network problems, and plan for network growth.

Figure 5-4 illustrates the network environment students create for this lab.

**Figure 5-4 Lab 5.4.5 Network Topology**

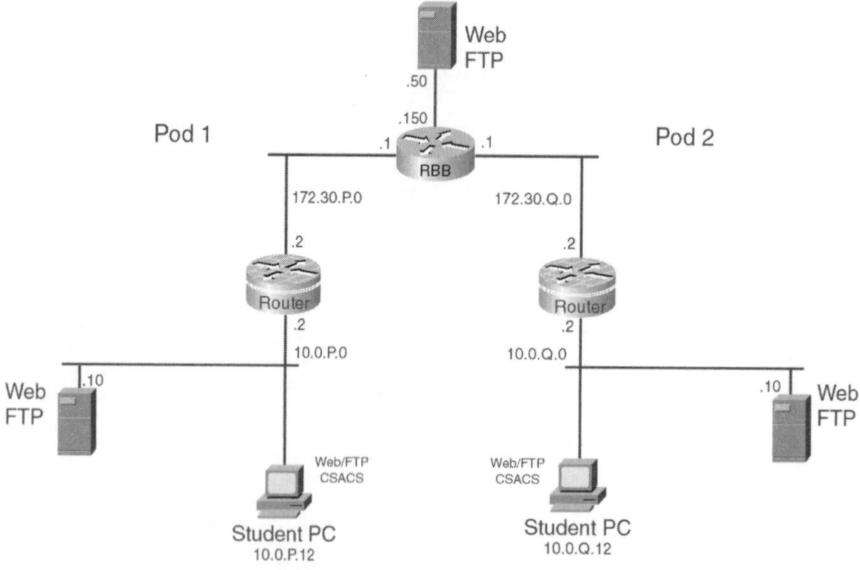


### Preparation

Begin with the standard lab topology and verify the standard router configuration on the Pod routers. Test the connectivity between the Pod routers. Access the perimeter router console port using the terminal emulator on the Windows 2000 server. If desired, save the router configuration to a text file for later analysis. Refer to the *Student Lab Orientation* (Lab 1.1.5) if you need more help.

## Tools and Resources or Equipment

In order to complete the lab, the standard lab topology is required:

- Two Pod routers
- Two student PCs
- Two servers
- Backbone switch and router
- Two console cables and HyperTerminal
- SNMP Trap Watcher

## Additional Materials

Further information about the objectives covered in this lab can be found at the following websites:

- http://www.cisco.com/en/US/products/sw/iosswrel/ps1831/products_configuration_guide_chapter09186a00800ca66b.html#57346
- http://www.cisco.com/en/US/products/sw/iosswrel/ps1834/products_feature_guide09186a008008026f.html
- http://www.bttsoftware.co.uk/snmptrap.html

## Command List

Table 5-4 lists the commands are used throughout this lab. Refer to this list if you need any assistance during the lab.

**Table 5-4 Lab 5.4.5 Command List**

| **Command** | **Description** |
|---|---|
| **no snmp-server** | Disables SNMP |
| **show snmp** | Monitors SNMP status |
| **snmp-server community** | Defines the community access string |
| **snmp-server contact** | Sets the system contact string |
| **snmp-server enable traps snmp** | Enables the sending of traps and specifies the type of notification to be sent |
| **snmp-server host** | Configures the recipient of an SNMP trap operation |

| Command | Description |
|---|---|
| **snmp-server location** | Sets the system location string |

**Task 1: Installing SNMP Application**

SNMP Trap Watcher is designed to be used to receive SNMP Traps from network equipment, including routers, switches, and workstations. Traps are sent when errors or specific events occur on the network.

Go to the following website to download the free copy of SNMP Trap Watcher: http://www.bttsoftware.co.uk/snmptrap.html

After downloading the application and installing it, run the application (see Figure 5-5).

**Figure 5-5 SNMP Trap Watcher Opening Screen**

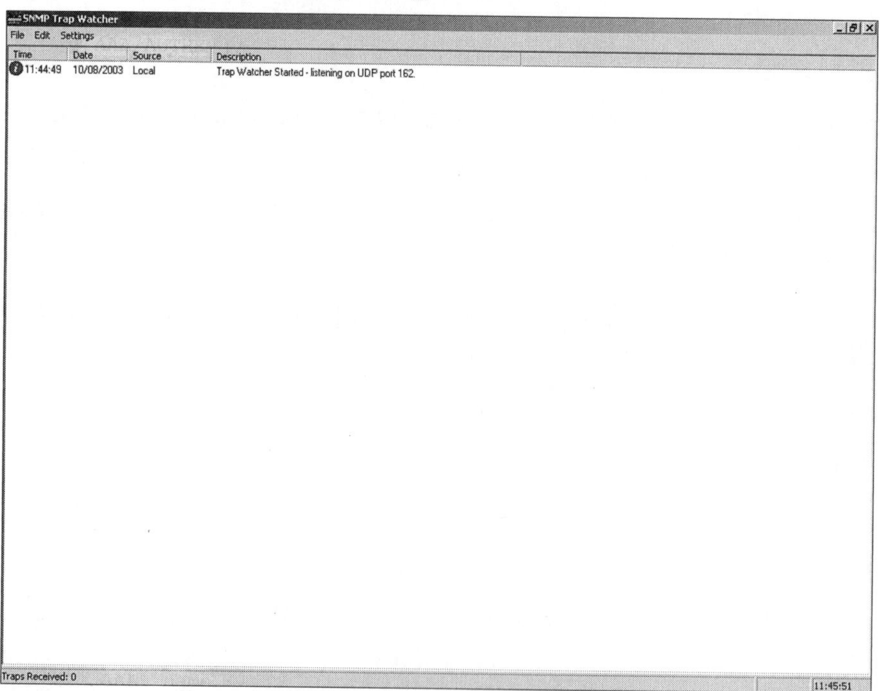


**Task 2: Enabling SNMP Community String**

Use an SNMP community string to define the relationship between the SNMP manager and the agent. The community string acts like a password to permit access to the agent on the router. Configure the community string by using the **snmp-server community** command. Let private be the read-write permission and public be the read-only permission:

```
RouterP(config)#snmp-server community private rw
RouterP(config)#snmp-server community public ro
```

If no permission is set, what will be the default permission?

_______________________________________________

### Task 3: Establishing the Contact and Location of the SNMP Agent

Set the system contact and location of the SNMP agent. To do so, use the following commands in global configuration mode:

```
RouterP(config)#snmp-server contact Dial System Operator at beeper # 27345
RouterP(config)#snmp-server location Floor 4 Room 20
```

What command displays this information on a router?

______________________________________________________________

### Task 4: Configuring the Router to Send Traps to a Host

To enable all the SNMP trap types at one time, use the **snmp-server enable traps snmp** command:

```
RouterP(config)# snmp-server enable traps snmp
```

Specify to the router what host the trap notifications will be sent to by using the **snmp-server host** *host community_string* **udp-port** *port_number* command:

```
RouterP(config)# snmp-server host 10.0.P.12 private udp-port 162
```

Look at the applications main window to see the udp-port on which it is listening.

If the default for an SNMP response is on port 162, what port is the request sent on?

______________________________________________________________

### Task 5: Testing the Configuration

Exit out of the router and log back in using the wrong password. After the failed attempts, log back into the router and issue the following commands:

```
RouterP(config)# int fa 0/1
RouterP(config-if)# shutdown
RouterP(config-if)# no shutdown
```

Now check the SNMP Trap Watcher software (see Figure 5-6).

There will now be entries of traps sent from the router to the manager.

Aside from the startup-config and running-config command outputs, where is another location to find information on the contact, location, and logging information for SNMP?

______________________________________________________________

**Figure 5-6 SNMP Trap Watcher Entries**

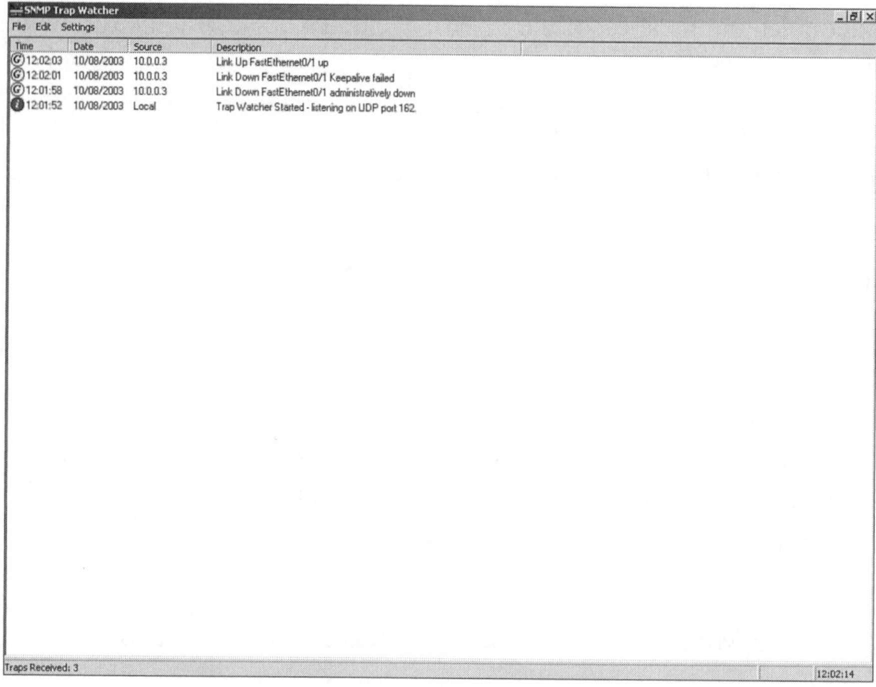


## Task 6: Limiting SNMP to Inside Server

Limit the SNMP access to the inside server located at 10.0.P.12 by creating a restrictive access list along with a read-only community string:

```
RouterP(config)#no snmp-server community private rw
RouterP(config)#no snmp-server community public ro
RouterP(config)#no access-list 70
RouterP(config)#access-list 70 permit 10.0.P.12
RouterP(config)#access-list 70 deny any
RouterP(config)#snmp-server community public ro 70
```

What command would be used to secure the SNMP **rw** access?

---

## Task 7: Disabling SNMP Traps

Disable the SNMP traps on the router by using the following commands:

```
RouterP(config)# no snmp-server enable traps
RouterP(config)# no snmp-server system-shutdown
RouterP(config)# no snmp-server trap-auth
```

By disabling SNMP trap notifications, network performance increases by freeing up bandwidth and eliminating unnecessary SNMP processing tasks.

## Task 8: Disabling SNMP and the Associated Access List

Disable the SNMP and the associated access list by using the following commands:

```
RouterP(config)# no snmp-server
RouterP(config)# no access-list 70
```

When should the SNMP be disabled?

---

## Review Questions

1. Describe the benefits of logging.

2. Describe the three component of SNMP.

3. Describe the security features in SNMP v3.

4. Describe CiscoView and its interaction in a network running SNMP.

5. List and describe the four types of Intrusion Detection covered in this chapter.

## Chapter 5 Quiz Questions

1. Which protocol can be described as a reliable, connection-oriented, byte-stream protocol?

   A. UDP

   B. NAT

   C. PAT

   D. TCP

2. Which of the following statements about TCP/UDP ports is *not* true?

   A. A port is virtual slot in the TCP and UDP stack that is used to map a connection between two hosts.

   B. Ports are numbered 0–65535.

   C. Ports 0-1023 are marked as reserved or privileged.

   D. Ports (1024-65535) are reserved for later use.

3. What does the SYN flag used in TCP mean?

   A. Open a new connection

   B. Close immediate connection

   C. Acknowledge previous packet

   D. Send data now

4. Which of the following is *not* a type of firewall discussed in this chapter?

   A. Circuit level

   B. Transport level

   C. Application layer

   D. Packet filter

5. Which type of firewall typically provides the highest performance?

   A. Application layer

   B. Packet filter

   C. Circuit level

   D. Dynamic packet filter

6. What is a disadvantage of a packet filter firewall?

   A. They require client computers to be specifically configured.

   B. They do not understand application layer protocols.

   C. They are typically slower than other firewalls.

   D. They are difficult to implement as hardware solutions.

7. Which of the following is *not* an advantage of circuit level firewalls?

   A. They are faster than application layer firewalls.

   B. They can prohibit connections between specific sources and destinations.

   C. They can restrict access to protocols other than TCP.

   D. They can implement network address translation.

8. Which of the following statements about TCP is *not* true?

   A. TCP is a connectionless protocol that includes acknowledgement and sequence numbers.

   B. A TCP packet contains the starting sequence number of the data in that packet and the sequence number of the last byte received from the remote peer.

   C. Forward and reverse sequence numbers are completely independent.

   D. Each TCP peer must track both its own sequence numbering and the numbering being used by the remote peer.

9. Which of the following is *not* a reason UDP is harder to secure than TCP?

   A. UDP has no handshaking or sequencing.

   B. It is difficult to determine the current state of a UDP transaction.

   C. UDP's sequencing and acknowledgement numbers can be randomly chosen.

   D. It is difficult to maintain the state of a session because it has no clear beginning, flow state, or end.

10. Which statement describes a SYN flood attack against a network server?

    A. An intruder generates TCP packets from multiple ports to the server, but fails to fully establish the connection by responding to the server's SYN + ACK packets.

    B. An intruder generates TCP packets from a single port, which are destined for multiple ports on the server, thus overloading the server's port buffer.

    C. An intruder generates many TCP packets with the SYN + ACK bits set to "ON," causing the server to generate multiple FIN packets.

    D. An intruder generates TCP packets from multiple ports to the server and responds to each of the server's SYN + ACK packets with FIN packets.

# Chapter 6

## Router Site-to-Site VPNs

This chapter contains some of the most important information the student needs to know. Cryptography is the basis of much of the security tasks used in a network. Having a good understanding of how cryptography works and where to apply the different types for encryption, authentication, and key management will be of great use to students.

Learning how to configure site-to-site Virtual Private Networks (VPNs) is an essential skill needed by most organizations. Those organizations with multiple locations want secure and reliable access to the corporate network. By being able to use the Internet to tunnel the network traffic, organizations can provide more services without the cost of dedicated lines. The students learn about the different tunneling protocols and are able to choose the best choice based on the needs of the organization.

One of the most common ways to secure a site-to-site VPN is with IP Security (IPSec). This protocol provides flexibility in determining the best way to protect the network traffic as it traverses the VPN. Within the IPSec framework, different protocols can be used to provide encryption, authentication, and key exchange. IPSec can be used with a VPN in two ways.

The first way is by using IPSec with preshared keys. This has the benefit of being faster, but has the drawback of exchanging the secret key. Recall that preshared keys need to be manually entered into each peer and do not scale very well. The other way of using IPSec is with digital certificates. By using digital certificates, there is greater scalability, but it has the possibility of more management involved. Choosing one way over the other depends on the organization's structure and type of workforce.

**Vocabulary Exercise**

CAR

______________________________________________

______________________________________________

cryptography

______________________________________________

______________________________________________

GRE

______________________________________________

______________________________________________

SONET

______________________________________________

______________________________________________

SSL

______________________________________________________________________________

______________________________________________________________________________

TLS

______________________________________________________________________________

______________________________________________________________________________

WFQ

______________________________________________________________________________

______________________________________________________________________________

WRED

______________________________________________________________________________

______________________________________________________________________________

## Lab Activities

The topology figures and lab examples contain **P** and **Q** values. The **P** value in the addressing and naming scheme refers to *your* assigned Pod number.

The following are examples of determining P values:

- Pod2 is looking at a topology figure and is trying to determine the P values in the figure. In this scenario, the P values would equal 2. 10.0.P.12 would become 10.0.2.12, 172.30.P.2 would become 172.30.2.2, and so on.
- Pod1 is looking at a topology figure and is trying to determine the P values in the figure. In this scenario, the P values would equal 1. 10.0.P.12 would become 10.0.1.12, 172.30.P.2 would become 172.30.1.2, and so on.

In both examples, the P values are directly related to the Pod number of the team.

The **Q** value in the naming and addressing scheme is used when testing the security or connectivity with the peer team.

The following are examples of determining Q values:

- In a lab, Pod2 has been asked to test connectivity to their peer inside host at IP address 10.0.Q.12. In this scenario, 10.0.Q.12 would equal 10.0.1.12.
- In a lab, Pod1 has been asked to test connectivity to their peer inside host at IP address 10.0.Q.12. In this scenario, 10.0.Q.12 would equal 10.0.2.12.

In both examples, the Q value is the directly related to the peer Pod number.

# Lab 6.4.5: Configuring Cisco IOS IPSec Using Preshared Keys

Estimated Time: 30 Minutes

Number of Team Members: Two teams with four students per team

## Objective

In this lab, students learn the following objectives:

- Prepare to configure Virtual Private Network (VPN) Support.
- Configure Internet Key Exchange (IKE) phase 1.
- Configure IKE parameters.
- Verify IKE and IP Security (IPSec) configuration.
- Configure IPSec parameters.
- Verify and test IPSec configuration.

## Overview

The XYZ Company has purchased Cisco routers and wants to create a secure VPN over the Internet between two sites. The company wants to configure a secure VPN gateway using IPSec between two Cisco routers to use preshared keys for authentication.

Figure 6-1 illustrates the network environment students create for this lab.

**Figure 6-1 Lab 6.4.5 Network Topology**

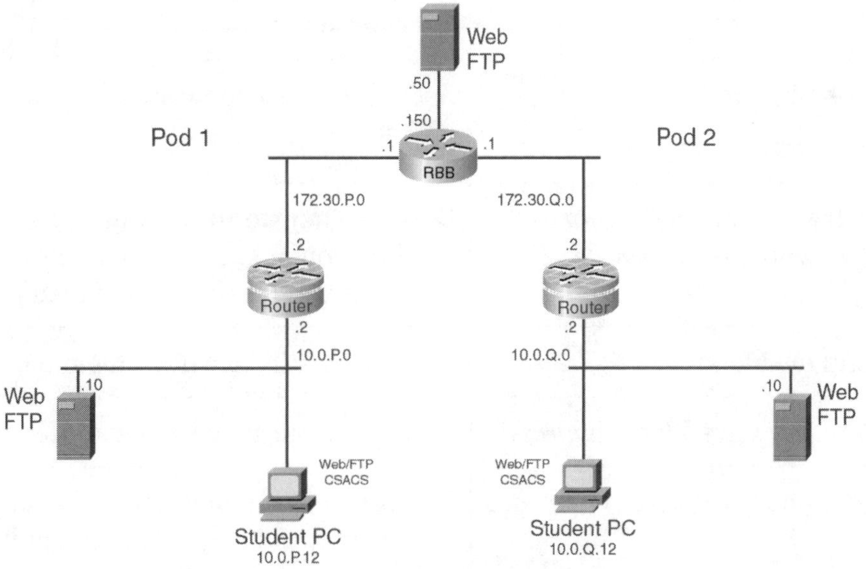


## Preparation

Begin with the standard lab topology and verify the standard router configuration on the Pod routers. Test the connectivity between the Pod routers. Access the perimeter router console port using the terminal emulator on the Windows 2000 server. If desired, save the router configuration to a text file for later analysis. Refer to the *Student Lab Orientation* (Lab 1.1.5) if you need more help.

## Tools and Resources or Equipment

To complete this lab, the standard lab topology is required:

- Two Pod routers
- Two student PCs
- Two servers
- Backbone switch and router
- Two console cables and HyperTerminal

## Additional Materials

Further information about the objectives covered in this lab can be found at the following websites:

- http://www.cisco.com/en/US/products/sw/secursw/ps2120/products_user_guide_chapter09186a0080089ba9.html
- http://www.cisco.com/en/US/products/sw/iosswrel/ps1834/products_feature_guide09186a008007fee4.html

## Command List

Table 6-1 lists the commands are used throughout this lab. Refer to this list if you need any assistance during the lab.

**Table 6-1 Lab 6.4.5 Command List**

| **Command** | **Description** |
|---|---|
| **authentication** *{rsa-sig \| rsa-encr \| preshare}* | Specifies the authentication method within an IKE policy |
| **crypto ipsec transform-set** *transform-set-name transform1 [ transform2 [ transform3]]* | Defines a transform set, which is an acceptable combination of security protocols and algorithms, and enters crypto transform configuration mode |
| **crypto isakmp enable** | Enables IKE/ISAKMP on the router |
| **crypto isakmp key** *key* **address** *address* | Sets up the preshared key and peer address |
| **crypto isakmp policy** *priority* | Defines an IKE policy and enters Internet Security Association and Key Management Protocol (ISAKMP) policy configuration mode |
| **crypto map** *map name* | Applies a previously defined crypto map set to an interface |
| **crypto map** *map-name seq-num* | Creates or modifies a dynamic crypto map entry, and enters the crypto map configuration mode |

| Command | Description |
|---|---|
| **ipsec-isakmp** | |
| **hash** {**sha** \| **md5**} | Specifies the hash algorithm within an IKE policy |
| **match** *address access-list number* | Specifies an extended access list for a crypto map entry |
| **mode** [**tunnel** \| **transport**] | Specifies the mode for the transform set |

**Task 1: Preparing to Configure VPN Support**

Perform the following steps to prepare for the IPSec configuration:

**Step 1.** Determine the IKE and IPSec policy. In this exercise, use the default values, except when directed to enter a specific value. The following are the overall policies used in the lab exercise:

- The IKE policy is to use preshared keys.
- The IPSec policy is to use Encapsulating Security Payload (ESP) mode with Data Encryption Standard (DES) encryption.
- The IPSec policy is to encrypt all traffic between perimeter routers.

**Step 2.** Verify that connectivity has been established to the peer router. Answer the following question:

```
RouterP> enable
password:cisco
RouterP# ping 172.30.Q.2
```

In a production environment, what other steps would need to be completed at this point?

_______________________________________________

**Task 2: Configuring IKE Parameters**

Work with the members of the Pod group to complete this lab. Perform the following steps to configure IKE on the Cisco router.

Be aware when the command line prompt changes while entering commands. This helps distinguish what configuration mode is active.

**Step 1.** Ensure configuration mode is enabled:

```
RouterP# config terminal
```

**Step 2.** Enable IKE/ISAKMP on the router:

```
RouterP(config)# crypto isakmp enable
```

**Step 3.** Create an IKE policy to use preshared keys by completing the following substeps.

a. Set the policy priority and enter config-isakmp mode:

```
RouterP(config)# crypto isakmp policy 110
```

b. Set authentication to use preshared keys:

```
RouterP(config-isakmp)# authentication preshare
```

c. Set IKE encryption:

```
RouterP(config-isakmp)# encryption des
```

d. Set the Diffie-Hellman group:

```
RouterP(config-isakmp)# group 1
```

e. Set the hash algorithm:

```
RouterP(config-isakmp)# hash md5
```

f. Set the IKE security association (SA) lifetime:

```
RouterP(config-isakmp)# lifetime 86400
```

g. Exit config-isakmp mode:

```
RouterP(config-isakmp)# exit
```

h. Set up the preshared key and peer address:

```
RouterP(config)# crypto isakmp key cisco1234 address 172.30.Q.2
```

i. Exit config mode:

```
RouterP(config)# exit
```

j. Examine the crypto policy suite:

```
RouterP# show crypto isakmp policy
Protection suite of priority 110
        encryption algorithm:   DES - Data Encryption Standard (56 bit keys).
        hash algorithm:         Message Digest 5
        authentication method:  Preshared Key
        Diffie-Hellman group:   #1 (768 bit)
        lifetime:               86400 seconds, no volume limit
Default protection suite
        encryption algorithm:   DES - Data Encryption Standard (56 bit keys).
        hash algorithm:         Secure Hash Standard
        authentication method:  Rivest-Shamir-Adleman Signature
        Diffie-Hellman group:   #1 (768 bit)
        lifetime:               86400 seconds, no volume limit
```

### Task 3: Configuring IPSec Parameters

Perform the steps in the following sections to configure IPSec on the Cisco router.

*Configure Transform Sets and Security Association Parameters*

**Step 1.** Ensure that configuration mode is enabled:

```
RouterP# config terminal
```

**Step 2.** View the available crypto IPSec command options. Answer the following question:

```
RouterP(config)# crypto ipsec ?
```

What options can be set at this level?

_______________________________________________________________________________

**Step 3.** Check the transform set options. Answer the following question:

```
RouterP(config)# crypto ipsec transform-set ?
```

Is it possible to configure a transform set without naming it first?

_______________________________________________________________________________

**Step 4.** Define a transform set. Use the following parameters:

- Transform name: **mine**
- ESP protocols: **des**
- Mode: **tunnel**

```
RouterP(config)# crypto ipsec transform-set mine esp-des
```

Has the command prompt changed? What can now be set? *Hint:* Type **?** to see the options.

---

**Step 5.** Set the mode to tunnel:

```
RouterP(cfg-crypto-trans)#mode tunnel
```

**Step 6.** Exit configuration mode:

```
RouterP(cfg-crypto-trans)#^Z
```

**Step 7.** Check the configuration:

```
RouterP# show crypto ipsec transform-set mine
Transform set mine: { esp-des   }
   will negotiate = { Tunnel,   },
```

*Configure Crypto Access Lists*

Perform the following steps to configure the crypto access lists. Create an access control list (ACL) to select traffic to protect. The ACL should encrypt traffic between perimeter routers. Use the following parameters:

- Traffic permitted: **all**
- Peer address: peer router external interface
- **ACL number: 102**
- Protocol: any Internet protocol

**Step 8.** Ensure that configuration mode is enabled:

```
RouterP(config)# config terminal
```

**Step 9.** Configure the ACL:

```
RouterP(config)# access-list 102 permit ip host 172.30.P.2 host 172.30.Q.2
```

(where P = the Pod number and Q = the peer's Pod number)

*Configure Crypto Maps*

Perform the following steps to configure a crypto map. Use the following parameters:

- Name of map: **mymap**
- Number of map: **10**
- Key exchange type: **isakmp**
- Peer: **172.30.Q.2**
- Transform set: **mine**
- Match address: **102**

**Step 10.** Set the name of the map, the map number, and the type of key exchange to be used:

```
RouterP(config)# crypto map mymap 10 ipsec-isakmp
```

**Step 11.** Specify the extended ACL to use with this map:

```
RouterP(config-crypto-map)# match address 102
```

**Step 12.** Specify the transform set defined earlier:

```
RouterP(config-crypto-map)# set transform-set mine
```

**Step 13.** Assign the VPN peer using the host name or IP address of the peer. Answer the following question:

```
RouterP(config-crypto-map)# set peer 172.30.Q.2
```

What other parameters can be set at this level? *Hint:* Type **set?**.

---

**Step 14.** Exit the crypto map configuration mode:

```
RouterP(config-crypto-map)# exit
```

*Apply the Crypto Map to an Interface*

Perform the following steps to assign the crypto map to the appropriate router interface. Use the following parameters:

- Interface to configure: **FastEthernet 0/1 (outside interface)**
- Crypto map to use: **mymap**

**Step 15.** Access interface configuration mode:

```
RouterP(config)# interface FastEthernet 0/1
```

**Step 16.** Assign the crypto map to the interface:

```
RouterP(config-if)# crypto map mymap
```

**Step 17.** Exit configuration crypto mode:

```
RouterP(config-if)# ^Z
```

**Task 4: Verifying and Testing IPSec Configuration**

Perform the following steps to verify and test the IPSec configuration. Coordinate the test with the peer router Pod group.

**Step 1.** Display the configured IKE policies:

```
RouterP# show crypto isakmp policy
Protection suite of priority 110
        encryption algorithm:   DES - Data Encryption Standard (56 bit keys)
        hash algorithm:         Message Digest 5
        authentication method:  Preshared Key
        Diffie-Hellman group:   #1 (768 bit)
        lifetime:               86400 seconds, no volume limit
Default protection suite
        encryption algorithm:   DES - Data Encryption Standard (56 bit keys)
        hash algorithm:         Secure Hash Standard
        authentication method:  Rivest-Shamir-Adleman Signature
        Diffie-Hellman group:   #1 (768 bit)
        lifetime:               86400 seconds, no volume limit
```

**Step 2.** Display the configured transform sets:

```
RouterP# show crypto ipsec transform-set
Transform set mine: { esp-des   }
   will negotiate = { Tunnel,   },
```

**Step 3.** Display the configured crypto maps:

```
RouterP# show crypto map
Crypto Map "mymap" 10 ipsec-isakmp
        Peer = 172.30.2.2
        Extended IP access list 102
access-list 102 permit ip host 172.30.1.2 host 172.30.2.2
        Current peer: 172.30.2.2
Security association lifetime: 4608000 kilobytes/3600 seconds
        PFS (Y/N): N
        Transform sets={ mine, }
```

**Step 4.** Display the current state of the IPSec SAs. The IPSec SAs may have been previously established by routing traffic. The following example shows initialized IPSec SAs before encryption traffic:

```
RouterP# show crypto ipsec sa
interface: FastEthernet0/1
    Crypto map tag: mymap, local addr. 172.30.1.2

    local  ident (addr/mask/prot/port): (172.30.1.2/255.255.255.255/0/0)
    remote ident (addr/mask/prot/port): (172.30.2.2/255.255.255.255/0/0)
    current_peer: 172.30.2.2
     PERMIT, flags={origin_is_acl,}
    #pkts encaps: 0, #pkts encrypt: 0, #pkts digest 0
    #pkts decaps: 0, #pkts decrypt: 0, #pkts verify 0
    #send errors 0, #recv errors 0

local crypto endpt.: 172.30.1.2, remote crypto endpt.: 172.30.2.2
     path mtu 1500, media mtu 1500
     current outbound spi: 0

     inbound esp sas:
     inbound ah sas:

     outbound esp sas:
     outbound ah sas:
```

**Step 5.** Clear any existing Sas:

```
RouterP# clear crypto sa
```

**Step 6.** Enable debug output for IPSec events:

```
RouterP# debug crypto ipsec
```

**Step 7.** Enable debug output for ISAKMP events:

```
RouterP# debug crypto isakmp
```

**Step 8.** Turn on console logging to see the debug output:

```
RouterP(config)# logging console
```

**Step 9.** Initiate a ping to the peer Pod perimeter router. Observe the IKE and IPSec debug output:

```
RouterP# ping 172.30.Q.2
```

**Step 10.** Verify the IKE and IPSec SAs. Note the number of packets encrypted and decrypted when viewing the IPSec SAs:

```
RouterP# show crypto isakmp sa
dst           src            state         conn-id   slot
172.30.1.2    172.30.2.2     QM_IDLE            16      0
RouterP#show crypto ipsec sa
interface: FastEthernet0/1
    Crypto map tag: mymap, local addr. 172.30.1.2

   local  ident (addr/mask/prot/port): (172.30.1.2/255.255.255.255/0/0)
   remote ident (addr/mask/prot/port): (172.30.2.2/255.255.255.255/0/0)
   current_peer: 172.30.2.2
     PERMIT, flags={origin_is_acl,}
    #pkts encaps: 6, #pkts encrypt: 6, #pkts digest 0
    #pkts decaps: 6, #pkts decrypt: 6, #pkts verify 0
    #send errors 4, #recv errors 0
```

```
    local crypto endpt.: 172.30.1.2, remote crypto endpt.: 172.30.2.2
    path mtu 1500, media mtu 1500
    current outbound spi: DB5049D

    inbound esp sas:
     spi: 0x26530A0D(642976269)
       transform: esp-des ,
       in use settings ={Tunnel, }
       slot: 0, conn id: 2, crypto map: mymap
       sa timing: remaining key lifetime (k/sec): (4607999/3542)
       IV size: 8 bytes
       replay detection support: N

    inbound ah sas:

    outbound esp sas:
     spi: 0xDB5049D(229967005)
       transform: esp-des ,
       in use settings ={Tunnel, }
       slot: 0, conn id: 3, crypto map: mymap
       sa timing: remaining key lifetime (k/sec): (4607999/3542)
       IV size: 8 bytes
       replay detection support: N

    outbound ah sas:
```

**Step 11.** Ensure that the encryption is working between routers by generating additional traffic. Then, observe that the packets encrypted and decrypted counter has incremented:

```
RouterP# ping 172.30.Q.2
RouterP# show crypto ipsec sa
interface: FastEthernet0/1
    Crypto map tag: mymap, local addr. 172.30.1.2

   local  ident (addr/mask/prot/port): (172.30.1.2/255.255.255.255/0/0)
   remote ident (addr/mask/prot/port): (172.30.2.2/255.255.255.255/0/0)
   current_peer: 172.30.2.2
     PERMIT, flags={origin_is_acl,}
    #pkts encaps: 11, #pkts encrypt: 11, #pkts digest 0
    #pkts decaps: 11, #pkts decrypt: 11, #pkts verify 0
    #send errors 4, #recv errors 0

     local crypto endpt.: 172.30.1.2, remote crypto endpt.: 172.30.2.2
     path mtu 1500, media mtu 1500
     current outbound spi: DB5049D

     inbound esp sas:
      spi: 0x26530A0D(642976269)
        transform: esp-des ,
        in use settings ={Tunnel, }
        slot: 0, conn id: 2, crypto map: mymap
        sa timing: remaining key lifetime (k/sec): (4607998/3506)
        IV size: 8 bytes
        replay detection support: N

     inbound ah sas:

     outbound esp sas:
      spi: 0xDB5049D(229967005)
        transform: esp-des ,
        in use settings ={Tunnel, }
        slot: 0, conn id: 3, crypto map: mymap
        sa timing: remaining key lifetime (k/sec): (4607998/3506)
        IV size: 8 bytes
        replay detection support: N

     outbound ah sas:
```

## Advanced Lab Portion of Lab 6.4.5: Fine-Tuning the ACL

Fine-tune the crypto ACLs used to determine interesting traffic to encrypt traffic only between the internal servers. Remember to work with the peer Pod group to make the ACLs symmetrical between the perimeter routers. Ensure that desired traffic is encrypted between peers.

**Step 1.** Ensure that configuration mode is enabled:

```
RouterP# config terminal
```

**Step 2.** Remove the previously configured ACL:

```
RouterP(config)# no access-list 102
```

**Step 3.** Configure a new ACL for the servers:

```
RouterP(config)# access-list 102 permit ip host 10.0.P.10 host 10.0.Q.10
```

**Step 4.** Verify the configuration by connecting to the peer web server at 10.0.Q.10, where Q = the peer Pod number, using the browser on the server.

## Lab 6.6.6: Configure IPSec Using Digital Certificates

Estimated Time: 30 Minutes

Number of Team Members: Two teams with four students per team

### Objective

In this lab, students learn the following objectives:

- Prepare for IKE and IPSec.
- Configure certification authority (CA) support.
- Configure IKE.
- Configure IPSec.
- Test and verify IPSec

### Overview

The XYZ Company has purchased Cisco routers and wants to create a secure VPN over the Internet between two sites. The company wants to configure a secure VPN gateway using IPSec between two Cisco routers using a CA server.

Figure 6-2 illustrates the network environment students create for this lab.

**Figure 6-2 Lab 6.6.6 Network Topology**

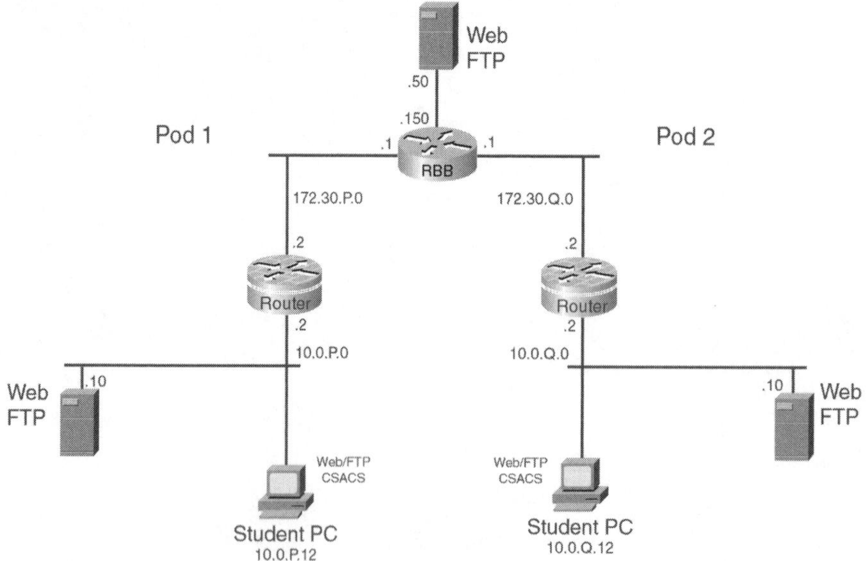


### Preparation

Begin with the standard lab topology and verify the standard router configuration on the Pod routers. Test the connectivity between the Pod routers. Access the perimeter router console port using the terminal emulator on the Windows 2000 server. If desired, save the router configuration to a text file for later analysis. Refer to the *Student Lab Orientation* (Lab 1.1.5) if you need more help.

## Tools and Resources or Equipment

To complete the lab, the standard lab topology is required:

- **Two Pod routers**
- **Two student PCs**
- **Two servers**
- **Backbone switch and router**
- **Two console cables and HyperTerminal**

## Additional Materials

Further information about the objectives covered in this lab can be found at this website:

- http://www.cisco.com/en/US/products/sw/iosswrel/ps1828/products_command_summary_chapter09186a00800eeaf4.html

## Command List

Table 6-2 lists the commands that are used throughout this lab. Refer to this list if you need any assistance during the lab.

**Table 6-2 Lab 6.6.6 Command List**

| Command | Description |
|---|---|
| **authentication** | Sets the IKE authentication method |
| **crl optional** | Specifies that the router can still accept other peers' certificates if the certificate revocation list (CRL) is not accessible. |
| **crypto ca authenticate labca** | Authenticates the CA server; verifies the fingerprint of the CA server with the CA administrator |
| **crypto ca enroll labca** | Obtains the router's certificate or certificates from the CA server |
| **crypto ca trustpoint** | Creates a name for the CA |
| **crypto isakmp ?** | Displays crypto ISAKMP options |
| **crypto isakmp enable** | Enables IKE on the router |
| **crypto isakmp policy** | Creates the IKE policy |
| **crypto isakmp trustpoint address** | Sets the ISAKMP trustpoint to address. |
| **crypto key generate rsa usage-keys** | Generates Rivest, Shamir, and Adelman (RSA) usage keys |

| Command | Description |
|---|---|
| **encryption** | Sets the IKE encryption method |
| **enrollment url http://vpnca** | Specifies the URL of the CA |
| **Group** | Sets the Diffie-Hellman group number |
| **Hash** | Sets the hash algorithm |
| **ip domain-name cisco.com** | Defines the router domain name |
| **ip host** | Defines the CA server's static hostname-to-IP address mapping |
| **lifetime** | Sets the lifetime in seconds and KB |
| **show crypto ca certificate** | Shows the CA certificates |

**Task 1: Preparing for IKE and IPSec**

Complete the following steps to prepare for IPSec configuration.

**Step 1.** Determine the IKE and IPSec policy. In this exercise, use the default values except when directed to enter a specific value:

- The IKE policy is to use RSA signature keys.
- The IPSec policy is to use ESP mode with DES encryption.
- The IPSec policy is to encrypt all traffic between perimeter routers.

**Step 2.** Set the router time zone, calendar, and time. Make sure to coordinate the time with the instructor who will set the time on the CA server. A time mismatch between the router and CA server will create invalid certificates and IPSec negotiation will fail during the main mode exchange of isakmp:

```
RouterP(config)# clock timezone zone hours [minutes]
RouterP# clock set hh:mm:ss day month year
```

**Step 3.** Verify connectivity with the peer router:

```
RouterP >ping 172.30.Q.2
```

(where Q = the peer Pod number)

**Step 4.** Ensure connectivity to the CA server from your router:

```
RouterP# ping 172.26.26.50
```

**Step 5.** Establish an HTTP session to the CA server. Test this capability from the 2000 server by opening a web browser and entering the location **http://172.26.26.50/certsrv**.

**Step 6.** Turn on console logging to see the debug output:

```
RouterP# terminal monitor
RouterP(config)# logging console
```

## Task 2: Configuring CA Support

Complete the following steps to configure CA support on the Cisco router. Make sure to work with the CA server administrator to complete this portion of the lab.

**Step 1.** Define the router domain name:

```
RouterP(config)# ip domain-name cisco.com
```

**Step 2.** Define the CA server static hostname-to-IP address mapping:

```
RouterP(config)# ip host vpnca 172.26.26.50
```

**Step 3.** Generate RSA usage keys:

```
RouterP(config)#crypto key generate rsa usage-keys
```

Follow the router prompts to complete the task. Use 512 for the number of bits for the modulus.

**Step 4.** Perform the following substeps to configure the CA server trustpoint.

a. Create a name for the CA and enter ca-trustpoint mode:

```
RouterP(config)# crypto ca trustpoint vpnca
```

b. Choose the registration authority mode:

```
RouterP(ca-trustpoint)# enrollment mode ra
```

c. Specify the URL of the CA.

For a Microsoft CA:

```
RouterP(ca-trustpoint)# enrollment url http://vpnca/certsrv/mscep/mscep.dll
```

Make sure this is spelled exactly as specified.

d. Specify that the router can still accept other peers certificates if the CRL is not accessible:

```
RouterP(ca-trustpoint)# crl optional
```

e. Exit CA configuration mode:

```
RouterP(ca-trustpoint)# ^Z
RouterP# copy running-config startup-config
```

f. Turn on public-key infrastructure (PKI) debugging to observe debug messages for the CA process:

```
RouterP# debug crypto pki messages
RouterP# debug crypto pki transactions
```

g. Authenticate the CA server. Verify the fingerprint of the CA server with the CA administrator:

```
RouterP# config term
RouterP(config)# crypto ca authenticate vpnca
Certificate has the following attributes:
Fingerprint: 527D8DCA 4D52A047 C8DA1DAD D5368629
% Do you accept this certificate? [yes/no]: y
```

Because **debug** is on, several full screen messages flash by, which may require the student to press **Enter** to see the question on the last line of the output.

h. Enroll to the CA server. Ensure that the CA administrator accepts the enrollment request. Answer the prompts as shown in the example.

*Caution*: Stop and ensure the instructor is ready to accept your enrollment request before continuing to the next step.

```
RouterP(config)# crypto ca enroll vpnca
% Start certificate enrollment ..
% Create a challenge password. You will need to verbally provide this
   password to the CA Administrator To revoke your certificate.
   For security reasons your password will not be saved in the configuration.
   Please make a note of it.
Password: cisco
Re-enter password: cisco

% The subject name in the certificate will be: r1.cisco.com
% Include the router serial number in the subject name? [yes/no]: n
% Include an IP address in the subject name? [yes/no]: n
Request certificate from CA? [yes/no]: y
% Certificate request sent to Certificate Authority
% The certificate request fingerprint will be displayed.
% The 'show crypto ca certificate' command will also show the fingerprint.
```

i. Verify the CA certificates:

```
RouterP(config)# exit
RouterP# copy running-config startup-config
RouterP# show crypto ca certificate
```

## Task 3: Configuring IKE

Complete the following steps to configure IKE on the Cisco router. Make sure to work with the members of the peer Pod to complete this section of the lab.

While you enter commands, notice when the command line prompt changes. This helps distinguish what configuration mode is active.

**Step 1.** Enable IKE/ISAKMP on the router:

```
RouterP(config)# crypto isakmp enable
```

**Step 2.** Create an IKE policy to use RSA signatures by completing the following substeps.

a. Set the policy priority:

```
RouterP(config)# crypto isakmp policy 110
```

b. Set authentication to use RSA signatures:

```
RouterP(config-isakmp)# authentication rsa-sig
```

c. Set the IKE encryption:

```
RouterP(config-isakmp)# encryption des
```

What other encryption choice can be used?

---

d. Set the Diffie-Hellman group:

```
RouterP(config-isakmp)# group 1
```

What would be the benefit of using Diffie-Hellman Group 2?

---

e. Set the hash algorithm:

```
RouterP(config-isakmp)# hash md5
```

f. Set the IKE SA lifetime:

```
RouterP(config-isakmp)# lifetime 86400
```

g. Exit config-isakmp mode:

```
RouterP(config-isakmp)# exit
```

## Task 4: Configuring IPSec

Complete the following steps to configure IPSec on the Cisco router.

*Configure Transform Sets and Security Association Parameters*

Complete the following steps to configure transform sets and SA parameters.

**Step 1.** Ensure that configuration mode is enabled:

```
RouterP# config terminal
```

**Step 2.** View the available crypto IPSec command options:

```
RouterP(config)# crypto ipsec ?
```

**Step 3.** Check the transform set options:

```
RouterP(config)# crypto ipsec transform-set ?
```

**Step 4.** Define a transform set. Use the following parameters:

- Transform name: **mine**
- ESP protocols: **des**
- Mode: **tunnel**

```
RouterP(config)# crypto ipsec transform-set mine esp-des
```

**Step 5.** Set the mode to tunnel:

```
RouterP(cfg-crypto-trans)# mode tunnel
```

**Step 6.** Exit configuration mode:

```
RouterP(cfg-crypto-trans)#^Z
```

**Step 7.** Check the configuration:

```
RouterP# show crypto ipsec transform-set mine
Transform set mine: { esp-des  }
   will negotiate = { Tunnel,  },
```

*Configure Crypto Access Lists*

Complete the following steps to configure the crypto access lists. Create an access list to select the traffic to protect. The access list should encrypt traffic between perimeter routers. Use the following parameters:

- **Traffic permitted:** all
- **Peer address: Peer router Ethernet interface**
- **Access list number:** 102
- **Protocol:** IP

**Step 8.** Ensure that configuration mode is enabled:

```
RouterP(config)# config terminal
```

**Step 9.** Configure the access list:

```
RouterP(config)# access-list 102 permit ip host 172.30.P.2 host 172.30.Q.2
```

(where P = the Pod number and Q = the peer's Pod number)

*Configure Crypto Maps*

Complete the following steps to configure a crypto map. Use the following parameters:

- Name of map: **mymap**
- Number of map: **10**
- Key exchange type: **isakmp**
- Peer: **172.30.Q.2**
- Transform set: **mine**
- Match address: **102**

**Step 10.** Set the name of the map, the map number, and the type of key exchange to be used:

```
RouterP(config)# crypto map mymap 10 ipsec-isakmp
```

**Step 11.** Specify the extended access list to use with this map:

```
RouterP(config-crypto-map)# match address 102
```

**Step 12.** Specify the transform set defined earlier:

```
RouterP(config-crypto-map)# set transform-set mine
```

**Step 13.** Assign the VPN peer using the hostname or IP address of the peer:

```
RouterP(config-crypto-map)# set peer 172.30.Q.2
```

**Step 14.** Exit crypto-map configuration mode:

```
RouterP(config-crypto-map)# exit
```

*Apply the Crypto Map to an Interface*

Complete the following steps to assign the crypto map to the appropriate router interface. Use the following parameters:

- **Interface to configure:** FastEthernet0/1
- **Crypto map to use:** mymap

**Step 15.** Access interface configuration mode:

```
RouterP(config)# interface FastEthernet0/1
```

**Step 16.** Assign the crypto map to the interface:

```
RouterP(config-if)# crypto map mymap
```

**Step 17.** Exit configuration crypto mode:

```
RouterP(config-if)# ^Z
```

### Task 5: Testing and Verifying IPSec

Complete the following steps to verify and test the IPSec configuration. Coordinate your test with the peer router's Pod group.

**Step 1.** Display the configured IKE policies:

```
RouterP# show crypto isakmp policy
Protection suite of priority 110
        encryption algorithm:   DES - Data Encryption Standard (56 bit keys).
        hash algorithm:         Message Digest 5
```

```
        authentication method:  Rivest-Shamir-Adelman Signature
        Diffie-Hellman group:   #1 (768 bit)
        lifetime:               86400 seconds, no volume limit
Default protection suite
        encryption algorithm:   DES - Data Encryption Standard (56 bit keys).
        hash algorithm:         Secure Hash Standard
        authentication method:  Rivest-Shamir-Adelman Signature
        Diffie-Hellman group:   #1 (768 bit)
        lifetime:               86400 seconds, no volume limit
```

**Step 2.** Display the configured transform sets:

```
RouterP# show crypto ipsec transform-set
Transform set mine: { esp-des  }
   will negotiate = { Tunnel,  },
```

**Step 3.** Display the configured crypto maps:

```
RouterP# show crypto map
Crypto Map "mymap" 10 ipsec-isakmp
        Peer = 172.30.2.2
        Extended IP access list 102
   access-list 102 permit ip host 172.30.1.2 host 172.30.2.2
        Current peer: 172.30.2.2
        Security association lifetime: 4608000 kilobytes/3600 seconds
        PFS (Y/N): N
        Transform sets={ mine, }
```

**Step 4.** Display the current state of the IPSec SAs. The IPSec SAs may have already been established by routing traffic:

```
RouterP# show crypto ipsec sa
interface: FastEthernet0/1
    Crypto map tag: mymap, local addr. 172.30.1.2

   local  ident (addr/mask/prot/port): (172.30.1.2/255.255.255.255/0/0)
   remote ident (addr/mask/prot/port): (172.30.2.2/255.255.255.255/0/0)
   current_peer: 172.30.2.2
     PERMIT, flags={origin_is_acl,}
    #pkts encaps: 21, #pkts encrypt: 21, #pkts digest 0
    #pkts decaps: 21, #pkts decrypt: 21, #pkts verify 0
    #send errors 0, #recv errors 0

local crypto endpt.: 172.30.1.2, remote crypto endpt.: 172.30.2.2
     path mtu 1500, media mtu 1500
     current outbound spi: 8AE1C9C

     inbound esp sas:
      spi: 0x1B781456(460854358)
        transform: esp-des ,
        in use settings ={Tunnel, }
        slot: 0, conn id: 17, crypto map: mymap
        sa timing: remaining key lifetime (k/sec): (4607997/3107)
        IV size: 8 bytes
        replay detection support: N

     inbound ah sas:

     outbound esp sas:
      spi: 0x8AE1C9C(145628316)
        transform: esp-des ,
        in use settings ={Tunnel, }
        slot: 0, conn id: 18, crypto map: mymap
        sa timing: remaining key lifetime (k/sec): (4607997/3107)
        IV size: 8 bytes
        replay detection support: N

     outbound ah sas:
```

**Step 5.** Clear any existing SAs:

```
RouterP# clear crypto sa
```

**Step 6.** Enable debug output for IPSec events:

```
RouterP# debug crypto ipsec
```

**Step 7.** Enable debug output for ISAKMP events:

```
RouterP# debug crypto isakmp
```

**Step 8.** Initiate a ping to the peer Pod perimeter router. Observe the IKE and IPSec debug output:

```
RouterP# ping 172.30.Q.2
```

**Step 9.** Verify the IKE and IPSec SAs. Note the number of packets encrypted and decrypted when viewing the IPSec SAs:

```
RouterP# show crypto isakmp sa
dst            src           state         conn-id   slot
172.30.1.2     172.30.2.2    QM_IDLE            16      0
```

The sample output that follows indicate if there is a misconfiguration with isakmp. This could also indicate a problem with certificate validity on either router. The MM Exchange indicates that the router cannot go beyond the main mode exchange of isakmp. This problem is also indicated by a continuous looping of debug output of isakmp exchange messages:

```
dst            src           state          conn-id   slot
172.30.1.2     172.30.2.2    MM Exchange    16        0

RouterP# show crypto ipsec sa
interface: FastEthernet0/1
    Crypto map tag: mymap, local addr. 172.30.1.2

   local  ident (addr/mask/prot/port): (172.30.1.2/255.255.255.255/0/0)
   remote ident (addr/mask/prot/port): (172.30.2.2/255.255.255.255/0/0)
   current_peer: 172.30.2.2
     PERMIT, flags={origin_is_acl,}
    #pkts encaps: 26, #pkts encrypt: 26, #pkts digest 0
    #pkts decaps: 26, #pkts decrypt: 26, #pkts verify 0
    #send errors 0, #recv errors 0

local crypto endpt.: 172.30.1.2, remote crypto endpt.: 172.30.2.2
     path mtu 1500, media mtu 1500
     current outbound spi: 8AE1C9C

     inbound esp sas:
      spi: 0x1B781456(460854358)
        transform: esp-des ,
        in use settings ={Tunnel, }
        slot: 0, conn id: 17, crypto map: mymap
        sa timing: remaining key lifetime (k/sec): (4607996/2963)
        IV size: 8 bytes
        replay detection support: N

      inbound ah sas:

     outbound esp sas:
      spi: 0x8AE1C9C(145628316)
        transform: esp-des ,
        in use settings ={Tunnel, }
        slot: 0, conn id: 18, crypto map: mymap
        sa timing: remaining key lifetime (k/sec): (4607996/2963)
        IV size: 8 bytes
        replay detection support: N

     outbound ah sas:
```

**Step 10.** Ensure that encryption is working between the routers by first generating additional traffic and then by observing that the packets encrypted and decrypted counter has incremented:

```
RouterP# ping 172.30.Q.2
RouterP# show crypto ipsec sa
interface: FastEthernet0/1
    Crypto map tag: mymap, local addr. 172.30.1.2

   local  ident (addr/mask/prot/port): (172.30.1.2/255.255.255.255/0/0)
   remote ident (addr/mask/prot/port): (172.30.2.2/255.255.255.255/0/0)
   current_peer: 172.30.2.2
     PERMIT, flags={origin_is_acl,}
    #pkts encaps: 31, #pkts encrypt: 31, #pkts digest 0
```

```
#pkts decaps: 31, #pkts decrypt: 31, #pkts verify 0
#send errors 0, #recv errors 0

 local crypto endpt.: 172.30.1.2, remote crypto endpt.: 172.30.2.2
 path mtu 1500, media mtu 1500
 current outbound spi: 8AE1C9C

 inbound esp sas:
  spi: 0x1B781456(460854358)
    transform: esp-des ,
    in use settings ={Tunnel, }
    slot: 0, conn id: 17, crypto map: mymap
    sa timing: remaining key lifetime (k/sec): (4607995/2954)
    IV size: 8 bytes
    replay detection support: N

 inbound ah sas:

 outbound esp sas:
  spi: 0x8AE1C9C(145628316)
    transform: esp-des ,
    in use settings ={Tunnel, }
    slot: 0, conn id: 18, crypto map: mymap
    sa timing: remaining key lifetime (k/sec): (4607996/2954)
    IV size: 8 bytes
    replay detection support: N

 outbound ah sas:
```

## Advanced Portion of Lab 6.6.6: Fine-Tuning the ACL

Fine-tune the crypto access lists used to determine interesting traffic to encrypt traffic only between the internal Windows 2000 servers. Remember to work with the peer Pod group to make the access lists symmetrical between the perimeter routers. Ensure that desired traffic is encrypted between the peers.

**Step 1.** Remove the previously configured access list:

```
RouterP(config)# no access-list 102
```

**Step 2.** Configure a new access list for the Windows 2000 servers:

```
RouterP(config)# access-list 102 permit ip host 10.0.P.12 host 10.0.Q.12
```

(where P = the Pod number, and Q = the peer Pod number)

**Step 3.** Verify the configuration by connecting to the web server at 10.0.Q.12 using the browser on the Windows 2000 server (where Q = peer Pod number).

## Review Questions

1. Describe MPLS.

_______________________________________________

_______________________________________________

_______________________________________________

_______________________________________________

2. Describe GRE.

_______________________________________________

_______________________________________________

_______________________________________________

_______________________________________________

3. Describe the importance of non-repudiation.

4. Describe a hash.

5. Describe IP authentication header (AH).

## Chapter 6 Quiz Questions

1. Which of the following statements about traffic flow between interfaces is correct?
   - A. Higher security interfaces can access lower security interfaces using conduits.
   - B. Lower security interfaces can access higher security interfaces using conduits.
   - C. Interfaces of the same security level can access each other without conduits.
   - D. Higher security interfaces can access lower security interfaces using an access control list.
2. What is the default security level of the outside interface?
   - A. 0
   - B. 25
   - C. 50
   - D. 100
3. What is the default security level of the inside interface?
   - A. 0
   - B. 25
   - C. 50
   - D. 100

4. What command is used to copy the current configuration of the primary firewall to the secondary unit?

   A. **copy primary secondary**

   B. **copy config standby**

   C. **write config standby**

   D. **write standby**

5. Which three commands are necessary to enable a firewall interface?

   A. **nameif, ip address, interface**

   B. **ip address, no shutdown, copy run start**

   C. **speed, ip address, enable**

   D. **conduit, route, static**

6. What commands are necessary for higher security interfaces to access lower security interfaces?

   A. **static** and **conduit**

   B. **nat** and **global**

   C. **nat** and **static**

   D. **global** and **conduit**

7. Which of the following is *not* an access mode on the firewall?

   A. Unprivileged

   B. Privileged

   C. Monitor

   D. Interface

8. What is the default password value for Telnet access?

   A. **Null**

   B. **<Return>**

   C. **cisco**

   D. **firewall**

9. What are the only two ways to gain access through the firewall?

   A. Valid user requests and predefined static and conduit statements

   B. Configured inside and outside NAT global and local pools

   C. PAT using a one-to-one static global-to-local mapping scheme

   D. Lower security interface requesting a web page from a higher security web server

10. How many hosts can theoretically share one global IP address using PAT?

    A. 512

    B. 1024

    C. 32,567

    D. 64,000

# Chapter 7

## Router Remote Access VPNs

Chapter 6, "Router Site-to-Site VPNs," discussed how to configure site-to-site VPNs between a company's remote offices and partners. This chapter discusses remote access VPNs. Remote access VPNs expand the company's network to its mobile workers or to those who telecommute. This ability gives a company a competitive advantage by being able to better meet the needs of its clients.

The configuration of a remote access VPN consists of configuring a remote access VPN server and the remote access client. You configure Cisco Easy VPN on the router to act as the remote access server and then configure the client using the Cisco VPN 3.5 client software.

After all the different VPNs have been established and are operational, managing each VPN individually can be confusing and time consuming. You are introduced to the Router Management Console (Router MC) as a way to improve the management of the company's VPNs.

**Vocabulary Exercise**

DSL

______________________________________________________________

______________________________________________________________

HTTPS

______________________________________________________________

______________________________________________________________

L2F

______________________________________________________________

______________________________________________________________

L2TP

______________________________________________________________

______________________________________________________________

MTU

______________________________________________________________

______________________________________________________________

VPN concentrator

______________________________________________________________

______________________________________________________________

## Lab Activities

The topology figures and lab examples contain **P** and **Q** values. The **P** value in the addressing and naming scheme refers to *your* assigned Pod number.

The following are examples of determining P values:

- Pod2 is looking at a topology figure and is trying to determine the P values in the figure. In this scenario, the P values would equal 2. 10.0.P.12 would become 10.0.2.12, 172.30.P.2 would become 172.30.2.2, and so on.
- Pod1 is looking at a topology figure and trying to determine the P values in the figure. In this scenario, the P values would equal 1. 10.0.P.12 would become 10.0.1.12, 172.30.P.2 would become 172.30.1.2, and so on.

In both examples, the P values are directly related to the Pod number of the team.

The **Q** value in the naming and addressing scheme is used when testing the security or connectivity with the peer team

The following are examples of determining Q values:

- In a lab, Pod2 has been asked to test connectivity to their peer inside host at IP address 10.0.Q.12. In this scenario, 10.0.**Q**.12 would equal 10.0.**1**.12.
- In a lab, Pod1 has been asked to test connectivity to their peer inside host at IP address 10.0.Q.12. In this scenario, 10.0.**Q**.12 would equal 10.0.**2**.12.

In both examples, the Q value is the directly related to the peer Pod number.

# Lab 7.3.6: Configure Remote Access Using Cisco Easy VPN

Estimated Time: 20 Minutes

Number of Team Members: Two teams with four students per team

## Objective

In this lab, students learn the following objectives:

- Change the IP address of the client PC.
- Create an IP address pool.
- Enable policy lookup via authentication, authorization, and accounting (AAA).
- Define group policy information for mode configuration push.
- Apply mode configuration and Xauth.
- Verify Easy VPN Server configuration.
- Install the Cisco VPN Client 3.5.
- Create a new connection entry.
- Launch the Cisco VPN Client.

## Overview

In this lab, the team configures a Cisco Easy VPN Server given a Cisco 2600 Series router, and a Cisco Virtual Private Network (VPN) Client 3.5 given a PC running Windows 2000. Upon completion of these configuration tasks, the group tests the connectivity between the VPN Client and the Easy VPN Server.

Figure 7-1 illustrates the network environment students create for this lab.

**Figure 7-1 Lab 7.3.6 Network Topology**

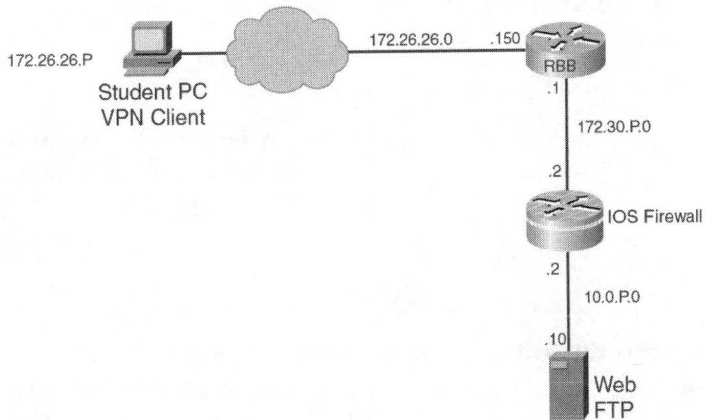


## Preparation

Begin with the topology in Figure 7-1 and verify the standard router configuration on the Pod routers. Access the perimeter router console port using the terminal emulator on the Windows

2000 server. If desired, save the router configuration to a text file for later analysis. Refer to the *Student Lab Orientation* if you need more help.

Before you begin this lab, it is imperative to change the static IP address of the laptop PC to **172.26.26.P** (P = the Pod number).The PC must be connected to a switch port on VLAN 1.

## Tools and Resources

In order to complete the lab, the standard lab topology is required:

- Two Pod routers
- Two student PCs
- Two servers
- Backbone switch and router
- Two console cables and HyperTerminal
- Cisco VPN Client 3.5

## Additional Materials

Further information about the objectives covered in this lab can be found at the following websites:

- www.cisco.com/en/US/products/sw/iosswrel/ps1834/products_feature_guide09186a008007feb8.html
- www.cisco.com/en/US/products/sw/iosswrel/ps1839/products_feature_guide09186a0080087d1e.html

### Command List

Table 7-1 lists the commands used throughout this lab. Refer to this list if you need any assistance during the lab.

**Table 7-1 Lab 7.3.6 Command List**

| Command | Description |
|---|---|
| **aaa authentication** | Use the **aaa authorization** global configuration command to set parameters that restrict a user's network access. |
| **aaa new-model** | Enables AAA. |
| **crypto isakmp client configuration group** *{group-name \| default}* | Specifies which group's policy profile will be defined and enters Internet Security Association Key Management Protocol (ISAKMP) group configuration mode.<br>If no specific group matches and a default group is defined, users will automatically be given the default group's policy. |

| Command | Description |
|---|---|
| **crypto map** *map-name* **client authentication list** *list-name* | Enforces Xauth.<br>The *list-name* argument is used to determine the appropriate username and password storage location (local or RADIUS), as defined in the **aaa authentication** login command. |
| **crypto map** *map-name* **client configuration address [initiate \| respond]** | Configures the router to initiate or reply to Mode Configuration requests.<br>Note that the Cisco clients require the **respond** keyword to be used. However, if the Cisco Secure VPN Client 1.x is used, the **initiate** keyword must be used. The **initiate** and **respond** keywords can be used simultaneously. |
| **crypto map** *map-name* **isakmp authorization list** *list-namen* | Enables Internet Key Exchange (IKE) querying for group policy when requested by the client.<br>The *list-name* argument is used by AAA to determine which storage source is used to find the policy (local or RADIUS), as defined in the **aaa authorization network** command. |
| **ip local pool** | Configures a group of local IP address pools. |
| **key** *name* | Specifies the IKE pre-shared key for group policy attribute definition.<br>Note that this command must be enabled if the client identifies itself with a pre-shared key. |
| **pool** *name* | Defines a local pool address.<br>Although a user must define at least one pool name, a separate pool may be defined for each group policy.<br>Note that this command must be defined and refer to a valid IP local pool address or the client connection will fail. |
| **username** *name* **password** *encryption-type encrypted-password* | Defines local users for Xauth if RADIUS or TACACS+ is not used.<br>Use this command only if no external validation repository will be used. |

## Task 1: Changing the IP Address of the Client PC

Before beginning this lab exercise, it is imperative to change the static IP address of the laptop PC to **172.26.26.P** (where P = the Pod number). Also, the PC must be physically connected to a switch port on VLAN 1.

## Task 2: Creating an IP Address Pool

Complete the following step to create an IP address pool for the remote clients on the perimeter router beginning in the global configuration mode.

**Step 1.** Configure a local pool of IP addresses to be used when a remote peer connects to a point-to-point interface. Use the **ip local pool global configuration** command, as shown here:

```
ip local pool {default | pool-name low-ip-address [high-ip-address]}
```

**Step 2.** Create the IP address pool:

```
RouterP(config)# ip local pool rempool 10.0.P.20 10.0.P.30
```

## Task 3: Enabling Policy Lookup Through AAA

To enable policy lookup through AAA, complete the following commands for the perimeter router beginning in global configuration mode.

**Step 1.** Enable AAA:

```
RouterP(config)# aaa new-model
```

**Step 2.** Set AAA authentication at login. Note that this command must be enabled to enforce Xauth:

```
RouterP(config)# aaa authentication login list-name method1 [method2...]
```

**Step 3.** Enable group policy lookup. A local and RADIUS server may be used together and will be tried in order:

```
RouterP(config)# aaa authorization network list-name local
```

What would the command be if a RADIUS server was used?

---

**Step 4.** (Optional) Define local users for Xauth if RADIUS or TACACS+ is not used. Note that this command is used only if no external validation repository will be used:

```
RouterP(config)# username name password encryption-type encrypted-password
```

## Task 4: Defining Group Policy Information for Mode Configuration Push

Define the policy attributes that are pushed to the VPN Client through mode configuration. Use the following commands beginning in global configuration mode.

**Step 1.** Specify which group policy profile will be defined and enter Internet Security Association Key Management Protocol (ISAKMP) group configuration mode. If no specific group matches and a default group is defined, users will automatically be given the default group policy. For this exercise, use a group name of "sales":

```
RouterP(config)# crypto isakmp client configuration group sales
```

**Step 2.** Specify the IKE pre-shared key for group policy attribute definition. Note that this command must be enabled if the VPN Client identifies itself with a pre-shared key. For this exercise, use a key name of cisco:

```
RouterP(isakmp-group)# key cisco
```

**Step 3.** Select a local IP address pool. Note that this command must refer to a valid local IP local address pool, or the VPN Client connection will fail. Use the rempool pool name:

```
RouterP(isakmp-group)# pool rempool
```

### Task 5: Applying Mode Configuration and Xauth

Mode Configuration and Xauth must be applied to a crypto map to be enforced. To apply Mode Configuration and Xauth to a crypto map, use the following commands in global configuration mode.

**Step 1.** Configure the router to initiate or reply to mode configuration requests. Note that VPN Clients require the **respond** keyword to be used. The **initiate** keyword was used with older VPN Clients and is no longer used with the 3.x version VPN Clients:

```
RouterP(config)# crypto map map-name client configuration address respond
```

**Step 2.** Enable IKE querying for group policy when requested by the VPN Client. AAA uses the list-name argument to determine which storage is used to find the policy, local or RADIUS, as defined in the **aaa authorization network** command:

```
RouterP(config)# crypto map map-name isakmp authorization list local
```

**Step 3.** Enforce Xauth. The list-name argument determines the appropriate username and password storage location, local or RADIUS, as defined in the **aaa authentication login** command:

```
RouterP(config)# crypto map map-name client authentication list list-name
```

### Task 6: Verifying Easy VPN Server Configuration

To verify the configurations for this feature, use the following command in EXEC mode:

```
Router#show crypto map {interface interface | tag map-name}
```

This command displays the crypto map configuration.

### Task 7: Installing the Cisco VPN Client 3.5

Complete the following steps to install the Cisco VPN Client version 3.5 on the Windows 2000 Server PC.

**Step 1.** Open the VPN Client desktop folder.

**Step 2.** Locate and run the Cisco VPN Client setup.exe executable. If this is the first time the VPN Client is installed, a window opens and displays the following message: Do you want the installer to disable the IPSec Policy Agent?

**Step 3.** Click **Yes** to disable the IPSec policy agent. The Welcome window opens.

**Step 4.** Read the Welcome window and click **Next**. The License Agreement window opens.

**Step 5.** Read the license agreement and click **Yes**. The Choose Destination Location window opens.

**Step 6.** Click **Next**. The Select Program Folder window opens.

**Step 7.** Accept the defaults by clicking **Next**. The Start Copying Files window opens.

**Step 8.** The files are copied to the hard disk drive of the PC and the InstallShield Wizard Complete window opens.

**Step 9.** Select **Yes, I want to restart my computer now** and click **Finish**. The PC restarts.

This completes the installation of the Cisco VPN Client (Software Client).

**Task 8: Creating a New Connection Entry**

Complete the following steps to create a new VPN connection entry.

Step 1. Choose **Start** > **Programs** > **Cisco Systems VPN Client** > **VPN Dialer**. The Cisco Systems VPN Client window opens.

**Step 2.** Click **New**. The New Connection Entry wizard opens.

**Step 3.** Enter **Boston Sales** in the connection entry field.

Step 4. Click **Next**.

**Step 5.** Enter a public interface IP address of **172.30.P.2** in the remote server field (where P = the Pod number).

**Step 6.** Click **Next**.

**Step 7.** Select **Group Access Information** and complete the following substeps. The following entries are always case sensitive:

a. Enter a group name, **sales**.

b. Enter the group password, **cisco**.

c. Confirm the password, **cisco**.

**Step 8.** Click **Next**.

**Step 9.** Click **Finish** and leave the Cisco Systems VPN Client window open.

The network parameters for the VPN Client have been configured and a new VPN private networking connection entry has been created successfully.

**Task 9: Launching the Cisco VPN Client**

Complete the following steps to launch the Cisco VPN client on the PC.

**Step 1.** Choose **Start** > **Programs** > **Cisco Systems VPN Client** > **VPN Dialer**.

**Step 2.** Verify that the connection entry is Boston Sales.

**Step 3.** Verify that the IP address of remote server is set to the perimeter router public interface IP address of 172.30.P.2 (where P = the Pod number).

**Step 4.** Click **Connect**. The Connection History window opens and several messages flash by quickly. Complete the following substeps:

a. When prompted for a username, enter **sales**.

b. When prompted to enter a password, enter **cisco**.

**Step 4.** Click **OK**. The following messages flash by quickly:

```
Initializing the connection
Contacting the security gateway at
Authenticating user
```

The window disappears and a VPN lock icon appears in the system tray. The VPN Client has been successfully launched.

## Review Questions

1. What are the two types of remote access VPNs? Describe each one.

_______________________________________________

_______________________________________________

_______________________________________________

_______________________________________________

2. What is the purpose the Cisco Easy VPN Server?

_______________________________________________

_______________________________________________

_______________________________________________

_______________________________________________

3. What is the Router MC?

_______________________________________________

_______________________________________________

_______________________________________________

_______________________________________________

4. Describe "building blocks" as they relate to the Router MC.

_______________________________________________

_______________________________________________

_______________________________________________

_______________________________________________

5. List and describe the tunneling protocols supported by the Router MC.

_______________________________________________

_______________________________________________

_______________________________________________

_______________________________________________

## Chapter 7 Quiz Questions

1. Which of the following interfaces provides character (line) mode access?

   A. Async

   B. BRI

   C. Console

   D. Serial

2. Which of the following is *not* a packet mode access method?

   A. Async

   B. Group-async

   C. BRI

   D. Telnet

3. Which of the following could be considered a NAS?

   A. Cisco IOS Router

   B. PIX Security Appliance

   C. Catalyst Switch

   D. All of these

4. If you are configuring a custom privilege level for a user or group of users, what aspect of AAA are you concerned with?

   A. Authentication

   B. Accounting

   C. Authorization

   D. All of the above

5. What command is used to initiate AAA configuration?

   A. **configure aaa**

   B. **aaa new-model**

   C. **aaa authentication-model**

   D. **interface aaa**

6. Which command could be used to create an AAA authentication list (newlist) that first tries to contact a TACACS+ server, but if an error is returned, the user is allowed access with no authentication?

   A. Router(config)# **aaa authentication login newlist tacacs+ none**

   B. Router(config)# **aaa authentication login newlist tacacs+ enable none**

C. Router(config)# **aaa authentication login newlist tacacs+ none enable**

D. Router(config)# **aaa authentication login newlist enable none tacacs+**

7. What kind of connections can be authenticated using Cisco IOS firewall authentication proxy?

A. Telnet

B. FTP

C. HTTP

D. All of these

8. Which of the following is an advantage of using authentication proxy over lock-and-key access lists?

A. Access lists are configured on the router only.

B. It requires users to log in from the same IP address each time, adding additional security.

C. It is triggered by Telnet connections.

D. It allows DHCP-based host IP addresses.

9. Which of the following is *not* one of the methods used by the PIX Security Appliance to authenticate remote users?

A. FTP

B. SMTP

C. HTTP

D. Telnet

10. What command is used to authorize other protocols on the PIX Security Appliance?

A. **aaa authorization include**

B. **aaa include authorization**

C. **aaa protocol include**

D. **aaa authorization protocol include**

# Chapter 8

## PIX Security Appliance

This chapter introduces the student to the concept of a firewall as well as the different types of firewall technologies. By learning about the different types of firewalls and their advantages and disadvantages, the student can better enforce the organization's security policy.

This chapter also covers the different firewall technologies, packet filtering, application layer or proxy server, and stateful packet filtering. Depending on the size and structure of an organization's network, more than one firewall may be used. The type of firewall used is determined by the location of the firewall and the resources it is protecting.

After the introduction to firewalls, the student is introduced to the PIX Security Appliance and the Finesse Operating System. The heart of the PIX Security Appliance is the Adaptive Security Algorithm (ASA); this is what protects the networks connected to the PIX Security Appliance.

After being introduced to the PIX Security Appliance and some of its capabilities, the student learns the basic configuration commands and some examples of their use. These commands enable the PIX Security Appliance to allow access to and from the networks as required. Leaving the PIX Security Appliance in this basic configuration is not recommended, but it does permit the student to test connectivity while further defining the rulesets.

Because some organizations might use the PIX Security Appliance as the perimeter device, different routing options are discussed to increase the functionality of the PIX Security Appliance. Static routes can be created to direct traffic to the appropriate interface or dynamic routing can be used to create the routing tables.

The PIX Security Appliance can be used as a Dynamic Host Configuration Protocol (DHCP) server, DHCP client, or both. This gives the PIX Security Appliance a lot of flexibility in its placement. With the increasing use of high-speed broadband access, the PIX Security Appliance can be set as a DHCP client on the WAN (untrusted) side and as a DHCP server on the LAN (trusted) side.

**Vocabulary Exercise**

application layer filtering

______________________________________________________________________

______________________________________________________________________

______________________________________________________________________

cut-through proxy

______________________________________________________________________

______________________________________________________________________

______________________________________________________________________

IGMP

______________________________________________________________________

______________________________________________________________________

______________________________________________________________________

packet filtering

______________________________________________________________________

______________________________________________________________________

______________________________________________________________________

SMR

______________________________________________________________________

______________________________________________________________________

______________________________________________________________________

stateful packet filtering

______________________________________________________________________

______________________________________________________________________

______________________________________________________________________

**Lab Activities**

The topology figures and lab examples contain **P** and **Q** values. The **P** value in the addressing and naming scheme refers to *your* assigned Pod number.

The following are examples of determining P values:

- Pod2 is looking at a topology figure and is trying to determine the P values in the figure. In this scenario, the P values would equal 2. 10.0.P.12 would become 10.0.2.12, 172.30.P.2 would become 172.30.2.2, and so on.
- Pod1 is looking at a topology figure and is trying to determine the P values in the figure. In this scenario, the P values would equal 1. 10.0.P.12 would become 10.0.1.12, 172.30.P.2 would become 172.30.1.2, and so on.

In both examples, the P values are directly related to the Pod number of the team.

The **Q** value in the naming and addressing scheme is used when testing the security or connectivity with the peer team.

The following are examples of determining Q values:

- In a lab, Pod2 has been asked to test connectivity to their peer inside host at IP address 10.0.Q.12. In this scenario, 10.0.**Q**.12 would equal 10.0.**1**.12.
- In a lab, Pod1 has been asked to test connectivity to their peer inside host at IP address 10.0.Q.12. In this scenario, 10.0.**Q**.12 would equal 10.0.**2**.12.

In both examples, the Q value is the directly related to the peer Pod number.

## Lab 8.3.3: Configure the PIX Security Appliance

Estimated Time: 25 Minutes

Number of Team Members: Two teams with four students per team

### Objective

In this lab, students complete the following tasks:

- Execute general maintenance commands.
- Configure the PIX Security Appliance inside and outside interfaces.
- Test and verify basic PIX Security Appliance operation.

### Overview

Students assign IP addresses and review all entries. Substitute the Pod number where the letter *P* displayed.

Perform the following steps in this lab:

- View the default configuration of the PIX Security Appliance
- Configure the PIX Security Appliance interfaces
- Test the inside, outside, and demilitarized zone (DMZ) interface connectivity

Figure 8-1 illustrates the network environment students create for this lab.

**Figure 8-1 Lab 8.3.3 Network Topology**

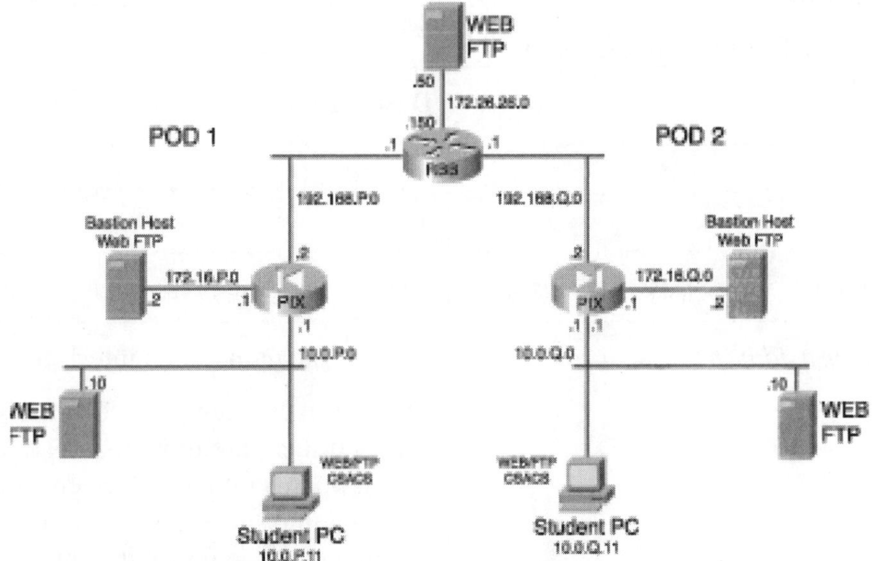

## Preparation

Verify that the standard PIX configuration on the Pod firewall is consistent with standard lab topology. Test connectivity between the Pod firewalls. Access the PIX console port using the terminal emulator on the student PC. If desired, save the configuration to a text file for later analysis. Refer to the *Student Lab Orientation* if you need more help.

## Tools and Resources

To complete the lab, the standard lab topology is required:

- Two Pod PIX Security Appliances
- Two student PCs
- One server
- Backbone switch and router
- Two console cables and HyperTerminal

## Additional Materials

Further information about the objectives covered in this lab can be found at this website:

- http://www.cisco.com/en/US/products/sw/secursw/ps2120/products_configuration_guide_chapter09186a00800eb0b0.html

## Command List

Table 8-1 lists the commands that are used throughout this lab. Refer to this list if you need any assistance during the lab.

**Table 8-1 Lab 8.3.3 Command List**

| **Command** | **Description** |
|---|---|
| **interface** | Identifies the speed and duplex settings of the network interface boards |
| **ip address** *if_name ip_address* [*netmask*] | Defines the IP address of each interface |
| **nameif** *hardware_id if_name security_level* | Defines the name of an interface<br>This command can be used to assign interface names if there are more than two network interface circuit boards on the PIX Security Appliance. The first two interfaces have the default names inside and outside. The inside interface has a default security level of 100, the outside interface has a default security level of 0. The **clear nameif** command reverts **nameif** command statements to default interface names and security levels. |

| Command | Description |
|---|---|
| **reload** | Reboots the PIX Security Appliance and reloads the configuration from a bootable floppy disk or, if a diskette is not present, from Flash memory |
| **route** *if_name ip_address netmask gateway_ip* [*metric*] | Enters a default or static route for an interface |
| **show history** | Displays previously entered commands |
| **show memory** | Displays a summary of the maximum physical memory and current free memory available to the PIX Security Appliance operating system<br>Memory in the PIX Security Appliance is allocated as needed. |
| **show running-config** | Displays the current configuration on the terminal |
| **show version** | Displays the following details of the PIX Security Appliance unit:<br>• Software version<br>• Operating time since last reboot<br>• Processor type<br>• Flash memory type<br>• Interface boards<br>• Serial number (BIOS ID)<br>• Activation key value<br>• Timestamp for when the configuration was last modified |
| **write erase** | Clears the Flash memory configuration |
| **write memory** | Stores the current configuration in Flash memory, along with the activation key value and timestamp for when the configuration was last modified |
| **write terminal** | Displays the current configuration on the terminal |

## Task 1: Executing General Commands

The instructor will provide the procedures for access to the PIX Security Appliance console port, as this varies according to the lab connectivity. After connecting to the PIX Security Appliance console port, the PIX Security Appliance prompt appears. If the prompt that appears is not the configuration mode prompt, enter configuration mode. The password should be null. Ask the instructor for assistance if necessary.

```
Pixfirewall> en
Pixfirewall# config t
Pixfirewall(config)#
```

**Step 1.** Erase the PIX Security Appliance default configuration. When prompted to confirm, press **Enter**:

```
Pixfirewall(config)# write erase
Erase PIX configuration in flash memory? [confirm] <Enter>
```

**Step 2.** Reboot the PIX Security Appliance. When prompted to confirm, press **Enter**:

```
Pixfirewall(config)# reload
Proceed with reload? [confirm} <Enter>
```

**Step 3.** The PIX Security Appliance begins to load through a series of interactive prompts. Press **Ctrl-Z** to escape. The unprivileged mode prompt appears:

```
Pre-configure PIX Security Appliance through interactive prompts [yes]? <Control>Z]
Pixfirewall>
```

**Step 4.** Display the list of help commands:

```
Pixfirewall> ?
```

**Step 5.** Enter the privilege mode of the PIX Security Appliance. When prompted for a password, press **Enter**:

```
Pixfirewall> enable

password:
Pixfirewall#
```

**Step 6.** Display the list of help commands:

```
Pixfirewall# ?
```

**Step 7.** Use the **write terminal** or **show run** command to display the PIX Security Appliance configuration on the terminal screen.

Press the **Q** key to escape the PIX Security Appliance output. Press the **Enter** key to go line by line. Press the **spacebar** to go page by page:

```
Pixfirewall# write terminal
nameif ethernet0 outside security0
nameif ethernet1 inside security100
nameif ethernet2 intf2 security10
nameif ethernet3 intf3 security15
nameif ethernet4 intf4 security20
nameif ethernet5 intf5 security25
enable password 8Ry2YjIyt7RRXU24 encrypted
passwd 2KFQnbNIdI.2KYOU encrypted
hostname pixfirewall
fixup protocol ftp 21
fixup protocol http 80
fixup protocol h323 h225 1720
fixup protocol h323 ras 1718-1719
fixup protocol ils 389
fixup protocol rsh 514
fixup protocol rtsp 554
fixup protocol smtp 25
fixup protocol sqlnet 1521
```

```
fixup protocol sip 5060
fixup protocol skinny 2000
names
pager lines 24
interface ethernet0 auto shutdown
interface ethernet1 auto shutdown
interface ethernet2 auto shutdown
interface ethernet3 auto shutdown
interface ethernet4 auto shutdown
interface ethernet5 auto shutdown
mtu outside 1500
mtu inside 1500
mtu intf2 1500
mtu intf3 1500
mtu intf4 1500
mtu intf5 1500
ip address outside 127.0.0.1 255.255.255.255
ip address inside 127.0.0.1 255.255.255.255
ip address intf2 127.0.0.1 255.255.255.255
ip address intf3 127.0.0.1 255.255.255.255
ip address intf4 127.0.0.1 255.255.255.255
ip address intf5 127.0.0.1 255.255.255.255
ip audit info action alarm
ip audit attack action alarm
no failover
failover timeout 0:00:00
failover poll 15
failover ip address outside 0.0.0.0
failover ip address inside 0.0.0.0
failover ip address intf2 0.0.0.0
failover ip address intf3 0.0.0.0
failover ip address intf4 0.0.0.0
failover ip address intf5 0.0.0.0
pdm history enable
arp timeout 14400
timeout xlate 3:00:00
timeout conn 1:00:00 half-closed 0:10:00 udp 0:02:00 rpc 0:10:00 h323 0:05:00
p 0:30:00 sip_media 0:02:00
timeout uauth 0:05:00 absolute
aaa-server TACACS+ protocol tacacs+
aaa-server RADIUS protocol radius
aaa-server LOCAL protocol local
no snmp-server location
no snmp-server contact
snmp-server community public
no snmp-server enable traps
floodguard enable
no sysopt route dnat
telnet timeout 5
ssh timeout 5
terminal width 80
Cryptochecksum:d41d8cd98f00b204e9800998ecf8427e
: end
[OK]
```

**Step 8.** Enter the **show memory** command:

```
Pixfirewall# show memory
```

How many bytes total does the PIX have? How many bytes free?

______________________________________________________________________

**Step 9.** Enter the **show version** command:

```
Pixfirewall# show version
Cisco PIX Security Appliance Version 6.2(0)
Cisco PIX Device Manager Version 2.1(1)
Compiled on Fri 01-Feb-02 15:14 by root
pixfirewall up 11 mins 46 secs
Hardware: PIX-515, 64 MB RAM, CPU Pentium 200 MHz
Flash i28F640J5 @ 0x300, 16MB
BIOS Flash AT29C257 @ 0xfffd8000, 32KB
0: ethernet0: address is 0003.e300.483a, irq 10
1: ethernet1: address is 0003.e300.483b, irq 7
2: ethernet2: address is 00e0.b602.3387, irq 11
3: ethernet3: address is 00e0.b602.3386, irq 11
4: ethernet4: address is 00e0.b602.3385, irq 11
5: ethernet5: address is 00e0.b602.3384, irq 11
```

```
Licensed Features:
Failover: Enabled
VPN-DES: Enabled
VPN-3DES: Enabled
Maximum Interfaces: 6
Cut-through Proxy: Enabled
Guards: Enabled
URL-filtering: Enabled
Inside Hosts: Unlimited
Throughput: Unlimited
IKE peers: Unlimited
Serial Number: 480430947 (0x1ca2cb63)
Running Activation Key: 0xdf113ba2 0x0afa876e 0xc7df24c3 0x2ae185bc
Configuration last modified by enable_15 at 09:15:28.668 UTC Tue Apr 23 2002
```

Step 10. Enter the **show history** command:

```
Pixfirewall# show history
```

What commands are displayed with the **show history** command?

______________________________________________________________________

______________________________________________________________________

**Step 11.** Enter configuration mode and change the hostname to **PixP** using the **hostname** command:

```
Pixfirewall# configure terminal
Pixfirewall(config)#
Pixfirewall(config)# hostname pixP
```

**Step 12.** Enable the use of names rather than IP addresses:

```
PixP(config)# names
```

**Step 13.** Assign the name bastionhost to the server on the DMZ:

```
PixP(config)# name 172.16.P.2 bastionhost
```

**Step 14.** Assign the name **insidehost** to the student PC.

Enter the following:

```
PixP(config)# name 10.1.P.11 insidehost
```

**Step 15.** Save the configuration to Flash memory:

```
PixP(config)# write memory
Building configuration...
Cryptochecksum: e901c202 27a9db19 7e3c2878 0fc0966b
[OK]
```

### Task 2: Configuring PIX Security Appliance Interfaces

To configure PIX Security Appliance Ethernet interfaces, complete the following steps.

**Step 1.** Assign the PIX Security Appliance DMZ interface the name dmz and security level 50:

```
PixP(config)# nameif e2 dmz security50
PixP(config)# show nameif
nameif ethernet0 outside security0
nameif ethernet1 inside security100
nameif ethernet2 dmz security50
nameif ethernet3 intf3 security15
nameif ethernet4 intf4 security20
nameif ethernet5 intf5 security25
```

**Step 2.** Enable the Ethernet 0, Ethernet 1, and Ethernet 2 interfaces for 100 Mbps Ethernet full-duplex communication.

*Note*: By default, the interfaces are disabled. All interfaces that are going to be used must be enabled.

```
PixP(config)# interface e0 100full
PixP(config)# interface e1 100full
PixP(config)# interface e2 100full
```

Make sure to check the switch or hub device, which connects to the PIX. A different hardware speed and duplex setting may be required. See the available settings in the list that follows:

- **10baset**: Set for 10 Mbps Ethernet half-duplex communication.
- **10full**: Set for 10 Mbps Ethernet full-duplex communication.
- **100basetx**: Set for 100 Mbps Ethernet half-duplex communication.
- **100full**: Set for 100 Mbps Ethernet full-duplex communication.
- **1000sxfull**: Set for 1000 Mbps Gigabit Ethernet full-duplex operation.
- **1000basesx**: Set for 1000 Mbps Gigabit Ethernet half-duplex operation.
- **1000auto**: Set for 1000 Mbps Gigabit Ethernet to auto-negotiate full- or half-duplex. It is recommended that you do not use this option to maintain compatibility with switches and other devices in your network.
- **aui**: Set 10 for Mbps Ethernet half-duplex communication with an AUI cable interface.
- **auto**: Set Ethernet speed automatically. The auto keyword can be used only with the Intel 10/100 automatic speed sensing network interface card.
- **bnc**: Set for 10 Mbps Ethernet half-duplex communication with a BNC cable interface.

```
PixP(config)#  show interface
interface ethernet0 "outside" is up, line protocol is up
Hardware is i82558 ethernet, address is 0090.2724.fd0f
IP address 127.0.0.1, subnet mask 255.255.255.255
MTU 1500 bytes, BW 100000 Kbit full duplex
6 packets input, 360 bytes, 0 no buffer
Received 6 broadcasts, 0 runts, 0 giants
0 input errors, 0 CRC, 0 frame, 0 overrun, 0 ignored, 0 abort
0 packets output, 0 bytes, 0 underruns
0 output errors, 0 collisions, 0 interface resets
0 babbles, 0 late collisions, 0 deferred
0 lost carrier, 0 no carrier
input queue (curr/max blocks): hardware (128/128) software (0/0)
output queue (curr/max blocks): hardware (0/0) software (0/0)
interface ethernet1 "inside" is up, line protocol is up
Hardware is i82558 ethernet, address is 0090.2716.43dd
IP address 127.0.0.1, subnet mask 255.255.255.255
MTU 1500 bytes, BW 100000 Kbit full duplex
22811 packets input, 3365905 bytes, 0 no buffer
Received 22811 broadcasts, 0 runts, 0 giants
0 input errors, 0 CRC, 0 frame, 0 overrun, 0 ignored, 0 abort
0 packets output, 0 bytes, 0 underruns
0 output errors, 0 collisions, 0 interface resets
0 babbles, 0 late collisions, 0 deferred
0 lost carrier, 0 no carrier
input queue (curr/max blocks): hardware (128/128) software (0/1)
output queue (curr/max blocks): hardware (0/0) software (0/0)
interface ethernet2 "dmz" is up, line protocol is up
Hardware is i82558 ethernet, address is 0090.2725.060d
IP address 127.0.0.1, subnet mask 255.255.255.255
MTU 1500 bytes, BW 100000 Kbit full duplex
20283 packets input, 3034748 bytes, 0 no buffer
Received 20283 broadcasts, 0 runts, 0 giants
0 input errors, 0 CRC, 0 frame, 0 overrun, 0 ignored, 0 abort
0 packets output, 0 bytes, 0 underruns
0 output errors, 0 collisions, 0 interface resets
0 babbles, 0 late collisions, 0 deferred
0 lost carrier, 0 no carrier
input queue (curr/max blocks): hardware (128/128) software (0/1)
output queue (curr/max blocks): hardware (0/0) software (0/0)
interface ethernet3 "intf3" is administratively down, line protocol is down
```

```
Hardware is i82558 ethernet, address is 0090.2716.43dc
IP address 127.0.0.1, subnet mask 255.255.255.255
MTU 1500 bytes, BW 100000 Kbit full duplex
184 packets input, 15043 bytes, 0 no buffer
Received 179 broadcasts, 0 runts, 0 giants
0 input errors, 0 CRC, 0 frame, 0 overrun, 0 ignored, 0 abort
0 packets output, 0 bytes, 0 underruns
0 output errors, 0 collisions, 0 interface resets
0 babbles, 0 late collisions, 0 deferred
0 lost carrier, 0 no carrier
input queue (curr/max blocks): hardware (128/128) software (0/1)
output queue (curr/max blocks): hardware (0/0) software (0/0)
interface ethernet4 "intf4" is administratively down, line protocol is down
Hardware is i82558 ethernet, address is 0090.2716.43db
IP address 127.0.0.1, subnet mask 255.255.255.255
MTU 1500 bytes, BW 100000 Kbit full duplex
184 packets input, 15043 bytes, 0 no buffer
Received 179 broadcasts, 0 runts, 0 giants
0 input errors, 0 CRC, 0 frame, 0 overrun, 0 ignored, 0 abort
0 packets output, 0 bytes, 0 underruns
0 output errors, 0 collisions, 0 interface resets
0 babbles, 0 late collisions, 0 deferred
0 lost carrier, 0 no carrier
input queue (curr/max blocks): hardware (128/128) software (0/1)
output queue (curr/max blocks): hardware (0/0) software (0/0)
interface ethernet5 "intf5" is administratively down, line protocol is down
Hardware is i82558 ethernet, address is 0090.2716.43da
IP address 127.0.0.1, subnet mask 255.255.255.255
MTU 1500 bytes, BW 100000 Kbit full duplex
184 packets input, 15043 bytes, 0 no buffer
Received 179 broadcasts, 0 runts, 0 giants
0 input errors, 0 CRC, 0 frame, 0 overrun, 0 ignored, 0 abort
0 packets output, 0 bytes, 0 underruns
0 output errors, 0 collisions, 0 interface resets
0 babbles, 0 late collisions, 0 deferred
0 lost carrier, 0 no carrier
input queue (curr/max blocks): hardware (128/128) software (0/1)
output queue (curr/max blocks): hardware (0/0) software (0/0)
```

**Step 3.** Assign IP addresses to the inside and DMZ network interface cards:

```
PixP(config)# ip address inside 10.0.P.1 255.255.255.0
PixP(config)# ip address dmz 172.16.P.1 255.255.255.0
```

**Step 4.** Configure the PIX Security Appliance to retrieve its outside IP address from a DHCP server using **ip address** *if_name* **dhcp [setroute] [retry retry_cnt].** Wait until the address appears before moving on to the next step:

```
PixP (config)# ip address outside dhcp
```

What IP address was assigned to the outside interface?

---

*Note*: If an address is not obtained, the server at 172.26.26.50 might not be configured as a DHCP server. If this is the case, assign a static address of 192.168.P.2/24 to the outside interface.

**Step 5.** Ensure that the IP addresses are correctly configured and are associated with the proper network interface:

```
PixP(config)# show ip address
System IP Addresses:
ip address outside 192.168.P.2 255.255.255.0
ip address inside 10.0.P.1 255.255.255.0
ip address dmz 172.16.P.1 255.255.255.0
ip address intf3 127.0.0.1 255.255.255.255
ip address intf4 127.0.0.1 255.255.255.255
ip address intf5 127.0.0.1 255.255.255.255
Current IP Addresses:
ip address outside 192.168.P.2 255.255.255.0
ip address inside 10.0.P.1 255.255.255.0
ip address dmz 172.16.P.1 255.255.255.0
ip address intf3 0.0.0.0 0.0.0.0
ip address intf4 0.0.0.0 0.0.0.0
ip address intf5 0.0.0.0 0.0.0.0
```

**Step 6.** Write the configuration to the Flash memory:

```
PixP(config)# write memory
```

## Task 3: Configuring Global Addresses, NAT, and Routing for Inside and Outside Interfaces

Complete the following steps to configure a global address pool, Network Address Translation (NAT), and routing.

**Step 1.** Assign one pool of NIC-registered IP addresses for use by outbound connections:

```
PixP(config)# global (outside) 1 192.168.P.20-192.168.P.254 netmask 255.255.255.0
PixP(config)# show global
global (outside) 1 192.168.P.20-192.168.P.254 netmask 255.255.255.0
```

**Step 2.** Configure the PIX Security Appliance to enable inside hosts to use NAT for outbound access:

```
PixP(config)# nat (inside) 1 10.0.P.0 255.255.255.0
```

**Step 3.** Display the currently configured NAT:

```
PixP(config)# show nat
nat (inside) 1 10.0.P.0 255.255.255.0 0 0
```

**Step 4.** Assign a default route:

```
PixP(config)# route outside 0 0 192.168.P.1
```

**Step 5.** Display the currently configured routes:

```
PixP(config)# show route
outside 0.0.0.0 0.0.0.0 192.168.P.1 1 OTHER static
inside 10.0.P.0 255.255.255.0 10.0.P.1 1 CONNECT static
dmz 172.16.P.0 255.255.255.0 172.16.P.1 1 CONNECT static
outside 192.168.P.0 255.255.255.0 192.168.P.2 1 CONNECT static
```

Is newly created default route shown? What is the difference between the newly created route and the other routes displayed?

---

**Step 6.** Write the current configuration to Flash memory:

```
PixP(config)# write memory
```

**Step 7.** Display a list of the most recently entered commands. The history inputs should be similar to the following:

```
PixP(config)#  show history
interface e0 100full
interface e1 100full
interface e2 100full
show interface
ip address inside 10.0.P.1 255.255.255.0
ip address dmz 172.16.P.1 255.255.255.0
ip address outside dhcp
show ip address
write memory
exit
configure terminal
global (outside) 1 192.168.P.20-192.168.P.254 netmask 255.255.255.0
show global
nat (inside) 1 10.0.P.0 255.255.255.0
show nat
route inside 10.1.1.0 255.255.255.0 10.0.1.102
route outside 0 0 192.168.P.1
show route
write memory
show history
```

*Note*: The up and down cursor keys on the keyboard can be used to recall commands. **Ctrl-P** and **Ctrl-N** can be used the same as the IOS shortcuts.

**Step 8.** Write the current configuration to the terminal and verify that the previous commands have been entered correctly:

```
PixP(config)# write terminal
nameif ethernet0 outside security0
nameif ethernet1 inside security100
nameif ethernet2 dmz security50
nameif ethernet3 intf3 security15
nameif ethernet4 intf4 security20
nameif ethernet5 intf5 security25
enable password 8Ry2YjIyt7RRXU24 encrypted
passwd 2KFQnbNIdI.2KYOU encrypted
hostname pix1
fixup protocol ftp 21
fixup protocol http 80
fixup protocol h323 h225 1720
fixup protocol h323 ras 1718-1719
fixup protocol ils 389
fixup protocol rsh 514
fixup protocol rtsp 554
fixup protocol smtp 25
fixup protocol sqlnet 1521
fixup protocol sip 5060
fixup protocol skinny 2000
names
name 172.16.1.2 bastionhost
name 10.0.1.11 insidehost
pager lines 24
interface ethernet0 100full
interface ethernet1 100full
interface ethernet2 100full
interface ethernet3 auto shutdown
interface ethernet4 auto shutdown
interface ethernet5 auto shutdown
mtu outside 1500
mtu inside 1500
mtu dmz 1500
mtu intf3 1500
mtu intf4 1500
mtu intf5 1500
ip address outside dhcp
ip address inside 10.0.P.1 255.255.255.0
ip address dmz 172.16.P.1 255.255.255.0
ip address intf3 127.0.0.1 255.255.255.255
ip address intf4 127.0.0.1 255.255.255.255
ip address intf5 127.0.0.1 255.255.255.255
ip audit info action alarm
ip audit attack action alarm
no failover
failover timeout 0:00:00
failover poll 15
failover ip address outside 0.0.0.0
failover ip address inside 0.0.0.0
failover ip address dmz 0.0.0.0
failover ip address intf3 0.0.0.0
failover ip address intf4 0.0.0.0
failover ip address intf5 0.0.0.0
pdm history enable
arp timeout 14400
global (outside) 1 192.168.P.20-192.168.P.254 netmask 255.255.255.0
nat (inside) 1 10.0.P.0 255.255.255.0 0 0
route outside 0.0.0.0 0.0.0.0 192.168.P.1 1
route inside 10.1.P.0 255.255.255.0 10.0.P.102 1
timeout xlate 3:00:00
timeout conn 1:00:00 half-closed 0:10:00 udp 0:02:00 rpc 0:10:00 h323 0:05:00 si
p 0:30:00 sip_media 0:02:00
timeout uauth 0:05:00 absolute
aaa-server TACACS+ protocol tacacs+
aaa-server RADIUS protocol radius
aaa-server LOCAL protocol local
no snmp-server location
no snmp-server contact
snmp-server community public
no snmp-server enable traps
```

```
floodguard enable
no sysopt route dnat
telnet timeout 5
ssh timeout 5
terminal width 80
Cryptochecksum:8509a41e9c58ce3e55b0197e89873006
: end
[OK]
```

**Step 9.** Test the operation of the global and NAT statements configured by originating connections through the PIX Security Appliance by completing the following substeps.

a. Ping the server at 172.26.26.50 from the student PC.

b. Open a web browser on the student PC.

c. Use the web browser to access the super server at IP address 172.26.26.50 by entering **http://172.26.26.50**.

**Step 10.** Observe the translation table:

```
PixP(config)# show xlate
```

The display should appear similar in the following:

```
1 in use, 1 most used
Global 192.168.P.20 Local insidehost
```

(where P = the Pod number)

A global address chosen from the low end of the global range has been mapped to the student PC.

## Task 4: Testing the Inside, Outside, and DMZ Interface Connectivity

To test and troubleshoot interface connectivity using the PIX Security Appliance **ping** command, complete the following steps.

**Step 1.** Ping the inside interface:

```
PixP(config)# ping 10.0.P.1
10.0.P.1 response received — 10ms
10.0.P.1 response received — 10ms
10.0.P.1 response received — 10ms
```

**Step 2.** Ping the inside host:

```
PixP(config)# ping insidehost
insidehost response received — 10ms
insidehost response received — 10ms
insidehost response received — 10ms
```

**Step 3.** Ping the outside interface:

```
PixP(config)# ping 192.168.P.2
192.168.P.2 response received — 10ms
192.168.P.2 response received — 10ms
192.168.P.2 response received — 10ms
```

**Step 4.** Ping the backbone router:

```
PixP(config)# ping 192.168.P.1
192.168.P.1 response received — 10ms
192.168.P.1 response received — 10ms
192.168.P.1 response received — 10ms
```

**Step 5.** Ping the DMZ interface:

```
PixP(config)# ping 172.16.P.1
172.16.P.1 response received — 10ms
172.16.P.1 response received — 10ms
172.16.P.1 response received — 10ms
```

**Step 6.** Ping the bastion host:

```
PixP(config)# ping bastionhost
bastionhost response received — 10ms
bastionhost response received — 10ms
bastionhost response received — 10ms
```

# Lab 8.5.3: Configuring the PIX Security Appliance as a DHCP Server

Estimated Time: 15 Minutes

Number of Team Members: Two teams with four students per team

## Objective

In this lab, students learn the following objectives:

- Define a DHCP address pool.
- Define a DHCP domain name.
- Verify DHCP settings on a PIX Security Appliance.
- Verify DHCP on a PC.

## Overview

DHCP is a method of automatically assigning a TCP/IP address from a pool of addresses to a requesting client. DHCP eliminates the need to manually assign static IP addresses. Implementing DHCP client and server features in the PIX significantly eases deployment into cable and digital subscriber line (DSL) broadband environments, where static IP addresses can be costly and cumbersome to maintain.

A PIX Security Appliance can provide DHCP services for hosts located on the trusted network, allowing it to automatically assign IP addresses to machines that are configured for dynamic addressing.

A DHCP server is simply a computer that provides configuration parameters to a DHCP client. A DHCP client is a computer or network device that uses DHCP to obtain network configuration parameters.

*Note*: The PIX Security Appliance DHCP server can be enabled only on the inside interface.

Figure 8-2 illustrates the network environment students create for this lab.

**Figure 8-2 Lab 8.5.3 Network Topology**

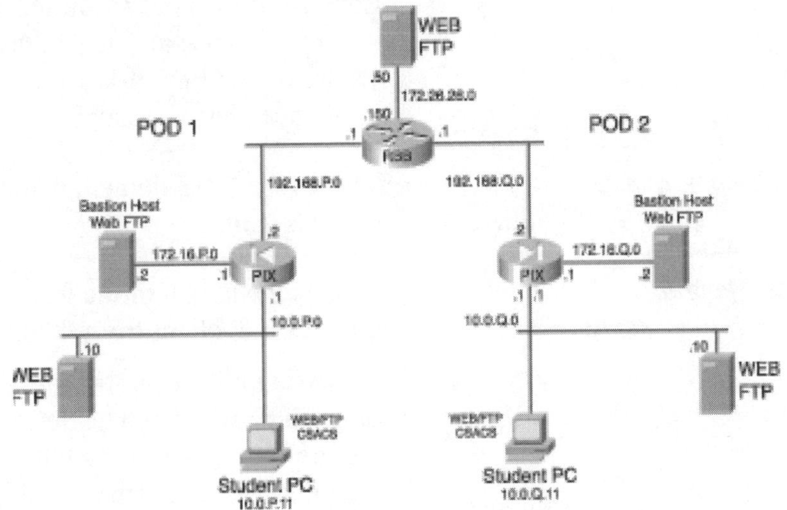

## Preparation

Verify the standard PIX configuration on the Pod firewall and test the connectivity. Access the PIX console port using the terminal emulator on the student PC. If desired, save the configuration to a text file for later analysis. Refer to the *Student Lab Orientation* (Lab 1.1.5) if you need more help.

## Tools and Resources

To complete the lab, the standard lab topology is required:

- Two Pod PIX Security Appliances
- Two student PCs
- One server
- Backbone switch and router
- Two console cables and HyperTerminal

## Additional Materials

Further information about the objectives covered in this lab can be found at this website:

- http://www.cisco.com/en/US/products/sw/secursw/ps2120/products_command_reference_book09186a0080104234.html

## Command List

Table 8-2 lists the commands that are used throughout this lab. Refer to this list if you need any assistance during the lab.

**Table 8-2 Lab 8.5.3 Command List**

| Command | Description |
|---|---|
| **dhcpd address** *ip1*[-*ip2*] [*if_name*] | Defines the IP pool address range<br>The size of the pool is limited to 32 addresses with a 10-user license and 128 addresses with a 50-user license on the PIX 501. All other PIX Security Appliance platforms support 256 addresses. |
| **dhcpd domain** *domain_name* | Defines the DNS domain name, such as **example.com** |
| **dhcpd lease** *lease_length* | Defines the length of the lease, in seconds, granted to the DHCP client from the DHCP server<br>The lease indicates how long the client can use the assigned IP address. The default is 3600 seconds. The minimum lease length is 300 seconds, and the maximum lease length is 2,147,483,647 seconds. |

| Command | Description |
|---|---|
| **show dhcpd [binding \| statistics]** | Displays the binding and statistics information associated with the **dhcpd** commands |

**Task 1: Verifying the PIX Security Appliance Inside IP Address**

Complete the following steps to verify the PIX Security Appliance inside IP address.

**Step 1.** Display the currently configured IP addresses:

```
pixP(config)# show ip address
```

**Step 2.** Ensure that the IP address on the inside interface is 10.0.P.1 (where P = the Pod number).

**Step 3.** Establish a connection to the web server at 172.26.26.50 by completing the following substeps.

a. Open a web browser on the student PC.

b. Use the web browser to access the web server by entering **http://172.26.26.50**.

**Task 2: Configuring the PIX Security Appliance DHCP Server Feature**

Complete the following steps to configure the PIX Security Appliance DHCP server feature.

**Step 1.** To configure the PIX as a DHCP server, the inside interface is required to be configured with an IP address. This IP address is required to be on the same subnet as the pool of dynamically assigned DHCP addresses. To configure the DHCP address pool, use the **dhcpd address** command in global configuration mode. The PIX Security Appliance assigns the client one of the addresses from this pool to use for a given length of time. The default is the **inside** interface. Specify a range of addresses for the DHCP server to distribute:

```
PixP (config)# dhcpd address 10.0.P.51-10.0.P.60 inside
```

**Step 2.** Specify the IP address of the Domain Name System (DNS) server the client will use:

```
PixP (config)# dhcpd dns 10.0.P.75
```

What is the maximum number of DNS servers that can be entered?

---

**Step 3.** Specify the IP address of the WINS server the client will use:

```
PixP (config)# dhcpd wins 10.0.P.76
```

**Step 4.** Specify the lease length to be granted to the client. This lease equals the amount of time in seconds the client can use its allocated IP address before the lease expires. To configure the DHCP lease length, use the **dhcpd lease *(lease length)*** command. The default value is 3600 seconds:.

Specify the lease length to grant the client as 3000:

```
PixP (config)# dhcpd lease 3000
```

**Step 5.** Configure the domain name the client will use:

```
PixP (config)# dhcpd domain cisco.com
```

**Step 6.** Enable the DHCP daemon within the PIX Security Appliance to listen for DHCP client requests on the enabled interface:

```
PixP (config)# dhcpd enable inside
```

**Step 7.** Display the DHCP configuration and binding:

```
PixP (config)# show dhcpd
dhcpd address 10.0.P.51-10.0.P.60 inside
dhcpd dns 10.0.P.75
dhcpd wins 10.0.P.76
dhcpd lease 3000
dhcpd ping_timeout 750
dhcpd domain cisco.com
dhcpd enable inside
```

**Step 8.** Save the DHCP configuration:

```
PixP (config)# write memory
```

### Task 3: Testing the PIX Security Appliance DHCP Server Feature

Complete the following steps to test the PIX Security Appliance DHCP server feature.

**Step 1.** Configure the student PC to obtain an IP address from a DHCP server.

**Step 2.** Open a Windows 2000 command prompt, and release and renew the IP address:

```
C:\> ipconfig /release
C:\> ipconfig /renew
```

**Step 3.** Verify that the PIX Security Appliance assigned an IP address, subnet mask, DNS address, WINS address, and domain name to the Windows 2000 server by opening a Windows 2000 command prompt and viewing the IP configuration:

```
C:\> ipconfig /all
```

Fill in the information in Table 8-3.

**Table 8-3 Record PIX Security Appliance Profile Information**

| | |
|---|---|
| **Connection-specific DNS suffix** | |
| **IP address** | |
| **Subnet mask** | |
| **Default gateway** | |
| **Primary WINS server** | |

**Step 4.** Establish a connection to the web server at 172.26.26.50 by completing the following substeps.

a. From the student PC, ping 172.26.26.50.

b. Open a web browser and access the web server by entering **http://172.26.26.50**.

### Task 4: Disabling the DHCP on the Student PC

Complete the following steps to reset the student PC.

**Step 1.** Disable DHCP on the student PC. Manually enter the following parameters:

- IP Address is **10.0.P.11** (where P = the Pod number).
- Subnet Mask is **255.255.255.0**.
- Default Gateway is **10.0.P.1** (where P = the Pod number).

**Step 2.** Restart the computer.

**Step 3.** Log back into the computer.

**Step 4.** At a command prompt, verify that the configuration supplied by the PIX Security Appliance DHCP server has been removed, and that the following IP configuration exists on the student PC:

```
C:\> ipconfig /all
```

- Hostname is **StudentPCP**
- DNS Server is (blank)
- DHCP Enabled is **no**
- IP Address is **10.0.P.11** (where P = the Pod number)
- Subnet Mask is **255.255.255.0**
- Default Gateway is **10.0.P.1** (where P = the Pod number)

### Task 5: Disabling the PIX Security Appliance DHCP Server Feature

Complete the following steps to disable the PIX Security Appliance DHCP server feature.

**Step 1.** Clear all **dhcpd** commands, binding, and statistics information:

```
PixP (config)# clear dhcpd
```

**Step 2.** Verify that the DHCP feature has been disabled:

```
PixP (config)# show dhcpd
```

**Step 3.** Save the current configuration:

```
PixP(config)# write memory
```

## Review Questions

1. What is the major difference between TCP and UDP that makes UDP harder to secure?

______________________________________________________________________

______________________________________________________________________

______________________________________________________________________

______________________________________________________________________

2. What is a firewall?

________________________________________________________________

3. How does an intruder use TCP packets to launch a SYN flood attack against a server?

4. Why might a network administrator choose a packet filter firewall over an application layer firewall?

5. What is one advantage of application layer firewalls over other technologies?

## Chapter 8 Quiz Questions

1. Which of the following is one of the most common VPN scenarios?

   A. Remote Access/Internet VPN

   B. Intranet VPN

   C. Extranet VPN

   D. All of these

2. Which of the following is *not* an advantage of VPNs?

   A. Cost savings

   B. Security

   C. Simplicity of design

   D. Scalability

3. What describes how two or more entities use services to communicate securely?

   A. SA

   B. IKE

   C. IPSec

   D. VPN

4. What is the maximum number of ESP transforms that can be configured for an IPSec transform set?

   A. 1

   B. 2

   C. 3

   D. 4

5. If you need data confidentiality, which part of the transform set provides it?

   A. Encapsulating security protocol

   B. Security association protocol

   C. Authentication header

   D. All of the above

6. What is the major difference between tunnel mode and transport mode?

   A. Transport mode is used to encrypt the entire IP datagram.

   B. Tunnel mode is used to encrypt the entire IP datagram.

   C. Transport mode encrypts the original IP header.

   D. Tunnel mode does not authenticate the original IP datagram.

7. What important step of IPSec establishment occurs in IKE Phase Two?

   A. Interesting traffic is generated.

   B. A secure tunnel is established between peers.

   C. IPSec SAs are negotiated.

   D. All of the above

8. What is the correct order for these configuration steps in IPSec implementation?

   1. Prepare for IKE and IPSec

   2. Configure IPSec

   3. Test and verify IPSec

   4. Configure IKE

A. 1, 4, 2, 3

B. 1, 2, 3, 4

C. 4, 3, 1, 2

D. 2, 3, 4, 1

9. How is a crypto access list different from regular access lists?

A. Crypto access lists define which traffic should be logged.

B. Crypto access lists define which traffic should be denied.

C. Crypto access lists define which traffic should be protected.

D. Crypto access lists define which traffic should be inspected.

10. Which of the following is *not* an acceptable transform combination?

A. **esp-des**

B. **ah-md5-hmac + ah-sha-hmac**

C. **esp-3des**

D. **ah-sha-hmac + esp-3des + esp-sha-hmac**

# Chapter 9

## PIX Security Appliance Translations and Connections

Because the PIX Security Appliance bases much of its decisions on the Transmission Control Protocol (TCP) and the User Datagram Protocol (UDP), it is imperative that the student thoroughly understands both TCP and UDP. This knowledge enables the student to better follow the process of packets moving through the firewall. One way to get a better understanding of how these and other protocols work is to use a sniffer type of tool. Capture some traffic and then view the results to see the interaction between the source and destination.

One of the important functions provided by the PIX Security Appliance is the ability to do Network Address Translation (NAT). It's important that the student understand the use of NAT when creating firewall rules. While NAT can be configured either inbound or outbound, a simple mistake can lead to an unintended exposure of the network. NAT can provide one-to-one, many-to-one, or many-to-many mappings of IP addresses.

Also covered is a form of NAT called Port Address Translation (PAT). PAT allows many inside hosts to share the same outside interface IP address. This is another way to conserve IP addresses. Port redirection is another feature of PAT. This enables administrators to allow access to a resource on the inside network from the outside interface using a nonstandard port. The firewall then matches up the request with the proper destination and forwards it along.

One of the issues of using NAT is trying to resolve domain names when the Domain Name System (DNS) server is located on the outside interface. The PIX Security Appliance has a feature called DNS Doctoring that resolves that issue.

Because hosts on the inside interface can send traffic to the outside interface by default, that's not true the other way around. By default, traffic from the outside interface is denied to the inside interface. To allow traffic from the outside interface in, specific connections need to be created. To create these connections, the student will learn to use the **static** and **conduit** commands.

Finally, students learn to configure multiple interfaces on the PIX Security Appliance to offer greater flexibility when allowing access to the trusted inside network.

**Vocabulary Exercise**

NAT

______________________________________________________________________

______________________________________________________________________

______________________________________________________________________

NFS

______________________________________________________________________

______________________________________________________________________

______________________________________________________________________

PAT

---

---

---

SSH

---

---

---

VoIP

---

---

---

**Lab Activities**

The topology figures and lab examples contain **P** and **Q** values. The **P** value in the addressing and naming scheme refers to *your* assigned Pod number.

The following are examples of determining P values:

- Pod2 is looking at a topology figure and is trying to determine the P values in the figure. In this scenario, the P values would equal 2. 10.0.P.12 would become 10.0.2.12, 172.30.P.2 would become 172.30.2.2, and so on.
- Pod1 is looking at a topology figure and is trying to determine the P values in the figure. In this scenario, the P values would equal 1. 10.0.P.12 would become 10.0.1.12, 172.30.P.2 would become 172.30.1.2, and so on.

In both examples, the P values are directly related to the Pod number of the team.

The **Q** value in the naming and addressing scheme is used when testing the security or connectivity with the peer team.

The following are examples of determining Q values:

- In a lab, Pod2 has been asked to test connectivity to their peer inside host at IP address 10.0.Q.12. In this scenario, 10.0.**Q**.12 would equal 10.0.**1**.12.
- In a lab, Pod1 has been asked to test connectivity to their peer inside host at IP address 10.0.Q.12. In this scenario, 10.0.**Q**.12 would equal 10.0.**2**.12.

In both examples, the Q value is directly related to the peer Pod number.

# Lab 9.5.6: Configure PAT

Estimated Time: 15 Minutes

Number of Team Members: Two teams with four students per team

## Objective

In this lab, students complete the objective of configuring PAT on the inside interface.

## Overview

Port address translation allows multiple hosts to share a single IP address. The PIX Security Appliance has the ability to allow as many as 4000 hosts to share an IP address by mapping TCP port numbers.

Figure 9-1 illustrates the network environment students create for this lab.

**Figure 9-1 Lab 9.5.6 Network Topology**

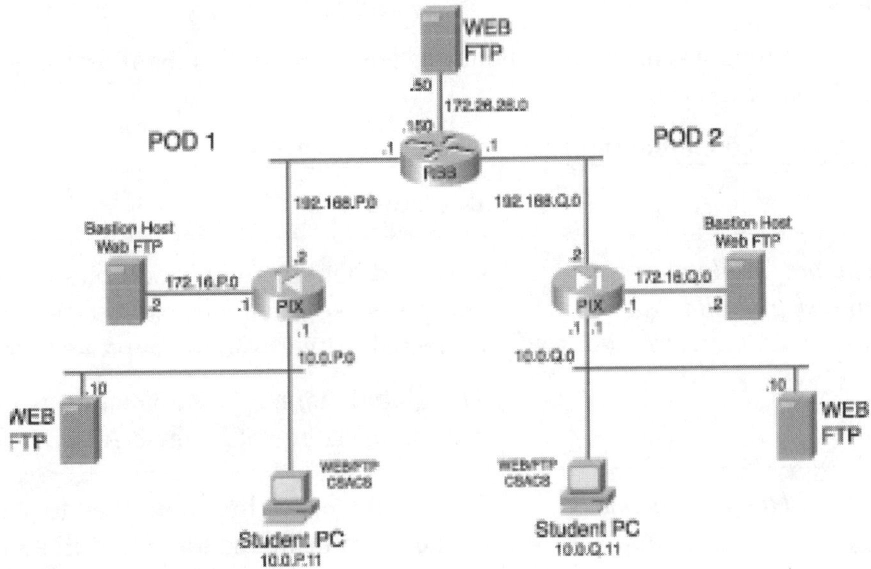


## Preparation

Begin with the standard lab topology in Figure 9-1 and verify the standard configuration on the Pod PIX Security Appliances. Access the PIX Security Appliance console port using the terminal emulator on the student PC. If desired, save the PIX Security Appliance configuration to a text file for later analysis.

## Tools and Resources

To complete the lab, the standard lab topology is required:

- Two Pod PIX Security Appliances
- Two student PCs

- Two servers
- Backbone switch and router
- Two console cables and HyperTerminal

## Additional Materials

Students can use the following links for more information on the objectives covered in this lab:

- http://www.cisco.com/en/US/products/sw/secursw/ps2120/prod_configuration_guide09186a008007da3b.html
- http://www.cisco.com/en/US/products/sw/secursw/ps2120/products_configuration_guide_chapter09186a00800eb721.html

Additional information on configuring firewalls can be found in *Cisco Secure PIX Security Appliances*, by David Chapman and Andy Fox (published by Cisco Press; ISBN: 1587050358).

## Command List

Table 9-1 lists the commands used throughout this lab. Refer to this list if assistance or help is needed during the lab exercise.

**Table 9-1 Lab 9.5.6 Command List**

| Command | Description |
|---|---|
| **global** *if_name nat_id global_ip-global_ip netmask global_mask* | Creates a pool of global addresses that translated addresses use when they exit the firewall from the protected networks to the unprotected networks<br>The **global** command statement is associated with a **nat** command statement by the NAT ID. |
| **nat** *if_name nat_id local_ip netmask* | Defines the inside host permitted to start outbound connections using the translated IP addresses from the global pool |
| **route** *if_name ip_address netmask gateway_ip* [*metric*] | Configures the default route |

## Task 1: Checking the Configuration

Before beginning, check the PIX Security Appliance for the following configurations:

- Name the Ethernet 2 interface "DMZ."
- Give each interface the appropriate IP address.
- Enable the Ethernet 0, Ethernet 1, and Ethernet 2 interfaces for an Intel 10/100 automatic speed-sensing network interface card.
- Set a default route for all internal hosts to the outside interface.

- Create a static mapping of host 172.16.P.2 to 192.168.P.10.
- Allow Internet Control Message Protocol (ICMP) traffic between all interfaces.
- Test the configuration by pinging all interfaces from the console.
- Save the configuration.

### Task 2: Preparing for PAT

The company has only four registered IP addresses. Three of these addresses have been assigned: the PIX outside interface, the perimeter router, and the bastion host. Therefore, a single registered IP address is available to use for translation for all inside hosts. PAT will allow all hosts on network 10.0.1.0 to share a single IP address, 192.168.1.9.

Check for any existing NAT or global configurations using the **show** command. If there are any inside NAT or outside global statements configured, remove them by using the **no** form of the statement. For example:

```
no nat (inside) 1 0.0.0.0 0.0.0.0 0 0
no global (outside) 1 192.168.P.12 - 192.168.P.254 netmask 255.255.255.0
```

### Task 3: Configuring NAT

All the hosts on the 10.0.1.0 network should be eligible for NAT translations. Create a NAT statement that identifies these hosts. Remember that the syntax for this command is **nat** *[(if_name)] nat_id local_ip [netmask]*.

Confirm the configuration using the **show nat** command. The NAT statement should look like this:

```
nat (inside) 1 10.0.P.0 255.255.255.0
```

### Task 4: Configuring a Global Pool of IP Addresses

Create a global pool to be used for traffic exiting the outside interface. This global pool will have a single IP address instead of a range of IP addresses. Remember that the syntax to create a global pool is **global** *[(if_name)] nat_id global_ip[-global_ip] [netmask global_mask]*.

Was there a message on the console indicating that this address will be port translated? If so, what was the message?

---

Confirm the configuration using the **show global** command. The global statement should look like this:

```
global (outside) 1 192.168.1.9 netmask 255.255.255.255
```

## Lab 9.6.3.1: Configure Access Through the PIX Security Appliance

Estimated Time: 25 Minutes

Number of Team Members: Two teams with four students per team

### Objective

In this lab, students complete the following tasks:

- Configure a PIX Security Appliance to protect an enterprise network from Internet access.
- Configure the PIX Security Appliance to allow inbound traffic to the inside host.
- Configure the PIX Security Appliance to allow inbound traffic to the bastion host.
- Test and verify correct PIX Security Appliance operation.

### Overview

In this exercise, the task is to configure the PIX Security Appliance to protect the campus network from intruders. One PIX Security Appliance is available for each Pod group of two students. Perform the following steps with Pod members to complete this exercise:

- Configure a global pool of addresses to assign to inside hosts accessing the demilitarized zone (DMZ).
- Configure statics and conduits to allow users on the outside interface to access the inside host and the bastion host.
- Test and verify correct PIX Security Appliance operation.

Figure 9-2 illustrates the network environment students will create for this lab.

**Figure 9-2 Lab 9.6.3.1 Network Topology**

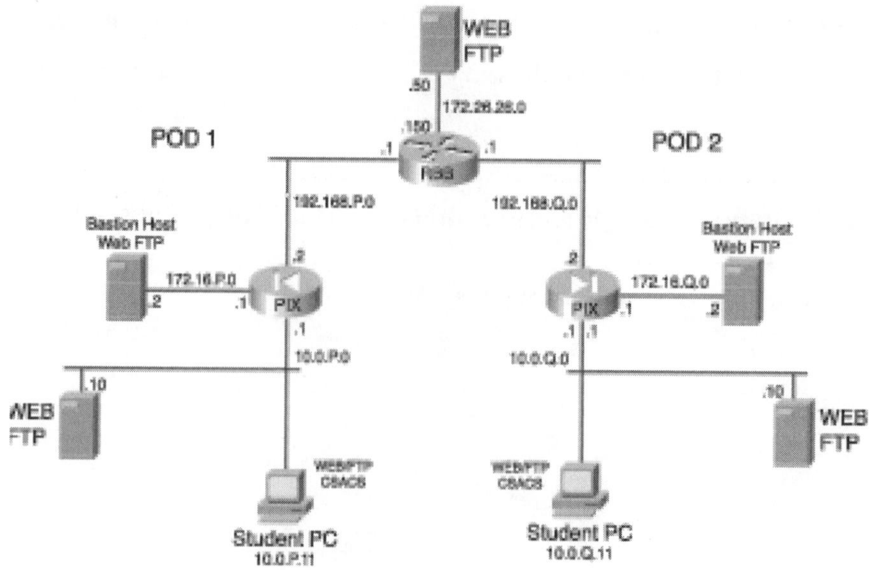

### Preparation

Begin with the standard lab topology in Figure 9-2 and verify the standard configuration on the Pod PIX Security Appliances. Access the PIX Security Appliance console port using the terminal emulator on the student PC. If desired, save the PIX Security Appliance configuration to a text file for later analysis.

### Tools and Resources

To complete the lab, the standard lab topology is required:

- Two Pod PIX Security Appliances
- Two student PCs
- One server
- Backbone switch and router
- Two console cables and HyperTerminal

### Additional Materials

Further information about the objectives covered in this lab can be found at this website:

- http://www.cisco.com/en/US/products/sw/secursw/ps2120/products_configuration_guide_chapter09186a00800eb0b1.html.

Additional information on configuring firewalls can be found in *Cisco Secure PIX Firewall,* by David Chapman and Andy Fox (published by Cisco Press; ISBN 1587050358).

### Command List

Table 9-2 lists the commands used throughout this lab. Refer to this list if you need any assistance during the lab.

**Table 9-2　Lab 9.6.3.1 Command List**

| Command | Description |
|---|---|
| **clear xlate** | Clears the contents of the translation slots. |
| **conduit permit** \| **deny** *protocol global_ip global_mask* [**operator port** [*port*]] *foreign_ip foreign_mask* [**operator port** [*port*]] | Denies or permits access if the conditions are matched. |
| **debug icmp trace** | Displays information about ICMP traffic. |
| **global** [*if_name*] *nat_id* {*global_ip* [-*global_ip*] [**netmask** *global_mask*]} \| **interface** | Creates or delete entries from a pool of global addresses. Configuration mode. |
| **show arp** | Changes or views the arp table, and sets the arp timeout value |

| Command | Description |
|---|---|
| **show conn** | Displays connection information. |
| **show xlate** | Displays current translation and connection slot information. |
| **static** [*prenat_interface*, *postnat_interface*] {**mapped_address**\| **interface**} *real_address* [**dns**] [**netmask** *mask*] [**norandomseq**] [*connection_limit* [*em_limit*]] | Configures a persistent one-to-one address translation rule by mapping a local IP address to a global IP address; known as Static PAT.<br>Configuration mode. |

### Task 1: Configuring a Conduit to Allow ICMP Through the PIX Security Appliance

Enter the following commands to configure PIX Security Appliance global address pools and routing.

**Step 1.** From the Windows command line, ping the backbone router:

```
C:\> ping 192.168.P.1
Pinging 192.168.P.1 with 32 bytes of data:
Request timed out.
Request timed out.
Request timed out.
Request timed out.
```

**Step 2.** Allow ICMP and ping packets through the PIX Security Appliance:

```
PixP(config)# conduit permit icmp any any
```

**Step 3.** From the Windows command line, ping the backbone route:

```
C:\> ping 192.168.P.1
Pinging 192.168.P.1 with 32 bytes of data:
Reply from 192.168.P.1: bytes=32 time<10ms TTL=128
Reply from 192.168.P.1: bytes=32 time<10ms TTL=128
Reply from 192.168.P.1: bytes=32 time<10ms TTL=128
Reply from 192.168.P.1: bytes=32 time<10ms TTL=128
```

### Task 2: Configuring the PIX Security Appliance to Allow Users on the Inside Interface to Access the Bastion Host

Configure the PIX Security Appliance to allow access to the DMZ from the inside network.

**Step 1.** Assign one pool of IP addresses for hosts on the public DMZ:

```
PixP(config)# global (dmz) 1 172.16.P.20-172.16.P.254 netmask 255.255.255.0
```

**Step 2.** Clear the translation table so that the global IP address will be updated in the table:

```
PixP(config)# clear xlate
```

**Step 3.** Write the current configuration to Flash memory:

```
PixP(config)# write memory
```

**Step 4.** Test connectivity to the bastion host from the Pod PC:

```
C:\> ping 172.16.P.2
```

**Step 5.** Test web access to the Pod bastion host from the Pod PC by completing the following substeps.

a. Open a web browser on the Pod PC.

b. Use the web browser to access the Pod bastion host by entering **http://172.16.P.2** (where P = the Pod number).

The home page of the bastion host should appear on the web browser.

**Step 6.** Use the **show arp**, **show conn,** and **show xlate** commands to observe the transaction:

```
PixP(config)# show arp
outside 192.168.P.1 00e0.1e41.8762
inside insidehost 00e0.b05a.d509
dmz bastionhost 00e0.1eb1.78df

PixP(config)# show xlate
Global 172.16.P.20 Local insidehost

PixP(config)# show conn
2 in use, 2 most used
TCP out bastionhost:80 in insidehost:1076 idle 0:00:07 Bytes 461 flags UIO
TCP out bastionhost:80 in insidehost:1075 idle 0:00:07 Bytes 1441 flags UIO
```

**Step 7.** Test the FTP access to the bastion host from the PC by completing the following substeps.

a. Establish an FTP session to the bastion host by choosing **Start** > **Run** > **ftp 172.16.P.2**. If the following message appears, the bastion host has been reached:

```
"Connected to 172.16.P.2."
```

b. Log into the FTP session:

```
User (172.16.P.2(none)): anonymous
331 Anonymous access allowed, send identity (e-mail name) as password.
Password: cisco
```

**Step 8.** Quit the FTP session after connecting and authenticating:

```
ftp> quit
```

### Task 3: Configuring the PIX Security Appliance to Allow Users on the Outside Interface to Access the Bastion Host

Configure a static translation so that traffic originating from the bastion host always has the same source address on the outside interface of the PIX Security Appliance. Then, configure a conduit to allow users on the outside interface to access the bastion host.

**Step 1.** Create a static translation for the Pod bastion host. Use the hostname configured in a previous lab step for the bastion host at 172.16.P.2:

```
PixP(config)# static (dmz,outside) 192.168.P.11 bastionhost
```

**Step 2.** Ping a peer bastion host from the internal host as allowed by the conduit via the static:

```
C:\> ping 192.168.Q.11
```

**Step 3.** View current static translations:

```
PixP(config)# show xlate
2 in use, 2 most used
Global 172.16.P.20 Local insidehost
Global 192.168.P.11 Local bastionhost
```

**Step 4.** Test the web access to the bastion hosts of peer Pod groups by completing the following substeps. The tests should fail.

a. Open a web browser on the client PC.

b. Use the web browser to access the bastion host of the peer Pod group by entering **http://192.168.Q.11** (where Q = peer Pod number).

c. Have a peer Pod attempt to access their peer bastion host in the same way.

Why did the connection fail?

---

**Step 5.** Test the FTP access to the bastion hosts of other Pod groups by completing the following substeps. The connection to the peer bastion host via the FTP should fail.

a. On the FTP client, attempt to get into the bastion host of another Pod group by choosing **Start**> **Run** > **ftp 192.168.Q.11** (where Q = peer Pod number).

b. Have a peer Pod group use the FTP to attempt to access their peer bastion host.

**Step 6.** Configure conduits to allow web and FTP access to the bastion host from the outside and then test the conduits. Configure the conduits to allow TCP traffic from clients on the outside network to access the DMZ bastion host using the previously configured static:

```
PixP(config)# conduit permit tcp host 192.168.P.11 eq www any
PixP(config)# conduit permit tcp host 192.168.P.11 eq ftp any
```

**Step 7.** Test web access to the bastion hosts of peer Pod groups by completing the following substeps. The test to access the peer Pod bastion host should be successful.

a. Open a web browser on the client PC.

b. Use the web browser to access the bastion host of the peer Pod group:

`http://192.168.Q.11.`

c. Have a peer Pod group test the static and conduit configuration in the same way.

d. Use the **show arp**, **show conn**, and **show xlate** commands to observe the transaction.

**Step 8.** Test the FTP access to the bastion hosts of other Pod groups by completing the following substeps.

a. On the student PC, use the FTP to get into the bastion host of another Pod group by choosing **Start** > **Run** > **ftp 192.168.Q.11** (where Q = peer Pod number).

b. Have a peer Pod group use FTP to get into the bastion host to test the static and conduit configuration.

c. Use the **show arp**, **show conn**, and **show xlate** commands to observe the transaction.

**Task 4: Configuring the PIX Security Appliance to Allow Users on the Outside Interface to Access the Inside Host**

Configure a static translation so that traffic originating from the student PC always has the same source address on the outside interface of the PIX Security Appliance. Then, configure a conduit to allow users on the outside interface to access the student PC.

**Step 1.** Create a static translation from the outside PIX Security Appliance interface to the internal host, and create a conduit to allow web connections from the outside to the PC on the inside:

```
PixP(config)# static (inside,outside) 192.168.P.10 insidehost
PixP(config)# conduit permit tcp host 192.168.P.10 eq www any
```

**Step 2.** Turn on ICMP monitoring at the PIX Security Appliance:

```
PixP(config)# debug icmp trace
ICMP trace on Warning: this may cause problems on busy networks
```

**Step 3.** Clear the translation table:

```
PixP(config)# clear xlate
```

**Step 4.** Ping the backbone router from the PC to test the translation. Observe the source and destination of the packets at the console of the PIX Security Appliance:

```
C:\> ping 192.168.P.1
```

Note the example display for pixP in the following:

```
Outbound ICMP echo request (len 32 id 2 seq 45056) insidehost > 192.168.P.10 > 192.168.P.1
Inbound ICMP echo reply (len 32 id 2 seq 45056) 192.168.P.1 > 192.168.P.10 > insidehost
Outbound ICMP echo request (len 32 id 2 seq 45312) insidehost > 192.168.P.10 > 192.168.P.1
Inbound ICMP echo reply (len 32 id 2 seq 45312) 192.168.P.1 > 192.168.P.10 > insidehost
Outbound ICMP echo request (len 32 id 2 seq 45568) insidehost > 192.168.P.10 > 192.168.P.1
Inbound ICMP echo reply (len 32 id 2 seq 45568) 192.168.P.1 > 192.168.P.10 > insidehost
```

Observe the source, destination, and translated addresses on the PIX Security Appliance console (where P = the Pod number).

**Step 5.** Ping a peer inside host from the inside host as allowed by the conduit via the static:

```
C:\> ping 192.168.Q.10
```

**Step 6.** Test web access to a peer Pod inside host as allowed by the static and conduit configured in this task by completing the following substeps:

a. Open a web browser on the Windows NT server.

b. Use the web browser to access the inside host of the peer Pod by entering **http://192.168.Q.10** (where Q = peer Pod number).

**Step 7.** Turn off **debug**:

```
PixP(config)#no debug icmp trace
```

**Step 8.** Write the current configuration to the terminal and verify that the previously entered commands are correct. The configuration should appear similar to the following:

```
PixP(config)# write terminal
Building configuration...
: Saved
:
PIX Version 6.2(0)
nameif ethernet0 outside security0
nameif ethernet1 inside security100
nameif ethernet2 dmz security50
nameif ethernet3 intf3 security15
nameif ethernet4 intf4 security20
nameif ethernet5 intf5 security25
enable password 8Ry2YjIyt7RRXU24 encrypted
passwd 2KFQnbNIdI.2KYOU encrypted
hostname pix6
fixup protocol ftp 21
fixup protocol http 80
fixup protocol h323 h225 1720
fixup protocol h323 ras 1718-1719
```

```
fixup protocol ils 389
fixup protocol rsh 514
fixup protocol rtsp 554
fixup protocol smtp 25
fixup protocol sqlnet 1521
fixup protocol sip 5060
fixup protocol skinny 2000
names
name 172.16.6.2 bastionhost
name 10.0.6.11 insidehost
pager lines 24
logging on
logging buffered debugging
logging trap debugging
logging host inside insidehost
interface ethernet0 100full
interface ethernet1 100full
interface ethernet2 100full
interface ethernet3 auto shutdown
interface ethernet4 auto shutdown
interface ethernet5 auto shutdown
mtu outside 1500
mtu inside 1500
mtu dmz 1500
mtu intf3 1500
mtu intf4 1500
mtu intf5 1500
ip address outside dhcp
ip address inside 10.0.6.1 255.255.255.0
ip address dmz 172.16.6.1 255.255.255.0
ip address intf3 127.0.0.1 255.255.255.255
ip address intf4 127.0.0.1 255.255.255.255
ip address intf5 127.0.0.1 255.255.255.255
ip audit info action alarm
ip audit attack action alarm
no failover
failover timeout 0:00:00
failover poll 15
failover ip address outside 0.0.0.0
failover ip address inside 0.0.0.0
failover ip address dmz 0.0.0.0
failover ip address intf3 0.0.0.0
failover ip address intf4 0.0.0.0
failover ip address intf5 0.0.0.0
pdm history enable
arp timeout 14400
global (outside) 1 192.168.6.20-192.168.6.254 netmask 255.255.255.0
global (dmz) 1 172.16.6.20-172.16.6.254 netmask 255.255.255.0
nat (inside) 1 10.0.6.0 255.255.255.0 0 0
static (dmz,outside) 192.168.6.11 bastionhost netmask 255.255.255.255 0 0
static (inside,outside) 192.168.6.10 insidehost netmask 255.255.255.255 0 0
conduit permit icmp any any
conduit permit tcp host 192.168.6.11 eq www any
conduit permit tcp host 192.168.6.11 eq ftp any
conduit permit tcp host 192.168.6.10 eq www any
route outside 0.0.0.0 0.0.0.0 192.168.6.1 1
route inside 10.1.6.0 255.255.255.0 10.0.6.102 1
timeout xlate 3:00:00
timeout conn 1:00:00 half-closed 0:10:00 udp 0:02:00 rpc 0:10:00 h323 0:05:00 si
p 0:30:00 sip_media 0:02:00
timeout uauth 0:05:00 absolute
aaa-server TACACS+ protocol tacacs+
aaa-server RADIUS protocol radius
aaa-server LOCAL protocol local
no snmp-server location
no snmp-server contact
snmp-server community public
no snmp-server enable traps
floodguard enable
no sysopt route dnat
telnet timeout 5
ssh timeout 5
terminal width 80
Cryptochecksum:65677978f6b81613892109e0f68af9d6
: end
```

## Lab 9.6.3.2: Configure Multiple Interfaces

Estimated Time: 25 Minutes

Number of Team Members: Two teams with four students per team

### Objective

In this lab, students complete the objective of configuring three PIX interfaces and configuring access through the PIX Security Appliance.

### Overview

The PIX Security Appliance can be physically configured with multiple interfaces. Each interface will have a security level somewhere between the outside interface security level of 0 and the inside interface security level of 100. It is common to have an interface called the DMZ. This interface will have a security level that is between 0 and 100. A typical application of the DMZ interface is for public servers, such as web servers.

In this lab, configure the PIX Security Appliance to allow inside and outside hosts to access the services of a web server on the DMZ interface. Review the topology carefully before beginning.

Figure 9-3 illustrates the network environment students create for this lab.

**Figure 9-3 Lab 9.6.3.2 Network Topology**

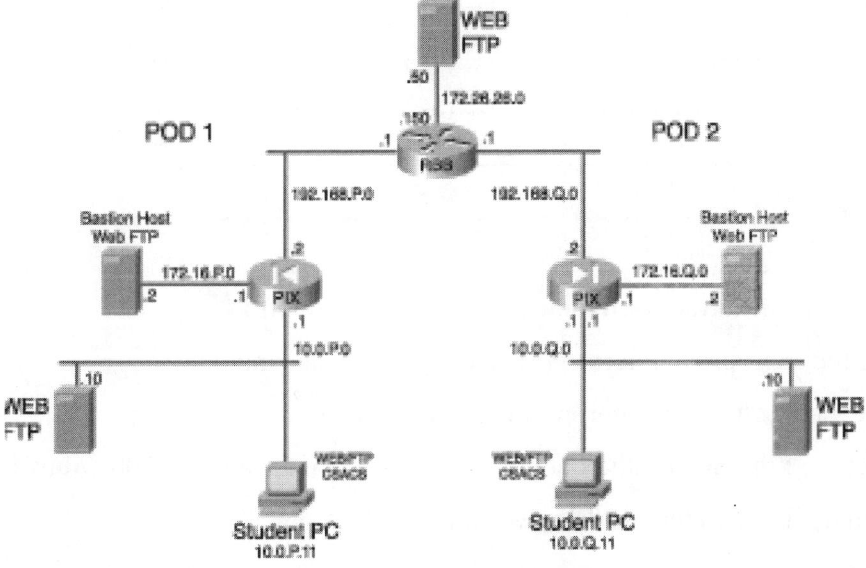


### Preparation

Begin with the standard lab topology in Figure 9-3 and verify the standard configuration on the Pod PIX Security Appliances. Access the PIX Firewall console port using the terminal emulator on the student PC. If desired, save the PIX Firewall configuration to a text file for later analysis.

## Tools and Resources

To complete the lab, the standard lab topology is required:

- Two Pod PIX Security Appliances
- Two student PCs
- Two servers
- Backbone switch and router
- Two console cables and HyperTerminal

## Additional Materials

Further information about the objectives covered in this lab can be found at this website:

- http://www.cisco.com/en/US/products/sw/secursw/ps2120/prod_configuration_guide09186a00801162ea.html#xtocid0.

**Task 1: Checking Configuration**

**Step 1.** Erase the existing configuration.

**Step 2.** What are the six basic commands to get the PIX operational?

______________________________________________________________________

______________________________________________________________________

______________________________________________________________________

______________________________________________________________________

______________________________________________________________________

______________________________________________________________________

Now, perform or confirm the configurations in Step 3 through 14.

**Step 3.** Name the appropriate interface(s) as inside, outside, and dmz.

**Step 4.** Give each interface the appropriate IP address.

**Step 5.** Enable the Ethernet 0, Ethernet 1, and Ethernet 2 interfaces as 100-Mbps full duplex.

**Step 6.** Assign all hosts on the inside network to a NAT pool.

**Step 7.** Define a global pool of IP addresses for inside hosts to use on the outside interface. Use IP addresses 192.168.P.20–192.168.P.254.

**Step 8.** Set a default route for all internal hosts to exit the outside interface.

**Step 9.** Allow ICMP traffic between all interfaces.

**Step 10.** Create a static mapping for the DMZ server at 172.16.P.2 to the global IP address 192.168.P.10.

**Step 11.** Define a global pool of IP addresses for inside hosts to access the DMZ interface. Here, the interface name will be DMZ and the range of IP addresses will be 172.16.1.20-172.16.1.254.

**Step 12.** Assign a name to a single host on the DMZ network. Because this host provides public services that protect the inside network from external connections, call this host "bastionhost." This host has an IP address of 172.16.P.2.

**Step 13.** Test the configuration by pinging all interfaces from the console and pinging the perimeter router from an inside host. FTP and WWW traffic should be able to reach the DMZ server.

**Step 14.** Use the following **show** commands to view information about the transaction: **show xlate, show conn,** and **show arp**.

a. What do these commands reveal?

______________________________________________________________________

______________________________________________________________________

______________________________________________________________________

b. What other **show** commands are useful to verify configuration and operation?

______________________________________________________________________

## Review Questions

1. Describe the how TCP hosts establish a connection.

______________________________________________________________________

______________________________________________________________________

______________________________________________________________________

______________________________________________________________________

2. What are the benefits of using NAT?

______________________________________________________________________

______________________________________________________________________

______________________________________________________________________

______________________________________________________________________

3. Describe static inside NAT.

______________________________________________________________________

______________________________________________________________________

______________________________________________________________________

______________________________________________________________________

4. Describe identity NAT.

______________________________________________________________________

______________________________________________________________________

______________________________________________________________________

______________________________________________________________________

5. Describe the two ways that traffic can get through a PIX security appliance.

______________________________________________________________________

______________________________________________________________________

______________________________________________________________________

______________________________________________________________________

## Chapter 9 Quiz Questions

1. The process of having outside hosts connect to a specific IP address or port and having the PIX Security Appliance redirect the request to a specific inside server is known as __________________.

   A. Port Address Redirection

   B. Port Address Translation

   C. Port Redirection

   D. Network Address Translation

2. What is the default destination port number of TFTP?

   A. TCP 21

   B. UDP 53

   C. TCP 23

   D. UDP 69

3. If a host and destination are communicating using TCP and the host sent a packet with a sequence number of 121 and a window size of 25, what will the destination send back as an acknowledgment number?

   A. 121

   B. 122

   C. 146

   D. 147

4. Based on a three-interface firewall with default security levels and the following configuration, which traffic would *not* be allowed through the PIX?

```
pix(config)# nat (inside) 1 10.0.0.0 255.255.255.0
pix(config)# nat (dmz) 1 172.16.0.0 255.255.255.0
pix(config)# global (outside) 1 192.168.0.20-192.168.0.62 netmask 255.255.255.0
pix(config)# global (dmz) 1 172.16.0.20-172.16.0.30 netmask 255.255.255.0
```

   A. Inside to dmz

   B. Inside to outside

   C. dmz to outside

   D. dmz to inside

5. Which answer provides a permanent, one-to-one mapping between an IP address on a less secure interface and an IP address on a more secure interface?

   A. Dynamic inside NAT

   B. Dynamic outside NAT

   C. Static inside NAT

   D. Static outside NAT

6. What is the command that translates one IP address to another?

   A. **route**

   B. **alias**

   C. **dnat**

   D. **xlate**

7. Which of the following commands associates a network with a pool of global IP addresses?

   A. **nat**

   B. **global**

   C. **ip address**

   D. **static**

8. Which of the following commands maps the e-mail server IP address (10.0.0.10) on the inside interface to the same IP address (192.168.0.9) on the outside interface?

   A. Pix(config)# **static (inside, outside) 192.168.0.9 10.0.0.10**

   B. Pix(config)# **static (outside, inside) 192.168.0.9 10.0.0.10**

   C. Pix(config)# **static (inside, outside) 10.0.0.10 192.168.0.9**

   D. Pix(config)# **static (outside, inside) 10.0.0.10 192.168.0.9**

9. Which of the following protocols uses UDP?

   A. SMTP

   B. FTP

C. SNMP

D. SSH

10. What commands are needed for traffic to flow from the outside interface to the inside interface?

A. None. It's allowed by default.

B. **static**

C. **conduit**

D. **dnat**

11. On a PIX Firewall, what command(s) enable NAT? (Choose all that apply.)

A. **nat**

B. **global**

C. **static**

D. **pat**

E. **local**

12. Which of the following is *not* a characteristic of UDP?

A. UDP is an unreliable but efficient transport protocol.

B. UDP has no handshaking or sequencing.

C. UDP guarantees delivery.

D. UDP has no connection setup and termination.

E. UDP has no congestion management or avoidance.

13. Which of the following is true regarding translations and connection? (Choose all that apply.)

A. Connections occur at the transport layer.

B. Translations occur at the transport layer.

C. Translations occur at the IP layer.

D. One translation can have multiple connections open.

14. What type of NAT is supported by a PIX Firewall? (Choose all that apply.)

A. IP/IPX

B. ARP/RARP

C. Static outside NAT

D. Dynamic outside NAT

15. What command configures NAT translation for all inside hosts?

    A. **nat inside 1 0.0.0.0 0.0.0.0**

    B. **nat inside 0.0.0.0 0.0.0.0**

    C. **nat 0**

    D. **nat (inside) 1 0.0.0.0 0.0.0.0**

16. What command clears an IP address in the translation table on a PIX?

    A. **clear uauth**

    B. **clear xlate**

    C. **clear ip routing**

    D. **clear route**

17. Which of the following is *not* a protocol used by UDP?

    A. TFTP

    B. SNMP

    C. DHCP

    D. DNS

    E. HTTP

18. Which of the following is *not* a protocol used by TCP?

    A. FTP

    B. HTTP

    C. SMTP

    D. SNMP

    E. SSL

19. At what layer of the OSI model do TCP and UPD reside?

    A. Application layer

    B. Transport layer

    C. Network layer

    D. Session layer

20. Which of the following are true regarding TCP? (Choose all that apply.)

    A. Layer 3 protocol

    B. Layer 4 protocol

    C. Connectionless

    D. Connection oriented

# Chapter 10

## PIX Security Appliance ACLs

Chapter 9, "PIX Security Appliance Translations and Connections," explained how to allow access through the PIX Security Appliance from a lower security level to a higher security level using the **static** and **conduit** commands. This chapter deals with using access control lists (ACLs) to do the same thing. Using ACLs is now the Cisco preferred way of allowing access through a PIX Security Appliance.

In this chapter, students learn how to use ACLs on the PIX Security Appliance. The traditional ACLs are covered, along with Turbo ACLs. Turbo ACLs enable the ACL to be compiled to improve search performance. This is a handy feature if ACLs consist of more than 20 entries. After covering the basics of ACLs, the differences between ACLs and conduits are discussed.

One of the important features of the PIX Security Appliance is the ability to do some filtering of malicious applets. This capability can be used to help protect the users from downloading destructive applets. The downside is that the filtering will also deny valid applets. This is another area where having a security policy in place will help to define allowable traffic. Also available to the administrator is the ability to deny access based on URL filtering. The PIX Security Appliance works in conjunction with a URL filtering application running on a separate server.

As the network grows and more resources are needed by different users, an ACL can multiply and grow. To help alleviate this, the administrator can use object grouping to help manage the size and number of ACLs. By using object grouping, you will find that services, servers, and clients can be assigned to a group instead of your having to create several separate entries.

**Vocabulary Exercise**

object groups

_______________________________________________

_______________________________________________

Turbo ACL

_______________________________________________

_______________________________________________

URL filtering

_______________________________________________

_______________________________________________

## Lab Activities

The topology figures and lab examples contain **P** and **Q** values. The **P** value in the addressing and naming scheme refers to *your* assigned Pod number.

The following are examples of determining P values:

- Pod2 is looking at a topology figure and is trying to determine the P values in the figure. In this scenario, the **P** values would equal **2**. 10.0.**P**.12 would become 10.0.**2**.12, 172.30.**P**.2 would become 172.30.**2**.2, and so on.
- Pod1 is looking at a topology figure and is trying to determine the P values in the figure. In this scenario, the **P** values would equal **1**. 10.0.**P**.12 would become 10.0.**1**.12, 172.30.**P**.2 would become 172.30.**1**.2, and so on.

In both examples, the P values are directly related to the Pod number of the team.

The **Q** value in the naming and addressing scheme is used when testing the security or connectivity with the peer team.

The following are examples of determining Q values:

- In a lab, Pod2 has been asked to test connectivity to their peer inside host at IP address 10.0.Q.12. In this scenario, 10.0.**Q**.12 would equal 10.0.**1**.12.
- In a lab, Pod1 has been asked to test connectivity to their peer inside host at IP address 10.0.Q.12. In this scenario, 10.0.**Q**.12 would equal 10.0.**2**.12.

In both examples, the Q value is directly related to the peer Pod number.

## Lab 10.1.2: Configure ACLs in the PIX Security Appliance

Estimated Time: 40 Minutes

Number of Team Members: Two teams with four students per team

### Objective

In this lab, students complete the following tasks:

- Disable pinging to an interface.
- Configure inbound and outbound ACLs.
- Configure malicious active code filtering.

### Overview

By default, the PIX Security Appliance denies access to an internal or perimeter network, which is the more secure network, from an external or less secure network. Network administrators specifically allow inbound connections by using access lists. Access lists work on a first-match basis. So for inbound access, administrators need to deny first and then permit after.

*Note*: Beginning with PIX Security Appliance version 5.3, access lists are the preferred method for managing network access. The **conduit** command was used in earlier versions. Access lists provide improved flexibility and greater ease of use for those familiar with Cisco IOS access control. However, the **conduit** command is still supported to maintain backward compatibility of configurations written for previous PIX Security Appliance versions.

The **access-list** and **access-group** commands permit access based on source or destination IP address, or by the protocol port number. Use the **access-list** command to create a single access list entry. Use the **access-group** command to bind one or more access list entries to a specific interface. Specify only one **access-group** command for each interface.

Figure 10-1 illustrates the network environment students create for this lab.

**Figure 10-1 Lab 10.1.2 Network Topology**

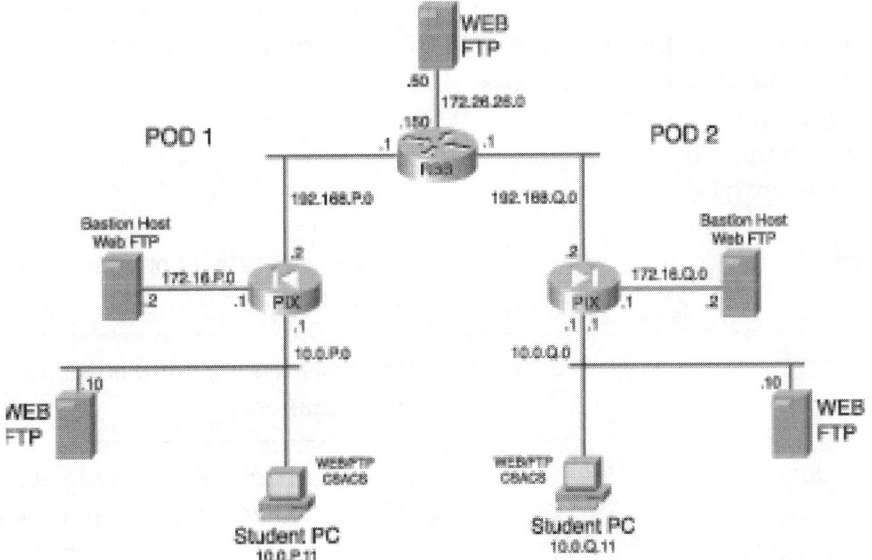

### Preparation

Begin with the standard lab topology in Figure 10-1 and verify the standard configuration on the Pod PIX Security Appliances. Access the PIX Security Appliance console port using the terminal emulator on the student PC. If desired, save the PIX Security Appliance configuration to a text file for later analysis.

### Tools and Resources

To complete the lab, the standard lab topology is required:

- Two Pod PIX Security Appliances
- Two student PCs
- One server
- Backbone switch and router
- Two console cables and HyperTerminal

### Additional Materials

Further information about the objectives covered in this lab can be found at this website:

- http://www.cisco.com/en/US/products/sw/secursw/ps2120/products_configuration_guide_chapter09186a00800eb0b0.html

Additional information on configuring firewalls can be found in *Cisco Secure PIX Security Appliances*, by David Chapman and Andy Fox (published by Cisco Press; ISBN 1587050358).

### Command List

Table 10-1 lists the commands used throughout this lab. Refer to this list if assistance or help is needed during the lab exercise.

**Table 10-1 Lab 10.1.2 Command List**

| Command | Description |
|---|---|
| **access-list** *acl_ID* {**deny** \| **permit**} **icmp** {*source_addr* \| *local_addr*} {*source_mask* \| *local_mask*} {*destination_addr* \| *remote_addr*} {*destination_mask* \| *remote_mask*} *icmp_type* | Configures an access list |
| **clear conduit** | Removes **conduit** command statements from the configuration |
| **clear icmp** | Removes **icmp** command statements from the configuration |
| **filter activex** *port local_ip mask foreign_ip mask* | Block outbound ActiveX, Java applets, and other HTML <object> tags from outbound packets |

| Command | Description |
|---|---|
| **filter java** *port*[*-port*] *local_ip mask foreign_ip mask* | Specifies to filter out Java applets returning from an outbound connection |
| **icmp permit** \| **deny** [**host**] *_addr* [*src_mask*] [*type*] *int_name* | Enables or disables the ability to ping a PIX Security Appliance interface |
| **show access-list** | Displays the configured access list |
| **show conduit** | Displays the configured conduit statements. |
| **show filter** | Displays URL, Java, and ActiveX filtering configurations. |
| **url-server** [*if_name*] **vendor websense host** *local_ip* [**timeout** *seconds*] [**protocol** {**TCP** \| **UDP**} *version*] | Defines Websense filtering |

### Task 1: Disabling Pinging to an Interface

Perform the following lab steps to configure an Internet Control Message Protocol (ICMP) ACL to prevent pinging to the PIX Security Appliance interfaces.

**Step 1.** Ping the inside interface of the PIX Security Appliance from the inside host:

```
C:\> ping 10.0.P.1
Pinging 10.0.P.1 with 32 bytes of data:
Reply from 10.0.P.1: bytes=32 time<10ms TTL=128
Reply from 10.0.P.1: bytes=32 time<10ms TTL=128
Reply from 10.0.P.1: bytes=32 time<10ms TTL=128
Reply from 10.0.P.1: bytes=32 time<10ms TTL=128
```

(where P = the Pod number)

**Step 2.** Ping the outside interface from the inside host. By default, pinging through the PIX to a PIX interface is not allowed:

```
C:\>ping 192.168.P.2
Pinging 192.168.P.2 with 32 bytes of data:
Request timed out.
Request timed out.
Request timed out.
Request timed out.
```

**Step 3.** Use the `icmp` command to prevent pinging the inside interface:

```
PixP(config)# icmp deny any echo inside
```

For what reason would this command be used?

___

**Step 4.** View the ICMP ACL:

```
PixP(config)# show icmp
icmp deny any echo inside
```

**Step 5.** Ping the inside PIX Security Appliance interface from the inside host. The ICMP ACL causes the ping to fail:

```
C:\>ping 10.0.P.1
Pinging 10.0.P.1 with 32 bytes of data:
Request timed out.
Request timed out.
Request timed out.
Request timed out.
```

**Step 6.** Enable pinging to the PIX Security Appliance inside interface:

```
PixP(config)# clear icmp
```

**Step 7.** Verify the inside interface by pinging the inside interface of the PIX Security Appliance:

```
C:\>ping 10.0.P.1
Pinging 10.0.P.1 with 32 bytes of data:
Reply from 10.0.P.1: bytes=32 time<10ms TTL=128
Reply from 10.0.P.1: bytes=32 time<10ms TTL=128
Reply from 10.0.P.1: bytes=32 time<10ms TTL=128
Reply from 10.0.P.1: bytes=32 time<10ms TTL=128
```

**Step 8.** From the inside host, ping an inside host of a peer Pod. Notice that the conduit created earlier allows the ping through the PIX Security Appliance:

```
C:\>ping 10.0.Q.12
Pinging 10.0.Q.12 with 32 bytes of data:
Reply from 10.0.Q.12: bytes=32 time<10ms TTL=128
Reply from 10.0.Q.12: bytes=32 time<10ms TTL=128
Reply from 10.0.Q.12: bytes=32 time<10ms TTL=128
Reply from 10.0.Q.12: bytes=32 time<10ms TTL=128
```

**Step 9.** From the inside host, ping a peer Pod outside the PIX Security Appliance interface:

```
C:\>ping 192.168.Q.2
Pinging 192.168.Q.2 with 32 bytes of data:
Reply from 192.168.Q.2: bytes=32 time<10ms TTL=128
Reply from 192.168.Q.2: bytes=32 time<10ms TTL=128
Reply from 192.168.Q.2: bytes=32 time<10ms TTL=128
Reply from 192.168.Q.2: bytes=32 time<10ms TTL=128
```

**Step 10.** Configure the PIX Security Appliance to deny all ping requests and permit all unreachable messages at the outside interface:

```
PixP(config)# icmp deny any echo outside
PixP(config)# icmp permit any unreachable outside
```

What is achieved by using these commands?

---

---

**Step 11.** Try again to ping the outside interface of a peer Pod PIX Security Appliance from the inside host. Notice that the ping fails due to the ICMP ACL that the peer created. Verify the neighboring Pod group has the ICMP ACL configured before attempting to ping:

```
C:\>ping 192.168.Q.2
Pinging 192.168.Q.2 with 32 bytes of data:
Request timed out.
Request timed out.
Request timed out.
Request timed out.
```

**Step 12.** Remove the ICMP ACL from the PIX Security Appliance outside interface:

```
PixP(config)# clear icmp
```

**Step 13.** Save the configuration:

```
PixP(config)# write memory
```

**Task 2: Configuring an Inbound ACL**

Perform the following lab steps to configure ACLs:

- Allow inbound web traffic from a peer Pod network to the bastion host.
- Allow inbound FTP traffic from an internal host of a peer Pod to the bastion host.
- Allow inbound web traffic to the inside host.
- Allow inbound pings to the inside host and bastion host.
- Allow icmp echo-replies from hosts on the outside and dmz interfaces.
- Deny all other inbound traffic.

**Step 1.** View the conduits using the **show conduit** command:

```
PixP(config)# show conduit
conduit permit tcp host 192.168.P.10 eq www any
conduit permit tcp host 192.168.P.11 eq www any
conduit permit tcp host 192.168.P.11 eq ftp any
conduit permit icmp any any
```

**Step 2.** If any conduits are configured, remove them using the **clear conduit** command:

```
PixP(config)# clear conduit
```

**Step 3.** Verify that the conduits have been removed:

```
PixP(config) show conduit
```

**Step 4.** Verify that statics are in place for the bastion host and for the inside host:

```
PixP(config)# show static
static (inside,outside) 192.168.P.10 insidehost netmask 255.255.255.255 0 0
static (dmz,outside) 192.168.P.11 bastionhost netmask 255.255.255.255 0 0
```

**Step 5.** Test web access to the bastion hosts of the peer Pod groups by completing the following substeps. The web request should fail to the peer bastion host via its static mapping.

a. Open a web browser on the student PC.

b. Use the web browser to access the bastion host of the peer Pod group by entering **http://192.168.Q.11** (where Q = the peer pod number).

c. Have a peer Pod group attempt to access the bastion host in the same way.

**Step 6.** Test web access to the inside host of the peer Pod by completing the following substeps. The web request should fail to access the inside host of the peer via its static mapping.

a. Open a web browser on the student PC.

b. Use the web browser to access the inside host of the peer Pod group by entering **http://192.168.Q.10** (where Q = the peer pod number).

c. Have a peer Pod group attempt to access the inside host in the same way.

**Step 7.** Test FTP access to the bastion hosts of the peer Pod groups by completing the following substeps. The FTP request should fail when accessing the peer bastion host via FTP.

a. On the FTP client, attempt to access the bastion host of another Pod group by using the following:

**Start>Run>ftp 192.168.Q.11**

b. Have a peer Pod group use the FTP to attempt to access their peer bastion host.

**Step 8.** Create an ACL to permit inbound web and FTP access to the bastion host.

```
PixP(config)# access-list ACLIN permit tcp 192.168.Q.0 255.255.255.0 host 192.168.P.11 eq www
PixP(config)# access-list ACLIN permit tcp host 192.168.Q.10 host 192.168.P.11 eq ftp
```

What command would be used to allow access to the mail server?

---

**Step 9.** Add commands to permit inbound web traffic to the inside host, permit inbound pings, permit icmp echo replies to the inside host, and deny all other traffic from the Internet:

```
PixP(config)# access-list ACLIN permit tcp any host 192.168.P.10 eq www
PixP(config)# access-list ACLIN permit icmp any any echo
PixP(config)# access-list ACLIN permit icmp any host 192.168.P.10 echo-reply
PixP(config)# access-list ACLIN deny ip any any
```

**Step 10.** Bind the ACL to the outside interface:

```
PixP(config)# access-group ACLIN in interface outside
```

**Step 11.** Create an access list to allow icmp echo-replies from the bastion host:

```
PixP(config)# access-list ICMPDMZ permit icmp host bastionhost any echo-reply
```

**Step 12.** Bind the new ACL to the dmz interface:

```
PixP(config)# access-group ICMPDMZ in interface dmz
```

**Step 13.** Display the access list and observe the hit counts:

```
PixP(config)# show access-list
access-list ACLIN; 6 elements
access-list ACLIN permit tcp 192.168.Q.0 255.255.255.0 host 192.168.P.11 eq www (hitcnt=0)
access-list ACLIN permit tcp host 192.168.Q.10 host 192.168.P.11 eq ftp (hitcnt=0)
access-list ACLIN permit tcp any host 192.168.P.10 eq www (hitcnt=0)
access-list ACLIN permit icmp any any echo (hitcnt=0)
access-list ACLIN permit icmp any host 192.168.P.10 echo-reply (hitcnt=0)
access-list ACLIN deny ip any any (hitcnt=0)
access-list ICMPDMZ; 1 elements
access-list ICMPDMZ permit icmp host bastionhost any echo-reply (hitcnt=0)
```

## Task 3: Testing and Verifying the Inbound ACLs

Perform the following steps to test the inbound ACL.

**Step 1.** Have a peer inside host ping the inside host:

```
C:\>ping 192.168.Q.10
Pinging 192.168.Q.10 with 32 bytes of data:
Reply from 192.168.Q.10: bytes=32 time<10ms TTL=128
Reply from 192.168.Q.10: bytes=32 time<10ms TTL=128
Reply from 192.168.Q.10: bytes=32 time<10ms TTL=128
Reply from 192.168.Q.10: bytes=32 time<10ms TTL=128
```

**Step 2.** Have a peer inside host ping the bastion host:

```
C:\>ping 192.168.Q.11
Pinging 192.168.Q.11 with 32 bytes of data:
Reply from 192.168.Q.11: bytes=32 time<10ms TTL=128
Reply from 192.168.Q.11: bytes=32 time<10ms TTL=128
Reply from 192.168.Q.11: bytes=32 time<10ms TTL=128
Reply from 192.168.Q.11: bytes=32 time<10ms TTL=128
```

**Step 3.** Ping the bastion host from the student PC:

```
C:\>ping 172.16.P.2
Pinging 172.16.P.2 with 32 bytes of data:
Reply from 172.16.P.2: bytes=32 time<10ms TTL=128
Reply from 172.16.P.2: bytes=32 time<10ms TTL=128
Reply from 172.16.P.2: bytes=32 time<10ms TTL=128
Reply from 172.16.P.2: bytes=32 time<10ms TTL=128
```

**Step 4.** Ping the super server from the student PC:

```
C:\>ping 172.26.26.50
Pinging 172.26.26.50 with 32 bytes of data:
Reply from 172.26.26.50: bytes=32 time<10ms TTL=128
Reply from 172.26.26.50: bytes=32 time<10ms TTL=128
Reply from 172.26.26.50: bytes=32 time<10ms TTL=128
Reply from 172.26.26.50: bytes=32 time<10ms TTL=128
```

**Step 5.** Test web access to the bastion hosts of peer Pod groups by completing the following substeps. The web request should be successful when accessing the peer bastion host via its static mapping.

a. Open a web browser on the student PC.

b. Use the web browser to access the bastion host of the peer Pod group by entering **http://192.168.Q.11** (where Q = the peer Pod number).

c. Have a peer Pod group attempt to access the bastion host in the same way.

**Step 6.** Test web access to the inside hosts of peer Pod groups by completing the following substeps. Access to the IP address of the static mapped to the inside host of the opposite Pod group should be successful.

a. Open a web browser on the client PC.

b. Use the web browser to access the inside host of the peer Pod group by entering **http://192.168.Q.10** (where Q = the peer Pod number).

c. Have a peer Pod group attempt to access the inside host in the same way.

**Step 7.** Test FTP access to the bastion hosts of peer Pod groups by completing the following substeps. Access to the peer bastion host via FTP should be successful.

a. On the FTP client, attempt to access the bastion host of a peer Pod group by using the following:

**Start** > **Run** > **ftp 192.168.Q.11**.

b. Have a peer Pod group use FTP to attempt to access their peer bastion host.

Were any of the preceding steps unsuccessful? Why?

---

**Step 8.** Display the access lists again and observe the hit counts:

```
PixP(config)# show access-list
access-list ACLIN; 6 elements
access-list ACLIN permit tcp 192.168.Q.0 255.255.255.0 host 192.168.P.11 eq www(hitcnt=2)
access-list ACLIN permit tcp host 192.168.Q.10 host 192.168.P.11 eq ftp (hitcnt=0)
access-list ACLIN permit tcp any host 192.168.P.10 eq www (hitcnt=2)
access-list ACLIN permit icmp any any echo (hitcnt=20)
access-list ACLIN permit icmp any host 192.168.P.10 echo-reply (hitcnt=12)
access-list ACLIN deny ip any any (hitcnt=0)
access-list ICMPDMZ; 1 elements
access-list ICMPDMZ permit icmp host bastionhost any echo-reply (hitcnt=12)
```

## Task 4: Configuring an Outbound ACL

Perform the following lab steps to configure ACLs:

- Deny outbound web traffic.
- Allow outbound FTP traffic from the internal network to 172.26.26.50.

**Step 1.** Test web access to the Internet by completing the following substeps. The test to access 172.26.26.50 should be successful.

a. Open a web browser on the student PC.

b. Use the web browser to access Internet host 172.26.26.50 by entering **http://172.26.26.50**.

**Step 2.** Test FTP access to Internet host 172.26.26.50. Access to the host 172.26.26.50 via FTP should be successful.

On the FTP client, attempt to access host 172.26.26.50 by using the following:

**Start>Run>ftp 172.26.26.50**

**Step 3.** Create an ACL that prevents users on the internal network from making outbound HTTP connections:

```
PixP(config)# access-list ACLOUT deny tcp any any eq www
```

This access list prevents all outbound connections.

**Step 4.** Enter the **access-group** command to create an access group that will bind the ACL to an interface:

```
PixP(config)# access-group ACLOUT in interface inside
```

**Step 5.** Display the configured access list, and observe the hit count:

```
PixP(config)# show access-list
access-list ACLIN; 6 elements
access-list ACLIN permit tcp 192.168.Q.0 255.255.255.0 host 192.168.P.11 eq www(hitcnt=4)
access-list ACLIN permit tcp host 192.168.Q.10 host 192.168.P.11 eq ftp (hitcnt=1)
access-list ACLIN permit tcp any host 192.168.P.10 eq www (hitcnt=4)
access-list ACLIN permit icmp any any echo (hitcnt=20)
access-list ACLIN permit icmp any host 192.168.P.10 echo-reply (hitcnt=12)
access-list ACLIN deny ip any any (hitcnt=0)
access-list ICMPDMZ; 1 elements
access-list ICMPDMZ permit icmp host bastionhost any echo-reply (hitcnt=12)
access-list ACLOUT; 1 elements
access-list ACLOUT deny tcp any any eq www (hitcnt=0)
```

**Step 6.** Test web access to the Internet by completing the following substeps. The test via HTTP should fail.

a. Open a web browser on the student PC.

b. Use the web browser to access the Internet by entering **http://172.26.26.50**.

**Step 7.** Test FTP access to an Internet host. The FTP connection should fail, as well as the HTTP, because of the implicit deny.

On the FTP client, attempt to access host 172.26.26.50:

**Start>Run>ftp 172.26.26.50**

**Step 8.** Display the access list again and note that the hit count has incremented:

```
PixP(config)# show access-list
access-list ACLIN; 6 elements
```

```
access-list ACLIN permit tcp 192.168.Q.0 255.255.255.0 host 192.168.P.11 eq www (hitcnt=4)
access-list ACLIN permit tcp host 192.168.Q.10 host 192.168.P.11 eq ftp (hitcnt=1)
access-list ACLIN permit tcp any host 192.168.P.10 eq www (hitcnt=4)
access-list ACLIN permit icmp any any echo (hitcnt=20)
access-list ACLIN permit icmp any host 192.168.P.10 echo-reply (hitcnt=12)
access-list ACLIN deny ip any any (hitcnt=0)
access-list ICMPDMZ; 1 elements
access-list ICMPDMZ permit icmp host bastionhost any echo-reply (hitcnt=12)
access-list ACLOUT; 1 elements
access-list ACLOUT deny tcp any any eq www (hitcnt=6)
```

**Step 9.** Add an additional command to the ACL to permit outbound FTP access to host 172.26.26.50:

```
PixP(config)# access-list ACLOUT permit tcp 10.0.P.0 255.255.255.0 host 172.26.26.50 eq ftp
```

**Step 10.** Add another access list command statement to deny other outbound IP traffic:

```
PixP(config)# access-list ACLOUT deny ip any any
```

This access list statement is needed only to enable viewing of the hit counts.

**Step 11.** View the access list again:

```
PixP(config)# show access-list ACLOUT
access-list ACLOUT deny tcp any any eq www (hitcnt=2)
access-list ACLOUT permit tcp 10.0.P.0 255.255.255.0 host 172.26.26.50 eq ftp(hitcnt=0)
access-list ACLOUT deny ip any any (hitcnt=0)
```

### Task 5: Testing and Verifying the Outbound ACL

Perform the following steps to test the outbound ACL.

**Step 1.** Test web access to the Internet by completing the following substeps. Accessing the Internet host fais because of the deny ACL.

a. Open a web browser on the student PC.

b. Use the web browser to access the Internet by entering **http://172.26.26.50**.

**Step 2.** Test FTP access to an Internet host by performing the following on the FTP client. At this point, a connection using FTP will work:

**Start>Run>ftp 172.26.26.50**

**Step 3.** Test the FTP access to a peer Pod bastion host by attempting to access the peer Pod bastion host on the FTP client. The connection using FTP should fail:

**Start>Run>ftp 192.168.Q.11**

**Step 4.** View the outbound access list again and observe the hit counts:

```
PixP(config)# show access-list ACLOUT
access-list ACLOUT deny tcp any any eq www (hitcnt=2)
access-list ACLOUT permit tcp 10.0.P.0 255.255.255.0 host 172.26.26.50 eq ftp (hitcnt=1)
access-list ACLOUT deny ip any any (hitcnt=3)
```

**Step 5.** Remove the outbound ACL.

Be sure to enter the following command exactly as shown. If the ACL name is omitted, all access list statements are removed:

```
PixP(config)# clear access-list ACLOUT
```

**Step 6.** Verify that the outbound ACL has been removed:

```
PixP(config)# show access-list
access-list ACLIN; 6 elements
access-list ACLIN permit tcp 192.168.Q.0 255.255.255.0 host 192.168.P.11 eq www(hitcnt=4)
access-list ACLIN permit tcp host 192.168.Q.10 host 192.168.P.11 eq ftp (hitcnt= 1)
```

```
access-list ACLIN permit tcp any host 192.168.P.10 eq www (hitcnt=4)
access-list ACLIN permit icmp any any echo (hitcnt=20)
access-list ACLIN permit icmp any host 192.168.P.10 echo-reply (hitcnt=12)
access-list ACLIN deny ip any any (hitcnt=0)
access-list ICMPDMZ; 1 elements
access-list ICMPDMZ permit icmp host bastionhost any echo-reply (hitcnt=12)
```

**Step 7.** Save the configuration:

```
PixP(config)# write memory
```

### Task 6: Filtering Malicious Active Code

Perform the following lab steps to configure ActiveX and filter Java. This task cannot be tested with the current setup.

**Step 1.** Enter the **filter activex** command to block ActiveX from any local host and for connections to any foreign host on port 80:

```
PixP(config)# filter activex 80 0 0 0 0
```

What is the significance of 0 0 0 0?

---

**Step 2.** Enter the **filter java** command to block Java applets:

```
PixP(config)# filter java 80 0 0 0 0
```

**Step 3.** Use the following command to show the filters:

```
PixP(config)# show filter
filter activex 80 0.0.0.0 0.0.0.0 0.0.0.0 0.0.0.0
filter java 80 0.0.0.0 0.0.0.0 0.0.0.0 0.0.0.0
```

### Task 7: Configuring the PIX Security Appliance to Work with a URL Filtering Server

Perform the following steps to configure the PIX Security Appliance to work with a URL-filtering server:

**Step 1.** Enter the **url-server** command to designate the URL-filtering server:

```
PixP(config)# url-server (inside) host insidehost timeout 5 protocol TCP version 4
```

**Step 2.** Show the designated url-server by entering the following command:

```
PixP(config)# show url-server
url-server (inside) vendor websense host insidehost timeout 5 protocol TCP version 4
```

**Step 3.** Enter the **filter url http** command to prevent outbound users from accessing WWW URLs that are designated with the filtering application:

```
PixP(config)# filter url http 0 0 0 0 allow
```

**Step 4.** Display the **filter url http** command by using the following command:

```
PixP(config)# show filter url
filter activex 80 0.0.0.0 0.0.0.0 0.0.0.0 0.0.0.0
filter java 80 0.0.0.0 0.0.0.0 0.0.0.0 0.0.0.0
filter url http 0.0.0.0 0.0.0.0 0.0.0.0 0.0.0.0 allow
```

**Step 5.** Remove the **url-server** command:

```
PixP(config)# no url-server (inside) host insidehost
```

**Step 6.** Remove the **filter url** command:

```
PixP(config)# no filter url http 0 0 0 0 allow
```

**Step 7.** Save the configuration:

```
PixP(config)# write memory
```

# Lab 10.4.4: Configure Object Groups

Estimated Time: 35 Minutes

Number of Team Members: Two teams with four students per team

## Objective

In this lab, students complete the following objectives:

- Configure a service object group.
- Configure an ICMP-Type object group.
- Configure a nested server object group.
- Configure an inbound ACL with object groups.
- Configure web and ICMP access to the inside host.
- Test and verify the inbound ACL.

## Overview

PIX code version 6.2 introduced the feature called object grouping, which allows objects such as IP hosts or networks, protocols, ports, and ICMP types to be grouped into objects. After it is configured, this object group can then be used with the standard **conduit** or **access-list** PIX commands to reference all objects within that group. This reduces the configuration size. When using an object group within a command, the keyword **object-group** must be used before the group name, as shown in the following example:

```
access-list 100 permit object-group protocols object-group  remotes object-group locals object-
  group services
```

In this example, protocols, remotes, locals, and services are previously defined object-group names. Object groups can also be nested, where one object group can be included as a subset of another object group.

Figure 10-2 illustrates the network environment students will create for this lab.

**Figure 10-2 Lab 10.4.4 Network Topology**

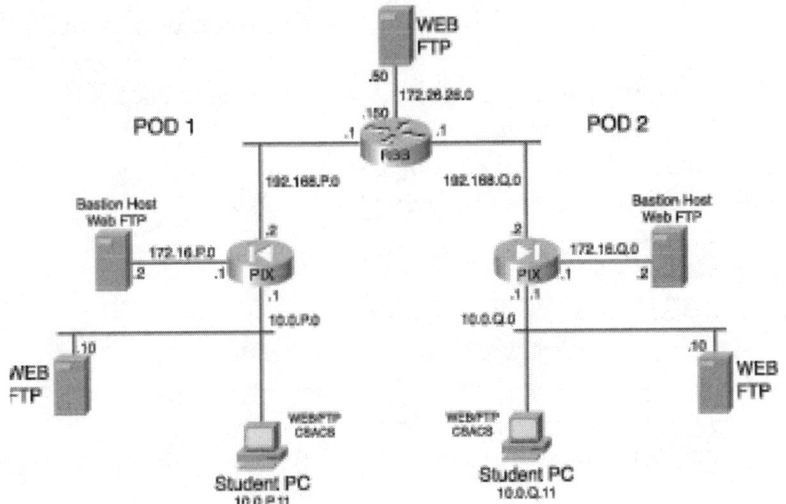

## Preparation

Begin with the standard lab topology and verify the standard configuration on the Pod PIX Security Appliances. Access the PIX Security Appliance console port using the terminal emulator on the student PC. If desired, save the PIX Security Appliance configuration to a text file for later analysis.

## Tools and Resources

To complete the lab, the standard lab topology is required:

- Two Pod PIX Security Appliances
- Two student PCs
- One server
- Backbone switch and router
- Two console cables and HyperTerminal

## Additional Materials

Further information about the objectives covered in this lab can be found at this website:

- http://www.cisco.com/en/US/products/hw/vpndevc/ps2030/products_tech_note09186a00800d641d.shtml.

Additional information on configuring firewalls can be found in *Cisco Secure PIX Security Appliances*, by David Chapman and Andy Fox (published by Cisco Press; ISBN 1587050358).

## Command List

Table 10-2 lists the commands used throughout this lab. Refer to this list if you need any assistance during the lab.

**Table 10-2 Lab 10.4.4 Command List**

| **Command** | **Description** |
|---|---|
| **access-group** *acl_ID* in **interface** *interface_name* | Binds the access list to an interface. Configuration mode. |
| **access-list** *id* {**deny** \| **permit**} {*protocol* \| object-group *protocol_obj_grp_id* {*source_addr* \| *local_addr*} {*source_mask* \| *local_mask*} \| object-group *network_obj_grp_id* [*operator port* [*port*] \| object-group *service_obj_grp_id*] {*destination_addr* \| *remote_addr*} {*destination_mask* \| *remote_mask*} \| object-group *network_obj_grp_id* [*operator port* [*port*] \| object-group *service_obj_grp_id*]} | Creates an access list |
| **object-group icmp-type** *grp_id* **icmp-group** *icmp_type* | Adds ICMP objects to an ICMP-type object group |

| Command | Description |
|---|---|
| **object-group network** *grp_id* **network-object host** *host_addr* **network-object** *host_addr netmask* | Defines a group of hosts or subnet IP addresses. After entering the main **object-group network** command, add network objects to the network group with the **network-object** and the **group-object** subcommands. |
| **object-group service** *grp_id* {**tcp** \| **udp** \| **tcp-udp**} **port-object eq** *service* **port-object range** *begin_service end_service* | Adds port objects to a service-object group |
| **show object-group** [**id** *grp_id* \| *grp_type*] | Displays object groups in the configuration |

### Task 1: Configuring a Service Object Group

To configure a service group containing HTTP and FTP, complete the following steps.

**Step 1.** Create a TCP service group named MYSERVICES. This step assigns a name to the group and enables the service object subcommand mode:

```
PixP(config)# object-group service MYSERVICES tcp
```

**Step 2.** Add HTTP and FTP to the service object group:

```
PixP(config-service)# port-object eq http
PixP(config-service)# port-object eq ftp
```

What is the command to group consecutive services?

______________________________________________________________

**Step 3.** Return to configuration mode:

```
PixP(config-network)# exit
```

**Step 4.** Verify that the object group has been configured successfully:

```
PixP(config)# show object-group
object-group service MYSERVICES tcp
port-object eq www
port-object eq ftp
```

### Task 2: Configuring an ICMP-Type Object Group

To configure an ICMP-Type group, complete the following steps.

**Step 1.** To assign a name to the group and enable the ICMP-Type subcommand mode, create an ICMP-Type object group named PING:

```
PixP(config)# object-group icmp-type PING
```

**Step 2.** Add ICMP echo to the ICMP-Type object group:

```
PixP(config-icmp-type)# icmp-object echo
```

**Step 3.** Add ICMP echo-reply to the ICMP-Type object group:

```
PixP(config-icmp-type)# icmp-object echo-reply
```

**Step 4.** Add ICMP unreachable messages to the ICMP-Type object group:

```
PixP(config-icmp-type)# icmp-object unreachable
```

**Step 5.** Return to configuration mode:

```
PixP(config-icmp-type)# exit
```

**Step 6.** Verify that the object group has been configured successfully:

```
PixP(config)# show object-group
object-group service MYSERVICES tcp
port-object eq www
port-object eq ftp
object-group icmp-type PING
icmp-object echo
icmp-object echo-reply
icmp-object unreachable
```

### Task 3: Configuring a Nested Server Object Group

To nest an object group within another object group, complete the following steps.

**Step 1.** Create a network object group named FTPSERVERS:

```
PixP(config)# object-group network FTPSERVERS
```

**Step 2.** Add the bastion host to the object group:

```
PixP(config-network)# network-object host 192.168.P.11
```

**Step 3.** Return to configuration mode:

```
PixP(config-network)# exit
```

**Step 4.** Create a network object group named ALLSERVERS:

```
PixP(config)# object-group network ALLSERVERS
```

**Step 5.** Nest the FTPSERVERS group within the ALLSERVERS group:

```
PixP(config-network)# group-object FTPSERVERS
```

**Step 6.** Add the following servers to the ALLSERVERS group:

- 192.168.P.10
- 192.168.P.6
- 192.168.P.7

```
PixP(config-network)# network-object host 192.168.P.10
PixP(config-network)# network-object host 192.168.P.6
PixP(config-network)# network-object host 192.168.P.7
```

**Step 7.** Verify that the object group has been configured successfully:

```
PixP(config-network)# show object-group
object-group service MYSERVICES tcp
    port-object eq www
    port-object eq ftp
object-group icmp-type PING
    icmp-object echo
    icmp-object echo-reply
    icmp-object unreachable
object-group network FTPSERVERS
    network-object host 192.168.P.11
object-group network ALLSERVERS
    group-object FTPSERVERS
    network-object host 192.168.P.10
    network-object host 192.168.P.6
    network-object host 192.168.P.7
```

## Task 4: Configuring an Inbound ACL with Object Groups

Complete the following steps to configure an inbound ACL:

- Allow inbound web traffic from a peer Pod network to the bastion host.
- Allow inbound FTP traffic from a peer Pod internal host to the bastion host.

**Step 1.** Remove the ACLs configured in the previous lab:

```
PixP(config-network)# clear access-list
```

**Step 2.** Verify that all ACLs have been removed:

```
PixP(config)# show access-list
```

**Step 3.** Test web access to the peer Pod bastion host by completing the following substeps. The test to the peer bastion host should fail.

a. Open a web browser on the student PC.

b. Use the web browser to access the bastion host of the peer Pod group by entering **http://192.168.Q.11** (where Q = the peer Pod number).

**Step 4.** Test web access to the inside host of the peer Pod by completing the following substeps. The test to the peer inside host should fail.

a. Open a web browser on the student PC.

b. Use the web browser to access the inside host of the peer Pod group by entering **http://192.168.Q.10** (where Q = the peer Pod number).

Why have these connection attempts failed?

______________________________________________________________

______________________________________________________________

**Step 5.** From the FTP client, test FTP access to the peer Pod bastion host. Access to the peer bastion host via FTP should fail:

**Start>Run>ftp 192.168.Q.11**

**Step 6.** Use the MYSERVICES group to create an ACL permitting inbound web and FTP access to the bastion host:

```
PixP(config)# access-list ACLIN permit tcp 192.168.Q.0 255.255.255.0 object-group FTPSERVERS
object-group MYSERVICES
```

**Step 7.** Bind the ACL to the outside interface:

```
PixP(config)# access-group ACLIN in interface outside
```

**Step 8.** Have a peer ping the inside host. The ping should fail:

```
C:\>ping 192.168.Q.10
Pinging 192.168.Q.10 with 32 bytes of data:
Request timed out.
Request timed out.
Request timed out.
Request timed out.
```

**Step 9.** Have a peer ping the bastion host. The ping should fail:

```
C:\>ping 192.168.Q.11
Pinging 192.168.Q.11 with 32 bytes of data:
```

```
Request timed out.
Request timed out.
Request timed out.
Request timed out.
```

**Step 10.** Test web access to the peer Pod bastion host by completing the following substeps. Access to the peer Pod bastion host should be successful.

a. Open a web browser on the student PC.

b. Use the web browser to access the bastion host of the peer Pod group by entering **http://192.168.Q.11** (where Q = the peer Pod number).

**Step 11.** Test web access to the peer Pod inside host by completing the following substeps. Access to the peer Pod inside host should fail.

a. Open a web browser on the client PC.

b. Use the web browser to access the inside host of the peer Pod group by entering **http://192.168.Q.10** (where Q = the peer Pod number).

**Step 12.** From the FTP client, test FTP access to the peer Pod bastion host. Access to the peer bastion host via FTP should be successful:

**`Start>Run>ftp 192.168.Q.11`**

**Step 13.** From the FTP client, test FTP access to the peer Pod inside hosts. Access to the peer inside host via FTP should fail:

**`Start>Run>ftp 192.168.Q.10`**

Why does the connection attempt to the peer Pod inside hosts fail?

___

___

### Task 5: Configuring Web and ICMP Access to the Inside Host

Complete the following steps to configure ACLIN:

- Permit inbound web and ICMP traffic to all hosts behind the PIX Security Appliance.
- Deny all other traffic from the Internet.

**Step 1.** Use a network hosts group to add an ACL entry permitting web traffic to all hosts behind the PIX Security Appliance:

```
PixP(config)# access-list ACLIN permit tcp any object-group ALLSERVERS eq www
```

**Step 2.** Permit ICMP traffic to all hosts behind the PIX Security Appliance:

```
PixP(config)# access-list ACLIN permit icmp any any object-group PING
```

**Step 3.** Deny all other traffic from the Internet:

```
PixP(config)# access-list ACLIN deny ip any any
```

**Step 4.** Bind the ACL to the outside interface:

```
PixP(config)# access-group ACLIN in interface outside
```

**Step 5.** Create an ACL to permit echo replies to the inside host from the bastion host:

```
PixP(config)# access-list ACLDMZ permit icmp any any object-group PING
```

**Step 6.** Bind the ACL to the demilitarized zone (DMZ) interface:

```
PixP(config)# access-group ACLDMZ in interface dmz
```

**Step 7.** Display the ACLs and observe the hit counts:

```
PixP(config)# show access-list
access-list ACLIN; 10 elements
access-list ACLIN permit tcp 192.168.Q.0 255.255.255.0 object-group FTPSERVERS o
bject-group MYSERVICES
access-list ACLIN permit tcp 192.168.Q.0 255.255.255.0 host 192.168.P.11 eq www (hitcnt=2)
access-list ACLIN permit tcp 192.168.Q.0 255.255.255.0 host 192.168.P.11 eq ftp (hitcnt=1)
access-list ACLIN permit tcp any object-group ALLSERVERS eq www
access-list ACLIN permit tcp any host 192.168.P.11 eq www (hitcnt=0)
access-list ACLIN permit tcp any host 192.168.P.10 eq www (hitcnt=0)
access-list ACLIN permit tcp any host 192.168.P.6 eq www (hitcnt=0)
access-list ACLIN permit tcp any host 192.168.P.7 eq www (hitcnt=0)
access-list ACLIN permit icmp any any object-group PING
access-list ACLIN permit icmp any any echo (hitcnt=0)
access-list ACLIN permit icmp any any echo-reply (hitcnt=0)
access-list ACLIN permit icmp any any unreachable (hitcnt=0)
access-list ACLIN deny ip any any (hitcnt=0)
access-list ACLDMZ; 3 elements
access-list ACLDMZ permit icmp any any object-group PING
access-list ACLDMZ permit icmp any any echo (hitcnt=0)
access-list ACLDMZ permit icmp any any echo-reply (hitcnt=0)
access-list ACLDMZ permit icmp any any unreachable (hitcnt=0)
```

## Task 6: Testing and Verifying the Inbound ACL

Complete the following steps to test the inbound ACL.

**Step 1.** Have a peer inside host ping the inside host:

```
C:\>ping 192.168.Q.10
Pinging 192.168.Q.10 with 32 bytes of data:
Reply from 192.168.Q.10: bytes=32 time<10ms TTL=128
Reply from 192.168.Q.10: bytes=32 time<10ms TTL=128
Reply from 192.168.Q.10: bytes=32 time<10ms TTL=128
Reply from 192.168.Q.10: bytes=32 time<10ms TTL=128
```

**Step 2.** Have a peer inside host ping the bastion host:

```
C:\>ping 192.168.Q.11
Pinging 192.168.Q.11 with 32 bytes of data:
Reply from 192.168.Q.11: bytes=32 time<10ms TTL=128
Reply from 192.168.Q.11: bytes=32 time<10ms TTL=128
Reply from 192.168.Q.11: bytes=32 time<10ms TTL=128
Reply from 192.168.Q.11: bytes=32 time<10ms TTL=128
```

**Step 3.** From the student PC, ping the bastion host:

```
C:\>ping 172.16.P.2
Pinging 172.16.P.2 with 32 bytes of data:
Reply from 172.16.P.2: bytes=32 time<10ms TTL=128
Reply from 172.16.P.2: bytes=32 time<10ms TTL=128
Reply from 172.16.P.2: bytes=32 time<10ms TTL=128
Reply from 172.16.P.2: bytes=32 time<10ms TTL=128
```

**Step 4.** From the student PC, ping the super server:

```
C:\>ping 172.26.26.50
Pinging 172.26.26.50 with 32 bytes of data:
Reply from 172.26.26.50: bytes=32 time<10ms TTL=128
Reply from 172.26.26.50: bytes=32 time<10ms TTL=128
Reply from 172.26.26.50: bytes=32 time<10ms TTL=128
Reply from 172.26.26.50: bytes=32 time<10ms TTL=128
```

**Step 5.** Test web access to the peer Pod bastion host by completing the following substeps. Access to the peer bastion host should be successful.

a. Open a web browser on the student PC.

b. Use the web browser to access the bastion host of the peer Pod group by entering **http://192.168.Q.11** (where Q = the peer Pod number).

**Step 6.** Test web access to the peer Pod inside host by completing the following substeps. Access to the peer Pod inside host should now be successful.

a. Open a web browser on the client PC.

b. Use the web browser to access the inside host of the peer Pod group by entering **http://192.168.Q.10** (where Q = the peer Pod number).

**Step 7.** From the FTP client, test FTP access to the peer Pod bastion host. Access to the peer bastion host via FTP should be successful:

**Start>Run>ftp 192.168.Q.11**

**Step 8.** From the FTP client, test FTP access to the peer Pod inside host. Access to the peer inside host via FTP should fail:

**Start>Run>ftp 192.168.Q.10**

**Step 9.** Display the ACLs again and observe the hit counts:

```
PixP(config)# show access-list
access-list ACLIN; 10 elements
access-list ACLIN permit tcp 192.168.Q.0 255.255.255.0 object-group FTPSERVERS object-group
MYSERVICES
access-list ACLIN permit tcp 192.168.Q.0 255.255.255.0 host 192.168.P.11 eq www (hitcnt=4)
access-list ACLIN permit tcp 192.168.Q.0 255.255.255.0 host 192.168.P.11 eq ftp (hitcnt=2)
access-list ACLIN permit tcp any object-group ALLSERVERS eq www
access-list ACLIN permit tcp any host 192.168.P.11 eq www (hitcnt=0)
access-list ACLIN permit tcp any host 192.168.P.10 eq www (hitcnt=2)
access-list ACLIN permit tcp any host 192.168.P.6 eq www (hitcnt=0)
access-list ACLIN permit tcp any host 192.168.P.7 eq www (hitcnt=0)
access-list ACLIN permit icmp any any object-group PING
access-list ACLIN permit icmp any any echo (hitcnt=12)
access-list ACLIN permit icmp any any echo-reply (hitcnt=4)
access-list ACLIN permit icmp any any unreachable (hitcnt=0)
access-list ACLIN deny ip any any (hitcnt=3)
access-list ACLDMZ; 3 elements
access-list ACLDMZ permit icmp any any object-group PING
access-list ACLDMZ permit icmp any any echo (hitcnt=0)
access-list ACLDMZ permit icmp any any echo-reply (hitcnt=8)
access-list ACLDMZ permit icmp any any unreachable (hitcnt=0)
```

## Review Questions

1. Describe the basic ACL usages guidelines for traffic passing through the PIX Security Appliance from a higher security area to lower security area.

_______________________________________________

_______________________________________________

_______________________________________________

_______________________________________________

2. Describe Turbo ACLs.

_______________________________________________

_______________________________________________

_______________________________________________

_______________________________________________

3. Describe the difference between conduits and ACLs.

4. Describe how the PIX Security Appliance supports VPNs.

5. Describe the difference between object groups and group objects.

## Chapter 10 Quiz Questions

1. Which of the following commands will filter Java applets through the PIX Security Appliance?
   - A. **ip inspect name** *inspection-name* **http java-list**
   - B. **ip inspect name java**
   - C. **filter java 80 0.0.0.0**
   - D. **ip inspect filter java**
2. Which of the following is not a valid object group type?
   - A. Network
   - B. Server
   - C. Service
   - D. Protocol
3. Which command will enable Turbo ACLs globally?
   - A. **access-list compiled**
   - B. **access list 102 complied**
   - C. **access-list global compile**
   - D. **enable turbo access-list**

4. If an access control list has both a **conduit** command and **access-list** and **access-group** commands, the **conduit** command takes precedence.

   A. True

   B. False

5. Denying ICMP unreachable messages can halt IPSec traffic.

   A. True

   B. False

6. What two commands are needed for the PIX Security Appliance to work with an URL filtering server?

   A. **url-server**

   B. **server-url**

   C. **filter url**

   D. **url filter**

7. In configuring an object group that will hold host IP addresses, which of the following commands is not a valid command?

   A. (config)# **object-group network** *WebAccess*

   B. (config)# **network-object host 10.1.1.14**

   C. (config-network)# **network-object host** *BobsPC*

   D. (config-network)# **network-object 10.1.1.32 255.255.255.224**

8. Which of the following are valid commands that can be used to nest group objects into the network object group *allservers*?

   A. (config-network)# **group-object SERVERS1**

   B. (config-service)# **group-object SERVERS2**

   C. (config-network)# **object-group SERVERS1**

   D. (config-network)# **group-object SERVERS3**

9. What would the command be to apply the object group *CLIENTS* TCP access anywhere to the access list called *ACLOUT*?

   ______________________________________________

10. A conduit applied to a single interface will affect all traffic, regardless of its security level.

   A. True

   B. False

# Chapter 11

## PIX Security Appliance AAA

This chapter covers authentication, authorization, and accounting (AAA) on the PIX Security Appliance. Remember that AAA can identify who the user is, what the user can do, and what the user did. Just like the router, the PIX Security Appliance can work with different TACACS+ and RADIUS AAA servers. Following a review of TACACS+ and RADIUS features that can be used with the PIX, students learn about using Cisco Secure Access Control Server (CSACS) with the PIX.

In this chapter, students learn how to configure the PIX Security Appliance to support authentication of the FTP, Telnet, and HTTP services. For support of non-FTP, Telnet, and HTTP traffic, virtual Telnet and virtual HTTP authentication is demonstrated. Also covered is authentication through the PIX Security Appliance consoles.

After the student learns how to configure different authentication methods, authorization and accounting is covered. The PIX Security Appliance uses TACACS+ authorization services to determine what resources the user can access. Also discussed is an overview of downloadable access control lists (ACLs). Downloadable ACLs are per-user ACLs that are downloaded from an AAA server to the PIX Security Appliance during authentication. To aid in the event that troubleshooting becomes necessary, we cover the commands that help verify and monitor the configuration.

With the increased availability of low-cost broadband access, a new feature in PIX software version 6.2 is for the PIX Security Appliance to act as a Point-to-Point Protocol over Ethernet (PPPoE) client. The student learns how to configure a PIX Security Appliance to support PPPoE in this chapter.

**Vocabulary Exercise**

PPPoE

___

___

**Lab Activities**

The topology figures and lab examples contain **P** and **Q** values. The **P** value in the addressing and naming scheme refers to *your* assigned Pod number.

The following are examples of determining P values:

- Pod2 is looking at a topology figure and is trying to determine the P values in the figure. In this scenario, the **P** values would equal **2**. 10.0.**P**.12 would become 10.0.**2**.12, 172.30.**P**.2 would become 172.30.**2**.2, and so on.
- Pod1 is looking at a topology figure and is trying to determine the P values in the figure. In this scenario, the **P** values would equal **1**. 10.0.**P**.12 would become 10.0.**1**.12, 172.30.**P**.2 would become 172.30.**1**.2, and so on.

In both examples, the P values are directly related to the Pod number of the team.

The **Q** value in the naming and addressing scheme is used when testing the security or connectivity with the peer team.

The following are examples of determining Q values:

- In a lab, Pod2 has been asked to test connectivity to their peer inside host at IP address 10.0.Q.12. In this scenario, 10.0.Q.12 would equal 10.0.1.12.
- In a lab, Pod1 has been asked to test connectivity to their peer inside host at IP address 10.0.Q.12. In this scenario, 10.0.Q.12 would equal 10.0.2.12.

In both examples, the Q value is directly related to the peer Pod number.

# Lab 11.3.5: Configure AAA on the PIX Security Appliance Using CSACS for Windows 2000

Estimated Time: 40 Minutes

Number of Team Members: Two teams with four students per team

## Objective

In this lab, students complete the following tasks:

- Install the CSACS for a Windows 2000 server.
- Add a user to the CSACS database.
- Identify the AAA server and protocol.
- Configure and test inbound authentication.
- Configure and test outbound authentication.
- Configure and test console access authentication.
- Configure and test virtual Telnet authentication.
- Change and test authentication timeouts and prompts.
- Configure and test authorization.
- Configure and test accounting.

## Overview

CSACS provides AAA services to network devices that function as AAA clients. These devices include a network access server, a PIX Security Appliance, and a router. An AAA client is any device that provides AAA client functionality and uses one of the AAA protocols supported by CSACS.

CSACS helps centralize access control and accounting, in addition to router and switch access management. With CSACS, network administrators can quickly administer accounts and globally change levels of service offerings for entire groups of users. Although the use of an external user database is optional, support for many popular user databases enables companies to put to use the working knowledge gained from and the investment already made in building their corporate user databases.

Figure 11-1 illustrates the network environment students create for this lab.

## Preparation

Begin with the standard lab topology in Figure 11-1 and verify the standard configuration on the Pod PIX Security Appliances. Access the PIX Security Appliance console port using the terminal emulator on the Student PC. If desired, save the PIX Security Appliance configuration to a text file for later analysis.

**Figure 11-1 Lab 11.3.5 Network Topology**

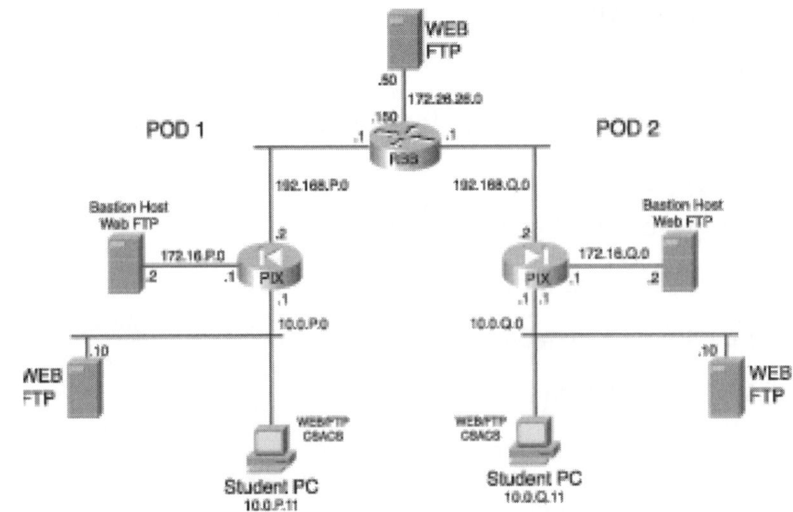


## Tools and Resources

To complete the lab, the standard lab topology is required:

- Two Pod PIX Security Appliances
- Two student PCs
- One server
- Backbone switch and router
- Two console cables and HyperTerminal

## Additional Materials

Students can use the following links for more information on the objectives covered in this lab:

- http://www.cisco.com/warp/public/cc/pd/sqsw/sq/prodlit/sacsd_ds.htm
- http://www.cisco.com/warp/public/cc/pd/sqsw/sq/prodlit/acsq_qp.htm

Additional information on configuring firewalls can be found in *Cisco Secure PIX Security Appliances*, by David Chapman and Andy Fox (published by Cisco Press; ISBN 1587050358).

## Command List

Table 11-1 lists the commands used throughout this lab. Refer to this list if you need any assistance during the lab.

**Table 11-1 Lab 11.3.5 Command List**

| Command | Description |
|---|---|
| **aaa accounting include** \| **exclude** *acctg_service* **inbound** \| **outbound** \| *if_name local_ip local_mask foreign_ip foreign_mask group_tag* | Enables, disables, or displays LOCAL, TACACS+, or RADIUS user accounting (on a server designated by the **aaa-server** command). Configuration mode. |

| Command | Description |
|---|---|
| **aaa authentication include \| exclude** *authen_service* **inbound \| outbound \|** *if_name local_ip local_mask foreign_ip foreign_mask group_tag* | Enables, disables, or displays LOCAL, TACACS+, or RADIUS user authentication (on a server designated by the **aaa-server** command)<br>The **aaa authentication** command has been modified to support PDM authentication.<br>(Configuration mode.) |
| **aaa authorization include \| exclude** *author_service* **inbound \| outbound \|** *if_name local_ip local_mask foreign_ip foreign_mask* | Enables or disables LOCAL or TACACS+ user authorization services. Configuration mode. |
| **aaa-server** *group_tag if_name* **host** *server_ip key* **timeout** *seconds* | Specifies an AAA server. Configuration mode. |
| **auth-prompt** [**accept** \| **reject** \| **prompt**] *string* | Changes the AAA challenge text. Configuration mode. |
| **clear aaa** | Removes **aaa** command statements from the configuration |
| **clear aaa-server** | Removes **aaa-server** command statements from the configuration |
| **clear uauth** | Removes an **auth-prompt** command statement from the configuration |
| **show aaa** | Displays the AAA authentication configuration |
| **show aaa-server** | Displays AAA server configuration |
| **show auth-prompt** | Displays authentication challenge, reject, or acceptance prompt |
| **show uauth** | Displays one or all currently authenticated users, the host IP to which they are bound, and, if applicable, any cached IP and port authorization information |
| **timeout** [**xlate** [*hh:mm:ss*]] [**conn** [*hh:mm:ss*]] [**half-closed** [*hh:mm:ss*]] [**udp** [*hh:mm:ss*]] [**rpc** [*hh:mm:ss*]] [**h323** [*hh:mm:ss*]] [**sip** [*hh:mm:ss*]] [**sip_media** [*hh:mm:ss*]][**uauth** [*hh:mm:ss*] [**absolute** \| **inactivity**]] | Sets the maximum idle time duration. Configuration mode. |

## Task 1: Installing CSACS for a Windows 2000 Server

If CSACS is already installed, skip Task 1 and proceed to Task 2. If CSACS is not installed, complete the following steps to install CSACS on the Windows 2000 server.

**Step 1.** To install CSACS on the student PC from the files on the hard drive, open the Cisco Secure ACS v3.0 folder on the desktop, and double-click the **setup.exe** program.

**Step 2.** Click **OK** in the Warning window.

**Step 3.** Click **Accept** to accept the Software License Agreement. The Welcome window opens.

**Step 4.** Read the Welcome frame. Click **Next** to continue. The Before You Begin window opens.

**Step 5.** Read and then select all four check boxes for the items in the Before You Begin frame. This is a reminder of tasks that should be completed prior to installation. Click **Next** to continue. The Choose Destination Location window opens.

**Step 6.** Use the default installation folder indicated in the Choose Destination Location windows by clicking **Next** to continue. The Authentication Database Configuration windows open.

**Step 7.** Verify that only the CSACS database is selected in the Authentication Database Configuration frame. Click **Next** to continue.

**Step 8.** Enter the following information in the Cisco Secure ACS Network Access Server Details frame:

- Authenticate users: TACACS+ (Cisco IOS)
- Access server name: PixP (where P = the Pod number)
- Access server IP address: 10.0.P.1 (where P = the Pod number)
- Windows 2000 Server IP address: For a local lab: 10.0.P.11 (where P = the Pod number)
- TACACS+ or RADIUS key: secretkey

**Step 9.** Click **Next** to start the file installation process.

**Step 10.** Select all six items displayed in the Advanced Options frame. Click **Next** to continue.

**Step 11.** Verify that **Enable Log-in Monitoring** is already selected in the Active Service Monitoring frame. Click **Next** to continue.

**Step 12.** De-select **Yes, I want to configure IOS software now**.

**Step 13.** Click **Next** to continue.

**Step 14.** Verify that the following are already selected in the Cisco Secure ACS Service Initiation frame:

- Yes, I want to start the Cisco Secure ACS Service now.
- Yes, I want Setup to launch the Cisco Secure ACS Administrator from my browser following installation.

**Step 15.** De-select Yes, I want to review the Readme file.

Step 16. Click **Next** to start the CSACS service.

Step 17. Read the Setup Complete frame and click **Finish** to end the installation wizard and start the web browser with CSACS.

**Task 2: Verifying Users in the CSACS Database**

Complete the following steps to verify users in the CSACS database.

**Step 1.** The CSACS interface should now be displayed in the web browser. Click **User Setup** to open the User Setup interface.

**Step 2.** To view the list of current users, click **Find**. The User List will appear on the right side of the interface.

Is there an entry for **aaauser**?

---

If there is an entry for **aaauser**, proceed to Task 3. If there is no entry for **aaauser**, continue to Step 3 to add a user in the CSACS database.

**Step 3.** Add a user by entering **aaauser** in the user field.

**Step 4.** Click **Add/Edit** to go into the User Information Edit window.

**Step 5.** Give the user a password by entering **aaapass** in both the Password and Confirm Password fields.

**Step 6.** Click **Submit** to add the new user to the CSACS database. Wait for the interface to return to the User Setup main window.

**Task 3: Verifying the AAA Client**

Complete the following steps to verify the existing AAA clients:

**Step 1.** The Cisco Secure ACS interface should be displayed in the web browser. Click **Network Configuration** to open the Network Configuration Setup interface. The Network Configuration Setup interface provides the ability to search, add, and delete AAA clients, AAA servers, and proxy distribution tables.

**Step 2.** The table at the top of the window displays all AAA clients that have been configured.

Is there an AAA client entry for PixP?

---

If there is an entry for PixP in the AAA client table, proceed to Task 4. If there is no entry for PixP, continue to Step 3 to configure PixP as an AAA client.

**Step 3.** To add PixP as an AAA client, click Add Entry. Enter the following information in the text boxes:

- AAA Client Hostname: **PixP**
- AAA Client IP Address: **10.0.P.1**
- Key: **secretkey**

**Step 4.** Verify that the authentication is TACACS+ (Cisco IOS). If any of check boxes are selected, uncheck them and press **Submit + Restart**.

**Step 5.** After a few moments, the Network Configuration Setup interface will refresh.

Is the PixP AAA client displayed?

---

### Task 4: Identifying the AAA Server and Protocol

Complete the following steps to identify the AAA server and the AAA protocol on the PIX Security Appliance.

**Step 1.** Create a group tag called MYTACACS and assign the TACACS+ protocol to it:

```
PixP(config)# aaa-server MYTACACS protocol tacacs+
```

**Step 2.** Assign the CSACS IP address and the encryption key secretkey:

```
PixP(config)# aaa-server MYTACACS (inside) host insidehost secretkey
```

**Step 3.** Verify the configuration:

```
PixP(config)# show aaa-server
aaa-server TACACS+ protocol tacacs+
aaa-server RADIUS protocol radius
aaa-server LOCAL protocol local
aaa-server MYTACACS protocol tacacs+
aaa-server MYTACACS (inside) host insidehost secretkey timeout 10
```

### Task 5: Configuring and Testing Inbound Authentication

Complete the following steps to enable the use of inbound authentication on the PIX Security Appliance.

**Step 1.** Configure the PIX Security Appliance to require authentication for all inbound traffic:

```
PixP(config)# aaa authentication include any inbound 0 0 0 0 MYTACACS
```

**Step 2.** Verify the configuration:

```
PixP(config)# show aaa authentication
aaa authentication include tcp/0 outside 0.0.0.0 0.0.0.0 0.0.0.0 0.0.0.0 MYTACACS
```

**Step 3.** Enable console logging of all messages:

```
PixP(config)# logging console debug
```

If the web browser is open, close it. Choose **File** > **Close** from the web browser's menu.

**Step 4.** Test a peer Pod inbound web authentication. Open the web browser, and go to a peer's demilitarized zone (DMZ) web server:

**http://192.168.Q.11**

(where Q = the peer Pod number)

**Step 5.** When the web browser prompts, enter **aaauser** for the username and **aaapass** for the password. On the PIX Security Appliance console, the following should be displayed:

```
302013: Built outbound TCP connection 126 for outside:192.168.Q.11/80 (192.168.Q.11/80) to
  inside:10.0.P.11/1337 (192.168.P.10/1337)
304001: 10.0.P.11 Accessed URL 192.168.Q.11:/
302014: Teardown TCP connection 126 for outside:192.168.Q.11/80 to inside:10.0.P.11/1337 duration
  0:00:36 bytes 359 TCP FINs
302013: Built outbound TCP connection 127 for outside:192.168.Q.11/80 (192.168.Q.11/80) to
  inside:10.0.P.11/1339 (192.168.P.10/1339)
```

```
304001: 10.0.P.11 Accessed URL 192.168.Q.11:/
302013: Built outbound TCP connection 128 for outside:192.168.Q.11/80 (192.168.Q.11/80) to
  inside:10.0.P.11/1340 (192.168.P.10/1340)
302013: Built outbound TCP connection 129 for outside:192.168.Q.11/80 (192.168.Q.11/80) to
  inside:10.0.P.11/1341 (192.168.P.10/1341)
302013: Built outbound TCP connection 130 for outside:192.168.Q.11/80 (192.168.Q.11/80) to
  inside:10.0.P.11/1342 (192.168.P.10/1342)
302014: Teardown TCP connection 127 for outside:192.168.Q.11/80 to inside:10.0.P.11/1339 duration
  0:00:03 bytes 1328 TCP FINs
304001: 10.0.P.11 Accessed URL 192.168.Q.11:/CISCOLOGO.GIF
304001: 10.0.P.11 Accessed URL 192.168.Q.11:/NETSENSOR.JPG
304001: 10.0.P.11 Accessed URL 192.168.Q.11:/PIX_PROD.JPG
302014: Teardown TCP connection 128 for outside:192.168.Q.11/80 to inside:10.0.P.11/1340 duration
  0:01:00 bytes 1734 TCP Reset-I
302014: Teardown TCP connection 129 for outside:192.168.Q.11/80 to inside:10.0.P.11/1341 duration
  0:01:00 bytes 11926 TCP Reset-I
302014: Teardown TCP connection 130 for outside:192.168.Q.11/80 to inside:10.0.P.11/1342 duration
  0:01:00 bytes 7323 TCP Reset-I
302010: 1 in use, 6 most used
```

**Step 6.** After a peer successfully authenticates to the PIX Security Appliance, display the PIX Security Appliance authentication statistics:

```
PixP(config)# show uauth
Current Most Seen
Authenticated Users    1    1
Authen In Progress     0    1
user 'aaauser' at 192.168.Q.10, authenticated
absolute timeout: 0:05:00
inactivity timeout: 0:00:00
```

What does the value in absolute timeout mean?

______________________________________________________________________

______________________________________________________________________

## Task 6: Configuring and Testing Outbound Authentication

Complete the following steps to enable the use of outbound authentication on the PIX Security Appliance.

**Step 1.** Configure the PIX Security Appliance to require authentication for all outbound traffic:

```
PixP(config)# aaa authentication include any outbound 0 0 0 0 MYTACACS
```

**Step 2.** Verify the configuration:

```
PixP(config)# show aaa authentication
aaa authentication include tcp/0 outside 0.0.0.0 0.0.0.0 0.0.0.0 0.0.0.0 MYTACACS
aaa authentication include tcp/0 inside 0.0.0.0 0.0.0.0 0.0.0.0 0.0.0.0 MYTACACS
```

**Step 3.** Test FTP outbound authentication from the Windows 2000 server:

```
C:\> ftp 172.26.26.50
Connected to 172.26.26.50
220-FTP server : (user 'aaauser')
220
User (172.26.26.50:(none)): aaauser@ftpuser
331-Password:
331
Password: aaapass@ftppass
230-220 172.26.26.50 FTP server ready.
331-Password required for ftpuser.
230-User ftpuser logged in.
230
ftp>
```

On the PIX Security Appliance console, the following should be displayed:

```
109001: Auth start for user '???' from 10.0.P.11/3142 to 172.26.26.50/21
109011: Authen Session Start: user 'aaauser', sid 13
109005: Authentication succeeded for user 'aaauser' from 10.0.P.11/3142 to 172.26.26.50/21 on
interface inside
302013: Built outbound TCP connection 218 for outside:172.26.26.50/21
(172.26.26.50/21) to inside:10.0.P.11/3142 (192.168.P.10/3142) (aaauser)
```

**Step 4.** Display authentication statistics on the PIX Security Appliance:

```
PixP(config)# show uauth
Current Most Seen
Authenticated Users    2    2
Authen In Progress     0    1
user 'aaauser' at insidehost, authenticated
absolute timeout: 0:05:00
inactivity timeout: 0:00:00
user 'aaauser' at 192.168.Q.10, authenticated
absolute timeout: 0:05:00
inactivity timeout: 0:00:00
```

**Step 5.** Clear the uauth timer:

```
PixP(config)# clear uauth
PixP(config)# show uauth
Current Most Seen
Authenticated Users    0    2
Authen In Progress     0     2
```

If the web browser is open, close it. Choose **File** > **Exit** from the web browser's menu.

**Step 6.** Test web outbound authentication. Open the web browser and go to the following URL:

**http://172.26.26.50**

**Step 7.** When the prompt appears asking for a username and password, enter **aaauser** as the username and **aaapass** as the password:

User Name: **aaauser**

Password: **aaapass**

**Step 8.** Display authentication statistics on the PIX Security Appliance:

```
PixP(config)# show uauth
Current Most Seen
Authenticated Users    1    1
Authen In Progress     0    1
user 'aaauser' at insidehost, authenticated
absolute timeout: 0:05:00
inactivity timeout: 0:00:00
```

### Task 7: Configuring and Testing Console Access Authentication

Complete the following steps to enable console Telnet authentication at the PIX Security Appliance.

**Step 1.** Configure the PIX Security Appliance to require authentication for Telnet console connections:

```
PixP(config)# aaa authentication telnet console MYTACACS
```

**Step 2.** Verify the configuration:

```
PixP(config)# show aaa authentication
aaa authentication include tcp/0 outside 0.0.0.0 0.0.0.0 0.0.0.0 0.0.0.0 MYTACACS
aaa authentication include tcp/0 inside 0.0.0.0 0.0.0.0 0.0.0.0 0.0.0.0 MYTACACS
aaa authentication include tcp/0 0.0.0.0 0.0.0.0 0.0.0.0 0.0.0.0 MYTACACS
```

**Step 3.** Configure the PIX Security Appliance to allow console Telnet logins:

```
PixP(config)# telnet insidehost 255.255.255.255 inside
```

**Step 4.** Verify the configuration:

```
PixP(config)# show telnet
insidehost 255.255.255.255 inside
```

**Step 5.** Clear the uauth timer:

```
PixP(config)# clear uauth
PixP(config)# show uauth
Current Most Seen
Authenticated Users 0 2
Authen In Progress 0 1
```

**Step 6.** Save the configuration:

```
PixP(config)# write memory
```

**Step 7.** Telnet to the PIX Security Appliance console:

```
C:\> telnet 10.0.P.1
Username: aaauser
Password: aaapass
Type help or '?' for a list of available commands.
PixP>
```

On the PIX Security Appliance console, the following should be displayed:

```
307002: Permitted Telnet login session from 10.0.P.11
111006: Console Login from aaauser at console
```

### Task 8: Configuring and Testing Virtual Telnet Authentication

Complete the following steps to enable the use of authentication with virtual Telnet on the PIX Security Appliance.

**Step 1.** Configure the PIX Security Appliance to accept authentication to a virtual Telnet service:

```
PixP(config)# virtual telnet 192.168.P.5
```

**Step 2.** Verify the virtual Telnet configuration:

```
PixP(config)# show virtual telnet
virtual telnet 192.168.P.5
```

**Step 3.** Clear the uauth timer:

```
PixP(config)# clear uauth
PixP(config)# show uauth
Current Most Seen
Authenticated Users     0     0
Authen In Progress      0     1
```

**Step 4.** Telnet to the virtual Telnet IP address to authenticate from the Windows 2000 server:

```
C:\> telnet 192.168.P.5
LOGIN Authentication
Username: aaauser
Password: aaapass
Authentication Successful
```

Why would a virtual Telnet IP address be created on the PIX Security Appliance?

_______________________________________________

_______________________________________________

If the web browser is open, close it. Choose **File** and then **Close** from the web browser's menu.

**Step 5.** Test the authentication. Open the web browser and enter the following in the URL field:

**http://172.26.26.50**

There should be no authentication prompt.

**Step 6.** Clear the uauth timer:

```
PixP(config)# clear uauth
PixP(config)# show uauth
Current Most Seen
Authenticated Users     0    1
Authen In Progress      0    1
```

If the web browser is open, close it. Choose **File** and then **Close** from the web browser's menu.

**Step 7.** Test that there is no authentication, and that there is no need to reauthenticate. Open the web browser and enter the following in the URL field:

**http://172.26.26.50**

**Step 8.** When prompted, enter **aaauser** for the username and **aaapass** for the password.

Why was authentication not needed this time?

______________________________________________________________________

______________________________________________________________________

### Task 9: Changing and Testing Authentication Timeouts and Prompts

Complete the following steps to change the authentication timeouts and prompts.

**Step 1.** View the current uauth timeout settings:

```
PixP(config)# show timeout uauth
timeout uauth 0:05:00 absolute
```

**Step 2.** Set the uauth absolute timeout to 3 hours:

```
PixP(config)# timeout uauth 3 absolute
```

**Step 3.** Set the uauth inactivity timeout to 30 minutes:

```
PixP(config)# timeout uauth 0:30 inactivity
```

**Step 4.** Verify the new uauth timeout settings:

```
PixP(config)# show timeout uauth
timeout uauth 3:00:00 absolute uauth 0:30:00 inactivity
```

**Step 5.** View the current authentication prompt settings:

```
PixP(config)# show auth-prompt
```

Nothing should be displayed.

**Step 6.** Set the prompt that users get when authenticating:

```
PixP(config)# auth-prompt prompt Please Authenticate
```

**Step 7.** Set the message that users get when successfully authenticating:

```
PixP(config)# auth-prompt accept You've been Authenticated
```

**Step 8.** Set the message that users get when their authentication is rejected:

```
PixP(config)# auth-prompt reject Authentication Failed, Try Again
```

**Step 9.** Verify the new prompt settings:

```
PixP(config)# show auth-prompt
auth-prompt prompt Please Authenticate
auth-prompt accept You've been Authenticated
auth-prompt reject Authentication Failed, Try Again
```

**Step 10.** Clear the uauth timer:

```
PixP(config)# clear uauth
PixP(config)# show uauth
Current Most Seen
Authenticated Users     0    1
Authen In Progress      0    1
```

**Step 11.** Telnet to the virtual Telnet IP address to test the new authentication prompts.

From the Windows 2000 server, enter the following:

```
C:\> telnet 192.168.P.5
LOGIN Authentication
Please Authenticate
Username: wronguser
Password: Authentication Failed, Try Again
LOGIN Authentication
Please Authenticate
Username: aaauser
Password: aaapass
You've been Authenticated
Authentication SUccessful
```

## Task 10: Configuring and Testing Authorization

Complete the following steps to enable the use of authorization on the PIX Security Appliance.

**Step 1.** Configure the PIX Security Appliance to require authorization for all outbound FTP traffic:

```
PixP(config)# aaa authorization include ftp outbound 0 0 0 0 MYTACACS
```

**Step 2.** Configure the PIX Security Appliance to require authorization for all outbound ICMP traffic:

```
PixP(config)# aaa authorization include http outbound 0 0 0 0 MYTACACS
```

What are some of the benefits of implementing authorization? Drawbacks?

______________________________________________________________________

______________________________________________________________________

**Step 3.** Verify the configuration:

```
PixP(config)# show aaa authorization
aaa authorization include ftp inside 0.0.0.0 0.0.0.0 0.0.0.0 0.0.0.0 MYTACACS
aaa authorization include http inside 0.0.0.0 0.0.0.0 0.0.0.0 0.0.0.0 MYTACACS
```

**Step 4.** Test FTP authorization failure from the Windows 2000 server:

```
C:\> ftp 172.26.26.50
Connected to 172.26.26.50
220-FTP Server : (user 'aaaserver')
220
User (172.26.26.50:(none)): aaauser@ftpuser
331-Password:
331
Password: aaapass@ftppass
530
Login failed
```

On the PIX Security Appliance console, the following should be displayed:

```
109001: Auth start for user 'aaauser' from 10.0.P.11/4442 to 172.2 6.26.50/21
109008: Authorization denied for user 'aaauser' from 10.0.P.11/4442 to 172.26.26.50/21 on
  interface inside
109001: Auth start for user '???' from 10.0.P.11/1867 to 172.26.26.50/21
109011: Authen Session Start: user 'aaauser', sid 5
109005: Authentication succeeded for user 'aaauser' from 10.0.P.11/1867 to 172.26.26.50/21 on
  interface inside
109008: Authorization denied for user 'aaauser' from 10.0.P.11/1867 to 172.26.26.50/21 on
  interface inside
```

```
106015: Deny TCP (no connection) from 10.0.P.11/1867 to 172.26.26.50/21 flags PS
H ACK on interface inside
106015: Deny TCP (no connection) from 10.0.P.11/1867 to 172.26.26.50/21 flags FI
N ACK on interface inside
```

**Step 5.** Test web authorization failure. Open the web browser and go to the following URL:

**http://172.26.26.50**

**Step 6.** When prompted for a username and password, enter aaauser as the username and aaapass as the password:

User Name: **aaauser**

Password: **aaapass**

On the PIX Security Appliance console, the following should be displayed:

```
109001: Auth start for user 'aaauser' from 10.0.P.11/1951 to 172.26.26.50/80
109008: Authorization denied for user 'aaauser' from 10.0.P.11/1951 to 172.26.26.50/80 on
interface inside
109001: Auth start for user 'aaauser' from 10.0.P.11/1951 to 172.26.26.50/80
109008: Authorization denied for user 'aaauser' from 10.0.P.11/1951 to 172.26.26.50/80 on
interface inside
109001: Auth start for user 'aaauser' from 10.0.P.11/1951 to 172.26.26.50/80
109008: Authorization denied for user 'aaauser' from 10.0.P.11/1951 to 172.26.26.50/80 on
interface inside
302010: 0 in use, 6 most used
```

**Step 7.** Click **Group Setup** to open the Group Setup interface.

**Step 8.** Choose **0: Default Group (1 user)** from the Group drop-down menu.

**Step 9.** Verify that the user belongs to the selected group. Click **Users in Group** to display the users under that group. The following information should be shown for the user:

- User: **aaauser**
- Status: **Enabled**
- Group: **Default Group (1 user)**

**Step 10.** Click **Edit Settings** to go to the Group Settings interface for the group.

**Step 11.** Scroll down in Group Settings until Shell Command Authorization Set is displayed, and select the **Per Group Command Authorization** button.

**Step 12.** Select the **Command** check box.

**Step 13.** Enter **ftp** in the Command field.

**Step 14.** Enter **permit 172.26.26.50** in the Arguments field.

**Step 15.** Click **Submit + Restart** to save the changes and restart CSACS. Wait for the interface to return to the Group Setup main window.

**Step 16.** Test FTP authorization success from the Windows 2000 server:

```
C:\> ftp 172.26.26.50
Connected to 172.26.26.50
220-FTP Server (user 'aaauser')
220
User (172.26.26.50:(none)): aaauser@ftpuser
331-Password:
331
Password: aaapass@ftppass
230-220 172.26.26.50 FTP server ready.
331-Password required for ftpuser
```

```
230-User ftpuser logged in.
230
ftp>
```

On the PIX Security Appliance console, the following should be displayed:

```
109001: Auth start for user 'aaauser' from 10.0.P.11/3535 to 172.26.26.50/21
109001: Auth start for user 'aaauser' from 10.0.P.11/3566 to 172.26.26.50/21
109011: Authen Session Start: user 'aaauser', sid 4
109007: Authorization permitted for user 'aaauser' from 10.0.P.11/3566 to 172.26.26.50/21 on
interface inside
302013: Built outbound TCP connection 6 for outside:172.26.26.50/21
(172.26.26.50/21) to inside:10.0.P.11/3566 (192.168.P.10/3566) (aaauser)
```

### Task 11: Configuring and Testing Accounting

If CSACS 3.0 is used to perform this lab, viewing the accounting records will not be possible as directed in this task. CSACS 3.0 does not populate the active.csv file.

Complete the following steps to enable the use of accounting on the PIX Security Appliance.

**Step 1.** Configure the PIX Security Appliance to perform accounting for all outbound traffic:

```
PixP(config)# aaa accounting include any outbound 0 0 0 0 MYTACACS
```

**Step 2.** Verify the configuration:

```
PixP(config)# show aaa accounting
aaa accounting include tcp/0 inside 0.0.0.0 0.0.0.0 0.0.0.0 0.0.0.0 MYTACACS
```

**Step 3.** Clear the uauth timer:

```
PixP(config)# clear uauth
PixP(config)# show uauth
Current Most Seen
Authenticated Users    0    1
Authen In Progress     0    1
```

**Step 4.** Test FTP outbound accounting from the Windows 2000 server:

```
C:\> ftp 172.26.26.50
Connected to 172.26.26.50
220-Please Authenticate :
220
User (172.26.26.50:(none)): aaauser@ftpuser
331-Password:
331
Password: aaapass@ftppass
230-220 172.26.26.50 FTP server ready.
331-Password required for ftpuser
230-User ftpuser logged in.
230
ftp>
```

**Step 5.** View the accounting records. On Cisco Secure ACS, click **Reports and Activity** to open the Reports and Activity interface.

**Step 6.** Click the **TACACS+ Accounting** link.

**Step 7.** Click the **TACACS+ Accounting** ***active.csv*** link to open the accounting records.

The following should be displayed.

| Date | Time | Username | Group-Name | Caller-ID | Acct-Flags | *** | NAS Portname | NAS IP Address | cmd |
|---|---|---|---|---|---|---|---|---|---|
| 4/27/00 | 11:14:45 | aaauser | Default Group | 10.0.P.11 | start | *** | PIX | 10.0.P.1 | ftp |

**Step 8.** Disable AAA by entering the following command:

```
PixP(config)# clear aaa
```

**Step 9.** Remove the aaa-server commands from the configuration:

```
PixP(config)# clear aaa-server
```

**Step 10.** Turn off the logging:

```
PixP(config)# no logging console debug
```

## Review Questions

1. Describe AAA.

_______________________________________________

_______________________________________________

_______________________________________________

_______________________________________________

2. Describe cut-through proxy operation.

_______________________________________________

_______________________________________________

_______________________________________________

_______________________________________________

3. Describe RADIUS.

_______________________________________________

_______________________________________________

_______________________________________________

_______________________________________________

4. Describe virtual Telnet.

_______________________________________________

_______________________________________________

_______________________________________________

_______________________________________________

5. Describe downloadable ACLs.

_______________________________________________

_______________________________________________

_______________________________________________

_______________________________________________

## Chapter 11 Quiz Questions

1. The PIX Security Appliance supports authorization with which of the following?

   A. NAS

   B. TACACS+

   C. RADIUS

   D. HTTP

2. A remote user can authenticate to the PIX Security Appliance using one of three services. Which of the following is not one of those services?

   A. Console

   B. FTP

   C. HTTP

   D. Telnet

3. The PIX Security Appliance uses which ports for RADIUS?

   A. 1645

   B. 1646

   C. 1812

   D. 1813

4. Which of the following commands is used to display a text message when users first try logging on to the firewall via Telnet access?

   A. (config-line)# **auth-prompt accept** *text string*

   B. (config)# **auth-prompt reject** *text string*

   C. (config)# **auth-prompt prompt** *text string*

   D. (config)# **auth-prompt accept** *text string*

5. What AAA service is configured to keep track of what resources a user is accessing?

   A. Authentication

   B. Authorization

   C. Accounting

   D. Auditing

6. You are configuring the firewall to require authentication for console access. The company's security policy requires all console access to use SSH. What command will require authentication to access the firewall?

   A. (config)# **aaa authentication console ssh** *group_tag*

   B. (config-line)# **aaa authentication ssh console** *group_tag*

C. (config)# **aaa authentication enable ssh** *group_tag*

D. (config)# **aaa authentication ssh console** *group_tag*

7. You want to modify the existing authentication timeouts on the PIX to a lower time limit. The translation slot idle timer value has been set to 6 minutes. Which of the following will be valid commands that can be entered at this time?

A. (config)# **uauth timeout 0:10:00 absolute**

B. (config)# **timeout uauth 0:05:00 absolute uuath 0:04:00 inactivity**

C. (config)# **uauth timeout 0:08:00 absolute**

D. (config)# **timeout uauth 0:05:00 inactivity**

8. What are the two commands needed to configure authentication using TACACS+ with the AAA server group *AAASRV01* server located in the DMZ with IP address 172.16.1.5?

______________________________________________________________________________

______________________________________________________________________________

9. What IOS commands are required to enable PPPoE on the PIX Security Appliance?

A. (config)# **vpdn group**

B. (config)# **vpdn username**

C. (config)# **ip address pppoe**

B. (config)# **enable pppoe**

10. PPPoE supports what authentication protocols?

A. MS-CHAP

B. DES

C. SHA-1

D. AH

# Chapter 12

## PIX Advanced Protocols and Intrusion Detection

The topics in this chapter help you improve the security of a network. Advanced protocol handling is done using the **fixup protocol** command. The **fixup protocol** command acts as an application-aware agent by monitoring the data stream to prevent protocol violations.

By watching for these protocols, the PIX Security Appliance can pass these packets by temporarily permitting the connection. When the connection is no longer needed, the connection is closed. This procedure is increasingly helpful as more networks start to implement greater multimedia use and Voice over IP (VoIP). These applications pose a special challenge because their nature requires the use of TCP and User Datagram Protocol (UDP) ports together, or the assigning of ports dynamically.

Another way the PIX Security Appliance can help in protecting the network from attack is through the use of attack guards. By using these different guards, an administrator can increase the protection of the network. Here is the concept of defense-in-depth. You cannot protect the network from every type of attack; however, the more layers an attacker has to go through, the longer the attack takes and the higher the chance that the attack will be discovered.

The PIX Security Appliance can provide another layer—intrusion detection—in the defense-in-depth approach. Offering basic intrusion detection capabilities, the PIX Security Appliance can match traffic against intrusion detection system (IDS) signatures and can be configured to take the appropriate action.

Finally, students learn how to configure the PIX Security Appliance to log messages to a Syslog server and use the Simple Network Management Protocol (SNMP) to monitor system events.

**Vocabulary Exercise**

H.323

______________________________________________________________________

______________________________________________________________________

ILS

______________________________________________________________________

______________________________________________________________________

rsh

______________________________________________________________________

______________________________________________________________________

RTP

______________________________________________________________________

______________________________________________________________________

RTSP

______________________________________________________________________

______________________________________________________________________

SIP

______________________________________________________________________

______________________________________________________________________

Skinny

______________________________________________________________________

______________________________________________________________________

SQL

______________________________________________________________________

______________________________________________________________________

SQL*NET

______________________________________________________________________

______________________________________________________________________

**Lab Activities**

The topology figures and lab examples contain **P** and **Q** values. The **P** value in the addressing and naming scheme refers to *your* assigned Pod number.

The following are examples of determining P values:

- Pod2 is looking at a topology figure and is trying to determine the P values in the figure. In this scenario the P values would equal 2. 10.0.P.12 would become 10.0.2.12, 172.30.P.2 would become 172.30.2.2, and so on.
- Pod1 is looking at a topology figure and is trying to determine the P values in the figure. In this scenario, the P values would equal 1. 10.0.P.12 would become 10.0.1.12, 172.30.P.2 would become 172.30.1.2, and so on.

In both examples, the P values are directly related to the Pod number of the team.

The **Q** value in the naming and addressing scheme is used when testing the security or connectivity with the peer team.

The following are examples of determining Q values:

- In a lab, Pod2 has been asked to test connectivity to their peer inside host at IP address 10.0.Q.12. In this scenario, 10.0.Q.12 would equal 10.0.1.12.
- In a lab, Pod1 has been asked to test connectivity to their peer inside host at IP address 10.0.Q.12. In this scenario, 10.0.Q.12 would equal 10.0.2.12.

In both examples, the Q value is directly related to the peer Pod number.

# Lab 12.1.7: Configure and Test Advanced Protocol Handling on the Cisco PIX Security Appliance

Estimated Time: 20 Minutes

Number of Team Members: Two teams with four students per team

## Objective

In this lab, students complete the following tasks:

- Display the fixup protocol configurations.
- Change the fixup protocol configurations.
- Test the outbound FTP fixup protocol.
- Test the inbound FTP fixup protocol.
- Set the fixup protocols to the default settings.

## Overview

Some applications embed addressing information into the application data stream and negotiate randomly picked TCP or UDP port numbers or IP addresses. In these cases, application inspection, also known as fixup, must be performed. This ensures that only proper and expected traffic is allowed through the filter inspection and that it is done in a secure manner. Application inspection is configured with the **fixup** command. The **fixup** function on a PIX Security Appliance enables a network administrator to configure specific ports used by various applications. In this lab, students will configure **fixup** for FTP.

Figure 12-1 illustrates the network environment students create for this lab.

**Figure 12-1 Lab 12.1.7 Network Topology**

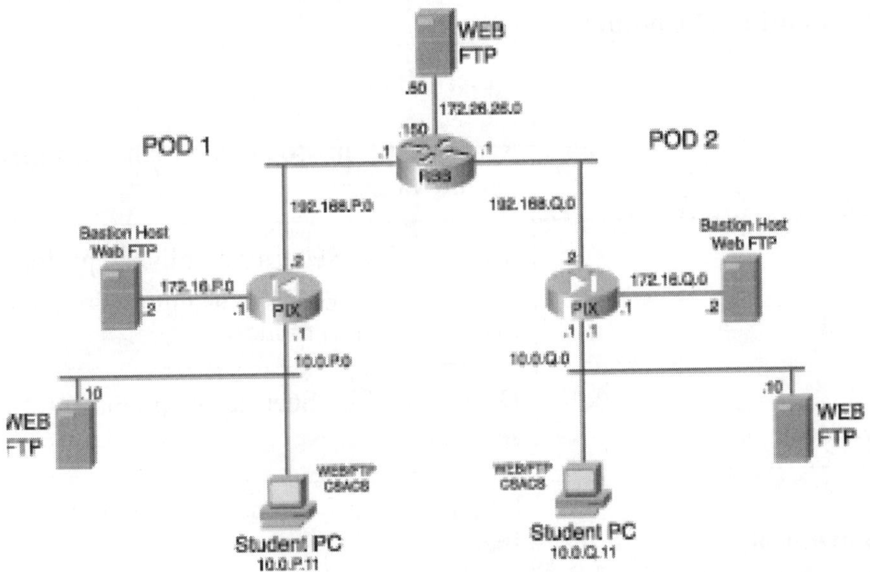

## Preparation

Begin with the standard lab topology in Figure 12-1 and verify the standard configuration on the Pod PIX Security Appliances. Access the PIX Security Appliance console port using the terminal emulator on the student PC. If desired, save the PIX Security Appliance configuration to a text file for later analysis.

## Tools and Resources

To complete the lab, the standard lab topology is required:

- Two Pod PIX Security Appliances
- Two student PCs
- One server
- Backbone switch and router
- Two console cables and HyperTerminal

## Additional Materials

Further information about the objectives covered in this lab can be found at this website:

- http://www.cisco.com/univercd/cc/td/doc/product/iaabu/pix/pix_sw/v_62/config/fixup.pdf.

Additional information on configuring firewalls can be found in *Cisco Secure PIX Firewalls*, by David Chapman and Andy Fox (published by Cisco Press; ISBN 1587050358).

## Command List

Table 12-1 lists the commands used throughout this lab. Refer to this list if you need any assistance during the lab.

**Table 12-1 Lab 12.1.7 Command List**

| Command | Description |
|---|---|
| **clear fixup** | Resets **fixup protocol** command statements to their default values |
| **fixup protocol** | Modifies PIX Security Appliance protocol fixups to add, delete, or change services and feature defaults; available in configuration mode |
| **no fixup protocol** | Deletes the PIX Security Appliance protocol fixups services |
| **show fixup protocol** | Displays the port values for the individual protocol specified |

## Task 1: Displaying the Fixup Protocol Configurations

Complete the following step and enter the command as directed to see the current configurations of the PIX Security Appliance.

**Step 1.** List the fixup protocols that are running on the PIX Security Appliance:

```
PixP(config)# show fixup protocol
```

Complete Table 12-2 with the ports assigned to the fixup protocols.

**Table 12-2 Fixup Protocol Port Assignments**

| Protocol | Port Assignment |
|---|---|
| ftp | |
| http | |
| h323 h225 | |
| h323 ras | |
| ils | |
| rsh | |
| rtsp | |
| smtp | |
| sqlnet | |
| sip | |
| skinny | |

## Task 2: Changing the Fixup Protocol Configurations

Complete the following steps and enter the commands as directed to change some of the current configurations of the PIX Security Appliance.

**Step 1.** Disable the following fixup protocols:

```
PixP(config)# no fixup protocol http 80
PixP(config)# no fixup protocol smtp 25
PixP(config)# no fixup protocol h323 h225 1720
PixP(config)# no fixup protocol sqlnet 1521
```

**Step 2.** Define a range of ports for SQL*Net connections:

```
PixP(config)# fixup protocol sqlnet 66-76
```

**Step 3.** Verify the fixup protocol settings by using the **show fixup protocol** command:

```
PixP(config)# show fixup protocol
fixup protocol ftp 21
fixup protocol h323 ras 1718-1719
fixup protocol ils 389
```

```
fixup protocol rsh 514
fixup protocol rtsp 554
fixup protocol sip 5060
fixup protocol skinny 2000
no fixup protocol http 80
no fixup protocol smtp 25
no fixup protocol h323 h225 1720
fixup protocol sqlnet 66-76
```

### Task 3: Testing the Outbound FTP Fixup Protocol

Complete the following steps and enter the commands as directed to test the outbound FTP fixup protocol.

**Step 1.** Enable console logging on the PIX Security Appliance:

```
PixP(config)# logging console debug
```

**Step 2.** FTP to the backbone server from the student PC using the Windows FTP client:

```
C:\> ftp 172.26.26.50
User (172.26.26.50:(none)): anonymous
Password: user@
```

**Step 3.** Do a directory listing at the FTP prompt:

```
ftp> dir
```

What logging messages were generated on the PIX Security Appliance console?

______________________________________________________________________________

______________________________________________________________________________

**Step 4.** Quit the FTP session:

```
ftp> quit
```

**Step 5.** Turn off the FTP fixup protocol on the PIX Security Appliance:

```
PixP(config)# no fixup protocol ftp
```

**Step 6.** Again, FTP to the backbone server from the student PC using the Windows FTP client:

```
C:\> ftp 172.26.26.50
User (172.26.26.50:(none)): anonymous
Password: user@
```

Was logging into the server successful? Why or why not?

______________________________________________________________________________

______________________________________________________________________________

**Step 7.** Do a directory listing at the FTP prompt:

```
ftp> dir
```

Was the file listing displayed? Why or why not?

______________________________________________________________________________

______________________________________________________________________________

**Step 8.** Quit the FTP session:

```
ftp> quit
```

*Note*: If the FTP client has stopped, press **Ctrl + C** to break back to the C:\ prompt or close the Command Prompt window.

**Step 9.** FTP to the backbone server from the student PC using the web browser. To do this, enter the following in the URL field:

```
ftp://172.26.26.50
```

a. Was the connection successful? Why or why not?

______________________________________________

______________________________________________

b. Was the file listing available? Why or why not?

______________________________________________

______________________________________________

**Step 10.** Close the web browser.

### Task 4: Testing the Inbound FTP Fixup Protocol

Complete the following steps and enter the commands as directed to test the inbound FTP fixup protocol.

**Step 1.** Reenable the FTP fixup protocol on the PIX Security Appliance:

```
PixP(config)# fixup protocol ftp 21
```

**Step 2.** FTP to a peer Pod bastion host from the student PC using the web browser. To do this, enter the following in the URL field:

```
ftp://192.168.Q.11
```

*Note*: The instructor assigns the peer Pod number.

What logging messages were generated on the PIX Security Appliance console?

______________________________________________

______________________________________________

______________________________________________

**Step 3.** Close the web browser.

**Step 4.** Turn off the FTP fixup protocol on the PIX Security Appliance:

```
PixP(config)# no fixup protocol ftp
```

**Step 5.** FTP to a peer Pod bastion host from the student PC using the web browser. To do this, enter the following in the URL field:

```
ftp://192.168.Q.11
```

*Note*: The instructor assigns the peer Pod number.

a. Was the connection to the peer Pod inside FTP server successful? Why or why not?

______________________________________________

______________________________________________

______________________________________________

b. Was the file listing available? Why or why not?

______________________________________________________________________

______________________________________________________________________

______________________________________________________________________

## Task 5: Setting the Fixup Protocols to the Default Settings

Complete the following steps and enter the commands as directed to set all fixups to the factory default.

**Step 1.** Set all fixup protocols to the factory defaults:

```
PixP(config)# clear fixup
```

**Step 2.** Verify the fixup protocol settings:

```
PixP(config)# show fixup protocol
fixup protocol ftp 21
fixup protocol http 80
fixup protocol h323 h225 1720
fixup protocol h323 ras 1718-1719
fixup protocol ils 389
fixup protocol rsh 514
fixup protocol rtsp 554
fixup protocol smtp 25
fixup protocol sqlnet 1521
fixup protocol sip 5060
fixup protocol skinny 2000
```

# Lab 12.4.3: Configure Intrusion Detection

Estimated Time: 30 Minutes

Number of Team Members: Two teams with four students per team

## Objective

In this lab, students complete the following tasks:

- Configure the use of Cisco IDS information signatures and send Cisco IDS Syslog output to a Syslog server.
- Configure the use of IDS attack signatures and send Cisco IDS Syslog output to a Syslog server.

## Overview

The PIX Security Appliance is interoperable with the Cisco IDS. The PIX Security Appliance traps IDS signatures and sends these as Syslog messages to the Syslog server. This feature supports only single-packet IDS signatures.

Figure 12-2 illustrates the network environment students create for this lab.

**Figure 12-2 Lab 12.4.3 Network Topology**

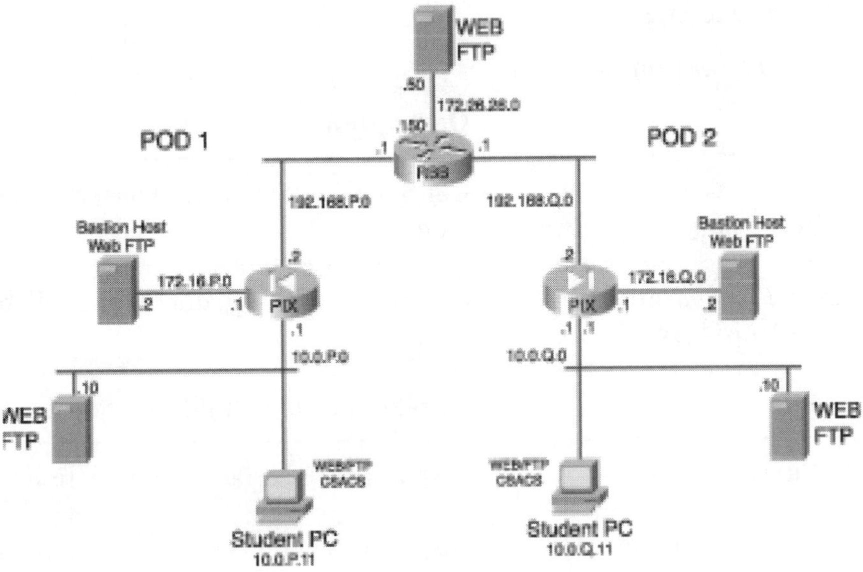


## Preparation

Begin with the standard lab topology in Figure 12-2 and verify the standard configuration on the Pod PIX Security Appliances. Access the PIX Security Appliance console port using the terminal emulator on the student PC. If desired, save the PIX Security Appliance configuration to a text file for later analysis.

### Tools and Resources

To complete the lab, the standard lab topology is required:

- Two Pod PIX Security Appliances
- Two student PCs
- One server
- Backbone switch and router
- Two console cables and HyperTerminal

### Additional Materials

Refer to *Cisco PIX Security Appliance System Log Messages* for a list of the supported IDS signature messages. The documentation can be viewed online at http://www.cisco.com/univercd/cc/td/doc/product/iaabu/pix/pix_61/syslog/index.htm.

Additional information on configuring firewalls can be found in *Cisco Secure PIX Firewalls,* by David Chapman and Andy Fox (published by Cisco Press; ISBN 1587050358).

### Command List

Table 12-3 lists the commands used throughout this lab. Refer to this list if assistance or help is needed during the lab exercise.

**Table 12-3 Lab 12.4.3 Command List**

| Command | Description |
|---|---|
| **ip audit interface** *if_name audit_name* | Configures IDS signature use; available in configuration mode |
| **ip audit name** *audit_name* **attack** [**action** [**alarm**] [**drop**] [**reset**]] | Configures IDS signature use; available in configuration mode |
| **show ip audit info** | Displays the default informational actions |
| **show ip audit interface** | Displays the interface configuration |
| **show ip audit name** [**name** [**info** \| **attack**]] | Displays all audit policies or specific policies referenced by name and possibly type |

### Task 1: Configuring the Use of IDS Information Signatures and Send Cisco IDS Syslog Output to a Syslog Server

Complete the following steps to configure the use of Cisco IDS signatures and to send Cisco IDS Syslog output to a Syslog server.

**Step 1.** Turn off console logging:

```
PixP(config)# no logging console debug
```

**Step 2.** Verify connectivity by pinging the peer Pod internal host from the Windows command prompt:

```
C:\> ping 192.168.Q.10
Pinging 192.168.Q.10 with 32 bytes of data:
Reply from 192.168.Q.10: bytes=32 time<10ms TTL=125
Reply from 192.168.Q.10: bytes=32 time<10ms TTL=125
Reply from 192.168.Q.10: bytes=32 time<10ms TTL=125
Reply from 192.168.Q.10: bytes=32 time<10ms TTL=125
```

(where Q = the peer Pod number)

**Step 3.** Specify the information signature policy on the PIX Security Appliance:

```
PixP(config)# ip audit name INFOPOLICY info action alarm reset
```

**Step 4.** Apply the information signature policy to the outside interface:

```
PixP(config)# ip audit interface outside INFOPOLICY
```

**Step 5.** Open and minimize the Kiwi Syslog Daemon on the desktop.

**Step 6.** Return to the Windows command line and attempt to ping the peer Pod internal host. The ping should fail:

```
C:\>ping 192.168.Q.10
Pinging 192.168.Q.10 with 32 bytes of data:
Request timed out.
Request timed out.
Request timed out.
Request timed out.
```

**Step 7.** Observe the messages that appear on the Kiwi Syslog Daemon display. The log should be similar to the following:

```
%PIX-4-400010: IDS:2000 ICMP echo request from 192.168.Q.10 to 192.168.P.10 on interface outside
%PIX-4-400010: IDS:2000 ICMP echo request from 192.168.Q.10 to 192.168.P.10 on interface outside
%PIX-4-400010: IDS:2000 ICMP echo request from 192.168.Q.10 to 192.168.P.10 on interface outside
%PIX-4-400010: IDS:2000 ICMP echo request from 192.168.Q.10 to 192.168.P.10 on interface outside
```

**Step 8.** Remove the information signature policy from the outside interface:

```
PixP(config)# no ip audit interface outside INFOPOLICY
```

**Step 9.** Remove the audit policy audit_name:

```
PixP(config)# no ip audit name INFOPOLICY
```

**Step 10.** Verify that the information signature policy has been removed from the outside interface, the default informational actions have been restored, and the ip audit name has been removed:

```
PixP(config)# show ip audit interface
PixP(config)# show ip audit info
ip audit info action alarm
PixP(config)# show ip audit name
```

### Task 2: Configuring the Use of IDS Attack Signatures and Send Cisco IDS Syslog Output to a Syslog Server

Complete the following steps to configure the use of IDS attack signatures and send IDS Syslog output to a Syslog server.

**Step 1.** Ping the bastion host with an Internet Control Message Protocol (ICMP) packet size of 10000 from the Windows 2000 command line:

```
C:\>ping -l 10000 172.16.P.2
Pinging 172.16.P.2 with 10000 bytes of data:
Reply from 172.16.P.2: bytes=10000 time<10ms TTL=128
```

```
Reply from 172.16.P.2: bytes=10000 time<10ms TTL=128
Reply from 172.16.P.2: bytes=10000 time<10ms TTL=128
Reply from 172.16.P.2: bytes=10000 time<10ms TTL=128
```

**Step 2.** Specify an attack policy:

```
PixP(config)# ip audit name ATTACKPOLICY attack action alarm reset
```

**Step 3.** Apply the attack policy to the inside interface:

```
PixP(config)# ip audit interface inside ATTACKPOLICY
```

**Step 4.** Ping the bastion host with an ICMP packet size of 10000 from the Windows 2000 command line:

```
C:\>ping -l 10000 172.16.P.2
Pinging 172.16.P.2 with 10000 bytes of data:
Request timed out.
Request timed out.
Request timed out.
Request timed out.
```

**Step 5.** Observe the messages that appear on the Kiwi Syslog Daemon display. The log should be similar to the following:

```
%PIX-4-400025: IDS:2154 ICMP ping of death from 10.0.P.11 to 172.16.P.2 on interface inside
%PIX-4-400023: IDS:2150 ICMP fragment from 10.0.P.11 to 172.16.P.2 on interface inside
%PIX-4-400023: IDS:2150 ICMP fragment from 10.0.P.11 to 172.16.P.2 on interface inside
%PIX-4-400023: IDS:2150 ICMP fragment from 10.0.P.11 to 172.16.P.2 on interface inside
%PIX-4-400023: IDS:2150 ICMP fragment from 10.0.P.11 to 172.16.P.2 on interface inside
%PIX-4-400023: IDS:2150 ICMP fragment from 10.0.P.11 to 172.16.P.2 on interface inside
%PIX-4-400023: IDS:2150 ICMP fragment from 10.0.P.11 to 172.16.P.2 on interface inside
%PIX-4-400025: IDS:2154 ICMP ping of death from 10.0.P.11 to 172.16.P.2 on interface inside
%PIX-4-400023: IDS:2150 ICMP fragment from 10.0.P.11 to 172.16.P.2 on interface inside
%PIX-4-400023: IDS:2150 ICMP fragment from 10.0.P.11 to 172.16.P.2 on interface inside
%PIX-4-400023: IDS:2150 ICMP fragment from 10.0.P.11 to 172.16.P.2 on interface inside
%PIX-4-400023: IDS:2150 ICMP fragment from 10.0.P.11 to 172.16.P.2 on interface inside
%PIX-4-400023: IDS:2150 ICMP fragment from 10.0.P.11 to 172.16.P.2 on interface inside
%PIX-4-400023: IDS:2150 ICMP fragment from 10.0.P.11 to 172.16.P.2 on interface inside
```

Why is the Syslog server showing the ICMP fragment in the log?

______________________________________________________________________

______________________________________________________________________

**Step 6.** Ping the bastion host with an increased ICMP packet size from the Windows 2000 command line:

```
C:\>ping -l 65000 172.16.P.2
Pinging 172.16.P.2 with 65000 bytes of data:
Request timed out.
Request timed out.
Request timed out.
Request timed out.
```

**Step 7.** Observe the messages that appear on the Kiwi Syslog Daemon display. The log should be similar to the following:

```
%PIX-4-400025: IDS:2154 ICMP ping of death from 10.0.P.11 to 172.16.P.2 on interface inside
%PIX-4-400025: IDS:2154 ICMP ping of death from 10.0.P.11 to 172.16.P.2 on interface inside
%PIX-4-400025: IDS:2154 ICMP ping of death from 10.0.P.11 to 172.16.P.2 on interface inside
%PIX-4-400025: IDS:2154 ICMP ping of death from 10.0.P.11 to 172.16.P.2 on interface inside
```

**Step 8.** Remove the attack policy from the inside interface:

```
PixP(config)# no ip audit interface inside ATTACKPOLICY
```

**Step 9.** Remove the audit policy:

```
PixP(config)# no ip audit name ATTACKPOLICY
```

**Step 10.** Verify that the attack policy has been removed from the inside interface, the default attack actions have been restored, and the ip audit name has been removed:

```
PixP(config)# show ip audit interface
PixP(config)# show ip audit attack
ip audit attack action alarm
PixP(config)# show ip audit name
```

**Step 11.** Save the configuration:

```
PixP(config)# write memory
```

## Review Questions

1. Describe the **fixup** command.

_______________________________________________

_______________________________________________

_______________________________________________

_______________________________________________

2. Describe why multimedia applications can cause issues with a network protected by a firewall.

_______________________________________________

_______________________________________________

_______________________________________________

_______________________________________________

3. Describe Mail Guard.

_______________________________________________

_______________________________________________

_______________________________________________

_______________________________________________

4. Describe DNS Guard.

_______________________________________________

_______________________________________________

_______________________________________________

_______________________________________________

5. Describe a SYN flood attack.

_______________________________________________

_______________________________________________

_______________________________________________

_______________________________________________

## Chapter 12 Quiz Questions

1. What is the command that enables fragmentation guard on the PIX Security Appliance?

    A. **fixup protocol fragguard 1500**

    B. **sysopt security fragguard**

    C. **fixup protocol fragguard 1858**

    D. **security sysopt fragguard**

2. The **fixup protocol ftp 21** command is enabled by default on the PIX Security Appliance.

    A. True

    B. False

3. The command **ip audit signature action alarm** performs what operation?

    A. Deletes the packet

    B. Generates a Syslog message

    C. Sends an alarm to the administrator's console

    D. Forwards the packet for further checking

4. Which of the following is an application layer protocol designed to facilitate the exchange of management information between network devices.

    A. SMTP

    B. DNS

    C. RTSP

    D. SNMP

5. Which of the following commands will disable the inspection of traffic on the indicated port for H.323 connections?

    A. **fixup protocol h323 1720**

    B. **clear fixup protocol h323**

    C. **no fixup protocol h323 1720**

    D. **clear fixup protocol h323 1720**

6. What command enables DNS guard on a PIX Security Appliance?

    A. **Enabled by default**

    B. **fixup protocol dns 53**

    C. **fixup protocol dnsguard**

    D. **enable dns guard**

7. Which of the following SNMP commands is incorrect?

   A. **snmp server host** *ipaddress*

   B. **snmp-server host** *ipaddress* poll

   C. **snmp-server community** *key*

   D. **clear snmp-server**

8. The PIX Security Appliance is capable of sending events to a Syslog server. Which of the following are valid events?

   A. Security

   B. Accounting

   C. Operating system

   D. Environmental

9. Passive Mode FTP uses port 20 for a data channel port.

   A. True

   B. False

10. What command enables the PIX Security Appliance to inspect streaming traffic on ports 16384-16399?

    A. **fix rtsp protocol rtsp 16384-16399**

    B. **rtsp 16384-16399 fix rtsp**

    C. **fixup protocol rtsp 16384-16399**

    D. None of the above

# Chapter 13

## PIX Failover and System Maintenance

This chapter deals with PIX failover and system maintenance. Both are important functions in providing ongoing protection of the network.

Failover provides those organizations that require protection all the time a method to meet that goal. The PIX failover solution has specific hardware requirements. To implement failover, two PIX Security Appliances of the same model running the same version of the software are required. There are two types of failover covered in the course: failover and stateful failover. These methods differ in how the client functions in the event of a failover.

The two failover connection methods of the PIX Security Appliance are serial-cable failover and LAN-based failover. The procedures for both methods are covered in this chapter.

After learning about failover, the student learns how to configure the PIX Security Appliance for Telnet access. In earlier chapters, the pitfalls of enabling Telnet access to routers were discussed. In addition, how Secure Shell (SSH) can be used to mitigate some of those issues was also discussed. The same is true for the PIX Security Appliance. In this chapter, students learn how to configure the PIX to allow remote access through an SSH client.

Command authorization is needed when administering the firewall, either locally or remotely. This enables the configuration of different privileged levels for assigning access permissions. It also requires the PIX to be configured for authentication, authorization, and accounting (AAA) authorization.

Finally in this chapter, students learn how to upgrade the software image and activation key.

**Vocabulary Exercise**

channeling

_______________________________________________

failover

_______________________________________________

_______________________________________________

PortFast

_______________________________________________

_______________________________________________

trunking

_______________________________________________

_______________________________________________

## Lab Activities

The topology figures and lab examples contain **P** and **Q** values. The **P** value in the addressing and naming scheme refers to *your* assigned Pod number.

The following are examples of determining P values:

- Pod2 is looking at a topology figure and is trying to determine the P values in the figure. In this scenario, the **P** values would equal **2**. 10.0.**P**.12 would become 10.0.**2**.12, 172.30.**P**.2 would become 172.30.**2**.2, and so on.
- Pod1 is looking at a topology figure and is trying to determine the P values in the figure. In this scenario, the **P** values would equal **1**. 10.0.**P**.12 would become 10.0.**1**.12, 172.30.**P**.2 would become 172.30.**1**.2, and so on.

In both examples, the P values are directly related to the Pod number of the team.

The **Q** value in the naming and addressing scheme is used when testing the security or connectivity with the peer team.

The following are examples of determining Q values:

- In a lab, Pod2 has been asked to test connectivity to their peer inside host at IP address 10.0.Q.12. In this scenario, 10.0.**Q**.12 would equal 10.0.**1**.12.
- In a lab, Pod1 has been asked to test connectivity to their peer inside host at IP address 10.0.Q.12. In this scenario, 10.0.**Q**.12 would equal 10.0.**2**.12.

In both examples, the Q value is directly related to the peer Pod number.

# Lab 13.3.3: Configure LAN-Based Failover (Optional)

Estimated Time: 30 Minutes

Number of Team Members: Two teams with four students per team

## Objective

In this lab, students complete the following tasks:

- Configure the primary PIX Security Appliance for LAN-based stateful failover to the secondary PIX Security Appliance.
- Configure the secondary PIX Security Appliance for LAN-based failover.
- Test LAN-based stateful failover.
- Make the primary PIX Security Appliance active.

## Overview

In an enterprise network, network outages are not an option. Many businesses and service providers must maintain continuous service; otherwise, the monetary loss can be high. In addition to redundant routers, the PIX supports failover capabilities.

Figure 13-1 illustrates the network environment students create for this lab.

**Figure 13-1 Lab 13.3.3 Network Topology**

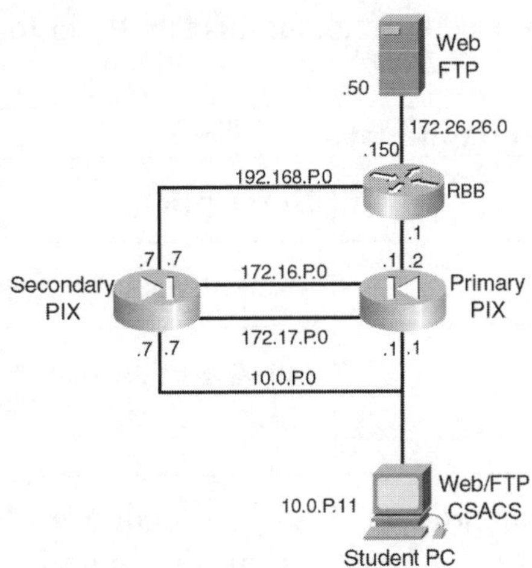


## Preparation

Begin with the failover lab topology and verify the standard configuration on the Pod PIX Security Appliances. Access the PIX Security Appliance console port using the terminal emulator on the student PC. If desired, save the PIX Security Appliance configuration to a text file for later analysis.

## Tools and Resources

To complete the lab, the standard lab topology is required:

- One primary unrestricted (UR) PIX Security Appliance
- One secondary PIX Security Appliance (failover, restricted, or unrestricted)
- One student PC
- One SuperServer
- Backbone switch and router
- Two console cables
- HyperTerminal

*Note*: Both PIX Security Appliances should be the same model and contain the same image and interface hardware. At least one must be an unrestricted model.

## Additional Materials

Students can use this link for more information on the objectives covered in this lab:

- http://www.cisco.com/en/US/products/hw/vpndevc/ps2030/products_tech_note09186a0080094ea7.shtml

## Command List

Table 13-1 lists the commands used throughout this lab. Refer to this list if you need any assistance during the lab.

**Table 13-1 Lab 13.5.3 Command List**

| **Command** | **Description** |
|---|---|
| **clock set** *hh*:*mm*:ss | Manually sets the system software clock |
| **failover** [**active**] | Initiates a failover switch from the standby unit |
| **failover ip address** *if_name ip_address* | Assigns a failover IP address for an interface to specify the standby unit's interface addresses |
| **failover lan interface** *if_name* | Configures LAN-based failover |
| **failover link** [*stateful_if_name*] | Enables stateful failover |
| **failover poll** [*seconds*] | Configures the primary to failover quicker |
| **interface** *hardware_id* [*hardware_speed*] [**shutdown**] | Identifies network interface speed and duplex |

| Command | Description |
|---|---|
| **ip address** *if_name ip_address* [*netmask*] | Identifies addresses for network interfaces |
| **nameif** *hardware_id if_name security_level* | Names interfaces and assigns a Security level |
| **show failover** | Verifies failover configuration and status |

### Task 1: Configuring the Primary PIX Security Appliance for LAN-Based Stateful Failover to the Secondary PIX Security Appliance

Complete the following steps to configure the primary PIX Security Appliance for failover to the secondary PIX Security Appliance.

**Step 1.** Assign an IP address to the outside interface of the PIX Security Appliance:

```
pixP(config)# ip address outside 192.168.P.2 255.255.255.0
```

**Step 2.** Use the **clock set** command on the active PIX Security Appliance to synchronize the time on both PIX Security Appliances:

```
clock set hh:mm:ss month day year
```

**Step 3.** Disable the unused interfaces:

```
pixP(config)# interface e4 shutdown
pixP(config)# interface e5 shutdown
```

**Step 4.** Assign the PIX Security Appliance interface name (MYFAILOVER) and security level (55):

```
pixP(config)# nameif e3 MYFAILOVER security55
```

**Step 5.** Enable the interface for an Intel full duplex:

```
pixP(config)# interface e3 100full
```

**Step 6.** Assign an IP address to the interface:

```
pixP(config)# ip address MYFAILOVER 172.17.P.1 255.255.255.0
```

**Step 7.** Use the **failover** command to enable failover on the primary unit:

```
pixP(config)# failover
```

**Step 8.** Change the failover poll time to 8 seconds so that the PIX Security Appliance triggers failover faster:

```
pixP(config)# failover poll 8
```

**Step 9.** Use the **show failover** command to verify that the primary PIX Security Appliance is active:

```
pixP(config)# show failover
Failover On
Cable status: My side not connected
Reconnect timeout 0:00:00
Poll frequency 3 seconds
This host: Secondary - Active
```

```
    Active time: 225 (sec)
    Interface intf5 (127.0.0.1): Link Down (Shutdown)
    Interface intf4 (127.0.0.1): Link Down (Shutdown)
    Interface MYFAILOVER (172.17.P.1): Link Down (Waiting)
    Interface dmz (172.16.P.1): Normal (Waiting)
    Interface outside (192.168.P.2): Normal (Waiting)
    Interface inside (10.0.P.1): Normal (Waiting)
Other host: Secondary - Standby
         Active time: 0 (sec)
    Interface intf5 (0.0.0.0): Unknown (Shutdown)
    Interface intf4 (0.0.0.0): Unknown (Shutdown)
    Interface intf3 (0.0.0.0): Unknown (Waiting)
    Interface intf2 (0.0.0.0): Unknown (Waiting)
    Interface outside (0.0.0.0): Unknown (Waiting)
    Interface inside (0.0.0.0): Unknown (Waiting)
```

**Step 10.** Assign a failover IP address for each interface to specify the standby unit's interface addresses:

```
pixP(config)# failover ip address inside 10.0.P.7
pixP(config)# failover ip address outside 192.168.P.7
pixP(config)# failover ip address dmz 172.16.P.7
pixP(config)# failover ip address MYFAILOVER 172.17.P.7
```

**Step 11.** Enter the **show failover** command to verify that the secondary unit now has IP addresses for each interface:

```
pixP(config)# show failover
Failover On
Cable status: My side not connected
Reconnect timeout 0:00:00
Poll frequency 3 seconds
This host: Secondary - Active
    Active time: 510 (sec)
    Interface intf5 (127.0.0.1): Link Down (Shutdown)
    Interface intf4 (127.0.0.1): Link Down (Shutdown)
    Interface MYFAILOVER (172.17.P.1): Link Down (Waiting)
    Interface dmz (172.16.P.1): Normal (Waiting)
    Interface outside (192.168.P.2): Normal (Waiting)
    Interface inside (10.0.P.1): Normal (Waiting)
Other host: Secondary - Standby
    Active time: 0 (sec)
    Interface intf5 (127.0.0.1): Unknown (Shutdown)
    Interface intf4 (127.0.0.1): Unknown (Shutdown)
    Interface MYFAILOVER (172.17.P.7): Unknown (Waiting)
    Interface dmz (172.16.P.7): Unknown (Waiting)
    Interface outside (192.168.P.7): Unknown (Waiting)
    Interface inside (10.0.P.7): Unknown (Waiting)
```

**Step 12.** Use the **failover link** command to specify the name of the dedicated interface:

```
pixP(config)# failover link MYFAILOVER
```

**Step 13.** Save all changes to Flash memory:

```
pixP(config)# write memory
```

**Step 14.** Configure LAN-based failover on the primary unit. Connect the LAN failover interface to the network, and complete the following substeps:

a. Disable failover:

```
pixP(config)# no failover
```

b. Specify the primary PIX Security Appliance to use for LAN-based failover:

```
pixP(config)# failover lan unit primary
```

c. Specify the interface name for LAN-based failover:

```
pixP(config)# failover lan interface MYFAILOVER
```

d. Enable encryption and authentication of LAN-based failover messages between PIX Security Appliances:

```
pixP(config)# failover lan key 1234567
```

e. Enable LAN-based failover:

```
pixP(config)# failover lan enable
```

f. Enable failover:

```
pixP(config)# failover
```

g. Save all changes to Flash memory:

```
pixP(config)# write memory
```

h. Make sure that the primary PIX Security Appliance is enabled for stateful failover by using the **show failover** command:

```
pixP(config)# show failover
Failover On
 Cable status: My side not connected
 Reconnect timeout 0:00:00
 Poll frequency 3 seconds
        This host: Primary - Active
                Active time: 510 (sec)
                Interface intf5 (127.0.0.1): Link Down (Shutdown)
                Interface intf4 (127.0.0.1): Link Down (Shutdown)
                Interface dmz (172.16.P.1): Normal (Waiting)
                Interface outside (192.168.P.2): Normal (Waiting)
                Interface inside (10.0.P.1): Normal (Waiting)
        Other host: Secondary - Standby (Failed)
                Active time: 0 (sec)
                Interface intf5 (127.0.0.1): Unknown (Shutdown)
                Interface intf4 (127.0.0.1): Unknown (Shutdown)
                Interface dmz (172.16.P.7): Unknown (Waiting)
                Interface outside (192.168.P.7): Unknown (Waiting)
                Interface inside (10.0.P.7): Unknown (Waiting)
  Stateful Failover Logical Update Statistics
        Link : MYFAILOVER
        Stateful Obj    xmit       xerr       rcv        rerr
        General         0          0          0          0
        sys cmd         0          0          0          0
        up time         0          0          0          0
        xlate           0          0          0          0
        tcp conn        0          0          0          0
        udp conn        0          0          0          0
        ARP tbl         0          0          0          0
        RIP Tbl         0          0          0          0

        Logical Update Queue Information
                        Cur     Max     Total
        Recv Q:         0       0       0
        Xmit Q:         0       0       0

  Lan Based Failover is Active

        Interface MYFAILOVER (172.17.P.1): Normal, peer (172.17.P.7) Down
```

i. Wait for the failover initialization process to complete. The following messages appears on the PIX Security Appliance console:

```
LAN-based Failover startup ping test failed!!
Wait for pix LAN-based failover init process to complete...
LAN-based Failover: Send hello msg and start failover monitoring
```

j. From the Student PC, verify connectivity to the SuperServer:

```
C:\> ping 172.26.26.50
```

k. From the student PC, Telnet to the backbone router to verify connectivity:

```
C:\> telnet 192.168.P.1
```

**Task 2: Configuring the Secondary PIX Security Appliance for LAN-Based Failover**

Complete the following steps to prepare the secondary PIX Security Appliance for failover.

**Step 1.** Power up the secondary PIX Security Appliance.

**Step 2.** Without the LAN-based failover interface connected, complete the following substeps on the secondary PIX Security Appliance.

a. When prompted to configure the PIX Security Appliance through interactive prompts, press **Control** > **Z** to escape.

b. Enter configuration mode.

c. Assign a name and security level to the failover interface:

```
pixP(config)# nameif e3 MYFAILOVER security55
```

d. Enable the interface for an Intel full duplex:

```
pixP(config)# interface e3 100full
```

e. Assign an IP address to the interface:

```
pixP(config)# ip address MYFAILOVER 172.17.P.1 255.255.255.0
```

f. Assign a failover IP address to the interface:

```
pixP(config)# failover ip address MYFAILOVER 172.17.P.7 255.255.255.0
```

g. Designate this firewall as the secondary firewall:

```
pixP(config)# failover lan unit secondary
```

h. Specify the name of the interface to be used for LAN-based failover:

```
pixP(config)# failover lan interface MYFAILOVER
```

i. Enter the secret key shared with the primary PIX Security Appliance:

```
pixP(config)# failover lan key 1234567
```

j. Enable LAN-based failover:

```
pixP(config)# failover lan enable
```

k. Enable failover:

```
pixP(config)# failover
```

l. Save the configuration to Flash memory:

```
pixP(config)# write mem
```

**Step 3.** Connect the secondary PIX Security Appliance to the network by connecting the LAN-based failover interface to the network.

**Step 4.** Reload the secondary PIX Security Appliance:

```
pixP(config)# reload
```

## Task 3: Testing LAN-Based Stateful Failover

Complete the following steps to test LAN-based stateful failover.

**Step 1.** After the message "Sync Complete" appears on the primary PIX Security Appliance console, Telnet to the backbone router from the student PC Windows command line:

```
C:\> telnet 192.168.P.1
```

**Step 2.** When prompted for a password, enter **cisco**:

```
User Access Verification
Password: cisco
rbb>
```

**Step 3.** From the student PC, start a continuous ping to 172.26.26.50:

```
C:\ ping 172.26.26.50 -t
```

**Step 4.** Reload the primary PIX Security Appliance:

```
pixP(config)# reload
```

**Step 5.** When asked to confirm the reload, press **Enter**.

**Step 6.** Verify that the continuous ping is still active.

**Step 7.** Return to the Telnet connection on the backbone router. Verify that it is still active by attempting to enter privileged mode. If the router accepts the command and a prompt for a privileged mode password is displayed, the session is still active:

```
rbb> en
```

**Step 8.** Enter the **show failover** command on the primary firewall and observe the output:

```
pixP(config)# show failover
Failover On
 Cable status: Normal
 Reconnect timeout 0:00:00
 Poll frequency 3 seconds
        This host: Primary - Standby
                Active time: 510 (sec)
                Interface intf5 (127.0.0.1): Link Down (Shutdown)
                Interface intf4 (127.0.0.1): Link Down (Shutdown)
                Interface dmz (172.16.P.7): Normal
                Interface outside (192.168.P.7): Normal
                Interface inside (10.0.P.7): Normal
        Other host: Secondary - Active
                Active time: 93 (sec)
                Interface intf5 (127.0.0.1): Link Down (Shutdown)
                Interface intf4 (127.0.0.1): Link Down (Shutdown)
                Interface dmz (172.16.P.1): Normal
                Interface outside (192.168.P.2): Normal
                Interface inside (10.0.P.1): Normal
  Stateful Failover Logical Update Statistics
        Link : MYFAILOVER
        Stateful Obj    xmit        xerr        rcv         rerr
        General         967         0          998          0
        sys cmd         675         0          897          0
        up time         4           0            2          0
        xlate           1006        0           65          0
        tcp conn        456         0          345          0
        udp conn        0           0            0          0
        ARP tbl         884         0            0          0
        RIP Tbl         0           0            0          0
```

```
Logical Update Queue Information
                       Cur      Max      Total
         Recv Q:       0        3        6740
         Xmit Q:       0        7        8665

  Lan Based Failover is Active

         Interface MYFAILOVER (172.17.P.1): Normal, peer (172.17.P.7) Normal
```

## Task 4: Making the Primary PIX Security Appliance Active

Complete the following steps to make the primary PIX Security Appliance the active PIX Security Appliance.

**Step 1.** Make the primary PIX Security Appliance the active PIX Security Appliance by using the **failover active** command. From the primary PIX Security Appliance's console port, enter the following:

```
pixP(config)# failover active
```

**Step 2.** Verify that the failover active command works by using the **show failover** command. The primary PIX Security Appliance should show that it is in active mode, and the secondary PIX Security Appliance should show that it is in standby mode:

```
pixP(config)# show failover
Failover On
Cable status: Normal
Reconnect timeout 0:00:00
        This host: Primary - Active
                  Active time: 7350 (sec)
                  Interface intf5 (127.0.0.1): Link Down (Shutdown)
                  Interface intf4 (127.0.0.1): Link Down (Shutdown)
                  Interface dmz (172.16.P.1): Normal (Waiting)
                  Interface outside (192.168.P.2): Normal (Waiting)
                  Interface inside (10.0.P.1): Normal (Waiting)
        Other host: Secondary - Standby
                  Active time: 7300 (sec)
                  Interface intf5 (0.0.0.0): Link Down (Shutdown)
                  Interface intf4 (0.0.0.0): Link Down (Shutdown)
                  Interface dmz (172.16.P.7): Normal
                  Interface outside (192.168.P.7): Normal
                  Interface inside (10.0.P.7): Normal
Stateful Failover Logical Update Statistics
         Link : MYFAILOVER
         Stateful Obj     xmit       xerr       rcv        rerr
         General          999        0          1256       0
         sys cmd          775        0          987        0
         up time          8          0          6          0
         xlate            2006       0          85         0
         tcp conn         656        0          445        0
         udp conn         0          0          0          0
         ARP tbl          1884       0          0          0
         RIP Tbl          0          0          0          0

Logical Update Queue Information
                       Cur      Max      Total
         Recv Q:       0        9        7860
         Xmit Q:       0        12       9875

  Lan Based Failover is Active

         Interface MYFAILOVER (172.17.P.1): Normal, peer (172.17.P.7) Normal
```

# Lab 13.5.3: Configure SSH, Command Authorization, and Local User Authentication

Estimated Time: 25 Minutes

Number of Team Members: Two teams with four students per team

## Objective

In this lab, students complete the following tasks:

- Configure SSH.
- Configure command authorization.
- Configure Local User Authentication.

## Overview

SSH is an application and a protocol that provides secure replacement for the suite of Berkeley r-tools. These tools include rsh, rlogin, and rcp. Cisco IOS supports rlogin. The protocol secures the sessions using standard cryptographic mechanisms.

LOCAL and TACACS+ command authorization is supported in PIX Security Appliance version 6.2. With the LOCAL command authorization feature, the PIX Security Appliance commands can be assigned to one of 16 levels. The PIX Security Appliance also supports defining users in the LOCAL database for authentication. In this lab, students configure these services.

Figure 13-2 illustrates the network environment students create for this lab.

**Figure 13-2 Lab 13.5.3 Network Topology**

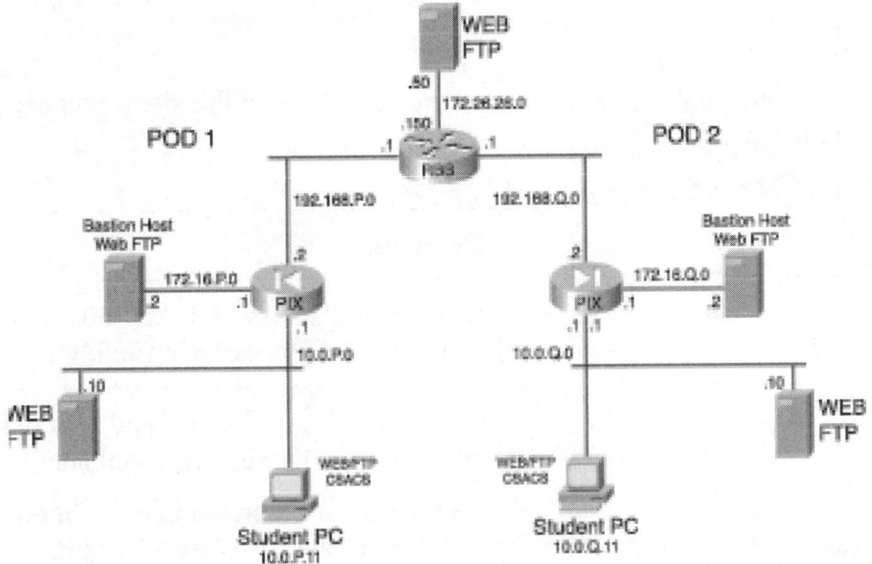

## Preparation

Begin with the standard lab topology and verify the standard configuration on the Pod PIX Security Appliances. Access the PIX Security Appliance console port using the terminal emulator on the student PC. If desired, save the PIX Security Appliance configuration to a text file for later analysis.

## Tools and Resources

To complete the lab, the standard lab topology is required:

- Two Pod PIX Security Appliances
- Two student PCs
- One server
- Backbone switch and router
- Two console cables and HyperTerminal

## Additional Materials

Students can use the following links for more information on the objectives covered in this lab:

- http://www.cisco.com/en/US/products/sw/secursw/ps2113/prod_configuration_guide09186a00800eea5a.html#xtocid15
- http://www.cisco.com/en/US/products/hw/vpndevc/ps2030/products_tech_note09186a00800949d6.shtml

Additional information on configuring firewalls can be found in *Cisco Secure PIX Firewalls,* by David Chapman and Andy Fox (published by Cisco Press; ISBN 1587050358).

### Command List

Table 132 lists the commands used throughout this lab. Refer to this list if you need any assistance during the lab.

**Table 13-2 Lab 13.5.3 Command List**

| Command | Description |
|---|---|
| **aaa authorization** {**LOCAL** \| *tacacs_server_tag*} | Enables or disables LOCAL or TACACS+ user authorization services. Configuration mode. |
| **ca generate rsa key** *modulus* | Generates Rivest, Shamir, and Adleman (RSA) key pairs for the PIX Security Appliance<br>RSA keys are generated in pairs of one public RSA key and one private RSA key. Configuration mode. |
| **clear aaa** | Removes **aaa** command statements from the configuration. |

| Command | Description |
|---|---|
| **debug ssh** | Provides debug information and error messages associated with the **ssh** command. |
| **privilege** [**show** \| **clear** \| **configure**] **level** *level* [mode *enable* \| *configure*] **command** *command* | Configures or displays command privilege levels. Configuration mode. |
| **show ca** | Displays information about Certificate Enrollment Protocol (CEP) |
| **show ssh** [**sessions** [*ip_address*]] | Displays active, all, or host-specific SSH sessions on the PIX Security Appliance |
| **ssh timeout** *mm* | Specifies a host for PIX Security Appliance console access through SSH Configuration mode. |
| **static** [(*internal_if_name*, *external_if_name*)] {**tcp** \| **udp**} {*global_ip* \| **interface**} *global_port local_ip local_port* [**netmask** *mask*][*max_conns* [*emb_limit* [**norandomseq**]]] | Configures a persistent one-to-one address translation rule by mapping a local IP address to a global IP address; also known as Static Port Address Translation (Static PAT) Configuration mode. |
| **username** *username {*[{**nopassword** \| **password** *password*} [**encrypted**]] [**privilege** *level*]*}* | Sets the username for the specified privilege level. Configuration mode. |

### Task 1: Enabling Authorization at the Enable Level

To enable command authorization with privileged mode passwords, complete the following steps.

**Step 1.** Set privilege level 10 for the enable mode **configure** command:

```
PixP(config)# privilege configure level 10 mode enable command configure
```

**Step 2.** Set privilege level 10 for the **nameif** command:

```
PixP(config)# privilege level 10 command nameif
```

**Step 3.** Set privilege level 12 for the **interface** command:

```
PixP(config)# privilege level 12 command interface
```

**Step 4.** Assign an enable password for privileged level 15:

```
PixP(config)# enable password prmode15
```

**Step 5.** Assign an enable password for privileged level 5:

```
PixP(config)# enable password prmode5 level 5
```

**Step 6.** Assign an enable password to privileged level 10:

```
PixP(config)# enable password prmode10 level 10
```

**Step 7.** Assign an enable password to privileged level 12:

```
PixP(config)# enable password prmode12 level 12
```

Why would different levels and passwords be assigned?

_______________________________________________

_______________________________________________

**Step 8.** Enable command authorization by entering the following command:

```
PixP(config)# aaa authorization command LOCAL
```

What other command authorization services can be used? Why can't RADIUS be used?

_______________________________________________

_______________________________________________

**Step 9.** Exit configuration mode:

```
PixP(config)# exit
PixP#
```

**Step 10.** Exit privileged mode:

```
PixP# exit
Logoff

Type help or '?' for a list of available commands.

PixP>
```

### Task 2: Testing Command Authorization at the Enable Level

To test the command authorization configured in Task 1, complete the following steps.

**Step 1.** Enter privileged mode level 12. When prompted for a password, enter **prmode12**:

```
PixP> enable 12
Password:
PixP#
```

**Step 2.** Enter configuration mode:

```
PixP# config t
```

**Step 3.** Verify that the **nameif** command is useable:

```
PixP(config)# nameif e3 PRIVTEST sec30
```

**Step 4.** View the configuration:

```
PixP(config)# show nameif
nameif ethernet0 outside security0
nameif ethernet1 inside security100
nameif ethernet2 dmz security50
nameif ethernet3 PRIVTEST security30
nameif ethernet4 intf4 security20
nameif ethernet5 intf5 security25
```

**Step 5.** Verify that the **interface** command is useable:

```
PixP(config)# interface e3 100full
```

**Step 6.** View the configuration:

```
PixP(config)# show interface
interface ethernet0 "outside" is up, line protocol is up
Hardware is i82559 ethernet, address is 0003.e300.483a
IP address 192.168.P.2, subnet mask 255.255.255.0
MTU 1500 bytes, BW 100000 Kbit full duplex
10640 packets input, 1374788 bytes, 0 no buffer
```

```
Received 7179 broadcasts, 0 runts, 0 giants
0 input errors, 0 CRC, 0 frame, 0 overrun, 0 ignored, 0 abort
3458 packets output, 348972 bytes, 0 underruns
0 output errors, 0 collisions, 0 interface resets
0 babbles, 0 late collisions, 0 deferred
0 lost carrier, 0 no carrier
input queue (curr/max blocks): hardware (128/128) software (0/6)
output queue (curr/max blocks): hardware (0/9) software (0/2)
interface ethernet1 "inside" is up, line protocol is up
Hardware is i82559 ethernet, address is 0003.e300.483b
IP address 10.0.P.1, subnet mask 255.255.255.0
MTU 1500 bytes, BW 100000 Kbit full duplex
11119 packets input, 1438842 bytes, 0 no buffer
Received 7554 broadcasts, 0 runts, 0 giants
0 input errors, 0 CRC, 0 frame, 0 overrun, 0 ignored, 0 abort
4153 packets output, 390555 bytes, 0 underruns
0 output errors, 0 collisions, 0 interface resets
0 babbles, 0 late collisions, 0 deferred
0 lost carrier, 0 no carrier
input queue (curr/max blocks): hardware (128/128) software (0/4)
output queue (curr/max blocks): hardware (0/15) software (0/14)
interface ethernet2 "dmz" is up, line protocol is up
Hardware is i82558 ethernet, address is 00e0.b602.3387
IP address 172.16.P.1, subnet mask 255.255.255.0
MTU 1500 bytes, BW 100000 Kbit full duplex
7024 packets input, 1050994 bytes, 0 no buffer
Received 6991 broadcasts, 0 runts, 0 giants
0 input errors, 0 CRC, 0 frame, 0 overrun, 0 ignored, 0 abort
98 packets output, 41652 bytes, 0 underruns
0 output errors, 0 collisions, 0 interface resets
0 babbles, 0 late collisions, 0 deferred
0 lost carrier, 0 no carrier
input queue (curr/max blocks): hardware (128/128) software (0/2)
output queue (curr/max blocks): hardware (0/9) software (0/1)
interface ethernet3 "PRIVTEST" is up, line protocol is down
Hardware is i82558 ethernet, address is 00e0.b602.3386
IP address 172.17.P.1, subnet mask 255.255.255.0
MTU 1500 bytes, BW 100000 Kbit full duplex
2510 packets input, 317593 bytes, 0 no buffer
Received 134 broadcasts, 0 runts, 0 giants
0 input errors, 0 CRC, 0 frame, 0 overrun, 0 ignored, 0 abort
2384 packets output, 223276 bytes, 0 underruns
0 output errors, 0 collisions, 0 interface resets
0 babbles, 0 late collisions, 0 deferred
0 lost carrier, 0 no carrier
input queue (curr/max blocks): hardware (128/128) software (0/38)
output queue (curr/max blocks): hardware (0/35) software (0/1)
interface ethernet4 "intf4" is administratively down, line protocol is down
Hardware is i82558 ethernet, address is 00e0.b602.3385
IP address 127.0.0.1, subnet mask 255.255.255.255
MTU 1500 bytes, BW 10000 Kbit half duplex
0 packets input, 0 bytes, 0 no buffer
Received 0 broadcasts, 0 runts, 0 giants
0 input errors, 0 CRC, 0 frame, 0 overrun, 0 ignored, 0 abort
0 packets output, 0 bytes, 0 underruns
0 output errors, 0 collisions, 0 interface resets
0 babbles, 0 late collisions, 0 deferred
0 lost carrier, 0 no carrier
input queue (curr/max blocks): hardware (128/128) software (0/0)
output queue (curr/max blocks): hardware (0/0) software (0/0)
interface ethernet5 "intf5" is administratively down, line protocol is down
Hardware is i82558 ethernet, address is 00e0.b602.3384
IP address 127.0.0.1, subnet mask 255.255.255.255
MTU 1500 bytes, BW 10000 Kbit half duplex
0 packets input, 0 bytes, 0 no buffer
Received 0 broadcasts, 0 runts, 0 giants
0 input errors, 0 CRC, 0 frame, 0 overrun, 0 ignored, 0 abort
0 packets output, 0 bytes, 0 underruns
0 output errors, 0 collisions, 0 interface resets
0 babbles, 0 late collisions, 0 deferred
0 lost carrier, 0 no carrier
input queue (curr/max blocks): hardware (128/128) software (0/0)
output queue (curr/max blocks): hardware (0/0) software (0/0)
```

**Step 7.** Exit configuration mode:

```
PixP(config)# exit
PixP#
```

**Step 8.** Exit privileged mode:

```
PixP# exit
Logoff
Type help or '?' for a list of available commands.
PixP>
```

**Step 9.** Enter privileged mode level 10. When prompted for a password, enter **prmode10**:

```
PixP> enable 10
Password:
PixP#
```

**Step 10.** Enter configuration mode:

```
PixP# config t
PixP(config)#
```

**Step 11.** Verify that the **nameif** command is useable:

```
PixP(config)# nameif e4 PRIVTEST2 sec35
```

**Step 12.** View the configuration:

```
PixP(config)# show nameif
nameif ethernet0 outside security0
nameif ethernet1 inside security100
nameif ethernet2 dmz security50
nameif ethernet3 PRIVTEST security30
nameif ethernet4 PRIVTEST2 security35
nameif ethernet5 intf5 security25
```

**Step 13.** Try to use the **interface** command:

```
PixP(config)# interface e4 100full
Command authorization failed.
```

**Step 14.** Exit configuration mode:

```
PixP(config)# exit
PixP#
```

**Step 15.** Exit privileged mode:

```
PixP# exit
Logoff
Type help or '?' for a list of available commands.
PixP>
```

**Step 16.** Enter privileged mode level 5. When prompted for a password, enter **prmode5**:

```
PixP> enable 5
Password:
PixP#
```

**Step 17.** Try to enter configuration mode:

```
PixP# config t
Command authorization failed.
```

**Step 18.** Exit privileged mode:

```
PixP# exit
Logoff
Type help or '?' for a list of available commands.
PixP>
```

**Step 19.** Enter privileged mode. When prompted for a password, enter **prmode15**:

```
PixP> enable
Password:
PixP#
```

**Step 20.** Enter configuration mode:

```
PixP# config t
PixP(config)#
```

### Task 3: Generating an RSA Key Pair for Encrypted SSH Sessions

To generate an RSA key pair to encrypt the SSH terminal session, complete the following steps.

**Step 1.** Delete any previously created RSA keys:

```
PixP(config)# ca zeroize rsa
```

**Step 2.** Save the certification authority (CA) state to complete the erasure of the old RSA key pair:

```
PixP(config)# ca save all
```

**Step 3.** Configure the domain name:

```
PixP(config)# domain-name cisco.com
```

**Step 4.** Generate an RSA key pair to use to encrypt SSH sessions:

```
PixP(config)# ca generate rsa key 1024
For <key_modulus_size> >= 1024, key generation could take up to several minutes. Please wait.
```

What are the modulus sizes that can be used?

---

**Step 5.** Save the keys to Flash memory:

```
PixP(config)# ca save all
```

**Step 6.** View the public key:

```
PixP(config)# sh ca mypubkey rsa
% Key pair was generated at: 18:34:29 UTC Apr 17 2002
Key name: pixP.cisco.com
Usage: General Purpose Key
Key Data:
30819f30 0d06092a 864886f7 0d010101 05000381 8d003081 89028181 00bc43bf
33d9c65d e508b6df ecf71e37 5574a21d 56185faf cbb9fe14 5a345222 42cd2927
604fd719 a58d4f82 dc382fc4 ae037d15 f4f11ca8 06020c8d 5cd350d1 9bf19457
a6dc1a86 f1e101ae 842b0281 f42f38c5 c8e5c095 711ac751 f28d693f ffdcb40f
2892169e 90be60dd 15c2fdc9 b8bda690 e55b29bf 670ed794 30e9c012 5f020301 0001
```

### Task 4: Establishing an SSH Connection to the PIX Security Appliance

To securely connect to the PIX Security Appliance through SSH, complete the following steps.

**Step 1.** Enable SSH debugging:

```
PixP(config)# debug ssh
SSH debugging on
```

**Step 2.** Grant SSH access to the inside subnet. For a local lab, do the following:

```
PixP(config)# ssh 10.0.P.0 255.255.255.0 inside
```

**Step 3.** Set the SSH inactivity timeout to 30 minutes:

```
PixP(config)# ssh timeout 30
```

**Step 4.** Minimize, but do not close, the Telnet session window. Double-click the **Shortcut to ttssh.exe** icon on the desktop.

**Step 5.** From the Host drop-down menu within the TCP/IP group box, choose the IP address of the PIX Security Appliance inside interface.

**Step 6.** Select the **SSH** radio button.

**Step 7.** Click **OK**. The Security Warning window opens.

**Step 8.** Select **Add this new key to the known hosts lists**.

**Step 9.** Click **Continue**. The SSH Authentication window opens.

**Step 10.** Enter **pix** as the username and **cisco** as the pass phrase. Click **OK**. The following should be displayed on the console terminal:

```
Device opened successfully.
SSH: host key initialised
SSH0: SSH client: IP = '10.0.P.11' interface # = 1
SSH0: starting SSH control process
SSH0: Exchanging versions - SSH-1.5-Cisco-1.25
SSH0: client version is - SSH-1.5-TTSSH/1.5.4 Win32
SSH0: begin server key generation
SSH0: complete server key generation, elapsed time = 2000 ms
SSH0: declare what cipher(s) we support: 0x00 0x00 0x00 0x0c
SSH0: SSH_SMSG_PUBLIC_KEY message sent
SSH0: SSH_CMSG_SESSION_KEY message received - msg type 0x03, length 144
SSH0: client requests 3DES cipher: 3
SSH0: keys exchanged and encryption on
SSH: Installing crc compensation attack detector.
SSH0: authentication request for userid pix
SSH(pix): user authen method is 'no AAA', aaa server group ID = 0
SSH0: authentication successful for pix
SSH0: starting exec shell
```

**Step 11.** Enter privileged mode. When prompted for a password, enter **prmode15**:

```
PixP>enable
Password:
PixP#
```

**Step 12.** Enter configuration mode:

```
PixP# config t
PixP(config)#
```

**Step 13.** To view the status the SSH session, enter the following command:

```
PixP(config)# show ssh sessions
Session ID Client IP Version Encryption State Username
0 insidehost 1.5 3DES 6 pix
```

**Step 14.** Disconnect the SSH session:

```
PixP(config)# ssh disconnect 0
```

**Step 15.** Click **OK** in the TTSSH window.

**Step 16.** Return to the Telnet session window, and change the PIX Security Appliance's Telnet password from **cisco** to **sshpass**:

```
PixP(config)# passwd sshpass
```

**Step 17.** Exit configuration mode:

```
PixP(config)# exit
PixP#
```

**Step 18.** Exit privileged mode:

```
PixP# exit
Logoff

Type help or '?' for a list of available commands.

PixP>
```

**Step 19.** Minimize the Telnet window. Do *not* close it.

*Note*: Leave this Telnet session open throughout the rest of this lab exercise.

**Step 20.** Establish another SSH session to the PIX Security Appliance. When prompted to authenticate, enter **pix** as the username and **sshpass** as the pass phrase.

## Task 5: Configuring Local User Authentication

To configure local user authentication through a secure SSH session, complete the following steps.

**Step 1.** Enter privileged mode. When prompted for a password, enter **prmode15**:

```
PixP>enable
Password:
PixP#
```

**Step 2.** Enter configuration mode:

```
PixP# config t
PixP(config)#
```

**Step 3.** Create three user accounts in the local database:

```
PixP(config)# username user10 password user10pass privilege 10
PixP(config)# username user12 password user12pass privilege 12
PixP(config)# username admin password adminpass privilege 15
```

What purpose is served by assigning different user privilege levels?

___

___

**Step 4.** Enable authentication using the LOCAL database:

```
PixP(config)# aaa authentication enable console LOCAL
```

**Step 5.** Disconnect the SSH session.

## Task 6: Testing Command Authorization with Local User Authentication

To test command authorization with local user authentication, complete the following steps.

**Step 1.** Return to the Telnet session.

**Step 2.** Enter privileged mode. When prompted for a username, enter **user12**. When prompted for a password, enter **user12pass**:

```
PixP> enable
Username:
Password:
PixP#
```

**Step 3.** Enter configuration mode:

```
PixP# config t
PixP(config)#
```

**Step 4.** View the user account that is currently logged in:

```
PixP(config)# show curpriv
Username : user12
Current privilege level : 12
Current Mode/s : P_PRIV P_CONF
```

**Step 5.** Verify that the **nameif** command is useable by attempting to change the Ethernet 4 name and security level:

```
PixP(config)# nameif e4 BOB sec36
```

**Step 6.** View the configuration:

```
PixP(config)# show nameif
nameif ethernet0 outside security0
nameif ethernet1 inside security100
nameif ethernet2 dmz security50
```

```
nameif ethernet3 PRIVTEST security30
nameif ethernet4 BOB security36
nameif ethernet5 intf5 security25
```

**Step 7.** Verify that the **`interface`** command is useable:

```
PixP(config)# interface e4 100full
```

**Step 8.** View the configuration:

```
PixP(config)# show int
interface ethernet0 "outside" is up, line protocol is up
Hardware is i82559 ethernet, address is 0003.e300.486a
IP address 192.168.P.2, subnet mask 255.255.255.0
MTU 1500 bytes, BW 100000 Kbit full duplex
0 packets input, 0 bytes, 0 no buffer
Received 0 broadcasts, 0 runts, 0 giants
0 input errors, 0 CRC, 0 frame, 0 overrun, 0 ignored, 0 abort
0 packets output, 0 bytes, 0 underruns
0 output errors, 0 collisions, 0 interface resets
0 babbles, 0 late collisions, 0 deferred
0 lost carrier, 0 no carrier
input queue (curr/max blocks): hardware (128/128) software (0/0)
output queue (curr/max blocks): hardware (0/0) software (0/0)
interface ethernet1 "inside" is up, line protocol is up
Hardware is i82559 ethernet, address is 0003.e300.486b
IP address 10.0.P.1, subnet mask 255.255.255.0
MTU 1500 bytes, BW 100000 Kbit full duplex
6197 packets input, 597517 bytes, 0 no buffer
Received 2231 broadcasts, 0 runts, 0 giants
0 input errors, 0 CRC, 0 frame, 0 overrun, 0 ignored, 0 abort
4698 packets output, 356441 bytes, 0 underruns
0 output errors, 0 collisions, 0 interface resets
0 babbles, 0 late collisions, 0 deferred
0 lost carrier, 0 no carrier
input queue (curr/max blocks): hardware (128/128) software (0/5)
output queue (curr/max blocks): hardware (1/3) software (0/2)
interface ethernet2 "dmz" is up, line protocol is up
Hardware is i82558 ethernet, address is 00e0.b602.375b
IP address 172.16.P.1, subnet mask 255.255.255.0
MTU 1500 bytes, BW 100000 Kbit full duplex
1890 packets input, 280534 bytes, 0 no buffer
Received 1890 broadcasts, 0 runts, 0 giants
0 input errors, 0 CRC, 0 frame, 0 overrun, 0 ignored, 0 abort
0 packets output, 0 bytes, 0 underruns
0 output errors, 0 collisions, 0 interface resets
0 babbles, 0 late collisions, 0 deferred
0 lost carrier, 0 no carrier
input queue (curr/max blocks): hardware (128/128) software (0/3)
output queue (curr/max blocks): hardware (0/0) software (0/0)
interface ethernet3 "PRIVTEST" is up, line protocol is down
Hardware is i82558 ethernet, address is 00e0.b602.375a
IP address 127.0.0.1, subnet mask 255.255.255.255
MTU 1500 bytes, BW 100000 Kbit full duplex
0 packets input, 0 bytes, 0 no buffer
Received 0 broadcasts, 0 runts, 0 giants
0 input errors, 0 CRC, 0 frame, 0 overrun, 0 ignored, 0 abort
0 packets output, 0 bytes, 0 underruns
0 output errors, 0 collisions, 0 interface resets
0 babbles, 0 late collisions, 0 deferred
0 lost carrier, 0 no carrier
input queue (curr/max blocks): hardware (128/128) software (0/0)
output queue (curr/max blocks): hardware (0/0) software (0/0)
interface ethernet4 "BOB" is up, line protocol is down
Hardware is i82558 ethernet, address is 00e0.b602.3759
IP address 127.0.0.1, subnet mask 255.255.255.255
MTU 1500 bytes, BW 100000 Kbit full duplex
0 packets input, 0 bytes, 0 no buffer
Received 0 broadcasts, 0 runts, 0 giants
0 input errors, 0 CRC, 0 frame, 0 overrun, 0 ignored, 0 abort
0 packets output, 0 bytes, 0 underruns
0 output errors, 0 collisions, 0 interface resets
0 babbles, 0 late collisions, 0 deferred
0 lost carrier, 0 no carrier
input queue (curr/max blocks): hardware (128/128) software (0/0)
output queue (curr/max blocks): hardware (0/0) software (0/0)
interface ethernet5 "intf5" is up, line protocol is down
Hardware is i82558 ethernet, address is 00e0.b602.3758
IP address 127.0.0.1, subnet mask 255.255.255.255
```

```
MTU 1500 bytes, BW 100000 Kbit full duplex
0 packets input, 0 bytes, 0 no buffer
Received 0 broadcasts, 0 runts, 0 giants
0 input errors, 0 CRC, 0 frame, 0 overrun, 0 ignored, 0 abort
0 packets output, 0 bytes, 0 underruns
0 output errors, 0 collisions, 0 interface resets
0 babbles, 0 late collisions, 0 deferred
0 lost carrier, 0 no carrier
input queue (curr/max blocks): hardware (128/128) software (0/0)
output queue (curr/max blocks): hardware (0/0) software (0/0)
```

**Step 9.** Try to create a static mapping for the demilitarized zone (DMZ) host 172.16.P.4:

```
PixP(config)# static (dmz,outside) 192.168.P.18 172.16.P.4 netmask 255.255.255.255
Command authorization failed
```

**Step 10.** Log out of the user12 account:

```
PixP(config)# logout
Logoff
Type help or '?' for a list of available commands.
PixP>
```

**Step 11.** Log in to the user 10 account. When prompted for a username, enter **user10**. When prompted for a password, enter **user10pass**:

```
PixP>login
Username:
Password:
PixP#
```

**Step 12.** Enter configuration mode:

```
PixP# config t
PixP(config)#
```

**Step 13.** Verify that the **nameif** command is useable by creating a name and security level for Ethernet 5:

```
PixP(config)# nameif e5 ALICE sec60
```

**Step 14.** View the configuration:

```
PixP(config)# show nameif
nameif ethernet0 outside security0
nameif ethernet1 inside security100
nameif ethernet2 dmz security50
nameif ethernet3 PRIVTEST security30
nameif ethernet4 BOB security36
nameif ethernet5 ALICE security60
```

**Step 15.** Try to use the **interface** command to enable Ethernet 5 for 100-Mbps Ethernet full-duplex communication:

```
PixP(config)# interface e5 100full
Command authorization failed
```

**Step 16.** Log out of the user10 account:

```
PixP(config)# logout
Logoff
Type help or '?' for a list of available commands.
PixP>
```

**Step 17.** Log in to the user admin account. When prompted for a username, enter **admin**. When prompted for a password, enter **adminpass**:

```
PixP>login
Username:
Password:
PixP#
```

**Step 18.** Enter configuration mode:

```
PixP# config t
PixP(config)#
```

**Step 19.** Clear the AAA configuration:

```
PixP(config)# clear aaa
```

**Step 20.** Save the configuration:

```
PixP(config)# write mem
Building configuration...
Cryptochecksum: a2d046eb daa27d65 f4a7a65f cdb3b13d
[OK]
```

## Lab 13.6.2 Perform Password Recovery

Estimated Time: 20 Minutes

Number of Team Members: Two teams with four students per team

### Objectives

In this lab, students complete the following tasks:

- Upgrade the PIX image.
- Perform password recovery procedures.

### Overview

One of the major job duties of a network administer is planning. Network administrators plan for new network design projects, future performance requirements, image upgrades, and contingency plans. Upgrading and performing password recovery are core skills needed by all network administrators. There may be situations when network administrators are locked out of their PIX Security Appliance. Password lockouts can occur from incorrectly configured enable passwords, incorrectly configured AAA parameters, and improperly documenting passwords. In this lab, students perform the steps involved in performing password recovery and upgrading the image of a PIX Security Appliance.

Figure 13-3 illustrates the network environment students create for this lab.

**Figure 13-3 Lab 13.6.2 Network Topology**

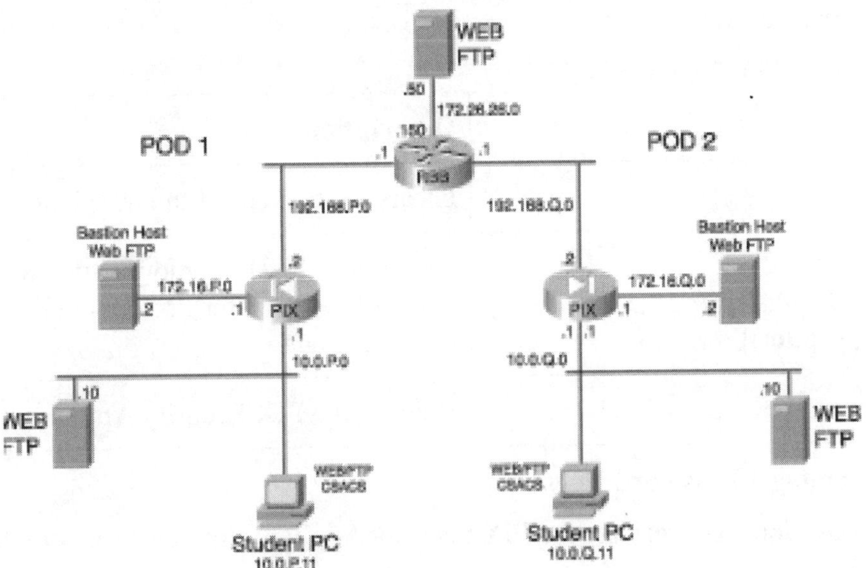


### Preparation

Begin with the standard lab topology and verify the standard configuration on the Pod PIX Security Appliances. Access the PIX Security Appliance console port using the terminal emulator on the student PC. If desired, save the PIX Security Appliance configuration to a text file for later analysis.

## Tools and Resources

To complete the lab, the standard lab topology is required:

- Two Pod PIX Security Appliances
- Two student PCs
- One server
- Backbone switch and router
- Two console cables and HyperTerminal

## Additional Materials

Students can use the following links for more information on the objectives covered in this lab:

- http://www.cisco.com/en/US/products/hw/vpndevc/ps2030/products_password_recovery09186a008009478b.shtml
- http://www.cisco.com/en/US/products/sw/secursw/ps2120/products_configuration_guide_chapter09186a00800eb0c5.html

Additional information on configuring firewalls can be found in *Cisco Secure PIX Firewalls,* by David Chapman and Andy Fox (published by Cisco Press; ISBN 1587050358).

## Command List

Table 13-3 lists the commands used throughout this lab. Refer to this list if assistance or help is needed during the lab exercise.

**Table 13-3 Lab 13.6.2 Command List**

| **Command** | **Description** |
|---|---|
| **clear xlate** | Clears the content of the translation slots |
| **copy tftp**[:[[//*location*] [/*tftp_pathname*]]] **flash**[:[**image** \| **pdm**]] | Downloads Flash memory software images through Trivial File Transfer Protocol (TFTP) without using monitor mode |
| **reload** | Reloads the PIX Security Appliance |

### Task 1: Performing a Password Recovery

To perform a password recovery for the PIX Security Appliance model 515, complete the following steps.

**Step 1.** Open and minimize the TFTP server on the desktop.

**Step 2.** Clear the translation table:

```
PixP(config)# clear xlate
```

**Step 3.** Create an enable password for entering into privileged mode:

```
PixP(config)# enable password badpassword
```

**Step 4.** Save the configuration:

```
PixP(config)# write memory
Building configuration...
Cryptochecksum: e18c684e d86c9171 9f63acf0 f64a8b43
[OK]
```

**Step 5.** Log out of the admin account:

```
PixP(config)# logout
Logoff
Type help or '?' for a list of available commands.
PixP>
```

**Step 6.** Attempt to enter privileged mode with the old password, **prmode15**:

```
PixP> enable
Password:
Invalid password:
```

**Step 7.** Enter privileged mode with the new password, **badpassword**:

```
Password:
PixP#
```

**Step 8.** Reboot the PIX Security Appliance and interrupt the boot process to enter monitor mode. To do this, press the **Escape** key or send a break character:

```
PixP# reload
```

**Step 9.** Specify the PIX Security Appliance interface to use for TFTP:

```
monitor> int 1
```

**Step 10.** Specify the PIX Security Appliance interface IP address:

```
monitor> address 10.0.P.1
```

**Step 11.** Verify connectivity to the TFTP server:

```
monitor> ping 10.0.P.11
```

**Step 12.** Name the server:

```
monitor> server 10.0.P.11
```

**Step 13.** Name the image filename:

```
monitor> file np62.bin
```

**Step 14.** Start the TFTP process:

```
monitor> tftp
tftp
np62.bin@10.0.P.11.............................................................................
.................................................................
Received 73728 bytes
Cisco Secure PIX Security Appliance password tool (3.0) #0: Wed Mar 27 11:02:16 PST 2002
Flash=i28F640J5 @ 0x300
BIOS Flash=AT29C257 @ 0xd8000
```

**Step 15.** When prompted, press **y** to erase the password:

```
Do you wish to erase the passwords? [yn] y
The following lines will be removed from the configuration:
enable password GlFe5rCOwv2JUi5H level 5 encrypted
enable password .7P6WvOReYzHKnus level 10 encrypted
enable password tgGMO76/Nf26X5Lv encrypted
passwd w.UT.4mPsVA418Ij encrypted
Do you want to remove the commands listed above from the configuration? [yn]
Please enter a y or n.
```

**Step 16.** When prompted, press **Y** to erase the passwords:

```
Do you want to remove the commands listed above from the configuration? [yn] y
Passwords and aaa commands have been erased.
```

The system automatically erases the passwords and starts rebooting.

**Step 17.** Verify that the password **badpassword** has been erased by entering privileged mode on the PIX Security Appliance:

```
Pix> enable
password: <Enter>
PixP#
```

**Task 2: Updating the PIX Image**

To load the PIX Security Appliance 515 image using TFTP, complete the following steps.

**Step 1.** Use the **copy tftp flash** command to load the image file pix621.bin:

```
PixP# copy tftp://10.0.P.11/pix621.bin flash:image
```

**Step 2.** After the PIX Security Appliance has received the image from the TFTP server and the message "Image installed" is displayed, reload the PIX Security Appliance. When prompted to confirm, press **Enter**:

```
PixP# reload
Proceed with reload? [confirm] <Enter>
```

**Step 3.** Enter the **show version** command to verify that the PIX Security Appliance software version 6.2(1) has been loaded:

```
PixP> show version
Cisco PIX Security Appliance Version 6.2(1)
Cisco PIX Device Manager Version 1.1(1)
Compiled on Fri 01-Feb-02 15:14 by root
PixP up 34 mins 52 secs
Hardware: PIX-515, 64 MB RAM, CPU Pentium 200 MHz
Flash i28F640J5 @ 0x300, 16MB
BIOS Flash AT29C257 @ 0xfffd8000, 32KB
0: ethernet0: address is 0003.e300.486a, irq 10
1: ethernet1: address is 0003.e300.486b, irq 7
2: ethernet2: address is 00e0.b602.375b, irq 11
3: ethernet3: address is 00e0.b602.375a, irq 11
4: ethernet4: address is 00e0.b602.3759, irq 11
5: ethernet5: address is 00e0.b602.3758, irq 11
Licensed Features:
Failover: Enabled
VPN-DES: Enabled
VPN-3DES: Enabled
Maximum Interfaces: 6
Cut-through Proxy: Enabled
Guards: Enabled
URL-filtering: Enabled
Inside Hosts: Unlimited
Throughput: Unlimited
IKE peers: Unlimited
Serial Number: 480430946 (0x1ca2cb62)
Running Activation Key: 0xf4e352a3 0xef857686 0x468be692 0xbd984b0b
Configuration last modified by enable_15 at 18:20:17.510 UTC Thu Apr 18 2002
```

## Review Questions

1. Describe configuration replication.

______________________________________________

______________________________________________

______________________________________________

______________________________________________

2. Describe non-stateful failover.

_______________________________________________

_______________________________________________

_______________________________________________

_______________________________________________

3. Describe stateful failover.

_______________________________________________

_______________________________________________

_______________________________________________

_______________________________________________

4. Describe the limitation of failover using a serial cable and how LAN-based failover overcomes this limitation.

_______________________________________________

_______________________________________________

_______________________________________________

_______________________________________________

5. What are the three ways to provide command authorization?

_______________________________________________

_______________________________________________

_______________________________________________

_______________________________________________

## Chapter 13 Quiz Questions

1. What is the command used to save the configuration file to the Flash memory of the PIX Security Appliance?

   A. **copy flash**

   B. **write flash**

   C. **write config**

   D. **write memory**

2. What is the command that will assign the password *secretpassword* for access to level 10 commands?

   A. **enable password** *secretPasSword* **level 10**

   B. **enable password SECRETPASSWORD level 10**

C. **enable password secretpassword level 10**

D. **enable password secretpassword 10**

3. What command creates the virtual MAC address for the PIX Security Appliance?

A. **virtual mac address**

B. **failover mac address**

C. **mac address** *mac_address*

D. **primary mac address**

4. LAN-based failover provides message encryption and authentication using a manual pre-shared key.

A. True

B. False

5. The PIX Security Appliance allows a maximum of _________ SSH client connections.

A. 1

B. 1 per interface

C. 2

D. 5

6. What is the command that will allow your assistant Bob to access the PIX Security Appliance's level 11 commands that are using the encrypted password TooManySecrets?

A. **username Bob password** *tooManysecrets* encrypted level 11

B. **username Bob password** *TooManySecrets* **encrypted level 11**

C. **username Bob password** *tooManySecrets* **encrypted level 11**

D. **username Bob password** *toomanysecrets* **encrypted level 11**

7. ACS command authorization uses usernames that are defined in the ______.

A. PIX Security Appliance local database

B. Remote TACACS+ server database

C. Remote RADIUS server database

D. Local user database

8. In a LAN-based failover setup, what is the recommended procedure after configuring the secondary PIX Security Appliance?

A. Reload the secondary firewall.

B. Connect the secondary firewall to the network.

C. Save the configuration to Flash memory.

D. Turn on the secondary firewall.

9. After configuring stateful failover between two PIX Security Appliances, no further commands are necessary to allow uninterrupted connections for all protocols if the primary PIX Security Appliance fails.

   A. True

   B. False

10. How many tests can the PIX Security Appliance perform to determine if either firewall has failed?

    A. 1

    B. 2

    C. 4

    D. 5

# Chapter 14

## PIX Security Appliance VPNs

This chapter covers using the PIX Security Appliance as part of a Virtual Private Network (VPN). After a brief overview of VPNs, the student learns of the different capabilities the PIX Security Appliance provides in VPN topologies.

IP Security (IPSec) is discussed as it applies to the PIX Security Appliance and the configuration tasks that are needed to implement IPSec support on the PIX. The terms should be familiar from the discussion of using IPSec with routers.

There are specific steps required in preparing to configure IPSec. The Internet Key Exchange (IKE) Phase 1 policy parameters and the IPSec policy parameters must be determined. After the policy parameters are determined, the firewall can be configured, tested, and verified for proper operation.

When the PIX Security Appliance configuration is completed, students learn about the different VPN clients that can be used. Several client platforms can be configured to operate a PIX-to-VPN client tunnel.

Finally, there is a brief overview of scaling PIX Security Appliance VPNs.

**Vocabulary Exercise**

AH

---

---

ESP

---

---

IKE

---

---

message authentication code

---

---

Oakley key exchange

---

---

SA

---

---

Skeme key exchange

---

---

SPI

---

---

## Lab Activities

The topology figures and lab examples contain **P** and **Q** values. The **P** value in the addressing and naming scheme refers to *your* assigned Pod number.

The following are examples of determining P values:

- Pod2 is looking at a topology figure and is trying to determine the P values in the figure. In this scenario, the P values would equal 2. 10.0.P.12 would become 10.0.2.12, 172.30.P.2 would become 172.30.2.2, and so on.
- Pod1 is looking at a topology figure and is trying to determine the P values in the figure. In this scenario, the P values would equal 1. 10.0.P.12 would become 10.0.1.12, 172.30.P.2 would become 172.30.1.2, and so on.

In both examples, the P values are directly related to the Pod number of the team.

The **Q** value in the naming and addressing scheme is used when testing the security or connectivity with the peer team.

The following are examples of determining Q values:

- In a lab, Pod2 has been asked to test connectivity to their peer inside host at IP address 10.0.Q.12. In this scenario, 10.0.**Q**.12 would equal 10.0.**1**.12.
- In a lab, Pod1 has been asked to test connectivity to their peer inside host at IP address 10.0.Q.12. In this scenario, 10.0.**Q**.12 would equal 10.0.**2**.12.

In both examples, the Q value is directly related to the peer Pod number.

# Lab 14.6.6: Configure a Secure VPN Gateway Using IPSec Between Two Cisco Secure PIX Security Appliances

Estimated Time: 45 Minutes

Number of Team Members: Two teams with four students per team

## Objective

In this lab, students complete the following tasks:

- Prepare to configure VPN support.
- Configure IKE parameters.
- Configure IPSec parameters.
- Test and verify an IPSec configuration.

## Overview

In this lab, students configure two Cisco Secure PIX Security Appliances to run a VPN tunnel from PIX to PIX over the network using IPSec. IPSec is a combination of open standards that provides data confidentiality, data integrity, and data origin authentication between IPSec peers.

IPSec negotiation can be broken down into five steps, including two IKE phases.

An IPSec tunnel is initiated by interesting traffic. Traffic is considered interesting when it is traveling between the IPSec peers.

In IKE Phase 1, the IPSec peers negotiate the established IKE security association (SA) policy. After the peers are authenticated, a secure tunnel is created using Internet Security Association and Key Management Protocol (ISAKMP).

In IKE Phase 2, the IPSec peers use the authenticated and secure tunnel to negotiate IPSec SA transforms. The negotiation of the shared policy determines how the IPSec tunnel will be established.

The IPSec tunnel is created and data is transferred between the IPSec peers based on the IPSec parameters configured in the IPSec transform sets.

The IPSec tunnel terminates when the IPSec SAs are deleted or when their lifetime expires.

*Note*: IPSec negotiation between the two PIXs will fail if the SAs in both IKE phases do not match on the peers.

Figure 14-1 illustrates the network environment students create for this lab.

## Preparation

Begin with the standard lab topology in Figure 14-1 and verify the standard configuration on Pod PIX Security Appliances. Access the PIX Security Appliance console port using the terminal emulator on the student PC. If desired, save the PIX Security Appliance configuration to a text file for later analysis.

**Figure 14-1 Lab 14.6.6 Network Topology**

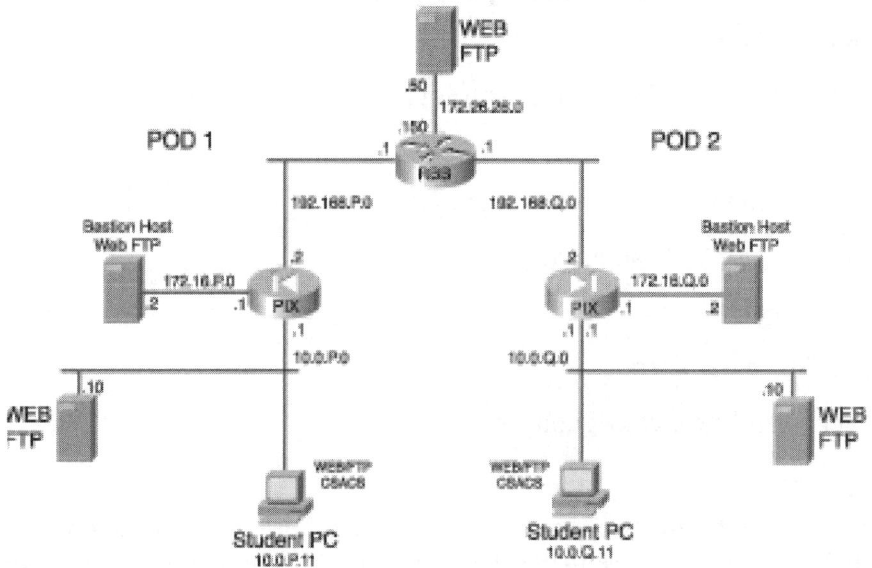


## Tools and Resources

To complete the lab, the standard lab topology is required:

- Two Pod PIX Security Appliances
- Two student PCs
- One server
- Backbone switch and router
- Two console cables and HyperTerminal

## Additional Materials

Students can use the following link for more information on the objectives covered in this lab:

- http://www.cisco.com/en/US/products/hw/vpndevc/ps2030/prod_configuration_examples_list.html

## Command List

Table 14-1 lists the commands used throughout this lab. Refer to this list if you need any assistance during the lab.

**Table 14-1 Lab 14.6.6 Command List**

| Command | Description |
|---|---|
| **clear** [**crypto**] **map** | Deletes all parameters entered through the **crypto map** command belonging to the specified map; does not delete dynamic maps. |

| Command | Description |
|---|---|
| **clear isakmp** | Removes **isakmp** command statements from the configuration. |
| **clear sysopt** | Removes **sysopt** command statements from the configuration. |
| **crypto ipsec transform-set** *transform-set-name transform1* [*transform2* [*transform3*]] | Creates, views, or deletes IPSec security associations, security association global lifetime values, and global transform sets. Configuration mode. |
| **crypto map** *map-name seq-num* **ipsec-isakmp** \| **ipsec-manual** [**dynamic** *dynamic-map-name*] | Creates, modifies, views, or deletes a crypto map entry; also deletes a crypto map set. Configuration mode. |
| **crypto map** *map-name* **interface** *interface-name* | Creates, modifies, views, or deletes a crypto map entry; also deletes a crypto map set. Configuration mode. |
| **debug crypto ipsec** [*level*] | Packets or Internet Control Message Protocol (ICMP) tracings can be debugged through the PIX Security Appliance. The **debug** command provides information that helps troubleshoot protocols operating with and through the PIX Security Appliance. Configuration mode. |
| **debug crypto isakmp** [*level*] | Packets or ICMP tracings can be debugged through the PIX Security Appliance. The **debug** command provides information that helps troubleshoot protocols operating with and through the PIX Security Appliance. Configuration mode. |
| **isakmp enable** *interface-name* | Negotiates IPSec security associations and enables IPSec secure communications. Configuration mode. |
| **isakmp identity address** \| **hostname** | Sets the IKE identity. |
| **isakmp key** *keystring* **address** *peer-address* [**netmask** *mask*] [**no-xauth**] [**no-config-mode**] | Negotiates IPSec security associations and enables IPSec secure communications. Configuration mode. |
| **isakmp policy** *priority* **authentication** *pre-share* \| *rsa-sig* | Configures a basic IKE policy using preshared keys for authentication. |

| Command | Description |
|---|---|
| **show crypto** | Displays the configured IPSec, IKE, and CA. |
| **show isakmp** | Displays the configured ISAKMP policy. |
| **show static** | Configures one-to-one address translation rules. |
| **sysopt connection permit-pptp \| permit-l2tp \| permit-ipsec** | Changes PIX Security Appliance system options. Configuration mode. |

### Task 1: Preparing to Configure VPN Support

Complete the following steps to prepare for the IKE and IPSec configuration. For this task, use default values except when directed to enter a specific value. Use preshared keys for the IKE policy, and use Encapsulating Security Payload (ESP) mode with DES encryption for the IPSec policy.

**Step 1.** Verify that a static translation is configured from a global IP address on the outside interface to the internal host:

```
PixP(config)# show static
static (dmz,outside) 192.168.P.11 bastionhost netmask 255.255.255.255 0 0
static (inside,outside) 192.168.P.10 insidehost netmask 255.255.255.255 0 0
```

**Step 2.** Verify that an access control list (ACL) permitting web access to the inside host has been configured:

```
PixP(config)# show access-list
access-list ACLIN; 10 elements
access-list ACLIN permit tcp 192.168.Q.0 255.255.255.0 object-group FTPSERVERS object-group
MYSERVICES
access-list ACLIN permit tcp 192.168.Q.0 255.255.255.0 host 192.168.P.11 eq www (hitcnt=4)
access-list ACLIN permit tcp 192.168.Q.0 255.255.255.0 host 192.168.P.11 eq ftp (hitcnt=2)
access-list ACLIN permit tcp any object-group ALLSERVERS eq www
access-list ACLIN permit tcp any host 192.168.P.11 eq www (hitcnt=0)
access-list ACLIN permit tcp any host 192.168.P.10 eq www (hitcnt=2)
access-list ACLIN permit tcp any host 192.168.P.6 eq www (hitcnt=0)
access-list ACLIN permit tcp any host 192.168.P.7 eq www (hitcnt=0)
access-list ACLIN permit icmp any any object-group PING
access-list ACLIN permit icmp any any echo (hitcnt=12)
access-list ACLIN permit icmp any any echo-reply (hitcnt=4)
access-list ACLIN permit icmp any any unreachable (hitcnt=0)
access-list ACLIN deny ip any any (hitcnt=3)
access-list ACLDMZ; 3 elements
access-list ACLDMZ permit icmp any any object-group PING
access-list ACLDMZ permit icmp any any echo (hitcnt=0)
access-list ACLDMZ permit icmp any any echo-reply (hitcnt=8)
access-list ACLDMZ permit icmp any any unreachable (hitcnt=0)
```

**Step 3.** Ensure a web connection can be established between Pods from the student PCs using the static and ACL.

**Step 4.** Enable the PIX Security Appliance to implicitly permit any packet from an IPSec tunnel and bypass checking with an associated conduit or **access-group** command for IPSec connections:

```
PixP(config)# sysopt connection permit-ipsec
```

### Task 2: Configuring IKE Parameters

Complete the following steps to configure IKE on the PIX Security Appliance.

**Step 1.** Ensure IKE is enabled on the outside interface:

```
PixP(config)# isakmp enable outside
```

**Step 2.** Configure a basic IKE policy using preshared keys for authentication:

```
PixP(config)# isakmp policy 10 authentication pre-share
```

**Step 3.** Set the IKE identity:

```
PixP(config)# isakmp identity address
```

**Step 4.** Configure the ISAKMP preshared key to point to the outside IP address of the peer PIX Security Appliance:

```
PixP(config)# isakmp key cisco123 address 192.168.Q.2 netmask 255.255.255.255
```

To test the command authorization configured in Task 1, complete the following steps:

**Step 1.** Enter privileged mode level 12. When prompted for a password, enter **prmode12**:

```
PixP> enable 12
Password:
PixP#
```

**Step 2.** Enter configuration mode:

```
PixP# config t
```

**Step 3.** Verify that the **nameif** command is useable:

```
PixP(config)# nameif e3 PRIVTEST sec30
```

**Step 4.** View the configuration:

```
PixP(config)# show nameif
nameif ethernet0 outside security0
nameif ethernet1 inside security100
nameif ethernet2 dmz security50
nameif ethernet3 PRIVTEST security30
nameif ethernet4 intf4 security20
nameif ethernet5 intf5 security25
```

**Step 5.** Verify that the **interface** command is useable:

```
PixP(config)# interface e3 100full
```

**Step 6.** View the configuration:

```
PixP(config)# show interface
interface ethernet0 "outside" is up, line protocol is up
Hardware is i82559 ethernet, address is 0003.e300.483a
IP address 192.168.P.2, subnet mask 255.255.255.0
MTU 1500 bytes, BW 100000 Kbit full duplex
10640 packets input, 1374788 bytes, 0 no buffer
Received 7179 broadcasts, 0 runts, 0 giants
0 input errors, 0 CRC, 0 frame, 0 overrun, 0 ignored, 0 abort
3458 packets output, 348972 bytes, 0 underruns
0 output errors, 0 collisions, 0 interface resets
0 babbles, 0 late collisions, 0 deferred
0 lost carrier, 0 no carrier
input queue (curr/max blocks): hardware (128/128) software (0/6)
output queue (curr/max blocks): hardware (0/9) software (0/2)
interface ethernet1 "inside" is up, line protocol is up
Hardware is i82559 ethernet, address is 0003.e300.483b
IP address 10.0.P.1, subnet mask 255.255.255.0
MTU 1500 bytes, BW 100000 Kbit full duplex
11119 packets input, 1438842 bytes, 0 no buffer
Received 7554 broadcasts, 0 runts, 0 giants
0 input errors, 0 CRC, 0 frame, 0 overrun, 0 ignored, 0 abort
4153 packets output, 390555 bytes, 0 underruns
0 output errors, 0 collisions, 0 interface resets
0 babbles, 0 late collisions, 0 deferred
0 lost carrier, 0 no carrier
input queue (curr/max blocks): hardware (128/128) software (0/4)
output queue (curr/max blocks): hardware (0/15) software (0/14)
```

```
interface ethernet2 "dmz" is up, line protocol is up
Hardware is i82558 ethernet, address is 00e0.b602.3387
IP address 172.16.P.1, subnet mask 255.255.255.0
MTU 1500 bytes, BW 100000 Kbit full duplex
7024 packets input, 1050994 bytes, 0 no buffer
Received 6991 broadcasts, 0 runts, 0 giants
0 input errors, 0 CRC, 0 frame, 0 overrun, 0 ignored, 0 abort
98 packets output, 41652 bytes, 0 underruns
0 output errors, 0 collisions, 0 interface resets
0 babbles, 0 late collisions, 0 deferred
0 lost carrier, 0 no carrier
input queue (curr/max blocks): hardware (128/128) software (0/2)
output queue (curr/max blocks): hardware (0/9) software (0/1)
interface ethernet3 "PRIVTEST" is up, line protocol is down
Hardware is i82558 ethernet, address is 00e0.b602.3386
IP address 172.17.P.1, subnet mask 255.255.255.0
MTU 1500 bytes, BW 100000 Kbit full duplex
2510 packets input, 317593 bytes, 0 no buffer
Received 134 broadcasts, 0 runts, 0 giants
0 input errors, 0 CRC, 0 frame, 0 overrun, 0 ignored, 0 abort
2384 packets output, 223276 bytes, 0 underruns
0 output errors, 0 collisions, 0 interface resets
0 babbles, 0 late collisions, 0 deferred
0 lost carrier, 0 no carrier
input queue (curr/max blocks): hardware (128/128) software (0/38)
output queue (curr/max blocks): hardware (0/35) software (0/1)
interface ethernet4 "intf4" is administratively down, line protocol is down
Hardware is i82558 ethernet, address is 00e0.b602.3385
IP address 127.0.0.1, subnet mask 255.255.255.255
MTU 1500 bytes, BW 10000 Kbit half duplex
0 packets input, 0 bytes, 0 no buffer
Received 0 broadcasts, 0 runts, 0 giants
0 input errors, 0 CRC, 0 frame, 0 overrun, 0 ignored, 0 abort
0 packets output, 0 bytes, 0 underruns
0 output errors, 0 collisions, 0 interface resets
0 babbles, 0 late collisions, 0 deferred
0 lost carrier, 0 no carrier
input queue (curr/max blocks): hardware (128/128) software (0/0)
output queue (curr/max blocks): hardware (0/0) software (0/0)
interface ethernet5 "intf5" is administratively down, line protocol is down
Hardware is i82558 ethernet, address is 00e0.b602.3384
IP address 127.0.0.1, subnet mask 255.255.255.255
MTU 1500 bytes, BW 10000 Kbit half duplex
0 packets input, 0 bytes, 0 no buffer
Received 0 broadcasts, 0 runts, 0 giants
0 input errors, 0 CRC, 0 frame, 0 overrun, 0 ignored, 0 abort
0 packets output, 0 bytes, 0 underruns
0 output errors, 0 collisions, 0 interface resets
0 babbles, 0 late collisions, 0 deferred
0 lost carrier, 0 no carrier
input queue (curr/max blocks): hardware (128/128) software (0/0)
output queue (curr/max blocks): hardware (0/0) software (0/0)
```

**Step 7.** Exit configuration mode:

```
PixP(config)# exit
PixP#
```

**Step 8.** Exit privileged mode:

```
PixP# exit
Logoff
Type help or '?' for a list of available commands.
PixP>
```

**Step 9.** Enter privileged mode level 10. When prompted for a password, enter **prmode10**:

```
PixP> enable 10
Password:
PixP#
```

**Step 10.** Enter configuration mode:

```
PixP# config t
PixP(config)#
```

**Step 11.** Verify the **nameif** command is useable:

```
PixP(config)# nameif e4 PRIVTEST2 sec35
```

**Step 12.** View the configuration:

```
PixP(config)# show nameif
nameif ethernet0 outside security0
nameif ethernet1 inside security100
nameif ethernet2 dmz security50
nameif ethernet3 PRIVTEST security30
nameif ethernet4 PRIVTEST2 security35
nameif ethernet5 intf5 security25
```

**Step 13.** Try to use the **interface** command:

```
PixP(config)# interface e4 100full
Command authorization failed.
```

**Step 14.** Exit configuration mode:

```
PixP(config)# exit
PixP#
```

**Step 15.** Exit privileged mode:

```
PixP# exit
Logoff
Type help or '?' for a list of available commands.
PixP>
```

**Step 16.** Enter privileged mode level 5. When prompted for a password, enter **prmode5**:

```
PixP> enable 5
Password:
PixP#
```

**Step 17.** Try to enter configuration mode:

```
PixP# config t
Command authorization failed.
```

**Step 18.** Exit privileged mode:

```
PixP# exit
Logoff
Type help or '?' for a list of available commands.
PixP>
```

**Step 19.** Enter privileged mode. When prompted for a password, enter **prmode15**:

```
PixP> enable
Password:
PixP#
```

**Step 20.** Enter configuration mode:

```
PixP# config t
PixP(config)#
```

Why were some commands accepted and others denied?

---

### Task 3: Configuring IPSec Parameters

Complete the following steps to configure IPSec (IKE Phase 2) parameters.

**Step 1.** Create an ACL to select traffic to protect. The ACL should protect IP traffic between Windows NT servers on the peer PIX Security Appliances:

```
PixP(config)# access-list 101 permit ip host 192.168.P.10 host 192.168.Q.10
```

**Step 2.** View the ACL:

```
PixP(config)# show access-list
access-list ACLIN; 10 elements
access-list ACLIN permit tcp 192.168.Q.0 255.255.255.0 object-group FTPSERVERS object-group
  MYSERVICES
```

```
access-list ACLIN permit tcp 192.168.Q.0 255.255.255.0 host 192.168.P.11 eq www (hitcnt=4)
access-list ACLIN permit tcp 192.168.Q.0 255.255.255.0 host 192.168.P.11 eq ftp (hitcnt=2)
access-list ACLIN permit tcp any object-group ALLSERVERS eq www
access-list ACLIN permit tcp any host 192.168.P.11 eq www (hitcnt=0)
access-list ACLIN permit tcp any host 192.168.P.10 eq www (hitcnt=2)
access-list ACLIN permit tcp any host 192.168.P.6 eq www (hitcnt=0)
access-list ACLIN permit tcp any host 192.168.P.7 eq www (hitcnt=0)
access-list ACLIN permit icmp any any object-group PING
access-list ACLIN permit icmp any any echo (hitcnt=12)
access-list ACLIN permit icmp any any echo-reply (hitcnt=4)
access-list ACLIN permit icmp any any unreachable (hitcnt=0)
access-list ACLIN deny ip any any (hitcnt=3)
access-list ACLDMZ; 3 elements
access-list ACLDMZ permit icmp any any object-group PING
access-list ACLDMZ permit icmp any any echo (hitcnt=0)
access-list ACLDMZ permit icmp any any echo-reply (hitcnt=8)
access-list ACLDMZ permit icmp any any unreachable (hitcnt=0)
access-list 101; 1 elements
access-list 101 permit ip host 192.168.P.10 host 192.168.Q.10 (hitcnt=0)
```

**Step 3.** Configure an IPSec transform set (IKE Phase 2 parameters) to use ESP and DES. Use a transform-set name of pixQ:

```
PixP(config)# crypto ipsec transform-set pixQ esp-des
```

What are some other IPSec security protocol combinations that can be used?

_______________________________________________________________________________

**Step 4.** Create a crypto map by completing the following substeps.

a. Create a crypto map entry. Use a map-name of peer Q:

```
PixP(config)# crypto map peerQ 10 ipsec-isakmp
```

b. Look at the crypto map and observe the defaults:

```
PixP(config)# show crypto map
Crypto Map "peerQ" 10 ipsec-isakmp
No matching address list set.
Current peer: 0.0.0.0
Security association lifetime: 4608000 kilobytes/28800 seconds
PFS (Y/N): N
Transform sets={ }
```

c. Assign the ACL to the crypto map:

```
PixP(config)# crypto map peerQ 10 match address 101
```

d. Define the peer. The peer IP address should be set to the peer's outside interface IP address:

```
PixP(config)# crypto map peerQ 10 set peer 192.168.Q.2
```

e. Specify the transform set used to reach the peer. Use the transform set name configured in substep b:

```
PixP(config)# crypto map peerQ 10 set transform-set pixQ
```

f. Apply the crypto map set to the outside interface:

```
PixP(config)# crypto map peerQ interface outside
```

## Task 4: Testing and Verifying IPSec Configuration

Complete the following steps to test and verify the VPN configuration.

**Step 1.** Verify the IKE policy. Note the default values:

```
PixP(config)# show isakmp
isakmp enable outside
```



```
isakmp key ******** address 192.168.Q.2 netmask 255.255.255.255
isakmp policy 10 authentication pre-share
isakmp policy 10 encryption des
```

```
isakmp policy 10 hash sha
isakmp policy 10 group 1
isakmp policy 10 lifetime 86400
```

**Step 2.** Examine the IKE policies in the PIX Security Appliance:

```
PixP(config)# show isakmp policy
Protection suite of priority 10
encryption algorithm: DES - Data Encryption Standard (56 bit keys).
hash algorithm: Secure Hash Standard
authentication method: Pre-Shared Key
Diffie-Hellman group: #1 (768 bit)
lifetime: 86400 seconds, no volume limit
Default protection suite
encryption algorithm: DES - Data Encryption Standard (56 bit keys).
hash algorithm: Secure Hash Standard
authentication method: Rivest-Shamir-Adleman Signature
Diffie-Hellman group: #1 (768 bit)
lifetime: 86400 seconds, no volume limit
```

**Step 3.** Verify the crypto ACL:

```
PixP(config)# show access-list 101
access-list 101; 1 elements
access-list 101 permit ip host 192.168.P.10 host 192.168.Q.10 (hitcnt=0)
```

**Step 4.** Verify that the IPSec parameters (IKE Phase 2) are correct:

```
PixP(config)# show crypto ipsec transform-set
Transform set pixQ: { esp-des }
will negotiate = { Tunnel, },
```

**Step 5.** Verify that the crypto map configuration is correct:

```
PixP(config)# show crypto map
Crypto Map: "peerQ" interfaces: { outside }
Crypto Map "peerQ" 10 ipsec-isakmp
Peer = 192.168.Q.2
access-list 101; 1 elements
access-list 101 permit ip host 192.168.P.10 host 192.168.Q.10 (hitcnt=0)
Current peer: 192.168.Q.2
Security association lifetime: 4608000 kilobytes/28800 seconds
PFS (Y/N): N
Transform sets={ pixQ, }
```

**Step 6.** Turn on debugging for IPSec and ISAKMP:

```
PixP(config)# debug crypto ipsec
PixP(config)# debug crypto isakmp
```

**Step 7.** Clear the IPSec SA by using the following command:

```
PixP(config)# clear crypto ipsec sa
```

**Step 8.** Initiate a web session from the student PC to the peer Pod's student PC. Observe the debug output and verify that the web session was established. The debug should state the following status indicating that IPSec was successful:

```
return status is IKMP_NO_ERROR
```

**Step 9.** Ensure that traffic between peers is being encrypted by completing the following substeps.

a. Examine the IPSec SAs. Note the number of packets encrypted and decrypted:

```
PixP(config)# show crypto ipsec sa
interface: outside
Crypto map tag: peerQ, local addr. 192.168.P.2
local ident (addr/mask/prot/port): (192.168.P.10/255.255.255.255/0/0)
remote ident (addr/mask/prot/port): (192.168.Q.10/255.255.255.255/0/0)
current_peer: 192.168.Q.2
PERMIT, flags={origin_is_acl,}
#pkts encaps: 11, #pkts encrypt: 11, #pkts digest 0
#pkts decaps: 6, #pkts decrypt: 6, #pkts verify 0
#pkts compressed: 0, #pkts decompressed: 0
```

```
#pkts not compressed: 0, #pkts compr. failed: 0, #pkts decompress failed: 0
#send errors 7, #recv errors 0
local crypto endpt.: 192.168.P.2, remote crypto endpt.: 192.168.Q.2
path mtu 1500, ipsec overhead 44, media mtu 1500
current outbound spi: be1be99e
inbound esp sas:
spi: 0x839aa69(137996905)
transform: esp-des ,
in use settings ={Tunnel, }
slot: 0, conn id: 2, crypto map: peer1
sa timing: remaining key lifetime (k/sec): (4607999/28604)
IV size: 8 bytes
replay detection support: N
inbound ah sas:
inbound pcp sas:
outbound esp sas:
spi: 0xbe1be99e(3189500318)
transform: esp-des ,
in use settings ={Tunnel, }
slot: 0, conn id: 1, crypto map: peer1
sa timing: remaining key lifetime (k/sec): (4607998/28595)
IV size: 8 bytes
replay detection support: N
outbound ah sas:
outbound pcp sas:
```

b. Generate additional traffic by clicking the **Reload** button of the web browser.

c. Examine the IPSec SAs again. Note that the packet counters have increased incrementally:

```
PixP(config)# show crypto ipsec sa
interface: outside
Crypto map tag: peerQ, local addr. 192.168.P.2
local ident (addr/mask/prot/port): (192.168.P.10/255.255.255.255/0/0)
remote ident (addr/mask/prot/port): (192.168.Q.10/255.255.255.255/0/0)
current_peer: 192.168.Q.2
PERMIT, flags={origin_is_acl,}
#pkts encaps: 35, #pkts encrypt: 35, #pkts digest 0
#pkts decaps: 20, #pkts decrypt: 20, #pkts verify 0
#pkts compressed: 0, #pkts decompressed: 0
#pkts not compressed: 0, #pkts compr. failed: 0, #pkts decompress failed: 0
#send errors 7, #recv errors 0
local crypto endpt.: 192.168.P.2, remote crypto endpt.: 192.168.Q.2
path mtu 1500, ipsec overhead 44, media mtu 1500
current outbound spi: be1be99e
inbound esp sas:
spi: 0x839aa69(137996905)
transform: esp-des ,
in use settings ={Tunnel, }
slot: 0, conn id: 2, crypto map: peerQ
sa timing: remaining key lifetime (k/sec): (4607996/28469)
IV size: 8 bytes
replay detection support: N
inbound ah sas:
inbound pcp sas:
outbound esp sas:
spi: 0xbe1be99e(3189500318)
transform: esp-des ,
in use settings ={Tunnel, }
slot: 0, conn id: 1, crypto map: peer1
sa timing: remaining key lifetime (k/sec): (4607993/28460)
IV size: 8 bytes
replay detection support: N
outbound ah sas:
outbound pcp sas:
```

**Step 10.** Clear the IPSec SAs with the **clear crypto sa** command:

```
PixP(config)# clear crypto sa
```

**Step 11.** Remove all **isakmp** command statements from the configuration with the **clear isakmp** command:

```
PixP(config)# clear isakmp
```

**Step 12.** Remove all parameters entered through the **crypto map** command with the **clear crypto map** command:

```
PixP(config)# clear crypto map
```

**Step 13.** Remove the **sysopt** command statements from the configuration with the **clear sysopt** command:

```
PixP(config)# clear sysopt
```

**Step 14.** Remove ACL 101 from the configuration:

```
PixP(config)# clear access-list 101
```

# Lab 14.7.5: Configure a Secure VPN Using IPSec Between a PIX and a VPN Client

Estimated Time: 30 Minutes

Number of Team Members: Two teams with four students per team

## Objective

In this lab, students complete the following tasks:

- Install and configure the Cisco VPN Client on a Microsoft Windows end-user PC.
- Configure the PIX Security Appliance for Cisco VPN Client remote access.

## Overview

CiscoSecure PIX Security Appliance (PIX) Software Release 6.0 supports connections from both the Cisco VPN Client 2.5.X and the Cisco VPN Client 3.x. The 2.5.X client uses Diffie-Hellman (DH) group 1 policy (PIX default) and the 3.x client uses DH group 2 policy. The **isakmp policy # group 2** command enables the 3.x clients to connect. Having the multiple ISAKMP policies (one for DH group 1 and one for DH group 2) is necessary only in a mixed client environment. In this lab, all clients will be running VPN Client 3.x.

Figure 14-2 illustrates the network environment students create for this lab.

**Figure 14-2 Lab 14.7.5 Network Topology**

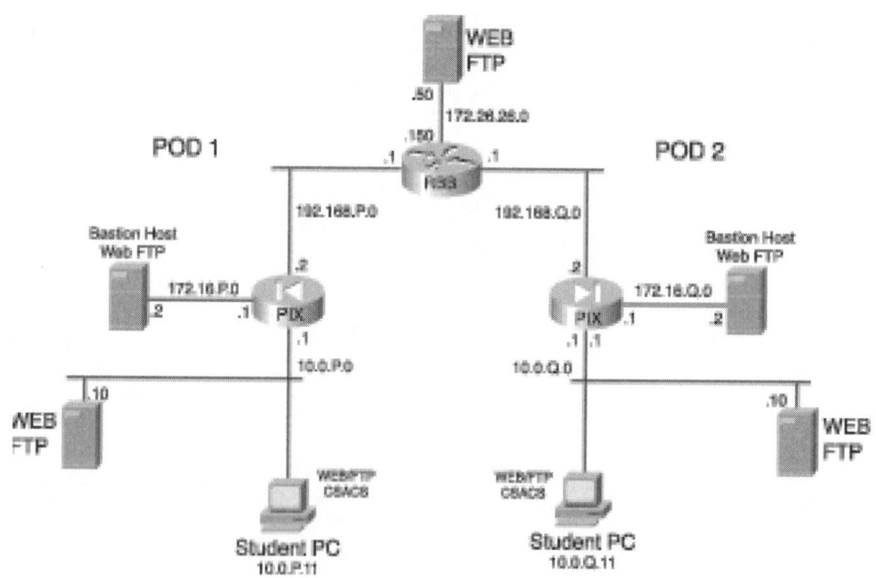


## Preparation

Begin with the standard lab topology in Figure 14-2 and verify the standard configuration on Pod PIX Security Appliances. Access the PIX Security Appliance console port using the terminal emulator on the student PC. If desired, save the PIX Security Appliance configuration to a text file for later analysis.

## Tools and Resources

To complete the lab, the standard lab topology is required:

- Two Pod PIX Security Appliances
- Two student PCs
- One server
- Backbone switch and router
- Two console cables and HyperTerminal

## Additional Materials

The student can use the following link for more information on the objectives covered in this lab:

- http://www.cisco.com/en/US/products/hw/vpndevc/ps2030/prod_configuration_examples_list.html

## Command List

Table 14-2 lists the commands used throughout this lab. Refer to this list if you need any assistance during the lab.

**Table 14-2 Lab 14.7.5 Command List**

| Command | Description |
|---|---|
| **aaa-server** *group_tag* **protocol** *auth_protocol* | Specifies an AAA server. Configuration mode. |
| **crypto dynamic-map** *dynamic-map-name dynamic-seq-num* **set transform-set** *transform-set-name1* [ *transform-set-name9*] | Creates a dynamic crypto map entry<br>Configuration mode. |
| **crypto ipsec transform-set** *transform-set-name transform1* [*transform2* [*transform3*]] | Creates IPSec transform sets<br>Configuration mode. |
| **crypto map** *map-name* **client [token] authentication** *aaa-server-name* | Configures Xauth to point to the TACACS+ server |
| **crypto map** *map-name* **interface** *interface-name* | Applies the crypto map to an interface |
| **ip local pool** *pool_name pool_start-address*[-*pool_end-address*] | Identifies addresses for a local pool<br>Configuration mode. |
| **isakmp client configuration address-pool local** *pool-name* [*interface-name*] | Configures IKE mode configuration-related parameters |

| Command | Description |
|---|---|
| **isakmp policy** *priority* **authentication** *pre-share* \| *rsa-sig* | Configures authentication for the IKE policy |
| **isakmp policy** *priority* **encryption** *des* \| *3des* | Specifies the encryption algorithm |
| **isakmp policy** *priority* **group1** \| **2** | Specifies the DH group |
| **isakmp policy** *priority* **hash** *md5* \| *sha* | Specifies the hash algorithm |
| **isakmp policy** *priority* **lifetime** *seconds* | Specifies the IKE SA's lifetime |

### Task 1: Configuring the Student PC Networking Parameters

Certain networking parameters must be configured before the student PC will operate in the lab environment. Complete the following steps to configure the student PC networking parameters. This procedure assumes that the Windows 2000 server is operating with an active network interface card (NIC).

**Step 1.** Change the IP address and default gateway of the student PC. Use the following configuration parameters:

- IP address: **172.26.26.*P*** (where P = the Pod number)
- Subnet mask: 255.255.255.0
- Default gateway: **172.26.26.100**

**Step 2.** Ping the backbone router's IP address. The ping should be successful:

```
C:\> ping 172.26.26.100
Pinging 172.26.26.100 with 32 bytes of data:
Reply from 172.26.26.100: bytes=32 time<10ms TTL=128
Reply from 172.26.26.100: bytes=32 time<10ms TTL=128
Reply from 172.26.26.100: bytes=32 time<10ms TTL=128
Reply from 172.26.26.100: bytes=32 time<10ms TTL=128
```

### Task 2: Configuring the PIX Security Appliance

The instructor will provide the procedures for access to the PIX Security Appliance console port. After accessing the PIX Security Appliance console port, enter configuration mode, and complete the following steps to configure the PIX Security Appliance.

**Step 1.** Set up a pool of IP addresses that will be assigned dynamically to the VPN clients through IKE mode configuration:

```
PixP(config)# ip local pool dealer 10.0.P.20-10.0.P.29
```

**Step 2.** Create a static translation that maps addresses from the local pool to addresses on the internal network:

```
PixP(config)# static (inside,outside) 10.0.P.0 10.0.P.0 netmask 255.255.255.0
```

**Step 3.** Configure the PIX Security Appliance for TACACS by completing the following substeps.

a. Create a group tag called MYTACACS and assign the TACACS+ protocol to it:

```
PixP(config)# aaa-server MYTACACS protocol tacacs+
```

b. Assign the CSACS IP address and the encryption key **secretkey**:

```
PixP(config)# aaa-server MYTACACS (inside) host 10.0.P.10 secretkey timeout 5
```

**Step 4.** Enable the PIX Security Appliance to implicitly permit any packet from an IPSec tunnel, and bypass checking with an associated conduit or **access-group** command for IPSec connections:

```
PixP(config)# sysopt connection permit-ipsec
```

**Step 5.** Set up a transform set that will be used for the VPN clients:

```
PixP(config)# crypto ipsec transform-set AAADES esp-des esp-md5-hmac
```

**Step 6.** Set up a dynamic crypto map to enable the VPN clients to connect to the PIX Security Appliance:

```
PixP(config)# crypto dynamic-map DYNOMAP 10 set transform-set AAADES
```

**Step 7.** Create a crypto map, and assign the dynamic crypto map to it:

```
PixP(config)# crypto map VPNPEER 20 ipsec-isakmp dynamic DYNOMAP
```

**Step 8.** Configure Xauth to point to the TACACS+ server:

```
PixP(config)# crypto map VPNPEER client authentication MYTACACS
```

**Step 9.** Apply the crypto map to the PIX Security Appliance interface:

```
PixP(config)# crypto map VPNPEER interface outside
```

**Step 10.** Enable IKE on the outside interface:

```
PixP(config)# isakmp enable outside
```

**Step 11.** Configure IKE mode configuration-related parameters:

```
PixP(config)# isakmp client configuration address-pool local dealer outside
```

**Step 12.** Configure the ISAKMP policy by completing the following substeps.

a. Configure a basic IKE policy using preshared keys for authentication:

```
PixP(config)# isakmp policy 10 authentication pre-share
```

What other authentication methods can be used?

___________________________________________________________________

b. Specify the encryption algorithm:

```
PixP(config)# isakmp policy 10 encryption des
```

c. Specify the hash algorithm:

```
PixP(config)# isakmp policy 10 hash md5
```

d. Specify the DH by group identifier:

```
PixP(config)# isakmp policy 10 group 2
```

e. Specify the IKE SA's lifetime:

```
PixP(config)# isakmp policy 10 lifetime 86400
```

**Step 13.** Configure the VPN group to support pushing mode configuration parameters to the VPN client. The VPN group name of *training* must match the group name in the VPN client. The VPN group password must match the password in the VPN client. Complete the following substeps.

a. Configure the IP address pool name:

```
PixP(config)# vpngroup training address-pool dealer
```

b. Configure the inactivity timeout in seconds:

```
PixP(config)# vpngroup training idle-time 1800
```

c. Configure the VPN group password:

```
PixP(config)# vpngroup training password training
```

## Task 3: Verifying the Configuration

Complete the following steps to verify the PIX Security Appliance's configuration.

**Step 1.** Verify the IP local pool:

```
PixP(config)# show ip local pool
Pool     Begin         End           Free    In use
dealer   10.0.P.20     10.0.P.29     10      0
Available Addresses:
10.0.P.20
10.0.P.21
10.0.P.22
10.0.P.23
10.0.P.24
10.0.P.25
10.0.P.26
10.0.P.27
10.0.P.28
10.0.P.29
```

**Step 2.** Verify the Network Address Translation (NAT) configuration:

```
PixP(config)# show nat
nat (inside) 1 10.0.P.0 255.255.255.0 0 0
```

**Step 3.** Verify the statics:

```
PixP(config)# show static
static (dmz,outside) 192.168.P.11 bastionhost netmask 255.255.255.255 0 0
static (inside,outside) 192.168.P.10 insidehost netmask 255.255.255.255 0 0
static (inside,outside) 10.0.P.0 10.0.P.0 netmask 255.255.255.0 0 0
```

**Step 4.** Verify the authentication, authorization, and accounting (AAA) server configuration:

```
PixP(config)# show aaa-server
aaa-server TACACS+ protocol tacacs+
aaa-server RADIUS protocol radius
aaa-server LOCAL protocol local
aaa-server MYTACACS protocol tacacs+
aaa-server MYTACACS (inside) host 10.0.P.10 secretkey timeout 5
```

**Step 5.** Verify the crypto map:

```
PixP(config)# show crypto map
Crypto Map: "VPNPEER" interfaces: { outside }
client authentication MYTACACS
Crypto Map "VPNPEER" 20 ipsec-isakmp
Dynamic map template tag: dynomap
```

**Step 6.** Verify the transform set:

```
PixP(config)# show crypto ipsec transform-set
Transform set AAADES: { esp-des esp-md5-hmac }
will negotiate = { Tunnel, },
```

**Step 7.** Verify the IKE policy:

```
PixP(config)# show isakmp policy
Protection suite of priority 10
encryption algorithm: DES - Data Encryption Standard (56 bit keys).
hash algorithm: Message Digest 5
authentication method: Pre-Shared Key
Diffie-Hellman group: #2 (1024 bit)
lifetime: 86400 seconds, no volume limit
Default protection suite
encryption algorithm: DES - Data Encryption Standard (56 bit keys).
hash algorithm: Secure Hash Standard
authentication method: Rivest-Shamir-Adleman Signature
Diffie-Hellman group: #1 (768 bit)
lifetime: 86400 seconds, no volume limit
```

**Step 8.** Verify the VPN group configuration:

```
PixP(config)# show vpngroup
vpngroup training address-pool dealer
vpngroup training idle-time 1800
vpngroup training password ********
```

What changes were made the to default ISAKMP policy?

______________________________________________________________________________

______________________________________________________________________________

______________________________________________________________________________

**Task 4: Installing the Cisco VPN Client**

In this lab exercise, the source files for the VPN client already reside on the hard disk drive of the student PC. Complete the following steps to install the VPN client:

**Step 1.** Open the Cisco VPN Client folder found on the student PC desktop.

**Step 2.** Double-click the **setup.exe** file in the Cisco VPN Client folder. The Cisco Systems VPN Client Setup window opens.

**Step 3.** Click **Next**. The License Agreement window opens.

**Step 4.** Read the license agreement and click **Yes**. Then choose a destination location.

**Step 5.** Accept the default destination folder by clicking **Next**. The Select Program Folder window opens.

**Step 6.** Accept the defaults by clicking **Next**. The Start Copying Files window opens.

**Step 7.** The files are copied to the hard disk drive of the student PC, and the InstallShield Wizard Complete window opens.

**Step 8.** Select **Yes, I want to restart my computer now** and click **Finish**. The student PC restarts.

**Step 9.** Log in to the student PC.

**Task 5: Configuring the Cisco VPN Client**

Use the following procedure to configure the networking parameters of the VPN client. This procedure assumes Windows 2000 is already running.

**Step 1.** Choose **Start** > **Programs** > **Cisco Systems VPN Client** > **VPN Dialer**. The Cisco Systems VPN Client window opens.

**Step 2.** Click **New**. The New Connection Entry wizard opens.

**Step 3.** Enter **vpnpeer*P*** as the name for the new connection entry in the Name of the New Connection Entry field (where P = the Pod number).

**Step 4.** Click **Next**.

**Step 5.** Enter the PIX Security Appliance's public interface IP address, **192.168.P.2**, as the IP address of the server (where P = the Pod number).

**Step 6.** Click **Next**.

**Step 7.** Select **Group Access Information** and complete the following substeps. The following entries are always case sensitive. Use lowercase characters for this lab.

a. Enter a group name: **training**.

b. Enter a group password: **training**.

c. Confirm the password: **training**.

**Step 8.** Click Next.

**Step 9.** Click Finish and leave the Cisco Systems VPN Client window open.

**Task 6: Verifying the Cisco VPN Client Properties**

Complete the following steps to verify the VPN client-configured parameters.

**Step 1.** Ensure that the Cisco Systems VPN Client window is open. If the Cisco Systems VPN Client window is not open, choose **Start>Programs>Cisco Systems VPN Client>VPN Dialer**.

**Step 2.** Select **vpnpeer*P*** within the Connection Entry group box (where P = the Pod number).

**Step 3.** Verify that the IP address of the remote server is set to the PIX Security Appliance's public interface IP address, 192.168.P.2 (where P = the Pod number).

**Step 4.** Click **Options**. A pop-up menu opens.

**Step 5.** Choose **Properties**. The Properties for vpnpeer*P* window opens (where P = the Pod number).

**Step 6.** Select the **General** tab and view the available options. Do not make any changes to the default settings.

**Step 7.** Select the **Authentication** tab and verify the spelling of the group name.

**Step 8.** Select the **Connections** tab and view the available options. Do not make any changes to the default settings.

**Step 9.** Click **OK**.

**Step 10.** Close the Cisco Systems VPN Client window.

**Task 7: Launching the Cisco VPN Client**

Complete the following steps to launch the VPN client on the student PC.

**Step 1.** Choose **Start** > **Programs** > **Cisco Systems VPN Client** > **VPN Dialer**.

**Step 2.** Verify that the Connection Entry is **vpnpeer*P*** (where P = the Pod number).

**Step 3.** Verify that the IP address of the remote server is set to the PIX Security Appliance's public interface IP address, 192.168.P.2 (where P = the Pod number).

**Step 4.** Click **Connect**. The Connection History window opens, and several messages flash by quickly. Complete the following substeps.

a. When prompted for a username, enter **student*P*** (where P = the Pod number).

b. When prompted to enter a password, enter **training**.

**Step 5.** Click **OK**. The following messages flash by quickly:

```
Initializing the connection
Contacting the security gateway at
Authenticating user
```

The window closes and a VPN (lock) icon appears in the system tray. This indicates that the VPN client has been successfully launched.

**Task 8: Verifying the VPN Connection**

Complete the following steps to verify the IPSec connection.

**Step 1.** Test access to the inside web server from the remote client by completing the following substeps.

a. Open a web browser on the VPN client PC.

b. Use the web browser to access the inside web server by entering: **http://10.0.P.10**.

c. The web server's home page should display.

**Step 2.** Double-click the VPN Dialer icon in the system tray and observe the IP address that was assigned to the student PC.

**Step 3.** Click the **Statistics** tab and view the information provided. Notice the number of packets encrypted and decrypted.

**Step 4.** Refresh the browser.

**Step 5.** Return to the Cisco Systems VPN Client Connection Status window and notice that the number of packets encrypted and decrypted has incremented.

**Step 6.** Click **OK** to close the window.

**Step 7.** Disconnect the VPN dialer session using the system tray VPN dialer icon.

**Step 8.** Remove the crypto map from the PIX Security Appliance's outside interface:

```
PixP(config)# no crypto map VPNPEER interface outside
```

# Lab 14.8.2: Configure IPSec Between Two PIX Security Appliances with CA Support

Estimated Time: 30 Minutes

Number of Team Members: Two teams with four students per team

## Objective

In this lab, students complete the following tasks:

- Configure CA support on a PIX Security Appliance.
- Configure IKE Phase 1 and Phase 2 using Rivest, Shamir, and Adelman (RSA) signatures for authentication between two PIX Security Appliances.
- Test and verify an IPSec configuration.

## Overview

The task in this lab is to configure a PIX Security Appliance to enable IPSec encrypted tunnels to another PIX Security Appliance using RSA signatures and a CA server. Work with a lab partner and the peer Pod's group to perform the following tasks in this lab:

Task 1: Prepare for configuring CA support.

Task 2: Configure CA support.

Task 3: Configure IKE parameters.

Task 4: Configure IPSec parameters.

Task 5: Verify IPSec configuration.

Figure 14-3 illustrates the network environment students create for this lab.

**Figure 14-3 Lab 14.8.2 Network Topology**

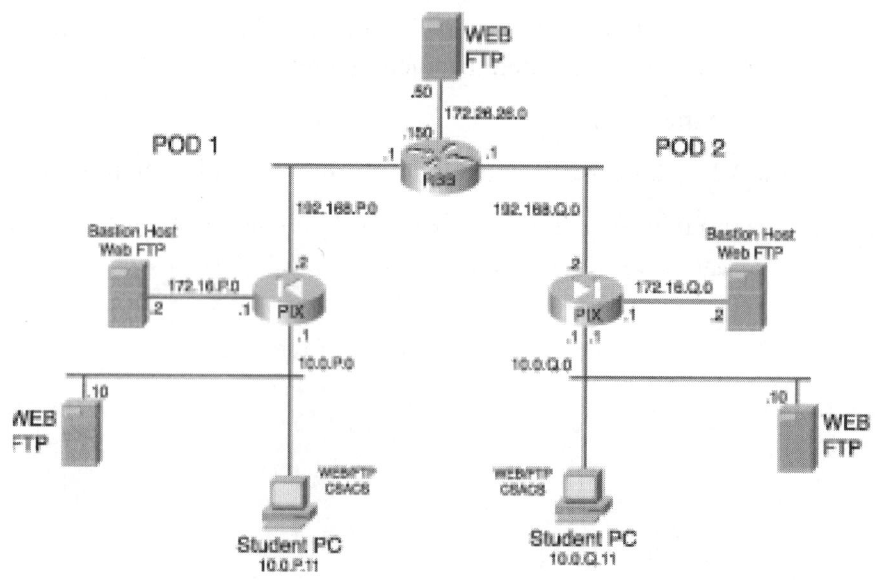

## Preparation

Begin with the standard lab topology and verify the standard configuration on the Pod PIX Security Appliances. Access the PIX Security Appliance console port using the terminal emulator on the student PC. If desired, save the PIX Security Appliance configuration to a text file for later analysis.

## Tools and Resources

To complete the lab, the standard lab topology is required:

- Two Pod PIX Security Appliances
- Two student PCs
- One SuperServer (CA server)
- Backbone switch and router
- Two console cables
- HyperTerminal

## Additional Materials

The student can use the following link for more information on the objectives covered in this lab:

- http://www.cisco.com/en/US/products/hw/vpndevc/ps2030/prod_configuration_examples_list.html

## Command List

Table 14-3 lists the commands used throughout this lab. Refer to this list if you need any assistance during the lab.

**Table 14-3 Lab 14.8.2 Command List**

| **Command** | **Description** |
|---|---|
| **clear [crypto] map** | Deletes all parameters entered through the **crypto map** command belonging to the specified map; does not delete dynamic maps. |
| **clear isakmp** | Removes **isakmp** command statements from the configuration. |
| **clear sysopt** | Removes **sysopt** command statements from the configuration. |
| **crypto ipsec transform-set** *transform-set-name transform1* [*transform2* [*transform3*]] | Creates, views, or deletes IPSec security associations, security association global lifetime values, and global transform sets. Configuration mode. |

| Command | Description |
|---|---|
| **crypto** map *map-name seq-num* **ipsec-isakmp** \| **ipsec-manual** [dynamic*dynamic-map-name*] | Creates, modifies, views, or deletes a crypto map entry; also used to delete a crypto map set. Configuration mode. |
| **crypto map** map-name **interface** *interface-name* | Creates, modifies, views, or deletes a crypto map entry; also used to delete a crypto map set. Configuration mode. |
| **debug crypto ipsec** [*level*] | Packets or ICMP tracings can be debugged through the PIX Security Appliance. The `debug` command provides information that helps troubleshoot protocols operating with and through the PIX Security Appliance. Configuration mode. |
| **debug crypto isakmp** [*level*] | Packets or ICMP tracings can be debugged through the PIX Security Appliance. The `debug` command provides information that helps troubleshoot protocols operating with and through the PIX Security Appliance. Configuration mode. |
| **isakmp enable** *interface-name* | Negotiates IPSec security associations and enables IPSec secure communications. Configuration mode. |
| **isakmp identity address** \| **hostname** | Sets the IKE identity. |
| **isakmp key** *keystring* **address** *peer-address* [**netmask** *mask*] [**no-xauth**] [**no-config-mode**] | Negotiates IPSec security associations and enables IPSec secure communications. Configuration mode. |
| **isakmp policy** *priority* **authentication** *pre-share* \| *rsa-sig* | Configures a basic IKE policy using preshared keys for authentication. |
| **show crypto** | Displays the configuration of IPsec, IKE, and CA. |
| **show isakmp** | Displays the configured ISAKMP policy. |
| **show static** | Configures one-to-one address translation rules. |
| **sysopt connection permit-pptp** \| **permit-l2tp** \| **permit-ipsec** | Changes PIX Security Appliance system options. Configuration mode. |

## Task 1: Preparing for Configuring CA Support

Determine the IKE and IPSec policy. In this exercise, default values are used except when directed to enter a specific value.

IKE policy is to use RSA signatures and MD5 for authentication.

IPSec policy is to use ESP mode with DES encryption.

Perform the following steps to prepare for the IPSec configuration.

**Step 1.** Verify that a static translation is configured from a global IP address on the outside interface to the internal Windows NT server:

```
pixP(config)# show static
static (inside,outside) 192.168.P.10 10.0.P.11 netmask 255.255.255.255 0 0
```

**Step 2.** Verify that a conduit permitting web access to the student PC has been configured:

```
pixP(config)# show conduit
conduit permit tcp host 192.168.P.10 eq www any
```

**Step 3.** Ensure that a web connection can be established between student PC Pods.

**Step 4.** Verify connectivity to the peer PIX Security Appliance:

```
pixP(config)# ping 192.168.Q.2
```

**Step 5.** Ensure connectivity to the CA server from the PIX Security Appliance:

```
pixP(config)# ping 172.26.26.50
```

**Step 6.** Ensure that an HTTP session can be established to the CA server. Test this capability from the student PC by opening a web browser and entering the following location: http://172.26.26.50/certserv.

**Step 7.** Enable the PIX Security Appliance to implicitly permit any packet that came from an IPSec tunnel and bypass the checking with an associated conduit or access-group command for IPSec connections:

```
pixP(config)# sysopt connection permit-ipsec
```

## Task 2: Configuring CA Support

Perform the following steps to configure CA support on the PIX Security Appliance. Work with the CA server administrator to complete this portion of the lab.

**Step 1.** Configure the PIX Security Appliance's host name:

```
pixP(config)# hostname pixP
```

**Step 2.** Set the time and date:

```
pixP(config)# clock set <set to current GMT time and date>
```

Check with the instructor for time and date settings:

**Step 3.** Define the PIX Security Appliance's domain name:

```
pixP(config)# domain-name cisco.com
```

**Step 4.** See if any RSA key pairs exist in Flash memory. Delete any existing RSA key pairs:

```
pixP(config)# show ca mypubkey rsa
      % Key pair was generated at: 12:12:12 Dec 31 2000
      Key name: pix1.cisco.com
       Usage: General Purpose Key
       Key Data:
       305c300d 06092a86 4886f70d 01010105 00034b00 30480241 00e24039 bc4e8b25
       4e13dbde 15ceb188 7ef89d43 e6707fd4 79e60447 386fe5d0 eedcc863 f718caa5
       fea0aec0 99620cbf 34a4b55f 208f8505 0dd44257 37bc5e7f ed02030  1001
pixP(config)# ca zeroize rsa
```

**Step 5.** Generate the PIX Security Appliance's own general purpose RSA key pair with the 512 bit modulus:

```
pixP(config)# ca generate rsa key 512
```

What other type of RSA key pairs can be generated for CA support?

---

**Step 6.** Generate the special-purpose RSA key pairs with the **specialkey** option, using the signature key pair for CA support. View the generated RSA key:

```
pixP(config)# show ca mypubkey rsa
% Key pair was generated at: 12:14:59 Dec 31 2000
Key name: pixP.cisco.com
Usage: General Purpose Key
Key Data:
305c300d 06092a86 4886f70d 01010105 00034b00 30480241 00c31f4a ad32f60d
6e7ed9a2 32883ca9 319a4b30 e7470888 87732e83 c909fb17 fb5cae70 3de738cf
6e2fd12c 5b3ffa98 8c5adc59 1ec84d78 90bdb53f 2218cfe7 3f020301 0001
```

**Step 7.** See if any certificates exist in memory. Delete any existing certificates:

```
pixP(config)# show ca certificate
Certificate
  Subject Name
    Name: pixP.cisco.com
  Status: Available
  Certificate Serial Number: 39108999
  Key Usage: General Purpose
pixP(config)# no ca identity labca
pixP(config)# no ca save all
```

**Step 8.** Declare a CA. For a Microsoft CA, use the following:

```
pixP(config)# ca identity labca 172.26.26.50:/certsrv/mscep/mscep.dll
```

**Step 9.** Configure the communication parameters between the PIX Security Appliance and the CA to use RA mode, a retry period of one minute, and a retry count of 20, making CRL optional:

```
pixP(config)# ca configure labca ra 1 20 crloptional
```

**Step 10.** Turn on PKI debugging and observe debug messages for the CA process:

```
pixP(config)# debug crypto ca
```

**Step 11.** Authenticate the CA by obtaining its public key and its certificate:

```
pixP(config)# ca authenticate labca
Certificate has the following attributes:
Fingerprint: 93700c31 4853ec4a ded81400 43d3c82c
```

**Step 12.** Request signed certificates from the CA server for the PIX Security Appliance's RSA key pair. Before entering this command, contact the CA to authenticate the PIX Security Appliance manually and grant its certificate:

```
pixP(config)# ca enroll labca passwordcisco
```

The argument **passwordcisco** in the example is a password, which is not saved with the configuration. The password is required in a production environment in the event the certificate needs to be revoked, so it is crucial that the password be recorded.

The **ca enroll** command requests as many certificates as there are RSA key pairs. The command should be performed once.

If the PIX Security Appliance reboots after the **ca enroll** command is issued, but before the certificates is received, the **ca enroll** command must be reissued.

*Note*: Notify the CA administrator to accept the pending certificate.

**Step 13.** Verify that the enrollment process was successful:

```
pixP(config)# show ca certificate
Certificate
  Subject Name
    Name: pixP.cisco.com
  Status: Available
  Certificate Serial Number: 39108997
  Key Usage: General Purpose

RA Signature Certificate
  Status: Available
  Certificate Serial Number: 391088d0
  Key Usage: Signature

CA Certificate
  Status: Available
  Certificate Serial Number: 391088c3
  Key Usage: Not Set

RA KeyEncipher Certificate
  Status: Available
  Certificate Serial Number: 391088cf
  Key Usage: Encryption
```

**Step 14.** Save the configuration:

```
pixP(config)# ca save all
pixP(config)# write memory
```

## Task 3: Configuring IKE Parameters

Perform the following steps to configure IKE to use RSA signatures on the PIX Security Appliance.

**Step 1.** Ensure IKE is enabled on the outside interface:

```
pixP(config)# isakmp enable outside
```

**Step 2.** Set the IKE identity to hostname:

```
pixP(config)# isakmp identity hostname
```

**Step 3.** Create an IKE policy. Complete the following substeps.

a. Specify the encryption algorithm:

```
pixP(config)# isakmp policy 5 encryption des
```

b. Specify the hash algorithm:

```
pixP(config-isakmp)# isakmp policy 5 hash md5
```

c. Specify the authentication method:

```
pixP(config-isakmp)# isakmp policy 5 authentication rsa-sig
```

d. Specify the DH group identifier:

```
pixP(config-isakmp)# isakmp policy 5 group 1
```

e. Specify the SA's lifetime:

```
pixP(config-isakmp)# isakmp policy 5 lifetime 86400
```

**Step 4.** View all existing IKE policies. Answer the following question:

```
pixP(config)# show isakmp policy
```

What other ISAKMP policy could be used?

---

---

### Task 4: Configuring IPSec Parameters

Perform the following steps to configure IPSec on the PIX Security Appliance.

**Step 1.** Create an access list to select traffic to protect. The access list should protect IP traffic between the internal NT servers of peer PIX Security Appliances. Use the following parameters:

- Traffic encrypted: Traffic between internal NT servers
- Peer address: IP address of peer PIX Security Appliance outside interface
- Access list number: 101
- Protocol: any Internet protocol

```
pixP(config)# access-list 101 permit ip host 192.168.P.10 host 192.168.Q.10
```

**Step 2.** Consider the example access list for PIX1 peering to PIX2:

```
pix1(config)# show access-list
access-list 101 permit ip host 192.168.1.10 host 192.168.2.3
```

**Step 3.** Configure an IPSec transform set, IKE Phase 2 parameters. Use the following parameters:

- Transform Set Name: **mine**
- ESP Protocols: **des**
- Mode: **tunnel**

```
pixP(config)# crypto ipsec transform-set mine esp-des
```

**Step 4.** Create a crypto map by performing the following substeps. Use the following parameters:

- Name of map: **peerQ**
- Number of map: **10**
- Key exchange type: **isakmp**
- Peer: **192.168.Q.2**
- Transform set: **mine**
- Match address: **101**

**Step 5.** Create a crypto map entry:

```
pixP(config)# crypto map peerQ 10 ipsec-isakmp
```

**Step 6.** Look at the crypto map at this point and observe the defaults. Answer the following question:

```
pixP(config)# show crypto map
Crypto Map "peerQ" 10 ipsec-isakmp
   Crypto Map: "peer2" interfaces: { }
        No matching address list set.
        Current peer: 0.0.0.0
        Security association lifetime: 4608000 kilobytes/28800 seconds
        PFS (Y/N): N
        Transform sets={ }
```

What is the default SA lifetime?

---

**Step 7.** Assign the access list to the crypto map:

```
pixP(config)# crypto map peerQ 10 match address 101
```

**Step 8.** Define the peer. The peer IP address should be set to the peer's outside interface IP address:

```
pixP(config)# crypto map peerQ 10 set peer 192.168.Q.2
```

**Step 9.** Specify the transform set used to reach the peer. Use the transform set name configured in substep b:

```
pixP(config)# crypto map peerQ 10 set transform-set mine
```

**Step 10.** Apply the crypto map set to the outside interface:

```
pixP(config)# crypto map peerQ interface outside
```

**Step 11.** Verify the crypto map configuration:

```
pixP(config)# show crypto map
```

### Task 5: Verifying IPSec Configuration

Perform the following steps to verify the IPSec configuration.

**Step 1.** Verify the IKE policy. Note the default values. Answer the following questions:

```
pixP(config)# show isakmp
isakmp enable outside
isakmp identity hostname
```

```
isakmp policy 5 authentication rsa-sig
isakmp policy 5 encryption des
isakmp policy 5 hash md5
isakmp policy 5 group 1
isakmp policy 5 lifetime 86400
```

a. What five policy items are configured in an IKE policy?

---

b. Which IKE policy value is required to support CA servers?

---

c. Which IKE policy values have defaults?

---

**Step 2.** Examine the IKE policies on the PIX Security Appliance. Answer the following questions:

```
pixP(config)# show isakmp policy
Protection suite of priority 5
        encryption algorithm:   DES - Data Encryption Standard (56 bit keys).
        hash algorithm:         Message Digest 5
        authentication method:  Rivest-Shamir-Adleman Signature
        Diffie-Hellman group:   #1 (768 bit)
        lifetime:               86400 seconds, no volume limit
Protection suite of priority 10
        encryption algorithm:   DES - Data Encryption Standard (56 bit keys).
        hash algorithm:         Secure Hash Standard
        authentication method:  Pre-Shared Key
        Diffie-Hellman group:   #1 (768 bit)
        lifetime:               86400 seconds, no volume limit
Default protection suite
        encryption algorithm:   DES - Data Encryption Standard (56 bit keys).
        hash algorithm:         Secure Hash Standard
        authentication method:  Rivest-Shamir-Adleman Signature
        Diffie-Hellman group:   #1 (768 bit)
        lifetime:               86400 seconds, no volume limit
```

a. How will the PIX Security Appliance know to use the IKE policy suite using RSA signatures instead of the one using a preshared key?

---

b. How did the default protection suite get configured?

---

**Step 3.** Verify the crypto access list. The list shown is for PIX2 connecting to PIX1:

```
pix2(config)# show access-list
access-list 101 permit ip host 192.168.2.10 host 192.168.1.10
```

**Step 4.** Verify the correct IPSec parameters, IKE Phase 2:

```
pixP(config)# show crypto ipsec transform-set
Transform set pixQ: { esp-des  }
will negotiate = { Tunnel,  },
```

**Step 5.** Verify the correct crypto map configuration. The crypto map shown is for PIX1:

```
pix1(config)# show crypto map
Crypto Map: "peer2" interface: "outside" local address: 192.168.1.2
Crypto Map "peer2" 10 ipsec-isakmp
```

```
Peer = 192.168.2.2
access-list 101 permit ip host 192.168.1.10 host 192.168.2.10 (hitcnt=0)
Current peer: 192.168.2.2
Security association lifetime: 4608000 kilobytes/28800 seconds
PFS (Y/N): N
Transform sets={ pix2, }
```

**Step 6.** Turn on debugging for IPSec and ISAKMP:

```
pixP(config)# debug crypto ipsec
pixP(config)# debug crypto isakmp
```

**Step 7.** Clear any IPSec SAs that might have been set up:

```
pixP(config)# clear crypto ipsec sa
```

**Step 8.** Initiate a web session from the student PC to the peer student PC. Observe the debug output and verify the web session was established.

**Step 9.** Ensure that traffic between peers is being encrypted by performing the following substeps.

a. Examine the IPSec SAs. Note the number of packets encrypted and decrypted:

```
pix1(config)# show crypto ipsec sa
interface: outside
    Crypto map tag: peer2, local addr. 192.168.1.2
local ident (addr/mask/prot/port): (192.168.1.10/255.255.255.255/0/0)
   remote ident (addr/mask/prot/port): (192.168.2.10/255.255.255.255/0/0)
   current_peer: 192.168.2.2
     PERMIT, flags={origin_is_acl,}
    #pkts encaps: 210, #pkts encrypt: 210, #pkts digest 0
    #pkts decaps: 201, #pkts decrypt: 227, #pkts verify 0
    #pkts compressed: 0, #pkts decompressed: 0
    #pkts not compressed: 0, #pkts compr. failed: 0, #pkts decompress failed: 0
    #send errors 29, #recv errors 0
```

b. Generate additional traffic by clicking the **Reload** button of the web browser.

c. Examine the IPSec SAs again. Note that the packet counters have incremented:

```
pix2(config)# show cry ipsec sa
interface: outside
    Crypto map tag: peer2, local addr. 192.168.1.2
local ident (addr/mask/prot/port): (192.168.2.10/255.255.255.255/0/0)
   remote ident (addr/mask/prot/port): (192.168.3.10/255.255.255.255/0/0)
   current_peer: 192.168.2.2
     PERMIT, flags={origin_is_acl,}
    #pkts encaps: 238, #pkts encrypt: 238, #pkts digest 0
    #pkts decaps: 239, #pkts decrypt: 267, #pkts verify 0
    #pkts compressed: 0, #pkts decompressed: 0
    #pkts not compressed: 0, #pkts compr. failed: 0, #pkts decompress failed: 0
    #send errors 31, #recv errors 0
```

## Review Questions

1. Describe the AH protocol.

______________________________________________________________________

______________________________________________________________________

______________________________________________________________________

______________________________________________________________________

2. Describe the ESP protocol.

___

___

___

___

3. Describe CA.

___

___

___

___

4. Describe the Diffie-Hellman key exchange.

___

___

___

___

5. Describe IPSec transform sets.

___

___

___

___

## Chapter 14 Quiz Questions

1. Put the following in the correct order when implementing IPSec on the PIX Security Appliance.

   A. Configure IKE Phase 1 policy

   B. Determine IPSec policy

   C. Configure IPSec policy

   D. Verify VPN configuration

2. IPSec works at what layer of the OSI model?

   A. Application

   B. Transport

   C. Network

   D. Data link

3. When a VPN client initiates ISAKMP with the PIX, what does the client send to the PIX?

   A. Public key

   B. VPN policy name

   C. VPN group name

   D. AAA server name

4. What is the command to view the parameters of each IKE policy?

   A. **show isakmp policy**

   B. **show ike policy**

   C. **show isakmp**

   D. **show ike**

5. What is the command that will create a transform set called *phoenixts* using ESP to provide the strongest authentication and encryption?

   A. **crypto transform-set** *phoenixts1* **esp-sha-hmac esp-3des**

   B. **crypto ipsec transform-set** *phoenixts1* **esp-3des**

   C. **crypto ipsec transform-set** *phoenixts1* **esp-sha-hmac**

   D. **crypto ipsec transform-set** *phoenixts1* **esp-sha-hmac esp-3des**

6. Which of the following commands will define an IKE policy on the PIX Security Appliance?

   A. **crypto isakmp policy 10 encryption md5**

   B. **crypto isakmp policy test authentication des**

   C. **isakmp policy test authentication pre-share**

   D. **isakmp policy 10 group 2**

7. Which commands will display the configured policies on the PIX Security Appliance?

   A. **write terminal**

   B. **show ike policies**

   C. **show isakmp policy**

   D. **show policy isakmp**

8. What command must be entered to activate a crypto map set to an interface?

   A. **set crypto map**

   B. **crypto map** *map_name* **interface** *interface-name*

   C. **crypto-map inside outside**

   D. **enable crypto** *map name* **interface**

9. When enrolling a PIX Security Appliance to a CA, the PIX Security Appliance must generate a RSA key pair.

   A. True

   B. False

10. Which of the following does IPSec *not* provide?

   A. Data confidentiality

   B. Data integrity

   C. Data availability

   D. Data authentication

# Chapter 15

## PIX Security Appliance Management

In this chapter, the different ways that a PIX Security Appliance can be managed are discussed. First, the student learns about the PIX Device Manager (PDM). The PDM is a GUI that can be accessed via a web browser. After an overview of the PDM, the student uses the PDM to configure the PIX Security Appliance.

After the PIX is configured, the PDM creates a site-to-site Virtual Private Network (VPN) and then a remote access VPN. This gives the student the opportunity to create VPNs on the PIX Security Appliance in two different ways.

Finally, the PIX Management Center (PIX MC) is discussed. The student learns how it can be used to monitor several PIX Security Appliances throughout the organization's network.

**Vocabulary Exercise**

AUS

____________________________________________________________________________________

____________________________________________________________________________________

CSPM

____________________________________________________________________________________

____________________________________________________________________________________

PIX MC

____________________________________________________________________________________

____________________________________________________________________________________

### Lab Activities

The topology figures and lab examples contain **P** and **Q** values. The **P** value in the addressing and naming scheme refers to *your* assigned Pod number.

The following are examples of determining P values:

- Pod2 is looking at a topology figure and is trying to determine the P values in the figure. In this scenario, the **P** values would equal **2**. 10.0.**P**.12 would become 10.0.**2**.12, 172.30.**P**.2 would become 172.30.**2**.2, and so on.
- Pod1 is looking at a topology figure and is trying to determine the P values in the figure. In this scenario, the **P** values would equal **1**. 10.0.**P**.12 would become 10.0.**1**.12, 172.30.**P**.2 would become 172.30.**1**.2, and so on.

In both examples, the P values are directly related to the Pod number of the team.

The **Q** value in the naming and addressing scheme is used when testing the security or connectivity with the peer team.

The following are examples of determining Q values:

- In a lab, Pod2 has been asked to test connectivity to their peer inside host at IP address 10.0.Q.12. In this scenario, 10.0.Q.12 would equal 10.0.1.12.
- In a lab, Pod1 has been asked to test connectivity to their peer inside host at IP address 10.0.Q.12. In this scenario, 10.0.Q.12 would equal 10.0.2.12.

In both examples, the Q value is directly related to the peer Pod number.

## Lab 15.6.3: Configuring the PIX Security Appliance with PDM

Estimated Time: 45 Minutes

Number of Team Members: Two teams with four students per team

### Objective

In this lab, students complete the following tasks:

- Install PDM and access it from the browser.
- Test PDM's warning for unsupported commands.
- Clear the PIX Security Appliance's configuration and access the PDM Startup Wizard.
- Use the PDM Startup Wizard to configure a privileged mode password.
- Configure outbound access with Network Address Translation (NAT).
- Test connectivity through the PIX Security Appliance.
- Configure and test inbound access.
- Configure and test logging to a Syslog server.
- Configure intrusion detection.
- Configure the PIX Security Appliance to monitor intrusion detection.
- Create a site-to-site VPN.
- Test and verify the VPN.

### Overview

The PDM is a browser-based configuration tool that enables you to configure and monitor the PIX Security Appliance graphically, without requiring an extensive knowledge of the PIX Security Appliance command-line interface (CLI). In this lab, students use PDM to test and verify a site-to-site VPN.

*Note*: In the following lab, bypass the initial security alert regarding the site security certificate. However, remember that when remotely configuring the PIX Security Appliance with PDM, the security certificate for secure encrypted communication between the PDM and the PIX Security Appliance can be used. To do this, install the certificate by clicking View Certificate in the initial Security Alert window and following the prompts. Because the certificate is assigned to the PIX Security Appliance by name rather than by IP address, a connection will need to be established with the PIX Security Appliance by entering its fully qualified domain name (FQDN), rather than the IP address, in the browser. Using the name rather than an IP address requires that name resolution is enabled through DNS or a hosts file.

Figure 15-1 illustrates the network environment students create for this lab.

**Figure 15-1 Lab 15.6.3 Network Topology**

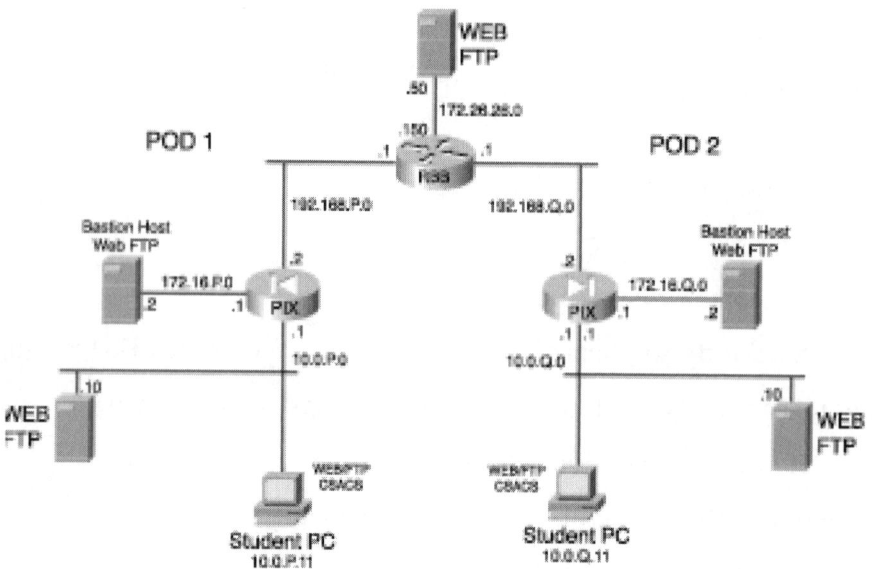


## Preparation

Begin with the standard lab topology in Figure 15-1 and verify the standard configuration on the Pod PIX Security Appliances. Access the PIX Security Appliance console port using the terminal emulator on the student PC. If desired, save the PIX Security Appliance configuration to a text file for later analysis.

## Tools and Resources

To complete the lab, the standard lab topology is required:

- Two Pod PIX Security Appliances
- Two student PCs
- One server
- Backbone switch and router
- Two console cables and HyperTerminal

## Additional Materials

Student can use the following link for more information on the objectives covered in this lab:

- http://www.cisco.com/en/US/products/sw/netmgtsw/ps2032/prod_release_note09186a00800e21a4.html

## Command List

Table 15-1 lists the commands used throughout this lab. Refer to this list if you need any assistance during the lab.

**Table 15-1 Lab 15.6.3 Command List**

| Command | Description |
|---|---|
| **conduit permit** \| **deny** *protocol global_ip global_mask [operator port* [*port*]] *foreign_ip foreign_mask* [*operator port* [*port*]] | Adds, deletes, or shows conduits through the PIX Security Appliance for incoming connections |
| **copy tftp**[**:**[[*//location*] [*/tftp_pathname*]]] **flash**[**:**[**image** \| **pdm**]] | Changes software images without requiring access to the TFTP monitor mode. |
| **http server enable** | Enables the PIX Security Appliance HTTP server |
| **route** *if_name ip_address netmask gateway_ip* [*metric*] | Enters a static or default route for the specified interface. Configuration mode. |

### Task 1: Installing PDM and Access It from the Browser

Complete the following steps to install PDM and access it from the browser.

**Step 1.** Load the PDM file into the PIX Security Appliance:

```
PixP(config)# copy tftp://10.0.P.11/pdm-201.bin flash:pdm
```

**Step 2.** Enable the HTTP server in the PIX Security Appliance:

```
PixP(config)# http server enable
```

**Step 3.** Grant permission for the inside host to initiate an HTTP connection to the PIX Security Appliance:

```
PixP(config)# http 10.0.P.11 255.255.255.0 inside
```

**Step 4.** Access the PDM console by completing the following substeps.

a. Open the browser and enter **https://10.0.P.1** (where P = the Pod number).

b. In the Security Alert window, click **Yes**.

c. When prompted for the username and password, do not enter a username or password. Click **OK** to continue.

d. Click **Yes** in the Security Warning window. If the Update Config window opens, click **Proceed**.

**Step 5.** Notice that the current PIX Security Appliance configuration has been imported. Examine the configuration by completing the following substeps.

a. Click the **Access Rules** tab. Notice that an access policy has been created to correspond to the access control lists (ACLs) configured earlier in the course.

b. Click the **Translation Rules** tab. Notice that the static mappings, NAT, and global pools appear here.

c. Click the **Hosts/Networks** tab and observe the network topology.

d. Click the **System Properties** tab. Notice that the configuration of the PIX Security Appliance interfaces is displayed.

**Step 6.** Close the browser. The Configuration Modified window opens.

**Step 7.** Click **Save**. The Save Successful window opens.

**Step 8.** Click **OK**. The "Are you sure" window opens.

**Step 9.** Click **Yes**.

### Task 2: Testing PDM's Warning for Unsupported Commands

To verify that PDM warns about unsupported commands, complete the following steps.

**Step 1.** Configure the PIX Security Appliance with a **conduit** command that permits IP traffic from a peer Pod's internal network to the internal network:

```
PixP(config)# conduit permit ip 192.168.Q.0 255.255.255.0 192.168.P.0 255.255.255.0
```

**Step 2.** Display the conduit:

```
PixP(config)# show cond
conduit permit ip host 192.168.P.10 192.168.Q.0 255.255.255.0
```

**Step 3.** Verify that conduits exist in the configuration along with ACLs by displaying the ACLs:

```
PixP(config)# show access-list
access-list ACLIN; 10 elements
access-list ACLIN permit tcp 192.168.Q.0 255.255.255.0 object-group FTPSERVERS object-group
MYSERVICES

access-list ACLIN permit tcp 192.168.Q.0 255.255.255.0 host 192.168.P.11 eq www(hitcnt=4)

access-list ACLIN permit tcp 192.168.Q.0 255.255.255.0 host 192.168.P.11 eq ftp(hitcnt=2)

access-list ACLIN permit tcp any object-group ALLSERVERS eq www
access-list ACLIN permit tcp any host 192.168.P.11 eq www (hitcnt=0)
access-list ACLIN permit tcp any host 192.168.P.10 eq www (hitcnt=2)
access-list ACLIN permit tcp any host 192.168.P.6 eq www (hitcnt=0)
access-list ACLIN permit tcp any host 192.168.P.7 eq www (hitcnt=0)
access-list ACLIN permit icmp any any object-group PING
access-list ACLIN permit icmp any any echo (hitcnt=12)
access-list ACLIN permit icmp any any echo-reply (hitcnt=4)
access-list ACLIN permit icmp any any unreachable (hitcnt=0)
access-list ACLIN deny ip any any (hitcnt=3)
access-list ACLDMZ; 3 elements
access-list ACLDMZ permit icmp any any object-group PING
access-list ACLDMZ permit icmp any any echo (hitcnt=0)
access-list ACLDMZ permit icmp any any echo-reply (hitcnt=8)
access-list ACLDMZ permit icmp any any unreachable (hitcnt=0)
```

**Step 4.** Access the PDM console by completing the following substeps.

a. In the browser, enter **https://10.0.P.1** (where P = the Pod number).

b. In the Security Alert window, click **Yes**.

c. When prompted for the username and password, do not enter a username or password. Click **OK** to continue.

d. The Unsupported Command Found window opens because PDM does not support configurations that use both conduits and ACLs.

e. Read the statement in the window.

f. Click **OK** in the Unsupported Command Found window.

g. Click the following tabs to verify that they are disabled: Access Rules, Translation Rules, VPN, Hosts/Networks, and System Properties.

h. Minimize but do *not* close the PDM console.

**Step 5.** In the Telnet window, remove the conduit to restore full PDM capability:

```
PixP(config)# clear conduit
```

**Step 6.** Verify that the conduit has been removed:

```
PixP(config)# show conduit
```

**Step 7.** Maximize the PDM console.

**Step 8.** Click **File** in the main menu. The drop-down File menu opens.

**Step 9.** Choose **Refresh PDM with the Running Configuration on the PIX**.

**Step 10.** Verify that the conduit has been removed by completing the following substeps.

a. Choose **Tools** and then **Command Line Interface** from the main menu.

b. In the Command field, enter **show conduit**.

c. Click **Send**.

**Step 11.** Close the browser.

### Task 3: Clearing the PIX Security Appliance's Configuration, and Access the PDM Startup Wizard

Complete the following steps to erase the current PIX Security Appliance configuration and access the PDM wizard.

**Step 1.** In the Telnet window, erase the current PIX Security Appliance configuration. When prompted to confirm, press **Enter**:

```
PixP(config)# write erase
Erase PIX configuration in flash memory? [confirm] <Enter>
```

**Step 2.** In the Telnet window, reload the PIX Security Appliance. When prompted to confirm, press **Enter**:

```
PixP(config)# reload
Proceed with reload? [confirm] <Enter>
```

**Step 3.** When prompted to preconfigure the PIX Security Appliance through interactive prompts, press **Enter**.

**Step 4.** Agree to use the current password by pressing **Enter**:

```
Enable password [<use current password>]: <Enter>
```

**Step 5.** Accept the default year by pressing **Enter**:

```
Clock (UTC):
Year [2002]: <Enter>
```

**Step 6.** Accept the default month by pressing **Enter**:

```
Month [Nov]: <Enter>
```

**Step 7.** Accept the default day by pressing **Enter**:

```
Day [14]: <Enter>
```

**Step 8.** Accept the default time stored in the host computer by pressing **Enter**:

```
Time [11:21:25]: <Enter>
```

**Step 9.** Enter the IP address of the PIX Security Appliance's inside interface:

```
Inside IP address: 10.0.P.1
```

**Step 10.** Enter the network mask that applies to inside IP address:

```
Inside network mask: 255.255.255.0
```

**Step 11.** Enter the hostname:

```
Host name: pixP
```

**Step 12.** Enter the DNS domain name of the network on which the PIX Security Appliance runs:

```
Domain name: cisco.com
```

**Step 13.** Enter the IP address of the host running PDM:

```
IP address of host running PIX Device Manager: 10.0.P.11
```

**Step 14.** Enter **y** at the prompt to save the information to the PIX Security Appliance's Flash memory.

**Step 15.** Create a static route to the 10.1.P.0 network:

```
PixP(config)# route inside 10.1.P.0 255.255.255.0 10.0.P.102
```

**Step 16.** Access the PDM console by completing the following substeps.

a. In the browser, enter **https://10.0.P.1** (where P = the Pod number).

b. In the Security Alert window, click **Yes**.

c. When prompted for the username and password, do not enter a username or password. Click **OK** to continue. The Update Config window opens.

d. Click **Proceed**. The PIX Device Manager Startup Wizard opens.

**Task 4: Using the PDM Startup Wizard to Configure a Privileged Mode Password**

Complete the following steps to configure a privileged mode password.

**Step 1.** In the PIX Device Manager Startup Wizard window, click **Next**. The Startup Wizard's Basic Configuration group box appears.

**Step 2.** Verify that pixP appears in the PIX Host Name field (where P = the Pod number).

**Step 3.** Verify that **cisco.com** appears in the Domain Name field.

**Step 4.** Select **Change Enable Password** within the Enable Password group box.

**Step 5.** Enter **cisco** in the New Enable Password text box.

**Step 6.** Enter **cisco** in the Confirm New Enable Password text box.

**Step 7.** Click **Finish**. The Enter Network Password window opens.

**Step 8.** Leave the Username field blank, and enter **cisco** in the password field. The main Cisco PIX Device Manager window opens.

**Task 5: Configuring Outbound Access with NAT**

Complete the following steps to configure the PIX Security Appliance's inside and outside interfaces, establish a default route, enable NAT for the internal network, and create a global pool of addresses for address translation.

**Step 1.** Select the System Properties tab.

**Step 2.** Configure the inside interface by completing the following substeps.

a. Double-click **ethernet1** in the Interfaces table. The Edit Interface window opens.

b. Verify that the Enable Interface check box is selected.

c. Verify that inside appears in the Interface Name field.

d. Verify that 10.0.P.1 appears in the IP Address field (where P = the Pod number).

e. Verify that 255.255.255.0 appears in the Subnet Mask drop-down menu.

f. Choose 100full from the Speed drop-down menu.

g. Verify that **100** appears in the Security Level field.

h. Click **OK**. This opens the Cisco PIX Device Manager main window.

**Step 3.** Configure the outside interface by completing the following substeps.

a. Double-click **ethernet0** in the Interfaces table. The Edit Interface window opens.

b. Select the **Enable Interface** check box.

c. Verify that **outside** appears in the Interface Name field.

d. Verify that the **Static IP Address** radio button is selected within the IP Address group box.

e. Enter **192.168.P.2** in the IP Address field (where P = the Pod number).

f. Choose **255.255.255.0** from the Subnet Mask drop-down menu.

g. Choose **100full** from the Speed drop-down menu.

h. Verify that **0** appears in the Security Level field.

i. Click **OK**. This opens the Cisco PIX Device Manager main window.

j. Click **Apply to PIX**.

**Step 4.** To establish a default route, complete the following substeps.

a. Verify that the System Properties tab is still active.

b. Expand the **Routing** branch in the Categories tree.

c. Choose **Static Route** from the Routing list.

d. Select **Add** from the Static Route group box. The Add Static Route window opens.

e. Choose **outside** from the Interface Name drop-down menu.

f. Enter **0.0.0.0** in the IP Address field.

g. Enter **192.168.P.1** in the Gateway IP field (where P = the Pod number).

h. Enter **0.0.0.0** in the Mask drop-down menu.

i. Verify that **1** appears in the Metric field.

j. Click **OK**. The static route appears in the Static Route table.

k. Click **Apply to PIX**.

**Step 5.** Configure a global pool of addresses to be used for address translation by completing the following substeps.

a. Select the **Translation Rules** tab.

b. Click the **Manage Pools** button. The Manage Global Address Pools window opens.

c. Click **Add**. The Add Global Pool Item window opens.

d. Choose **outside** from the Interface drop-down menu.

e. Enter **1** in the Pool ID field.

f. Verify that the **Range** radio button is selected.

g. Enter **192.168.P.20** in the first IP address field (where P = the Pod number).

h. Enter **192.168.P.254** in the second IP address field (where P = the Pod number).

i. Enter **255.255.255.0** in the Network Mask field.

j. Click **OK**. This opens the Manage Global Address Pools window.

k. Click **OK**. This opens the Cisco PIX Device Manager main window.

l. Click **Apply to PIX**.

**Step 6.** Configure NAT by completing the following substeps:

a. Verify that the **Translation Rules** tab is still active.

b. Verify that the **Translation Rules** radio button is selected.

c. Choose **Rules>Add** from the main menu. The Add Address Translation Rule window opens.

d. Verify that the inside interface is chosen in the Interface drop-down menu.

e. Click **Browse**. The Select host/network window opens.

f. Verify that the inside interface is chosen in the drop-down menu.

g. Select the inside network by clicking **10.0.P.0**.

h. Click **OK**. This will open the Add Address Translation Rule window.

i. Verify that **outside** is chosen in the Translate address on less secure interface drop-down menu.

j. Verify that **Dynamic** is selected in the Translate Address to group box.

k. Choose **1** from the Address Pool drop-down menu.

l. Verify the global pool configured earlier (192.168.P.20–192.168.P.254) appears under Address.

m. Click **OK** in the Add Address Translation Rule window. The new rule appears on the Translation Rules tab.

n. Click **Apply to PIX**.

**Task 6: Testing Connectivity Through the PIX Security Appliance**

Complete the following steps to test interface connectivity and NAT.

**Step 1.** Test interface connectivity by completing the following substeps.

a. Choose **Tools** > **Ping**.

b. In the IP Address field, enter **10.0.P.1** (where P = the Pod number).

c. Click **Ping**.

d. The output on your screen should appear similar to the following:

```
10.0.P.1 response received -- 0ms
10.0.P.1 response received -- 0ms
10.0.P.1 response received -- 0ms
```

e. Click Clear Screen.

**Step 2.** Repeat Step 1 for the following IP addresses. A response for all pings should be received:

- The inside host: 10.0.P.11 (where P = the Pod number)
- The outside interface: 192.168.P.2 (where P = the Pod number)
- The backbone router: 192.168.P.1 (where P = the Pod number)

**Step 3.** Exit the Ping window by clicking Close.

**Step 4.** Test the operation of the global and NAT configured by originating connections through the PIX Security Appliance. To do this, complete the following substeps.

a. Open a web browser on the student PC.

b. Use the web browser to access the SuperServer at IP address 172.26.26.50 by entering **http://172.26.26.50**.

**Step 5.** Observe the translation table by completing the following substeps.

a. Choose **Tools > Command Line Interface**. The Command Line Interface window opens.

b. In the Command field, enter **show xlate**.

c. Click **Send**.

d. Observe the output in the Response field. It should appear similar to the following:

```
Result of the PIX command: "show xlate"
1 in use, 1 most used
Global 192.168.P.20 Local 10.0.P.11
```

*Note*: A global address chosen from the low end of the global range has been mapped to the student PC.

**Step 6.** Exit the Command Line Interface window by clicking **Close**.

### Task 7: Configuring and Testing Inbound Access

Complete the following steps to configure the PIX Security Appliance to permit inbound access to hosts on the inside interface.

**Step 1.** Enable command preview by completing the following substeps.

a. Choose **Options** and then **Preferences** from the main menu. The Preferences window opens.

b. Select **Preview Commands Before Sending to PIX**.

c. Click **OK**.

**Step 2.** Create a static translation for the inside host by completing the following substeps.

a. Select the **Translation Rules** tab.

b. Select the **Add New Rule** icon in the toolbar. The Add Address Translation Rule window opens.

c. Verify that the inside interface is chosen in the Interface drop-down menu.

d. Click **Browse**. The Select host/network window opens.

e. Verify that the inside interface is chosen in the drop-down menu.

f. Select the inside host: Click **10.0.P.11**. (where P = the Pod number).

g. Click **OK**. This opens the Add Address Translation Rule window.

h. Verify that **outside** is chosen in the Translate Address on Less Secured Interface drop-down menu.

i. Select **Static** in the Translate address to group box.

j. Enter **192.168.P.10** in the IP Address field (where P = the Pod number).

k. Click **OK**. The new rule appears on the Translation Rules tab.

l. Click **Apply to PIX**. The Preview CLI Commands window opens.

m. Click **Send**.

**Step 3.** Ping a peer Pod's inside host from the internal host. The ping should fail because the access policy does not yet allow it:

```
C:\> ping 192.168.Q.10
Pinging 192.168.Q.10 with 32 bytes of data:
Request timed out.
Request timed out.
Request timed out.
```

**Step 4.** Configure an ACL to allow pinging through the PIX Security Appliance by completing the following substeps.

a. Select the **Access Rules** tab.

b. Choose **Rules** from the main menu.

c. Click **Add**. The Add Rule window opens.

d. Verify that permit is chosen in the Select an action drop-down menu.

e. Choose **outside** from the Interface drop-down menu in the Source Host/Network group box.

f. Choose **inside** from the Interface drop-down menu in the Destination Host/Network group box.

g. Select **ICMP** in the Protocol or Service group box.

h. Verify that **any** is selected in the ICMP type group box.

i. Click **OK**. The new rule appears on the Access Rules tab.

j. Click **Apply to PIX**. The Preview CLI Commands window opens.

k. Observe the ACLs to be sent to the PIX Security Appliance.

l. Click **Send**.

**Step 5.** Ping a peer Pod's inside host from the internal host. Be sure to coordinate with the peer Pod:

```
C:\> ping 192.168.Q.10
Pinging 192.168.Q.10 with 32 bytes of data:
Reply from 192.168.Q.10: bytes=32 time<10ms TTL=125>
Reply from 192.168.Q.10: bytes=32 time<10ms TTL=125>
Reply from 192.168.Q.10: bytes=32 time<10ms TTL=125>
Reply from 192.168.Q.10: bytes=32 time<10ms TTL=125>
```

**Step 6.** Configure an ACL to allow web access to the inside host from the outside by completing the following substeps.

a. Select the **Access Rules** tab.

b. Choose **Rules** and then **Add**. The Add Rule window opens.

c. Verify that **permit** is chosen in the Select an action drop-down menu.

d. Choose **outside** from the Interface drop-down menu within the Source Host/Network group box.

e. Choose **inside** from the Interface drop-down menu within the Destination Host/Network group box.

f. Click **Browse** in the Destination Host/Network group box. The Select host/network window opens.

g. Verify that inside is chosen in the interface drop-down menu.

h. Select the IP address of the inside host: **`10.0.P.11`** (where P = the Pod number).

i. Click **OK**. The Add Rule window becomes active.

j. Select **TCP** in the Protocol and Service group box.

k. Verify that = is chosen in the Service drop-down menu within the Source Port group box.

l. Verify that any appears in the Service field within the Source Port group box.

m. Verify that = is chosen in the Service drop-down menu within the Destination Port group box.

n. Click the ellipsis button within the Destination Port group box. The Service window opens.

o. Choose **http** from the Service list.

p. Click **OK**. This opens the Add Rule window.

q. Click **OK**.

r. Click **Apply to PIX**. The Preview CLI Commands window opens.

s. Observe the ACLs to be sent to the PIX Security Appliance.

t. Click **Send**.

**Step 7.** Clear the current translations by completing the following substeps.

a. Choose **Tools** and then **Command Line Interface**. The Command Line Interface window opens.

b. Enter **clear xlate** in the Command field.

c. Click **Send**.

d. Verify that the output in the Response field is similar to the following:

```
Result of PIX command: "clear xlate"
The command has been sent to PIX.
```

**Step 8.** View current translations by completing the following substeps.

a. Click **Clear Screen** in the Command Line Interface window.

b. Enter **show xlate** in the Command field.

c. Click **Send**.

d. Verify that the output in the Response field is similar to the following:

```
Result of PIX command: "show xlate"
0 in use, 3 most used
```

e. Click **Close** in the Command Line Interface window.

**Step 9.** Test web access to the inside hosts of opposite Pod groups by completing the following substeps.

a. Open a web browser on the student PC.

b. Use the web browser to access the inside host of the peer Pod group **http://192.168.Q.10** (where Q = the peer Pod number). The web connection to the peer's inside host should be successful.

**Step 10.** Test FTP access to the inside hosts of other Pod groups by completing the following substeps.

a. On the client PC, use FTP to get into the inside host of another Pod group by choosing **Start> Run > ftp 192.168.Q.10** (where Q = the peer Pod number). Accessing the peer's inside host through FTP should fail.

b. Have an opposite Pod group use FTP to attempt to get into the inside host.

**Step 11.** Observe the transactions by completing the following substeps.

a. Choose **Tools > Command Line Interface**. The Command Line Interface window opens.

b. Enter **show arp** in the Command field.

c. Click **Send**.

d. Verify that the output in the Response box is similar to the following:

```
result of PIX command: "show arp"
outside 192.168.P.1 0003.6ba4.ca60
inside 10.0.P.11 0050.da31.6130
```

e. Click Clear Screen.

f. Enter **show conn** in the Command field.

g. Click Send.

h. Verify that the output in the Response field is similar to the following:

```
result of PIX command: "show conn"
0 in use, 6 most used
```

i. Click Clear Screen.

j. Enter **show xlate** in the Command field.

k. Click Send.

l. Verify that the output in the Response field is similar to the following:

```
result of PIX command: "show xlate"
2 in use, 3 most used
Global 192.168.P.10 Local 10.0.P.11 static
```

m. Click **Close**.

**Task 8: Configuring and Testing Logging to a Syslog Server**

Complete the following steps to configure the PIX Security Appliance to send messages to a Syslog server.

**Step 1.** Select the System Properties tab.

**Step 2.** Expand Logging from the Categories tree on the left side of the panel. Logging Setup appears under Logging.

**Step 3.** Select Logging Setup.

**Step 4.** Select Enable logging in the Logging Setup group menu.

**Step 5.** Click Apply to PIX. The Preview CLI Commands window opens.

**Step 6.** Click Send. This opens the System Properties tab.

**Step 7.** Select Syslog under Logging from the Categories tree on the left side of the panel. The Syslog group box appears.

**Step 8.** Choose Debugging from the Level drop-down menu.

**Step 9.** Select Include Timestamp.

**Step 10.** Click Add. The Add Syslog Server window opens.

**Step 11.** Verify that inside is chosen in the Interface drop-down menu.

**Step 12.** Enter the IP address of the Syslog server in the IP Address field. Use 10.0.P.11 (where P = the Pod number).

**Step 13.** Click **OK**. This opens the System Properties tab.

**Step 14.** Click **Apply to PIX**. The Preview CLI Commands window opens.

**Step 15.** Click Send.

**Step 16.** Open the Kiwi Syslog Daemon on the desktop.

**Step 17.** From the Windows command line, Telnet to the perimeter router to generate traffic to be logged:

```
C:\> telnet 192.168.P.1
```

**Step 18.** Close the Telnet window that opens.

**Step 19.** The Kiwi Syslog Daemon display should be similar to the following:

```
<166> Jun 20 2001 16:19:14: %PIX-6-302001: Built outbound TCP connection 38 for
faddr 192.168.P.1/23 gaddr 192.168.P.10/1815 laddr 10.0.P.11/1815
```

### Task 9: Configuring Intrusion Detection

Complete the following steps to configure the PIX Security Appliance to detect Internet Control Message Protocol (ICMP) packet attacks, drop the packets, and send an alarm to a Syslog server.

**Step 1.** Verify that the System Properties tab is still active.

**Step 2.** Expand **Intrusion Detection** from the Categories tree on the left side of the panel. IDS Policy appears under Intrusion Detection.

**Step 3.** Select **IDS Policy**. The IDS Policy group box opens on the right.

**Step 4.** Click **Add**. The Add IDS Policy window opens.

**Step 5.** Enter **ATTACKPOLICY** in the Policy Name field.

**Step 6.** Verify that **Attack** is selected in the Policy Type group box.

**Step 7.** Select **Drop** and **Alarm** in the Action group box.

**Step 8. Click OK**. This opens the System Properties tab.

**Step 9.** Choose **ATTACKPOLICY** from the drop-down menu for the inside interface under Attack Policy.

**Step 10.** Click **Apply to PIX**. The Preview CLI Commands window opens.

**Step 11.** Click **Send**.

### Task 10: Configuring PDM to Monitor Intrusion Detection

Complete the following steps to configure monitoring of intrusion detection.

**Step 1.** Select the Monitoring tab.

**Step 2.** Expand Miscellaneous Graphs from the Categories tree on the left side of the panel. IDS appears under Miscellaneous Graphs.

**Step 3.** Select IDS.

**Step 4.** Choose ICMP Attacks from the Available Graphs list.

**Step 5.** Click Add.

**Step 6.** Click Graph It. The New Graph window opens.

**Step 7.** Verify that Real-time, data every 10 sec is chosen in the View drop-down menu.

**Step 8.** From the Windows command line, ping the bastion host with an ICMP packet size of 10000:

```
C:\> ping -l 10000 172.16.P.2
Pinging 172.16.P.2 with 10000 bytes of data:
Request timed out.
Request timed out.
Request timed out.
Request timed out.
```

**Step 9.** From the Windows command line, ping the bastion host with an ICMP packet size of 65,000:

```
C:\> ping -l 65000 172.16.P.2
Pinging 172.16.P.2 with 65000 bytes of data:
Request timed out.
Request timed out.
Request timed out.
Request timed out.
```

**Step 10.** Observe the graph in the Graph tab.

**Step 11.** Select the **Table** tab and observe the statistics in the table.

**Step 12.** Save the PIX Security Appliance configuration to Flash memory by clicking the **Save Running Config to Flash** icon in the PDM toolbar. The Save Running Configuration to Flash window opens.

**Step 13.** Click **Apply to PIX**. The Preview CLI Commands window opens.

**Step 14.** Click **Send**. The Save Successful window opens.

**Step 15.** Click **OK**.

**Task 11: Configuring a Site-to-Site VPN**

To create a secure site-to-site VPN between the PIX Security Appliance and the peer Pod's PIX Security Appliance, complete the following steps.

**Step 1.** Choose **Wizards > VPN Wizard** from the main menu. The VPN Wizard window opens.

**Step 2.** Verify that the **Site-to-Site VPN** radio button is selected. Verify that the outside interface is chosen from the drop-down box.

**Step 3.** Click **Next**. The Remote Site Peer window opens. Enter **192.168.Q.2** in the Peer IP Address field (where Q = the peer Pod number).

**Step 4.** Verify that the **Preshared Key** radio button is selected from the Authentication group box.

**Step 5.** Enter **cisco123** in the Pre-shared Key field. Enter **cisco123** in the Reenter Key field. Click **Next**. The IKE Policy window opens.

**Step 6.** Choose **DES** from the Encryption drop-down menu. Choose **SHA** from the Authentication drop-down menu. Choose **Group 1 (768-bit)** from the DH Group drop-down menu. Click **Next**. The Transform Set window opens.

**Step 7.** Choose **DES** from the Encryption drop-down menu. Choose **SHA** from the Authentication drop-down menu. Click **Next**. The IPSec Traffic Selector window opens.

**Step 8.** Verify that the **IP Address** radio button is selected within the Host/Network group box. Verify that **inside** is chosen from the Interface drop-down menu. Enter **192.168.P.10** in the IP Address field (where P = the Pod number).

**Step 9.** Choose **255.255.255.255** from the Mask drop-down menu.

**Step 10.** Click the arrow to move the host address to the Selected list. The Add host/network window opens. Click **OK**. The Create host/network window opens. The IP address and netmask for the inside host appear in the Basic Information group box. Verify that **inside** appears in the Interface drop-down menu.

**Step 11.** Click **Next**. The Static Route frame appears. Click **Next**. The NAT (Network Address Translation) frame appears. Click **Finish**. This will open the IPSec Traffic Selector window.

**Step 12.** Click the arrow button to move the IP address 192.168.P.10 to the Selected list (where P = the Pod number).

**Step 13.** Click **Next**. The IPSec Traffic Selector (Continue) window opens. Verify that the **IP Address** radio button is selected within the Host/Network group box.

**Step 14.** Verify that outside is chosen in the Interface drop-down menu. Enter the statically mapped IP address of the peer's inside host, **192.168.Q.10,** in the IP Address field (where Q = the peer Pod number).

**Step 15.** Choose **255.255.255.255** from the Mask drop-down menu. Click the arrow button to move the IP address **192.168.Q.10** to the Selected list.

**Step 16.** Click **OK**. The Create host/network window opens. The IP address and netmask for the peer's inside host appears in the Basic Information group box.

**Step 17.** Verify that outside appears in the Interface drop-down menu. Click **Next**. A reminder appears in the Create host/network window. Click **Finish**. This opens the IPSec Traffic Selector (Continue) window.

**Step 18.** Click the arrow button to move the IP address of the peer's inside host to the selected list. Click **Finish**. The Preview CLI Commands window opens. Click **Send**. This opens the Cisco PIX Device Manager main window.

**Step 19.** Click the **Save Config to Flash** icon. The Save Running Configuration to Flash window opens. Click **Apply to PIX**. The Preview CLI Commands window opens.

**Step 20.** Click **Send**. The Save Successful window opens. Click **OK**.

**Task 12: Testing and Verifying the VPN**

To test the site-to-site VPN, complete the following steps:

**Step 1.** Test the web access to the peer's inside host from the Windows NT server by completing the following substeps.

a. Open a web browser on the student PC.

b. Use the web browser to access the peer's inside host by entering **http://192.168.Q.10** (where Q = the peer Pod number).

The home page of the peer's inside host should open in the web browser.

**Step 2.** Observe the IKE security association (SA):

```
PixP(config)# show crypto isakmp sa
```

**Step 3.** Display the IPSec SA, and observe the number of encrypted and decrypted packets:

```
PixP(config)# show crypto ipsec sa
```

**Step 4.** Refresh the browser.

**Step 5.** Display the IPSec SA again and observe the number of encrypted and decrypted packets. The number should have incremented:

```
PixP(config)# show crypto ipsec sa
```

## Review Questions

1. Describe the PIX Management Center.

_______________________________________________

_______________________________________________

_______________________________________________

_______________________________________________

2. List the requirement that a PIX Security Appliance must meet in order to successfully run PDM.

_______________________________________________

_______________________________________________

_______________________________________________

_______________________________________________

3. Describe the Translation Rules tab in PDM and its function.

_______________________________________________

_______________________________________________

_______________________________________________

_______________________________________________

4. List and describe the four types of elements that are configurable with the PIX MC.

_______________________________________________

_______________________________________________

_______________________________________________

_______________________________________________

5. Describe the function of the Auto Update Server (AUS).

______________________________________________________________________

______________________________________________________________________

______________________________________________________________________

______________________________________________________________________

## Chapter 15 Quiz Questions

1. Which of the following is a policy management system for Cisco firewalls and IDS sensors?
   - A. PIX Device Manager
   - B. Cisco ACS
   - C. Cisco Secure Policy Manager
   - D. Cisco Policy Management System
2. The PDM supports the Secure Socket Layer (SSL) protocol with the encryption standards DES or 3DES.
   - A. True
   - B. False
3. You are using the PDM to change the configuration of the firewall.What command or step needs to be completed to save the configuration changes you have just made?
   - A. **write memory**
   - B. Click File > Write configuration to Flash
   - C. **enable flash copy**
   - D. Click File > Save configuration to Flash
4. Which of the following is not a valid parameter that the PIX Security Appliance will issue to a VPN client?
   - A. Host name
   - B. DNS server
   - C. WINS server
   - D. Domain name
5. The System Properties tab in the PDM has three types of routing configurations. Which of the following is not a valid routing type?
   - A. Static
   - B. ARP

C. RIP

D. Dynamic

6. The **sysopt connection permit-ipsec** command allows L2TP traffic to pass through the PIX Security Appliance.

   A. True

   B. False

7. To enable the PIX Security Appliance to connect to a central-site Cisco VPN concentrator, you must select the Enable VPN Hardware Client check box.

   A. True

   B. False

8. The PDM cannot be used to send logging messages to a Syslog server.

   A. True

   B. False

9. The PDM is capable of producing summary graphs to assist with the monitoring of the PIX Security Appliance.

   A. True

   B. False

10. While configuring the PIX Security Appliance through the PDM, how are the changes sent to the PIX?

   A. By using **copy config flash**

   B. By clicking Apply to PIX

   C. By using **save config flash**

   D. By using **save memory**

# Notes

## Notes

# Notes

# Notes

# Notes

## Notes

# Notes

## Notes

# Notes

# Notes

# Notes

# Notes